The Foundations of Arab Linguistics V

Studies in Semitic Languages and Linguistics

VOLUME 107

The titles published in this series are listed at *brill.com/ssl*

The Foundations of Arab Linguistics V

Kitāb Sībawayhi, *The Critical Theory*

Edited by

Manuel Sartori
Francesco Binaghi

BRILL

LEIDEN | BOSTON

Cover illustration: Manuscript of *al-Kāfiya* of Ibn al-Ḥāǧib (d. 646/1249), 1005/1596-97. Paris, Bibliothèque universitaire des Langues et Civilisations (BULAC), MS.ARA.11, fol. 25b.

The Library of Congress Cataloging-in-Publication Data is available online at http://catalog.loc.gov
LC record available at http://lccn.loc.gov/2012007523

Typeface for the Latin, Greek, and Cyrillic scripts: "Brill". See and download: brill.com/brill-typeface.

ISSN 0081-8461
ISBN 978-90-04-51584-0 (hardback)
ISBN 978-90-04-51589-5 (e-book)

This book is printed on acid-free paper and produced in a sustainable manner.

Contents

Notes on Contributors VII

Introduction 1
Manuel Sartori and Francesco Binaghi

PART 1
***The Critical Theory of Sībawayhi's* Kitāb**

1 *Ṭūl al-kalām* in the *Kitāb* 13
Michael G. Carter

2 'A Little Yesterday': The "Canonical" Text of Sībawayhi's Teaching Confronted to Two Unedited Manuscripts of the *Kitāb* 37
Ilyass Amharar and Jean N. Druel

3 Arabic Grammar and Qur'ānic Scholarship in 2nd/8th Century's Basra: A Comparative Analysis of the Qur'ānic Material Found in the *Kitāb Sībawayhi* and in al-'Aḫfaš al-'Awsaṭ's *Ma'ānī al-Qur'ān* 52
Raoul Villano and Giuliano Lancioni

4 The Arabic Linguistic Tradition after Sībawayhi: A Study in the Profile of the Speaker 97
Hanadi Dayyeh

5 Referencing Sībawayhi: The Reception of the *Kitāb* as a Source 114
Simona Olivieri

6 Grammar and the *radd* Genre in al-Andalus 135
Francesco Binaghi

PART 2
Further Developments of the Critical Theory

7 Fārābī against the Grammarians?? 157
Wilfrid Hodges and Manuela E.B. Giolfo

8 Ibn al-Sarrāǧ's Classification of Pseudo-Objects and the Grammatical Concept of *faḍla* 179
Hideki Okazaki

9 Suprasegmental Criteria in Medieval Arabic Grammar 198
Manuel Sartori

10 On Interpretation of the Pronoun *huwa* in 112/1 of the Qurʾān: *Tafsīr* and Grammar 223
Haruko Sakaedani

Index Operum 245
Index Nominum 248
Index Rerum 252

Notes on Contributors

Ilyass Amharar
is Franco-Moroccan and shares his time between Casablanca and Paris. He graduated from Sorbonne University in Paris (2017) with a Master thesis on Ibn Mālik's (d. 672/1274) *ʾAlfiyya* and Ibn Tūmart's (d. 524/1146) *Muršida*. In 2021, he completed a PhD at Aix-Marseille University on the relationship between Arabic language and theology among ʾAšʿarī authors, based on a treatise by al-Qāḍī Ibn al-ʿArabī (d. 543/1148), under the supervision of late lamented Prof. Éric Chaumont. He also works on the critical edition of Ibn Ḫarūf's manuscript of Sībawayhi's (d. 180/796?) *Kitāb*.

Francesco Binaghi
obtained his PhD in Arabic linguistics (Aix-Marseille University, 2015) with a dissertation on the history of grammatical studies in al-Andalus and the Maghreb. He is currently lecturer (associate professor) at the university Sorbonne Nouvelle in Paris, and researcher at the Laboratoire d'Histoire des Théories Linguistiques (Université Paris Cité/Université Sorbonne Nouvelle/CNRS, F-75005 Paris, France). His research interests mainly deal with the history and epistemology of the Arabic grammatical tradition, notably in al-Andalus and the Islamic West, and he has recently edited a thematic issue of the journal *Histoire Épistémologie Langage* (40/2, 2018) on the contribution of Andalusi grammarians to the Arabic linguistic tradition. In the broader field of Arabic linguistics, he has also co-edited Fuṣḥā *écrit contemporain. Usages et nouveaux développements* (Diacritiques Éditions, 2019, with Manuel Sartori) on the exploration of linguistic features specific to Contemporary Written *Fuṣḥā*.

Michael G. Carter
after a D.Phil. (Oxon.), taught at Sydney University (1968–1985), New York University (1986–1996) and Oslo University (from 1996 until retirement in 2004). Research interests are Sībawayhi and early Arabic grammatical theory, and the relationship between grammar, law and philosophy in early Islam.

Hanadi Dayyeh
PhD at the American University of Beirut, is a researcher in the field of Arabic Historical Linguistics. Her research concentrates on Sībawayhi's linguistic theory and its impact on the evolution of the Arabic linguistic tradition. In the field of Arabic Linguistics, she also focuses on language acquisition and its implications on the teaching of Arabic. Her work experience in the field of

teaching and researching teaching methods in Arabic language, both to native and non-native speakers, extends over 15 years and she has produced a number of textbooks in this field.

Jean N. Druel

is French and lives in Cairo. He graduated in Teaching Arabic as a Foreign Language at the American University in Cairo (AUC, 2006), and in 2012 he completed a PhD in the history of Arabic grammar at the University of Nijmegen, in the Netherlands, under the supervision of Prof. Kees Versteegh. He currently works on the edition of the Milan, Ambrosiana X 56 *sup.* manuscript which contains one fourth of Sībawayhi's (d. 180/796?) *Kitāb*.

Manuela E.B. Giolfo

holds an M.A. in philosophy from Milan University, and a PhD in Arabic linguistics from Aix-Marseille University. She was lecturer in Arabic at Exeter University (2008–2013) before moving to the University of Genoa, where she is lecturer in Arabic language and philology. She edited *Arab and Arabic linguistics* (Oxford, 2014), and co-edited *Approaches to the history and dialectology of Arabic in honor of Pierre Larcher* (Leiden, 2016, with Manuel Sartori and late lamented Philippe Cassuto). She is also the author of *Les systèmes hypothétiques de l'arabe classique* (Rome, 2017).

Wilfrid Hodges

is Emeritus Professor of Mathematics at Queen Mary, University of London, specializing in mathematical logic and logical semantics. Since his retirement he has been working on Medieval Arabic logic, in particular that of Ibn Sīnā (d. 427/1037). Books on the logic of Ibn Sīnā and Fārābī (d. 339/950) are in preparation (one joint with Saloua Chatti). He also has a project with Manuela E.B. Giolfo to compare the views of Sīrāfī and Ibn Sīnā in areas where linguistics and logic overlap.

Giuliano Lancioni

PhD in Linguistics (Roma Tre University), is full professor of Arabic language and literature at Roma Tre University. His research interests include the history of the Arabic linguistic thinking, Arabic corpus and computational linguistics, and information retrieval from Arabic texts. He co-edited the collective monographs *The Word in Arabic* (Brill, 2011, with Lidia Bettini) and *Dār al-islām / dār al-ḥarb: Territories, People, Identities* (Brill, 2017, with Vanna Calasso).

Hideki Okazaki
his research field is Arabic grammatical thought. Articles published in Japanese include "Ibn al-Sarrāǧ, *Kitāb al-ʾUṣūl fī al-Naḥw* Kara Mita Arabu Bunpou Ronsou [The Arab Grammatical Controversies in the Light of Ibn al-Sarrāǧ's *Kitāb al-ʾUṣūl fī al-Naḥw*]," *Journal of Arabic and Islamic Studies* 7, 2009, and "9-Seiki No Arabu Bunpougaku Niokeru Shishi Shoujyou: Kufa Gakuha No Bunpouka Ṯaʿlab Ni Kansuru Ichikousatsu [A Succession from Teachers to Deciples in the 9th-century Arab Grammar: A Study of the Kufan Grammarian Ṯaʿlab]," *Shitennoji University Bulletin* 51, 2010.

Simona Olivieri
holds a PhD in Arabic language and linguistics (2016) from Sapienza University of Rome. She is currently postdoctoral research associate and lecturer at the Seminar für Semitistik und Arabistik at Freie Universität Berlin, where she does research on classical Arabic and the Arabic linguistic tradition. Her research interests include Arabic language and linguistics, historical linguistics, corpus linguistics, and digital humanities.

Haruko Sakaedani
is a part-time lecturer in Arabic at Keio University, the University of Tokyo, Tokai University and Waseda University. She holds an M.A. in Teaching Arabic as a Foreign Language from the American University in Cairo and a PhD in Arabic linguistics from the Research Institute for Languages and Cultures of Asia and Africa, Tokyo University of Foreign Studies.

Manuel Sartori
after graduating in comparative politics at the Institute of Political Studies (IEP, Aix-en-Provence, 1999) and in Arabic studies at Aix-Marseille University (AMU, 2004), Manuel Sartori became senior teacher (professeur agrégé) in Arabic (2009) and completed a PhD in Arabic language and linguistics at AMU (2012). Formerly lecturer at IEP, he is currently Professor of Arabic grammar and linguistics at AMU and researcher at IREMAM. His research interests include Arabic grammar and linguistics (diachronic and synchronic, medieval and contemporary) and the history of the Arabic language. He notably co-edited *Approaches to the History and Dialectology of Arabic in Honor of Pierre Larcher* (Brill, 2016, with Manuela E.B. Giolfo and late lamented Philippe Cassuto), *Case and Mood Endings in Semitic Languages—Myth or Reality?* (Harrassowitz, 2018, with Lutz Edzard and late lamented Philippe Cassuto) and Fuṣḥā *écrit contemporain. Usages et nouveaux développements* (Diacritiques Éditions, 2019, with Francesco Binaghi). For more details please visit https://iremam.cnrs.fr/fr/sartori-manuel

Raoul Villano
PhD in Islamic Civilization, History and Philology (Sapienza University of Rome), he is now associate professor at Roma Tre University where he teaches Arabic language and literature. His main research interests are Qurʾānic studies, the history of the Arabic linguistic tradition and *Ṭabaqāt* biographical literature. He has published a monograph on the Qurʾān (*La struttura binaria del Corano,* Istituto per l'Oriente C.A. Nallino, 2018) and he is now editing a special issue of *Language & History* on "Formal Models in the History of Arabic Linguistic Tradition" (forthcoming).

Introduction

Manuel Sartori and Francesco Binaghi

This volume contains a selection of papers presented at the Fifth Conference on the Foundations of Arab Linguistics (FAL V), hosted by Amal E. Marogy at the Faculty of Asian and Middle Eastern Studies, University of Cambridge on September 20–21, 2018. This conference constituted a sequel to the first four of the series: FAL I and FAL II had already been organized in Cambridge by Amal E. Marogy, respectively on September 3–4, 2010 and on September 13–14, 2012; afterwards, Georgine Ayoub convened the third conference (FAL III) in Paris on October 23–24, 2014, and Manuela E.B. Giolfo the fourth one (FAL IV) in Genoa on September 8–9, 2016 (for the proceedings of these conferences, cf. Marogy 2012, Marogy & Versteegh 2015, Ayoub & Versteegh 2018, Giolfo & Versteegh 2019).[1]

This fifth opus of the Foundations of Arabic Linguistics conference series is special in several ways. First and foremost, the title is no longer exactly the same as the four previous editions. In the present title, *Arab* Linguistics replaces the previous *Arabic* Linguistics, which is an echo of the distinction sketched by Michael G. Carter in a prominent article of his (1987–1988); since this fifth conference was convened in his honor, it was then entitled *Foundations of Arab Linguistics*.

Far from an essentialist view of what the study of language is in the Arab and in the Western worlds, Carter defines these two approaches in terms of their object, the theoretical and epistemological framework in which they are elaborated, and finally their scope. He defines *Arab Linguistics* as encompassing not only this language's own linguistic tradition ("the study of the native science of grammar that has been continuously active since at least the eighth century A.D.", Carter 1987–1988: 205), but also the contribution of all those inter-

1 Cf. also the reviews by Larcher 2015, Larcher 2018, Larcher 2019a, and Larcher 2019b. In the present volume, the same editorial guidelines as in the previous volumes have generally been followed, the only notable exception being the use of *ǧ* instead of *j* for the transliteration of *ǧīm*. The transcription of Arabic follows the system of *Arabica*, with one major difference: the initial *hamza* is systematically transcribed when it is morphological (*hamzat al-qaṭʿ*), but not when it is merely phonetic (*hamzat al-waṣl*, thus: *wa-ktub* "and write!", but *wa-ʾaktib* "and make write!"). Inflectional endings are fully transcribed in Qurʾānic and poetic quotations, as well as in grammatical examples; in other quotations and book titles we have opted for a simplified system, in which pausal rather than contextual forms are used. Yet, in some papers, full transcription can be used for specific needs.

 | DOI:10.1163/9789004515895_002

ested in it, including therefore Western scholars ("*all* those whose concern is with indigenous grammatical theory, whether in the Muslim world or in the long-established tradition of Arabic studies in the West, are counted as 'Arab' linguists", ibid). By contrast, *Arabic Linguistics* identifies the study of Arabic through the lenses of modern linguistics, whose theories, standards and methods have started to be developed in Europe in the 18th century ("for the 'Arabic' linguist, whether a native speaker or not, the choice of Arabic as the object language is [at least in principle] a matter of total indifference, since the whole purpose is to deduce or apply a theory or test a model", Carter 1987–1988: 206). Carter argues that this opposition is particularly flagrant when it comes to the difference in attitude to linguistic data: on the one side, traditional Arab grammarians—and henceforth Arab linguists—work on a defined and atemporal set of data, while Arabic linguists adapt their corpora to their needs or even produce as much data as is required (Carter 1987–1988: 213). Arabic linguistics' goal is ultimately identified as context-free universality, whereas Arab linguistics is presented as a "humanistic discipline in the fullest sense" (ibid),[2] as it is concerned with the development of our knowledge of the Arabs themselves: their civilization, thought, etc.

Nevertheless, even if Carter considers that Arab linguistics' and Arabic linguistics' development will continue separately,[3] he acknowledges that they represent the two ends of a scale between which one can find considerable overlap and sometimes confusion. Giolfo (2014: 3–4) stresses the importance of bringing together these two approaches and proposes to see Arab(ic) linguistics as a single discipline: in her view, such different approaches should be considered nothing more than the expression of the complexity of the phenomena they investigate. This is indeed the spirit of the papers presented in this volume, whose authors delve into medieval Arabic grammatical treatises and develop analysis mixing the two approaches and addressing both types of audience. In the same spirit as Giolfo (2014: 3), we consider that "the word 'and' between 'Arab Linguistics' and 'Arabic Linguistics' is not meant to carry an adversative meaning but rather a meaning that goes beyond 'dangers of confusing the two'

2 This excerpt and the philosophical approach more broadly presented in this article certainly explain the title (*Grammar as a Window onto Arabic Humanism*) of the *Festschrift* offered to Michael G. Carter in 2006 (Edzard & Watson, eds.).

3 As it goes for Larcher (1992, also mentioned in 2014:V-VI), who sketches a similar dichotomy between, on the one side, Arab(ic) linguistics made in departments of Arabic studies by Arabists who do not always have a background in linguistics and, on the other side, Arab(ic) linguistics made in departments of linguistics by scholars who lack a solid background in Arabic studies (whom Larcher identifies as mainly being Arabic mother-tongue speakers with a background in French or English studies).

[Carter 1987–1988: 205]." However, if a label was needed, the FAL series would indeed be an expression of *Arab Linguistics*, rather than that of *Arabic Linguistics*: all the chapters take Medieval Arabic grammatical sources as the starting point for analysis.

If we wanted to go further down the description of our field, its history and its methods, we should also note that *Arab Linguistics* actually encompasses—without distinguishing between them—two different traditions. On the one hand, we have *Arabs' Linguistics*, that is to say the tradition of studies elaborated in the Islamicate world, written in Arabic and ultimately dealing with the Classical Arabic language.[4] It broadly corresponds to what is known as the Arabic Grammatical Tradition. This is not only the intellectual product of the Medieval periods and pre-modern times, but some prolongations can be found until today, in that most of today's (Arabic-language) grammars of Arabic reproduce not only the closed and atemporal corpus of Classical Arabic, but also the methods and the theoretical framework of Medieval grammarians, and even some of their examples. This tradition is unresponsive to the developments of modern linguistics.

On the other hand, we have *Arabists' Linguistics*, that is to say the tradition of studies on Arabic grammar that has developed outside the Islamicate world since the late Medieval times, and whose works are mainly written in other languages than Arabic (i.e. the long-established tradition of Arabic studies in the West). While paying the due respect to the work of Medieval Arabic grammarians and acknowledging their extremely important contribution for the study of this language, the Arabists' tradition takes into account the new theories, concepts and methods developed by modern linguistics to enlighten, complete and enrich the description provided by medieval Arabic grammatical treatises. Moreover, since it addresses a non-Arabic speaking audience, it sometimes tends to adapt to the Greek and Latin grammatical system and adopt its taxonomy and terminology for the grammatical description.[5]

If this cycle of conferences can—in some of its contributions—address the latter, it nevertheless deals primarily with the former, focusing on its production and material, starting from the tutelary figure of Sībawayhi (d. 180/796?).

---

4 The term *Arabs'* should not conceal the very important fact that most of these scholars were actually not of Arab descent, and that for some of them Arabic was not a mother tongue (Sībawayhi in the first place!), even though they had all been arabized linguistically. Just as the term *Linguistics* should not be taken here in the primary sense of a specific modern science, but rather in a wider way as "the study of language". The reader will forgive us here for this anachronistic use, which simply occurs for the sake of debate around Carter's label *Arab Linguistics*.

5 For an example of such a development, cf. Guillaume 2020.

Contributors to this series are mainly historians of the grammatical and more generally linguistic tradition of the "Arabs", rather than of the Arabists' one (a history which is still to be done). Because of this, it might even be more accurate to speak here—at least for the moment being—of *Arabs' Linguistics*.

The volume is also innovatory in the organization of its contents, which are no longer presented in the sheer alphabetical order of the contributors, as it was the case in the last three editions. Here, a thematic arrangement has been preferred, thus reviving the approach of the opening book of the series. The contributions are organized in two sections. The first one focuses on the status of Sībawayhi's *Kitāb* and tries to evaluate its impact on following grammarians, as well as the debates and refutations it raised. It is this interest for the reception of the *Kitāb* that explains the subtitle "*Kitāb Sībawayhi*: The Critical Theory" given to the FAL V conference and, subsequently, to the present proceedings. The second section explores later developments in the grammatical and linguistic thought, and deals more precisely with the constitution of some grammatical categories.

Furthermore, if this volume is particular, it is also because none of its editors were involved in the organization of the FAL V conference. Just as Kees Versteegh stepped in to help with the edition of the proceedings of the last three editions (FAL II to FAL IV)—and this is also an opportunity to pay tribute to him—, we also intervened and replaced the conference organizer who was prevented from carrying out this task.

Last but not least, the end of this editing process has taken place during the Covid-19 pandemic, which has been imposing upon us a series of unprecedented containment measures. This will certainly mark the spirit of the beginning of the third decade of the 21st century. In this context, the sixth conference of the series (FAL VI), initially planned for September 2020, has had to be postponed twice, thus breaching the biennial rhythm of these meetings. Nevertheless, we hope that the FAL conference cycle will pass through this ordeal and continue for a long time, leaving its enduring mark on Arabic studies.

We wish to thank the contributors for their hard work and their commitment besides us in this adventure—commitment being a rare value that we have to cherish. Let those who act with commitment be warmly thanked. Credits would not be complete without mentioning Elisa Perotti from Brill, who has been enthusiastic about this project since the very first moment, welcoming and accompanying us on behalf of Brill publishing house, as well as Noortje Maranus for the production of this book.

The papers in the present volume are organized into two main sections: the first one deals explicitly with the critical theory of Sībawayhi's *Kitāb*, while the second one addresses further developments of the grammatical analysis. Michael G. Carter (chapter 1) inaugurates the first part with the examination of Sībawayhi's notion of "*ṭūl al-kalām*", which appears some two dozen times in the *Kitāb* with reference to the length of utterances or parts of utterances, as well as a number of other occurrences connected with the length of individual sounds. After outlining the contexts in which the term is used, the paper makes some interpretative comments and shows that *ṭūl al-kalām*, in common with the rest of the terminology of the *Kitāb*, is applied to elements at all levels of analysis from phoneme to syntagmeme. Furthermore, the feature of *ṭūl al-kalām* is strongly associated with Sībawayhi's master, Ḫalīl (d. 170/786 or 175/791), who displays a refined concept of morpheme boundaries in association with the rules of pause (*waqf*). Its link with vocative constructions lends weight to the assumption that the language under analysis was indeed a spoken form of Arabic. In conclusion, a few sporadic examples of *ṭūl al-kalām* from later grammar are presented, though the literature needs a more thorough examination, and the paper ends with some remarks about a possible echo in the treatment of the demonstratives in the modern pronunciation of Classical Arabic.

Ilyass Amharar and Jean N. Druel (chapter 2) approach the question of Sībawayhi's heritage through the lenses of the textual tradition, confronting the "canonical" text of Sībawayhi's teaching to two unedited manuscripts of the *Kitāb*. The investigation focuses on the specific question of whether is it permissible to form the diminutive of the names of the days of the week, as in *ṯunayyāni* 'a little Monday' or *ṯulayṯāʾ* 'a little Tuesday'. Sībawayhi denies this possibility, arguing that these words ('Monday', 'Tuesday', etc.), along with the names of the months, are proper names that refer to only one item, not to a whole genus (*ʾumma*): there can be many Zayds and ʿAmrs, some being smaller than others, but there is only one 'Monday', just like there is only one 'yesterday' or one 'tomorrow'; in other words, the names of the days of the week have less *tamakkun* ('declinability, flexibility, potentiality') than *zayd* and *ʿamr*. Ǧarmī (d. 225/839) and Māzinī (d. 249/863), followed by Mubarrad (d. 285/898 or 286/899), criticize Sībawayhi's position, while Ibn Wallād (d. 332/944) defends it. In this paper, the authors shed new light on this very specific debate thanks to fresh data from so far unedited manuscripts of Sībawayhi's *Kitāb* (Milan, Ambrosiana x 56 *sup.*; Paris, Bibliothèque nationale de France ar. 6499). The many variant readings give an insight into the gradual elaboration of the 'canonical' version of Sībawayhi's *Kitāb*, in dialogue with the early grammatical treatises, their commentaries, and their refutations.

Back to the origin of Sībawayhi's grammatical activity, Raoul Villano and Giuliano Lancioni (chapter 3) address the issues of his early reputation as a grammatical authority and of his relationship with his alleged most outstanding pupil, al-ʾAḫfaš al-ʾAwsaṭ (d. 215/830). The analysis of biographical and historical sources clearly shows that Sībawayhi's reputation is already well established between the end of the 2nd/8th and the beginning of the 3rd/9th centuries. As for ʾAḫfaš, he is described, already in the first half of the 3rd/9th century, not only as the transmitter of the *Kitāb*, but also as the heir and successor of Sībawayhi's teachings. Moreover, all biographical and historical sources persistently record that the two scholars were part of, if not the same grammatical school, at least the same scholarly circle in Basra. Based on these considerations, the second and third sections of the paper offer a comparative analysis of the Qurʾānic material found in Sībawayhi's *Kitāb* and in ʾAḫfaš's *Maʿānī al-Qurʾān*. Evidence demonstrates that the two books are rooted in a common ground originated in the 2nd/8th century's Basran intellectual milieu, and emerged from the same scholarly tradition, which should be identified with the circle of the *naḥwiyyūn*.

Shifting attention to the Arabic Linguistic Tradition after Sībawayhi, Hanadi Dayyeh (chapter 4) addresses the 'profile of the speaker' as a case study of how the critical theory examines and reinterprets Sībawayhi's heritage. Where the speaker appears in Sībawayhi's *Kitāb* as an originator and arbiter, it comes across as a learner in the works of his successors. This process begins with Mubarrad's *Muqtaḍab* and is achieved with Ibn al-Sarrāǧ's (d. 316/929) *ʾUṣūl*. Notwithstanding some later attempts at restoring the profile of the speaker as an originator, notably in Ibn Ǧinnī's (d. 392/1002) treatises, the study argues that such a change reveals a shift in approach to linguistic analysis away from Sībawayhi's. The causes of this shift and its impact on the development of the Arabic Linguistic Tradition will be examined.

Simona Olivieri's contribution (chapter 5) reminds that Sībawayhi's *Kitāb* epitomizes the linguistic debate that took place among the scholars of Arabic during the first and second centuries after the *hiǧra*, and that it constitutes the evident result of the way the earliest grammarians interpreted substantial linguistic themes. According to the author, Sībawayhi's contribution to the development of the Arabic grammatical tradition is such that his view and approach lays the foundations of the subsequent linguistic thinking, becoming a grammatical source itself, together with the Qurʾān and the *kalām al-ʿarab*. Indeed, the data discussed in Sībawayhi's investigation are also included in numbers of examples provided by later grammarians, becoming a self-standing corpus. Hence, both the pioneering terminology he establishes and his data are to be adopted by scholars belonging to later and diverse traditions. On this basis, the paper investigates how the *qurʾān al-naḥw* is spoken of in later grammarians' works and to what extent the exploitation of Sībawayhi's arguments is specious to defend Basran or Kufan theories. As a matter of fact, although the data available in later grammarians' treatises are substantially the same as those already presented and discussed by Sībawayhi, their interpretation sometimes shows interesting variations, usually functional to the specific theory they want to support.

The issue of Sībawayhi's *Kitāb* heritage and textual tradition is also evoked in Francesco Binaghi's contribution (chapter 6), which closes the first section of the book. The paper evaluates the *radd* genre that, nowadays overshadowed by the most famous *al-Radd ʿalā al-nuḥāt* by Ibn Maḍāʾ (d. 592/1196), seems to have been particularly flourishing in al-Andalus and attests to the Andalusi intellectual activity in the field of grammatical studies. It presents a list of 25 titles, which include the name of some of the most important Andalusi grammarians either as authors or as targets of these refutations, and tries to evaluate the content and impact of these treatises: even though almost all these texts (with the notable exception of Ibn Maḍāʾ's *Radd*) have not been preserved, indirect information provided by other grammatical works or biobibliographical sources sheds some light on the issue. Two opposing groups emerge, on the basis of which the author proposes a first sketch of scholarly trends in al-Andalus. The fraction lines among them seem to develop along two main issues: the question of the primary reference for grammatical studies—the *Ǧumal* of Zaǧǧāǧī (d. 337/949), or the *ʾĪḍāḥ* of Fārisī (d. 377/989)—, and the epistemological definition of grammar's purpose: an instrumental discipline or a speculative science? The author ends his investigation wondering whether these fraction lines are eventually linked to the textual history of Sībawayhi's *Kitāb* and to a struggle for Sībawayhi's heritage.

The second part of this volume opens with a contribution that goes back to the period of standardization of the grammatical theory (4th/10th century) and focuses on the encounter between grammar and philosophy. Wilfrid Hodges and Manuela E.B. Giolfo (chapter 7) analyze some of the sources presenting this encounter as an open confrontation with a notable interest for the figure of Fārābī (d. 339/950). As a matter of fact, it has sometimes been suggested that Fārābī's views about grammar put him in conflict with the Arabic grammarians of his time. The authors examine the evidence and conclude that, although not a grammarian himself, Fārābī is closely in touch with leading grammarians of his time, and describes features of Arabic which can be illustrated in detail with examples from Sībawayhi or Sīrāfī (d. 368/979): no points of conflict are thus to be noticed. However, although Fārābī casts his explanations in terms that should apply to any language, the authors suspect he may not have had a fluent knowledge of any language other than Arabic.

The books continues with a contribution focusing on taxonomic issues in the Arabic grammatical tradition. Hideki Okazaki (chapter 8) examines the classification of *mušabbah bi-l-mafʿūl* ("pseudo-object") by Ibn al-Sarrāǧ based on the grammatical concept of *faḍla*, which corresponds to *laġw* in the *Kitāb* of Sībawayhi. Ibn al-Sarrāǧ's major 4th/10th-century work, *Kitāb al-ʾUṣūl fī al-naḥw*, is one of the oldest grammatical works that classified *mafʿūl* into five categories with well-defined terminologies. His treatise is characterized by the classification of each grammatical category based on the principles of comprehensive divisions, and by the arrangement of chapters according to this classification. However, his manner of dividing *mušabbah bi-l-mafʿūl* is less assertive than his clear-cut classification of *mafʿūl*. According to his description, one may say that he recognizes five types of "objects" (the five *mafʿūl*-s), as well as five types of "pseudo-objects" (*ḥāl, tamyīz, istiṯnāʾ, ḫabar kāna wa-ʾaḫawātihā*, and *ism ʾinna wa-ʾaḫawātihā*). Ibn al-Sarrāǧ classifies these pseudo-objects based on two aspects: the semantic relation between *manṣūb* and *marfūʿ*, and the grammatical category of *ʿāmil* (operator). However, the paper argues that he fails to account for the reason why *nidāʾ* (vocative) and *nafy bi-lā* (negation with *lā*) are excluded from the category of pseudo-objects. Although Ibn al-Sarrāǧ's taxonomy of *mušabbah bi-l-mafʿūl* is accepted by Ibn Ǧinnī and Ǧurǧānī (d. 471/1078), the classification of some of the categories is modified, at least after the 7th/13th century, by grammarians like Ibn Mālik (d. 672/1274), ʾAstarābāḏī (d. 688/1289?), and their successors.

Classical Arabic falling essentially within the written level of the language, this one takes precedence in its descriptions, even if Medieval Arab Grammarians sing praises of an effective and relevant *ʾiʿrāb* which is supposed to be regularly uttered. However, it does not seem possible to identify clear traces of the integration of suprasegmental elements in medieval Arabic grammatical thought, such as intonation for example. This is the purpose of Manuel Sartori's paper (chapter 9), which takes the distinction to be made between *badal* and *ʿaṭf al-bayān* as a practical case study. Interestingly enough, not only does this question not find an immediate answer, but there is nothing to differentiate two examples given by Ibn Ǧinnī and illustrating respectively *badal* and *ʿaṭf al-bayān*: *qāma ʾaḫūka zaydun* and *qāma ʾaḫūka muḥammadun*. Moreover, a grammarian and logician like ʾAstarābāḏī states explicitly that he does not see any clear difference between *badal al-kull min al-kull* and *ʿaṭf al-bayān*. In fact, the answer given by the Medieval Arabic grammars may seem in some ways confusing, *ʿaṭf al-bayān* being an intersection between the *badal* and the *ṣifa*. This might be the reason why Arabists' grammars of Arabic often avoid addressing the difference between *badal* and *ʿaṭf al-bayān*. Two criteria are traditionally exhibited by medieval Arabic grammarians to differentiate between them: an inflectional criterion in the very restricted context of the vocative (*nidāʾ*), and a semantic and pragmatic criterion. This latter is based on the fact that the *badal* is the essential term compared to its *mubdal minhu*, whereas the

ʿaṭf al-bayān is only an accessory element. The paper underlines, however, that another criterion of distinction between these two appositions exists if one wants to *listen carefully* to the old Arabic grammarians: this criterion is neither distributional, nor inflectional (therefore syntactical), nor even semantic and pragmatic, but suprasegmental. In conclusion, the author argues that medieval Arabic grammarians were actually not *deaf* to suprasegmental criteria and considerations.

Finally, Haruko Sakaedani (chapter 10) closes this volume with a study on the pronoun *huwa* in Q. 112/1, where she indicates that *qul huwa llāhu ʾaḥadun* is often interpreted as a subject, *allāhu* being its predicate, and *ʾaḥadun* this latter's apposition or the second predicate. Her paper examines interpretations of *huwa* both in *tafsīr*-s and in Arabic grammatical books. The author underlines that, around the time of Zamaḫšarī (d. 538/1144), this *huwa* comes to be recognized as a cataphoric *ḍamīr al-šaʾn* (a pronoun of the matter). According to the author, there are two more "pronouns of the matter" in the Qurʾān: Q. 18/38 *lākinnā huwa llāhu rabbī* and Q. 34/27 *bal huwa llāhu l-ʿazīzu l-ḥakīmu*; here, however, *huwa* is not explained as a *ḍamīr al-šaʾn* either. The paper postulates that also in the case of these last two verses the reasons for such an analysis are that the *ḍamīr al-šaʾn* in the Qurʾān mainly appear as suffix pronouns, and that preceding contexts of these two verses enable *huwa* to be interpreted as an anaphoric pronoun.

Even though the title of this fifth chapter of the series recalls once more the name and central place of Sībawayhi within the grammatical tradition, the papers successfully prove that his heritage and the critical theory that develops around his *Kitāb* are far more complex than a simple reorganization of its grammatical matter, to the point that—after all—Sībawayhi can almost be considered as a potential divisive factor among later grammarians. The articles also provide some new interpretative tools which will certainly contribute to deepen our understanding of the Arabic grammatical tradition.

Bibliography

Ayoub, Georgine & Kees Versteegh (eds.). 2018. *The Foundations of Arabic Linguistics III. The Development of a Tradition: Continuity and Change*. Leiden & Boston: Brill, coll. "Semitic Studies in Languages and Linguistics" 94.

Carter, Michael G. 1987–1988. "Arab Linguistics and Arabic Linguistics". *Zeitschrift für Geschichte der Arabisch-Islamischen Wissenschaften* 4. 205–218.

Edzard, Lutz & Janet Watson (eds.). 2006. *Grammar as a Window onto Arabic Humanism: A Collection of Articles in Honour of Michael G. Carter*. Wiesbaden: Harrassowitz.

Giolfo, Manuela E.B. (ed.). 2014. *Arab and Arabic Linguistics: Traditional and New Theoretical Approaches*. Manchester: Oxford University Press, coll. "Journal of Semitic Studies. Supplement" 34.

Giolfo, Manuela E.B. & Kees Versteegh (eds.). 2019. *The Foundations of Arabic Linguistics IV. The Evolution of Theory*. Leiden & Boston: Brill, coll. "Semitic Studies in Languages and Linguistics" 97.

Guillaume, Jean-Patrick. 2020. "Entre grammaire arabe et grammaires arabisantes : Heurs et malheurs de la phrase nominale." *Histoire Épistémologie Langage* 42/1 (La grammaire arabe étendue). 93–114.

Larcher, Pierre. 1992. "Où en est la linguistique arabe en France ? État des lieux et bilan critique." *Lettre d'information de l'AFEMAM* 7 (Compte-rendu de la réunion "Langues et Littératures dans le monde arabe et musulman" 26–28 Juin 1989-La Baume Les Aix). 15–42.

Larcher, Pierre. 2014. "Foreword". *Arab and Arabic Linguistics: Traditional and New Theoretical Approaches*, ed. by Manuela E.B. Giolfo, v–vi. Manchester: Oxford University Press, coll. "Journal of Semitic Studies. Supplement" 34.

Larcher, Pierre. 2015. Review of *The Foundations of Arabic Linguistics. Sībawayhi and Early Arabic Grammatical Theory*, ed. by Amal E. Marogy. Leyde & Boston: Brill, coll. "Studies in Semitic Languages and Linguistics" 65 (2012). *Arabica* 62/2–3. 411–415.

Larcher, Pierre. 2018. Review of *The Foundations of Arabic Linguistics II. Kitāb Sībawayhi: Interpretation and Transmission*, ed. by Amal E. Marogy & Kees Versteegh. Leiden & Boston: Brill, coll. "Studies in Semitic Languages and Linguistics" 83 (2015). *Arabica* 65/1–2. 259–263.

Larcher, Pierre. 2019a. Review of *The Foundations of Arabic Linguistics III. The Development of a Tradition: Continuity and Change*, ed. by Georgine Ayoub & Kees Versteegh. Leiden & Boston: Brill, coll. "Studies in Semitic Languages and Linguistics" 94 (2018). *Arabica* 66/1–2. 185–189.

Larcher, Pierre. 2019b. Review of *The Foundations of Arabic Linguistics IV. The Evolution of Theory*, ed. by Manuela E.B. Giolfo & Kees Versteegh. Leiden & Boston: Brill, coll. "Studies in Semitic Languages and Linguistics" 97 (2019). *Arabica* 66/5. 543–548.

Marogy, Amal E. (ed.). 2012. *The Foundations of Arabic Linguistics. Sībawayhi and Early Arabic Grammatical Theory*. Leiden & Boston: Brill, coll. "Studies in Semitic Languages and Linguistics" 65.

Marogy, Amal E. & Kees Versteegh (ed.). 2015. *The Foundations of Arabic Linguistics II. Kitāb Sībawayhi: Interpretation and Transmission*. Leiden & Boston: Brill, coll. "Studies in Semitic Languages and Linguistics" 83.

PART 1

The Critical Theory of Sībawayhi's Kitāb

CHAPTER 1

Ṭūl al-kalām in the *Kitāb*

Michael G. Carter

Introduction*

The notion of *ṭūl al-kalām* is applied, in the manner typical of the *Kitāb*, to phenomena at all linguistic levels, phonological, morphological, and syntactical. Furthermore, it is conspicuously associated with Sībawayhi's (d. 180/796?) master, al-Ḫalīl b. ʾAḥmad (d. 170/786?).

Thanks to Gérard Troupeau's (1927–2010) *Lexique-Index du* Kitāb *de Sībawayhi*[1] it is easy to trace all the occurrences of the term in the *Kitāb* in its various stems, *ṭāla*, *ṭawwala*, *ʾaṭāla* and *istaṭāla* and their derivatives. The roots *maṭala* and *maṭṭaṭa*, which occur just a few times, evidently in the same sense as *ṭāla*, are also taken into account. The data are representative rather than exhaustive, and there will be minimal discussion of the grammatical points at issue.

Unless the context requires it, *ṭūl al-kalām* will stand for the concept in general, regardless of the actual expression used, such as *ṭāla al-kalām*, *ṭawwaltahu*, *ʾaṭalta al-naʿt* etc.[2] References are to the chapter number of the *Kitāb* with the Derenbourg (D.) and Būlāq (B.) pagination, from which Jahn's translation and the Hārūn edition respectively are easily accessed.

1 Phonological

1.1 *Long Sounds*

§ 495, D. II, 311 l. 4/B. II, 285 l. 7 لأنّك لا تدع صوت الفم يطول حتى تبتدئ صوتا

When pronouncing unvowelled *mahmūsa* sounds in juncture across word boundaries, e.g. *ʾaḫriǧ ḥātiman* "send out Ḥātim", the sound is not prolonged.

---

* This paper is an expansion, with corrections, of Carter 2016:180 at note [202] (a), and id. 207.

1 Online versions of the text of the *Kitāb* were not consulted for this paper. Troupeau's *Index* is more informative than the electronic alternatives (but cf. 3.13 below).

2 A reviewer correctly notes that the expression *ṭūl al-kalām* does not occur explicitly in the *Kitāb*. It is used here following the practice of the later grammarians. I am grateful to both

 | DOI:10.1163/9789004515895_003

1.2 *Extension of Speech Organs*

§ 567, D. II, 462 l. 1/B. II, 412 l. 16 والشين لا تُدغَم في الجيم لانّ الشين استَطال مَخْرَجُها لرَخاوتها

The sound of the [character] *šīn* does not assimilate to *ǧīm* because the point of articulation of *šīn* is "long", i.e. stretched or extended.[3]

1.3 *Long Sounds (with* maṭl)

§ 567, D. II, 461 l. 7/B. II, 412 l. 2 يكونان كالألف في المدّ والمطْل

The length of final *–ū* and *–ī* inhibits sandhi assimilation, because they share the properties of *ʾalif* (i.e. *ā*) in being "extended" sounds.

The phrase *al-madd wa-l-maṭl* raises a problem: is it merely a variant of *al-madd wa-l-līn*, the standard designation of the weak consonants *ʾalif*, *wāw* and *yāʾ*, or does it refer to a special feature of *ʾalif* alone? Jahn ad loc. omits *maṭl* in his translation, as if it were a synonym of *madd*; see also comment in 1.4.

1.4 *Long Sounds (with* mamṭūl)

§ 566, D. II, 456 l. 10/B. II, 407 l. 19 حرفُ مدّ ولينٍ كأنه يعوّض ذلك لأنه حرف ممطول

We also find *mamṭūl*, describing the lengthening effect of a "long" consonant *ḥarf mamṭūl* on the vowels. As in 1.3, the relationship between *maṭl* and *madd* is unexplained.

Given the rarity of *maṭala*, and the fact that Ḫalīl is not named in this context, it may be a relic of pre-Sībawayhian terminology which never established itself. Ḫalīl certainly knew the word, but does not associate it with speech when defining *maṭala* in the *Kitāb al-ʿAyn* (VII, 433–434).

1.5 *Long Sounds (with* maṭṭata)

§ 506, D. II, 324 l. 15 f. /B. II, 297 l. 4 f. أما الذين يشبعون فيمططون وعلامتها واو وياء

reviewers for their comments and corrections, which, where relevant, have been incorporated below, mostly without further acknowledgment.

3 Either in the acoustic or the articulatory sense, cf. Fleischer 1885–1888:I, 9, fn. 1, and I, 14.

A similar verb, *maṭṭaṭa*, occurs once in the *Kitāb*, in the statement *yušbiʿūna fa-yumaṭṭiṭūna* "[those who] saturate [the sound] excessively prolong it", referring to the overextended pronunciation of the inflectional vowels, as in *yaḍribūhā* for 3rd sing. *yaḍribuhā*. This time there is a possibility of the influence of Ḫalīl, with whom Sībawayhi discusses this topic in the course of the chapter, and it is noteworthy that in the *Kitāb al-ʿAyn* (VII, 409; cf. Talmon 1997: 347) the cognate verb *maṭṭa* in *maṭṭa kalāmahu* is glossed as *maddahu wa-ṭawwalahu*. But again *maṭṭa*, like *maṭala*, is a marginal term. At some stage the noun *maṭṭa* came to denote the calligraphic lengthening of a line or a character to achieve the justification of the written text, and it also serves as a Qurʾānic diacritic, marking the overlong recitation of *ʾalif mamdūda*.[4]

2 Morphological

2.1 *Single Noun Status (with* mamṭūl)

§ 159, D. I, 282 l. 8/B. I, 324 l. 19 — الاسمان فيه بمنزلة اسم واحد ممطول

This time *mamṭūl* refers to such long compounds as [*yā*] *ṯalāṯatan wa-ṯalāṯīna*, which are compared with [*yā*] *ḍāriban raǧulan* in their equivalence to single nouns.

Here again it is not clear whether *mamṭūl* is a technical term: it appears in the chapter title, but in the body of the text it is the notion of *ṭūl al-kalām* which is invoked to account for the morphology.

2.2 *Second Element as End of Compound Noun*

§ 317, D. II, 63 l. 23/B. II, 68 l. 16 — لأنّ الاسم قد طال ولم يكن الأول المنتهى

A familiar general principle is invoked, that an element can function as the end of a compound word, in this case the coordinated vocative *yā zaydan wa-ʿamran*. As Sībawayhi puts it, "the noun is long and its first element [*zaydan*] is not the end [of the word]".

4 According to Antonin Goguyer (1846–1909) (Ibn Mālik *ʾAlfiyya*(2) 321, s.v. *maṭṭa*), but he provides no sources.

2.3 *Long Qualifiers*

§ 39, D. I, 78 l. 16/B. I, 95 l. 8

كما حذفوها من اللذَيْن والّذين حين طال الكلام
وكان الاسم الأول منتهاه الاسمُ الآخِر

The same principle applies to long qualifiers, which may be shortened by elision. The trigger for this observation is the poetic elision seen in *al-ḥāfiẓū ʿawrata l-ʿašīrati* "those protecting the [vulnerable] gaps of the tribe", where the participle loses the final *nūn* which would mark the end of the word, but retains the verbal operation of the full form *al-ḥāfiẓūna ʿawrata l-ʿašīrati*.[5]

2.4 *Elision of Definiteness Markers in Proper Names*

§ 123, D. I, 228 l. 4/B. I, 267 l. 8

جمعتْ ما ذكرنا من التطويل وحذفوا

This quotation was chosen simply to illustrate the perils of translation. Troupeau correctly identifies *taṭwīl* as a morphological lengthening, referring to the affixes and qualifiers of personal names which have been discussed exhaustively in the preceding pages of the *Kitāb*,[6] thus "[these nouns] combine the lengthening which we have already mentioned." But Jahn (1895: I, 338) has misunderstood *taṭwīl* here to mean "going on at length about something", and accordingly translated it as "a wide-ranging description" (eine weitläufige Beschreibung).

Sībawayhi's point is that personal names are a special case: to adapt Marogy's formulation, they are "pragmatically definite" because of their "deictic accessibility",[7] so the presence of these "lengthening" elements is irrelevant to the definiteness of personal names, cf. *al-ḥasanu* and *ḥasanun*.

3 Syntactical

3.1 *Coordination of Noun to Pronoun*

§ 216, D. I, 342 l. 14/B. I, 390 l. 5

وذلك أنّك لما وصفته حسن الكلام حيث
طوّلته ووكّدته

5 Sībawayhi compares it to another poetic licence, the reduction of the relative nouns *allaḏāni* and *allaḏīna* to *allaḏā* and *allaḏī*, e.g. *ʾinna ʿammayya llaḏā qatalā l-mulūka* for *allaḏāni qatalā l-mulūka* "my two uncles are the ones who killed kings".

6 Namely the definite article, *tanwīn*, annexation and quasi-annexation, adjectival and relative qualification, cf. below 7.6.

7 Marogy 2010:101, fn. 8, and 113 respectively.

This is a simple example of the principle of the "long" constituent produced by co-ordinating a pronoun agent and an overt noun agent, as in the Qurʾān (Q. 2/35 and elsewhere) *uskun ʾanta wa-zawǧuka l-ǧannata* etc., where the agent is extended (*ṭawwaltahu*) by the addition of a second agent.

3.2 *Inversion*

§ 31, D. I, 49 l. 18/B. I, 61 l. 14 كلّما طال الكلام ضعف التأخير إذا أعملت

It is unacceptable to delay the operating verb for too long in inverted sentences, thus **zaydan ʾaḫāka ʾaẓunnu* *"Zayd to be your brother I believe" is rejected (the translation echoes the incorrect syntax). But if the sentential clause is not the object of the verb, inversion is permitted, as in *ʿabdu llāhi ṣāḥibu ḏālika balaġanī* "ʿAbd Allāh is the owner of that has reached me". Sībawayhi specifically states that *ʿabdu llāhi ṣāḥibu ḏālika* is not operated on by *balaġanī*, presumably because in this fronted position it is the subject of a nominal sentence, and the agent of *balaġanī* is the referential pronoun contained in the verb.

3.3 *Elliptical Exclamations*

§ 54, D. I, 117 l. 7/B. I, 139 l. 1 فشبّهت بإيّاك حيث طال الكلام

Because exclamations of warning are typically a single word, e.g. *al-ḥiḏāra* "beware!" the compound warning *raʾsaka wa-l-sayfa* "[look out for] your head and the sword!" is regarded as a "long" form. Sībawayhi explains that the first element, *raʾsaka*, has been assimilated to the syntax of another compound warning, *ʾiyyāka wa-l-ʾasada* "[look out for] yourself and the lion!", where *ʾiyyāka* has dependent case as the direct object of the verb for which *ʾiyyāka* here acts as a substitute (*badal*), namely *ittaqi* "be careful!". In both structures the second element has dependent form by coordination.

3.4 *Separation of Elements*

§ 37, D. I, 74 l. 8/B. I, 89 l. 3 كلّما طال الكلام كان أقوى وذلك أنّك لا تفصل بين الجارّ وما يعمل فيه

This illustrates the consequences of separating bound elements, as in *hāḏā ḍāribu zaydin fīhā wa-ʿamran* "this man is the striker of Zayd in it and ʿAmr [dep.]", i.e. not "and of ʿAmr" because the intrusive *fīhā* breaks the syntactic bond, forcing the change of case to the default *ʿamran*.

3.5 *Agreement Issues*

§ 111, D. I, 202 l. 3–4/B. I, 235 l. 12–13

كلّما طال الكلام فهو أحسن نحو قولك حضر القاضيَ امرأةٌ لأنّه إذا طال الكلام كان الحذف أجمل

In *ḥaḍara l-qāḍiya imraʾatun* "[there] attended [masc.] the judge, a woman" (the translation replicates the anomalous structure), the distance between the verb and its agent allows the elision of the fem. agent marker. When Mubarrad (d. 285/898 or 286/899) discusses this phenonemon he inserts *al-yawma* into the text, *ḥaḍara l-qāḍiya l-yawma imraʾatun* "there attended [masc.] the judge, today, a woman" (cf. 5.1). This insertion is unnecessary, but Mubarrad's made-up example immediately following, *nazala dāraka wa-dāra zaydin ǧāriyatun* "[there] dwelt [masc.], in your house and the house of Zayd, a slave-girl" shows that he wanted to stress the separation (*al-tafriqa bayn al-ism wa-l-fiʿl*) rather than the distance of the verb from its agent. Perhaps for this reason he does not invoke *ṭūl al-kalām* here.[8]

3.6 *Long Vocatives*

§ 148 D. I, 270 l. 7, l. 11 f./B. I, 311 l. 13, l. 18 f.

وكذلك نداء النكرة لمّا لحقها التنوين وطالت صارت بمنزلة المضاف

With the indefinite vocative *yā rākiban* "O any rider" the dependent form is accounted for by Ḫalīl himself as due to the similarity between a dependent vocative noun in annexation (e.g. *yā ʿabda llāhi*) and a noun with a *tanwīn* suffix acting as the completion of that noun, both regarded as "long" forms compared with the simple vocative *yā rākibu*, where unmarked *rākibu* is defined by position. He draws a parallel between the vocatives and the behaviour of the word *qabl*: we find *qablu* and *yā rākibu* in isolation, *qabla* and *yā ʿabda llāhi* in annexation, and *qablan* and *yā rākiban* with *tanwīn*.

8 In effect Mubarrad has discarded or failed to take account of Sībawayhi's analysis, where the issue is not separation but the hierarchy of definiteness, whereby delaying the indefinite agent creates a longer than minimal utterance. Similar agreement issues are dealt with elsewhere in *Muqtaḍab* III, 349, again invoking separation. For a brief discussion of definiteness and word order issues in the *Kitāb*, cf. Carter 2015:38 and 2016:107 f. = note [123] (b).

3.7 *Irregular* tanwīn

§ 148, D. I, 271 l. 17 f./B. 1, 313 l. 10 يجعله إذا نُون وطال كالنكرة

The lengthening effect of *tanwīn* also explains the anomalous vocative *yā maṭarun* in a line of verse. This time the dependent form is not permitted because the *tanwīn* is not an indefiniteness marker contrasting with a definite *yā maṭaru* (unlike *yā rākibu* versus *yā rākiban*). Instead it is a marker of *tamakkun*, so the regular *ḍamma* of the simple vocative is retained in *yā maṭarun*. Needless to say this is disputed among grammarians, but that is not our problem.[9]

3.8 *Further Long Vocatives with* tanwīn

§ 159, D. I, 282 l. 15/B. 1, 324 l. 25 كما لزم يا ضاربًا رجلا حين طال الكلام

Vocatives of compound words have to follow the pattern of *yā ḍāriban raǧulan* to avoid giving the listener the impression that two separate people are intended: thus *yā ṯalāṯatan wa-ṯalāṯīna* "O Mr. 33" and not *yā ṯalāṯatun wa-ṯalāṯūna* "O Mr. 3 and Mr. 30". The presence of the *tanwīn* on the first element marks the unity of the whole phrase, as if *ḍāriban* were the "middle of the noun" *wasaṭ al-ism* and *raǧulan* the completion of it *tamām al-ism*.

3.9 *Exceptives*

§ 188, D. I, 318 l. 7–8/B. 1, 363 l. 4–5 ولكنّه لمّا طال الكلام قَوِي واحتُمل ذلك كأشياء تجوز في الكلام إذا طال

In the exceptive constructions *mā ʾanta ʾillā ḏāhiban* and *lā ʾaḥada raʾaytuhu ʾillā zaydun* the irregular case of *ḏāhiban* (instead of *ḏāhibun*) and *zaydun* (instead of *zaydan*) is permitted because the length of the utterance carries the excepted element beyond the reach of case agreement.[10]

---

9 ʿĪsā b. ʿUmar al-Ṯaqafī (d. 149/766) argues for *yā maṭaran*, appealing to the model of *yā rākiban* etc., but this is rejected by Sībawayhi, perhaps echoing or siding with Ḫalīl.

10 Sībawayhi links this topic with several other constructions displaying the same (dialectal) inconsistency in agreement, implicitly because of their length, e.g. the alternation of *mā ʾanta ʾillā sayran* (D. I, 140 l. 16/B. 1, 168 l. 15) and *mā ʾanta ʾillā sayrun* (D. I, 319 l. 11/B. 1, 364 l. 5), which he compares to the inconsistency of agreement between *mā fīhā ʾaḥadun*

3.10 *Long Bound Forms*

§ 188, D. I, 348 l. 1/B. 1, 395 l. 14 حتى يكون ما بعدها معرفة أو ما أشبه المعرفة ممّا طال

The principle of extended utterances also applies to "long" constituents such as *ḫayrun minka, ʾafḍalu minka* and others. The bond between *ḫayrun* and *minka* is strong enough for Ḫalīl to equate it with the bond between subject and predicate: just as a subject arouses in the listener the expectation of a predicate (*Kitāb* I, 346 l. 20 f./B. 1, 394 l. 16), so *minka* is obligatory after *ḫayrun* because the listener will be waiting for it.

3.11 *Compensation Issues,* ʿiwaḍ

§ 223, D. I, 352 l. 14/B. 1, 399 l. 15 لأنّه إذا طال الكلام فهو أمثل قليلا وكأن طوله عوض من ترك هو

The question revolves around the omission of the referential pronoun *huwa* in *iḍrib ʾayyahum [huwa] qāʾilun laka šayʾan* "strike whichever of them is saying something to you".[11] Ḫalīl explains that the length of the utterance compensates for the absence of *huwa*.[12]

3.12 *Qurʾānic* ṭūl al-kalām

§ 272, D. I, 423 l. 20/B. 1, 474 l. 20 وكان في هذا حسناً حين طال الكلام

Even the Qurʾān exhibits *ṭūl al-kalām*, namely Q. 91/9, *qad ʾaflaḥa man zakkāhā* "[God] has caused to prosper him who purified [his soul]", dropping the asseverative *la-* required on *la-qad ʾaflaḥa*. But it is correct to elide it because of the length of the utterance, in this case the eight preceding verses, all of them oaths, "by the sun and its brightness, by the moon when it follows it" and so on.[13]

ʾillā ḥimāran (D. I, 319 l. 7/B. 1, 363 l. 24) and *lā ʾaḥada fīhā ʾillā ḥimārun* (D. I, 319 l. 4/B. 1, 364 l. 1).

11 A very similar example occurs in D. I, 231 l. 7/B. 1, 270 l. 11, *mā ʾanā bi-llaḏī [huwa] qāʾilun laka sūʾan*, this time with *sūʾan* instead of *šayʾan*, which would make more sense, and is confirmed by a repetition of this example, now with *qabīḥan*.

12 ʾAbū ʿAlī al-Fārisī (d. 377/987) accounts similarly for the elision of a relative pronoun in a "long" utterance, cf. Baalbaki 2000 [2004]:201f.

13 The prose model for this is *wa-llāhi ʾinnahu la-ḏāhibun* "by God, verily he is going away".

3.13 *Overlap of Object Language and Metalanguage*

§149, D. I, 263 l. 2/B. I, 304 l. 4 ولم يكن فيه ما كان في الطويل لطوله

The problem lies in the vocative phrase *ʾa-zaydu ʾaḫā warqāʾa* "O Zayd, brother of Warqāʾ" (a poetic example), where the second vocative *ʾaḫā warqāʾa* has dependent form even though it is in apposition to *zaydu* and should therefore agree in case, as in *yā zaydu l-ṭawīlu* "O Zayd the tall one" with independent qualifier *al-ṭawīlu*. Ḫalīl declares that *ʾaḫā warqāʾa* is not like *zaydu l-ṭawīlu*, because annexed vocative phrases, such as *ʾaḫā warqāʾa*, must be formally inflected for their dependent function, while in *yā zaydu l-ṭawīlu* the independent form of *al-ṭawīlu* is permitted "because of the length [of the utterance]", *li-ṭūlihi*.

Jahn (1900: II, 2) and Reuschel (1959: 22 f.) correctly reproduce the concept of morphological length, but Troupeau seems to have been distracted by the context. In his *Lexique-Index* he does count four occurrences of *ṭūl* in the *Kitāb*, of which this is the second, but he gives no page number for it: perhaps he understood *li-ṭūlihi* literally "because he is tall" and not as a technical term.

4 *Ṭūl al-kalām* in Farrāʾ (d. 207/822)

The subsequent history of the concept is outside the scope of this paper, but a few examples will be offered. Thanks to the monumental concordance of the late Naphtali Kinberg, we can easily trace *ṭūl al-kalām* in the *Maʿānī al-Qurʾān*.

4.1 *In Phonological Contexts*

An intriguing asymmetry emerges between his and Sībawayhi's use of the concept: for example, both invoke *ṭūl al-kalām* in phonological contexts, but do not apply it to the same sounds. Whereas Sībawayhi applies it to the weak consonants *ʾalif*, *wāw* and *yāʾ* generally (1.1) and to *šīn* and *ǧīm* (1.2), Farrāʾ restricts it to problems of pronunciation of *ʾalif* in combination with *hamza* or in pausal positions (cf. Kinberg 1996 s.v. *ṭāla*). We may speculate that the two grammarians are drawing on different traditions.

4.2 *With Durative Verbs*

Maʿānī I, 133 l. 1 فإذا كان الفعل الذي قبل حتى لا يتطاول وهو ماض رُفع الفعل بعد حتى

idem I, 133 l. 4 فإذا طال ما قبل حتى ذُهِب بما بعدها إلى النصب

Here Farrāʾ discusses *ḥattā* with durative verbs in the context of Q. 2/214, using *ṭāla* and *taṭāwala* several times in a meaning unconnected with *ṭūl al-kalām* (cf. Talmon 1993: 84–87 and 2003: 39, 105, 146, 209 on this passage). But although Sībawayhi's treatment of *ḥattā* quotes the same Qurʾānic passage as Farrāʾ and indeed the same poetic *šāhid* (*Kitāb* D. I, 327 l. 3ff./B. I, 417 l. 12) he makes no use of *ṭāla* in any sense.

4.3 *"Long"* naʿt *in* madḥ

Maʿānī I, 106 l. 6ff.	نصب المقيمين على أنه نعت للراسخين فطال نعته فنصب
idem I, 107 l. 8	لا ينصب الممدوح إلا عند تمام الكلام

There is a considerable overlap between Sībawayhi and Farrāʾ in their analysis of the same two Qurʾānic verses. The issue is the dependent case of *al-ṣābirīna fī l-baʾsāʾi* (Q. 2/177) where *al-ṣābirūna* would be expected, and of *wa-l-muqīmīna l-ṣalāta* (Q. 4/162) for the expected *al-muqīmūna*. Both grammarians attribute the dependent forms to the structure of praise and blame. However, their explanations differ. Sībawayhi (D. I, 213/B. I, 248f.) agrees with Ḫalīl that the dependent case is due to an implicit *uḏkur* "bear in mind, think of", while Farrāʾ states that in these expressions of praise and blame "the qualifier is long" (*ṭāla naʿtuhu*), and moreover occurs only "at the completion of the utterance" (*ʿinda tamām al-kalām*). Again it seems that both are drawing on independent traditions, but this time the principle of *ṭūl al-kalām* is invoked by Farrāʾ (following Kisāʾī, d. 189/805), while Sībawayhi's treatment of the same verses lacks all reference to the length of the qualifiers.

Curiously Sībawayhi does use the concept of "long adjectival qualifiers" in an entirely different context elsewhere, namely adjectival agreement in a series of adjectives. As Sībawayhi puts it, *ʾin ʾaṭalta l-naʿt* lit. "if you lengthen the qualifier [or the qualifying process]",[14] then the adjectives must all agree, e.g. *marartu bi-rağulin ʿāqilin karīmin muslimin* (*Kitāb* D. I, 178 l. 17/B. I, 210 l. 5). Significantly Ḫalīl takes no part in the discussion.

4.4 *Morphological Length*

Maʿānī I, 390 l. 7	وهو على التوهم إذا طالت الكلمة بعض الطول

A poetic use of *ʾimmā* "or" by itself instead of the normal paired *ʾimmā … ʾimmā* "either … or" is said to be based on the assumption that although *ʾimmā* is

14 Here, as often in the *Kitāb*, it is not clear whether the term refers to the class of speech act or its linguistic output.

"somewhat longer" than the shorter word *ʾaw* "or" it can still mean the same. Farrāʾ's formulation, *ʿalā l-tawahhum*, is essentially negative, implying a false assumption, but since it is applied here to a Qurʾānic usage as well, it must be interpreted more broadly, along the lines of "on the understanding that", see the detailed study by Baalbaki (1982 [2004]).

5 *Ṭūl al-kalām* in Mubarrad

5.1 *Lack of Gender Agreement*

Muqtaḍab II, 148 l. 5, 338 l. 1 — حضر القاضيَ اليومَ امرأة

The lack of gender agreement in *ḥaḍara l-qāḍiya* [*l-yawma*] *mraʾatun* has already been dealt with in 3.5 (cf. *Muqtaḍab* III, 349 for related examples).

5.2 *Link between* ṭūl *and* ʿiwaḍ

Muqtaḍab II, 338 l. 2 — فيجيزون الحذف مع طول الكلام لأنّهم يرون ما زاد عوضًا ممّا حذف

This too has been dealt with above, cf. 3.5.

5.3 *Elision with Long Utterances*

Muqtaḍab II, 337 l. 9 on Q. 91/9 — وحذفت اللام لطول القصّة لأنّ الكلام إذا طال كان الحذف أجمل

Dealt with above, cf. 3.12.

5.4 *On* al-ḥāfiẓū ʿawrata l-ʿašīrati

Muqtaḍab IV, 145 l. 10 — حذف النون لطول الاسم
idem IV, 146 l. 1 — يحذفون لطول الصلة

Likewise dealt with above, cf. 2.3. Note that in all cases Mubarrad is more or less paraphrasing Sībawayhi.

What is relevant to our topic is the fact that Mubarrad finds four different ways of referring to the length of an utterance, as *ṭūl al-kalām* (5.2), then as *ṭūl al-qiṣṣa* in (5.3), and *ṭūl al-ism* and *ṭūl al-ṣila* in (5.4). None of the last three is found in the *Kitāb*. Presumably Mubarrad is aiming to identify different types of long utterances, but whether these subcategories were ever adopted remains to be explored.

6 *Ṭūl al-kalām* in ʾAbū Ḥayyān al-Ġarnāṭī (d. 745/1344)

A more or less random example from ʾAbū Ḥayyān is interesting in that it applies the concept to a feature not discussed in those terms in the *Kitāb*.

6.1 Rubbamā *and* ṭūl/ʿiwaḍ

Irtišāf 464, l. 13 فطول الكلام بالتركيب عوض من الفعل المحذوف

The issue is the poetic use of *rubbamā* without a following verb,[15] exactly like the elliptical English "maybe". ʾAbū Ḥayyān argues that the extra length of the compound *rubba* + *mā* compensates for the elided verb. Note the connection between *ṭūl* and *ʿiwaḍ*, on which see further below, 7.8.

7 *Ṭūl al-kalām* as Part of the Grammatical System

When Sībawayhi says in 3.9, "but when the speech is long there is the capacity and the potential for that [i.e. to vary the inflection], just as other things are permitted in speech when it is long", he is telling us that *ṭūl al-kalām* is a general operating principle of the language he is describing.

The remainder of this paper reviews the place of *ṭūl al-kalām* in Sībawayhi's system, starting with some speculations about the nature of Ḫalīl's contribution, then examining the nexus of concepts to which *ṭūl al-kalām* belongs. Space limits us to bullet points, though something with a less military tone would be preferable, so the following comments are strung together in medieval Arab fashion like pearls on a necklace, *laʾālī al-marām fī ṭūl al-kalām*, as Suyūṭī (d. 911/1505) might have put it.

15 The verse rhymes in *rubbamā*, and is by ʾAbū Tammām (d. 231/845; *Dīwān* 260). ʾAbū Ḥayyān claims that he knows of no other such verse, though the standard reference sources also attribute a different verse with the same rhyme to Ḥātim al-Ṭāʾī (d. 578 CE) or ʿUrwa b. al-Ward (d. 607 CE).

7.1 *Ḫalīl as a Prosodist*

Ḫalīl's contribution to the *Kitāb* is usually assessed in terms of his achievements in phonology, morphology and lexicography, but here we shall consider his role as the founder of Arabic prosody.

Arabic poetry is a purely oral phenomenon, a particular register of speech. The phonological unit of poetry is the line, *bayt*, a single indivisible acoustic event, marked by a first syllable containing no initial consonant clusters (as dictated by the law[16] of syllable structure), and a final syllable exhibiting a rhyme only partially (and if so, then only coincidentally) the same as the pausal forms of ordinary speech. Everything in between is a continuum of uninterrupted junctural forms, and no pause is permitted in recitation.[17]

The corresponding unit of prose discourse, *kalām*, shares with poetry the property of being a single phonological event, bearing formal initial and final markers, but, unlike poetry, *kalām* is of indeterminate length, metrically unstructured and, most importantly, it allows internal pause, either at breath groups or for rhetorical reasons.[18]

This paper argues that Ḫalīl's analysis of *kalām* is fundamentally that of a prosodist. The key feature of his approach is what might nowadays be termed "suprasegmental", that is to say, he accepted the word classes set out at the beginning of the *Kitāb*, but he was primarily interested in the behaviour of spoken words in combination, where the listener identifies the constituents by means of audible clues, similar to the way the metrical structure of a poem is perceived while it is being recited.

As a prosodist, Ḫalīl would surely have agreed with Frolov (2000: 61) on "the prosodic irrelevance of word junctures" in poetry, but when dealing with prose as a grammarian Ḫalīl inverted this principle to use the **potential** pauses in *kalām* to extract its syntactic units.

In a process probably unconnected with Ḫalīl (and certainly irrelevant to his purpose), it was these same pauses, potential and actual, which enabled

---

16 Borrowing Frolov's term, 2000:60f., for this inexorable prosodic rule. This paper owes much to Frolov, especially 61–68.

17 The end of the first *miṣrāʿ*, for example, is always in juncture with the beginning of the second *miṣrāʿ*, except in the opening line of a *qaṣīda*, when both are pronounced with the full rhyming form, e.g. … *manzilī* … *ḥawmalī* (Imruʾ al-Qays, d. 540? CE). For metrical reasons *manzilī* cannot be reduced to *manzil*, the pausal form it would have in prose.

18 Qurʾānic recitation is not considered here, except to observe that its spellings are junctural, even at the end of the verse, regardless of the recitation. However there are also internal pauses, marked as optional or obligatory by additional signs superimposed on the junctural spelling. To this extent the Qurʾān provides rare documentary evidence of suprasegmental speech patterns, cf. Larcher 2017:74 for the parsing implications.

the division of *kalām* into written words. As is well known, the Arabic writing system represents each word as if it were dictated in isolation, relying on the speaker's intuition as to where pauses could be made.[19]

In their conversations about Arabic, Ḫalīl and Sībawayhi were in fact describing a preliterate, virtually pre-literary language, with all the data being oral. We see this clearly in Ḫalīl's treatment of *ʾišmām*, where the inflectional *ḍamma* is reduced to the point of inaudibility: this speech act, says Ḫalīl, is only discernible in the pursing of the speaker's lips, hence imperceptible to a blind listener (*Kitāb*, D. II, 309 l. 1–7/B. II, 283 l. 9–15).[20] Likewise we see in 1.3 that it is the sound of the language which interests Ḫalīl when he describes *ʾišbāʿ* as "saturating by prolonging" the inflectional vowels, as in *yaḍribūhā*, probably with extra stress on those vowels.[21]

Arabic orthography is not alone in lacking a notation for stress, tone or vowel quality: in English, for example, we say "not every black bird is a blackbird" but the difference in stress is not graphically marked. Likewise in "not every noble man is a nobleman", neither the stress nor the vowel gradation are indicated: unlike the free noun "man" [mæn], the suffix "-man" is virtually enclitic, unstressed, short, and pronounced [mən]. Likewise in French singing, final silent /e/ creates an additional syllable by being pronounced [ə]. For Ḫalīl such suprasegmental features were taken for granted: as a native speaker he would use the appropriate intonation and stress patterns when citing the data, without the need to provide any written symbols for them.

7.2 *Morpheme Boundaries*

Although he accepted the word classes set out at the beginning of the *Kitāb*, words themselves *kalimāt* (or *kalim*) are not Ḫalīl's primary unit of discourse: he speaks quite frequently of *ṭūl al-kalām* in the *Kitāb*, but never of *ṭūl al-kalima*.[22]

---

19 Ghersetti (2011:95, fn. 31) points out that the same technique is used in modern Western linguistics.

20 Perhaps Sībawayhi had this in mind when he reversed the idea to state that even a blind man can use the verb *raʾā* in the sense of "consider, regard" as one of the *ʾafʿāl al-qulūb* (D. I, 13 l. 21/B. I, 18 l. 13).

21 *Ad hoc* notations for these and other phonological features were, of course, devised for use in the *Kitāb* and the *Qirāʾāt*, but only the *madda* sign was incorporated into the standard orthographical repertoire. The IPA has equally failed to penetrate Western writing systems.

22 It will be apparent here and elsewhere that the collection of papers edited by Lancioni & Bettini (2011), with its focus on *kalima*, has little overlap with the present article, one exception being the contribution of Ghersetti.

To be sure he does use *ṭūl al-kalima* in the *Kitāb al-ʿAyn* to refer to the length of a word, but only at the morphological/lexical, not syntactical level, see Talmon (1997: index s.v. *ṭāla*, and p. 145), where it is glossed as "conditioned by word length" without further explanation. In fact the absolute length of the syntactical "word" is irrelevant to what Ḫalīl meant by *ṭūl al-kalām*. We see this in Sīrāfī's (d. 368/979) scornful refutation of Farrāʾ's assertion that the loss of *tanwīn* in the vocative is due to the length of the noun. To this Sīrāfī responds that length plays no part in the process: just as vocative *zaydu* alternates with non-vocative *zaydun*, so do the fanciful and doubtless fictitious vocatives [*yā*] *fazaʿbulānatu, mazanbazānu, ǧūḏābadanatu, ʾušnābadabatu* "and other names with many letters" alternate with their non-vocative forms *fazaʿbulānatun* and *ǧūḏābadanatun*, quoted a few lines below.[23]

Note also that Ḫalīl's term for compound elements with the status of single words is *ism wāḥid* "a single noun", not *kalima wāḥida* (cf. 7.4).[24] We conclude that he preferred to focus on the constituents of *kalām* as elements which could be isolated (and hence quoted as data and discussed in the metalanguage) by segmenting the utterance at the appropriate pausal points. This method is independent of orthographical conventions, and avoids the need to define the parts of speech formally.

7.3 *The Role of* tanwīn

The major unit of *kalām*, the complete sentence, can be taken for granted: under well-defined semantic conditions, such utterances formally break the silence with a vocative element (usually omitted in practice, D. I, 274 l. 1/B. I, 316 l. 5), and end with a pausal form, *waqf*, returning to silence.

Within this string of sounds the *tanwīn* acquires an importance which has generally been underestimated: as well as marking morphosyntactic fullness,

23 Sīrāfī, cmt. on D. I, 262 l. 10/B. I, 303 l. 12, at MS fol. 201b et seq. The passage could not be traced in the one printed edition accessed on line. Note that Sīrāfī's paraphrase of Farrāʾ does use *ṭāla*, but this is no guarantee that the Kufan himself did so—the item is not listed in Kinberg. Cf. also 4.4 above for another use of *ṭūl al-kalima* by Farrāʾ.

24 A reviewer correctly points out that Ḫalīl does use [*manzilat*] *kalima wāḥida* to refer to the compound word *ka-ʾanna* (*Kitāb* D. I, 423 l. 21/B. I, 474 l. 21) but this is in a morphological sense, in keeping with what seems to be Ḫalīl's predominant analytical focus. Moreover he also uses *manzilat ḥarf wāḥid* for *lan* etc. (D. I, 361 l. 17 /B. I, 407 l. 16f.) and *manzilat ism wāḥid* for *māḏā* (D. I, 359, l. 1/B. I, 405, l. 4), while *ism wāḥid* is also used regularly for compound nouns such as *ḥaḍramawt* (D, I, 298 l. 2/B. I, 341 l. 16 and elsewhere), again in a morphological sense. At first sight *kalima wāḥida* looks rather isolated in the *Kitāb*, in contrast with Farrāʾ, who uses *kalima wāḥida* a number of times in a syntactic sense (cf. Kinberg 1996 s.v.).

tamakkun, and indefiniteness (historically a secondary function), *tanwīn* also indicates that the utterance is not yet complete, and is thus complementary to *waqf*,[25] the marker of completeness.[26]

Waqf audibly signals to the listener that the utterance thus far is complete (without affecting the speaker's right to continue),[27] and that it is now the listener's turn to speak. In contrast, *tanwīn* audibly signals that the speaker has not finished, and it is not yet the listener's turn to speak.

This role of the *tanwīn* is confirmed by Sībawayhi's report of the situation where a *tanwīn* is, as it were, put on hold, because the speaker cannot think of what to say next, but does not want the listener to interrupt. By adding an arbitrary syllable, as in *hāḏā sayfun-ī* "this is a sword, um", the speaker retains control of the conversation (cf. Carter 2015: 47, 60).

7.4 Ism wāḥid

The notion that compound elements can have the status of a single noun, *ism wāḥid*, is too well known to need discussion: it will suffice to note that the second element of such groups is morphologically "the end of that [compound] noun" *muntahā al-ism*, cf. 2.2, 2.3.

It is here that the non-pausal function of *tanwīn* is most prominent. In the words of Ḫalīl, speaking of the vocative *yā ḍāriban rağulan* (3.8), the *tanwīn* of *ḍāriban* cannot be elided because "it is the middle of the noun and *rağulan* belongs to the completion of the noun" *al-tanwīn wasaṭ al-ism wa-rağulan min tamām al-ism* (D. I, 282 l. 17/B. 1, 325 l. 1, and cf. 2.1 or 2.2)

As already noted (7.2) the term *ism wāḥid* is preferred over *kalima wāḥida*, as if to avoid problems of the definition of *kalima*.[28] There is no phonological or morphological uniformity in what constitutes *ism wāḥid* beyond the fact that the string can function in the place of a single word.

---

25 Naturally words which never have *tanwīn* (the *ġayr munṣarif* etc.) will not display the formal opposition with *waqf*, but these are covered by the general principle of the *lafẓī* versus the *maḥallī*, i.e. as allomorphs of *tanwīn*.

26 Regarding *tamakkun* two recent studies of *tanwīn* offer a more refined perspective, namely Marogy 2015 and Ayoub 2018.

27 Larcher 2017, index s.v. segment, segmentée etc., introduces a concept borrowed from theoretical linguistics, namely segmentation, the principle that certain syntactic structures contain potential pauses at the boundaries of major constituents. These pauses are not marked by punctuation in Arabic, but it is interesting that translations of Arabic into French often have a comma at this boundary. These are precisely the points at which a listener might choose to interrupt the speaker.

28 The term *kalima wāḥida* is indeed found, but only in later grammar, cf. Guillaume 2011:61 and remarks above in 7.2.

The relationship between *ṭūl al-kalām* and *ism wāḥid* depends on the constituents involved: broadly constituents which do not themselves form complete sentences are classified as *ism wāḥid*, while complete sentences, although they may exhibit *ṭūl al-kalām*, are not treated as *ism wāḥid*, for example *ḥaḍara l-qāḍiya mraʾatun* in 3.5, and the series of Qurʾānic verses in 3.12, which are all "long" but are not *ism wāḥid*.[29] The difference can be appreciated by contrasting the two phrases *lā rağula* and *yā rağulu*: the negative unit *lā rağula* is considered to be *ism wāḥid* of the same nature as a compound noun such as *ḫamsata ʿašara* and the like,[30] while the vocative unit *yā rağulu* is equivalent to an elliptical verbal sentence and therefore cannot be replaced by a single noun.[31]

7.5 Baʿd al-tamām

The length of a self-sufficient (*mustaġnī*) utterance cannot be specified in advance, though the point at which it is "correct to be silent" (*yaḥsun al-sukūt ʿalayhi*) is governed by rules of formal structural correctness (*ḥusn/qubḥ*) and semantic adequacy (*istiqāma*), on which see *Kitāb* § 6. In this respect *ṭūl al-kalām* and *baʿd al-tamām* are complementary: *ṭūl al-kalām* refers to elements which are longer than minimal, without regard to their function, while *baʿd al-tamām* invokes the functional status of elements (termed *ʿumda* and *faḍla* in later grammar), without regard to their length. The listener thus performs two interpretative acts simultaneously, (1) identifying the boundaries of constituents with indeterminate length, and (2) distinguishing the two obligatory constituents of the minimal utterance from any structurally redundant elements (including those with no function at all, *laġw*).

The archetype for this, which has been covered in the secondary literature, is the phrase *ʿišrūna dirhaman*: the *tanwīn* (more precisely its allomorph here) on *ʿišrūna* signals the formal and syntactic completeness of that constituent, after which, *baʿd al-tamām* "after the completion", further elements are excluded from this syntagm. Such structurally extraneous elements usually default to the dependent form, for example in *ʿalayhi miʾatun bīḍan* "he owes a hundred, in

29 The grammarians were well aware that some types of sentence could indeed function as a single element, but the distinction is not relevant to the data in this paper.

30 The issue is dealt with by Sībawayhi, D. I, 306/B. I, 351 and succeeding chapters, and is conveniently paraphrased by Mubarrad, especially *Muqtaḍab* IV, 364 ff.

31 Vocative utterances are construed by Sībawayhi as verbal sentences with a permanently elided verb (D. I, 292 l. 8 f./B. I, 303 l. 11 f.). This adumbrates the more complex analysis of the later grammarians, who treated vocatives explicitly as performative utterances, cf. Kasher 2013, cf. also Larcher 2014:107 ff.

silver [coins]" (D. I, 262 l. 3/B. I, 299 l. 7), where the *tanwīn* on *mi'atun* is the marker of syntactic completeness at that point.

In principle every such *tanwīn* can be converted to pausal form if the utterance is permitted to end there, e.g. *ʿalayhi mi'ah*. A prominent exception is the type *ḫayrun minka* etc. in 3.10, where, as Ḫalīl puts it, for semantic reasons *minka* is indispensable to *ḫayrun*, hence its *tanwīn* must always be preserved.

Note that *ʿišrūna dirhaman* itself contains two *tanwīn*-s. The *nūn* on the first word, pronounced in full junctural form as *ʿišrūna*, signals that there is still more to come, like *ḍāriban rağulan*, in contrast with pausal *ʿišrūn*, which can only occur at the end of an utterance or segment. The other *tanwīn*, on *dirhaman*, is a grammatical fiction which does not exist outside the metalanguage: in natural language only the pausal form *dirhamā* can occur in this position, marking the end of the whole utterance, for example as an elliptical answer to the question, "what is the price of those sheep?". In Carter (2016: 196–200 = [261–268] in thesis pagination) this distinction was not given its proper weight.

Grammarians were aware of the artificiality of terminal junctural forms when citing data: frequently a seemingly unnecessary phrase is attached to a quoted example, e.g. *ḥaḍara l-qāḍiya l-yawma mra'atun yā fatā* (Mubarrad *Muqtaḍab* III, 338, cf. 5.1 above). The intention is to ensure that the final word of the data retains its junctural form with the relevant inflection. Another example is *yā 'ayyuhā l-rağulu zaydun 'aqbil* "O that man Zayd, come here!" (*Kitāb* D. I, 190 l. 19/B. I, 223 l. 12, cf. Marogy 2010: 177), where *'aqbil* protects the inflection of *zaydun*, which would disappear in the pausal *zayd*, thereby removing the point of the example, which is to illustrate agreement with *al-rağulu*.

7.6 Mufrad

In his typical manner Ḫalīl uses the category *mufrad* without actually defining it, and has no comprehensive term for elements which are not *mufrad*.

Fortunately we have a de facto definition of non-*mufrad* elements in the treatment of the qualification (*waṣf*) of definite nouns and related agreement issues in §104, especially starting at D. I, 188 l. 10/B. I, 220 l, 16. From this we may deduce that a word is *mufrad* if it lacks all the following features: definite article, *tanwīn*, coordination, annexation and quasi-annexation, adjectival and relative qualifiers (cf. 2.4 above).

In effect this leaves only two categories of word which are *mufrad*, the vocative [*yā*] *rağulu* and categorical negative [*lā*] *rağula*, which are morphologically isolated single words, while all other words are compound by affixation of or collocation with the above markers. This property was already pointed out by

Silvestre de Sacy (1758–1838) (Ibn Mālik *ʾAlfiyya* 142) to distinguish *mufrad* from its more common meaning of "singular [in number]".[32]

Note that the morphological pattern and case markers are included in the *mufrad* form, whether the latter are true inflections (dep. in *lā raǧula*) or not inflections at all (in *yā raǧulu*, also dep., but *mabnī ʿalā al-ḍamma*). A translation of *mufrad* as "bare" might be a useful approximation, but it would still only apply to [*yā*] *raǧulu* and [*lā*] *raǧula*. At the same time *mufrad* represents a radically different concept from what is implied by *kalima*.

7.7 Murakkab

It was left to later grammarians to invent the complementary term for *mufrad*, namely *murakkab*.[33] There is no trace of *murakkab* in the *Kitāb*, not even of the root *rakkaba*, and Mubarrad, and also Ibn al-Sarrāǧ (d. 316/929) (based on a superficial examination), manage to discuss the issues involving *mufrad* and non-*mufrad* elements without coining a general term for the latter. At this stage in the history of grammar there was no need to name the default category of non-*mufrad* items, as they had already been adequately defined by enumeration, cf. 7.6.[34]

The *Mufaṣṣal* of Zamaḫšarī (d. 538/1144) may represent a transitional stage. In §48 he lists *yā ʾayyuhā l-raǧulu* in the *mufrad* category, leaving us to work out for ourselves in §51 that only *ʾayyuhā* is covered by this term, and that the full phrase *yā ʾayyuhā l-raǧulu* belongs to the demonstrative category, following the analysis of Ḫalīl (*Kitāb* D. I, 295 l. 3–6/B. I, 306 l. 6–8). It is thus by default non-*mufrad*, but Zamaḫšarī does not use the term *murakkab* in this context.

7.8 Ṭūl al-kalām *and* ʿiwaḍ

References to compensation *ʿiwaḍ* in the context of *ṭūl al-kalām* above (2.3, 3.11, 5.2, 6.1), point to a complementarity between the length of an utterance and the ability to elide parts of it. As we know from his explicit statements, Ḫalīl believed that speakers are under an obligation to fulfil the listener's expectations (cf. 3.10), and this paper will draw a parallel between the process by which a listener recovers elided elements in prose and the reception of recited poetry.

---

32 As Silvestre de Sacy points out, a plural word can still be *mufrad*, as in *yā riǧālu*, cf. Q. 34/10, *yā ǧibālu* "O mountains".

33 The term *muṭawwal* is also found, for example in Ibn Mālik *ʾAlfiyya*(2) glossary 299. It appears to be more limited in scope than *murakkab*, applying only to extended phrases of the pattern *lā ḫayran min zaydin ʿindanā*, but has not been explored for this paper.

34 For a recent survey of the topic, cf. Lancioni & Bettini (2011), passim, especially the chapters by Ghersetti and Guillaume.

In both cases an acoustic structure is interpreted in terms of the listener's expectations, and the listener's knowledge of the conventions enables missing elements in prose to be restored, and poetry to be mentally scanned, whether to confirm its metrical integrity or to detect metrical errors in the length and number of syllables.

It is tempting to assume that elision cannot occur with *mufrad* items, since these are already minimal forms, and there is nothing to compensate for. There is one possible case, however, in the phenomenon of *tarḫīm*, such as *yā māli* a hypercorism of *yā māliku* "O Mālik!", where the emotional intensity of the utterance overrides the morphological rules.

8 Conclusion

It is time to apply the principle of *ṭūl al-kalām* to this paper and bring it to a close.

The terms discussed above are, to be sure, used relatively infrequently in the *Kitāb*, but it is also apparent that they represent a nexus of interrelated concepts which are applied systematically and coherently to a wide range of linguistic phenomena, in a significant number of cases in association with the name of Ḫalīl b. ʾAḥmad.

Bear in mind that these phenomena are all oral, acoustic events which could only be segmented into constituents by hearing them, using the alternation of audible *tanwīn* and pause to establish the boundaries, and measuring them against a principle of minimal length determined by their function in the utterance. As a prosodist, Ḫalīl was predisposed to perform such an analysis. He would have been more sensitive than most to those orthographically unmarked suprasegmental features outlined in 7.1, while his use of the complementary notions of *ism wāḥid* (7.4) and *baʿd al-tamām* (7.5) suggest that he was intuitively aware of what might nowadays be termed domains, the extent of the effect of one element upon another beyond the constituent, even over some distance.

The case argued above about the role of prosody in Ḫalīl's analysis is admittedly speculative. If correct, it goes some way to explaining the cluster of terms around *ṭūl al-kalām* and more generally Ḫalīl's role as the provider not only of most of Sībawayhi's data but also his method of processing it as an oral corpus. This in no way diminishes Sībawayhi's originality, which is asserted from the very first line of the *Kitāb*, and we should also take into account that occasionally Sībawayhi uses the principle of *ṭūl al-kalām* without reference to his master (Ḫalīl is not cited, for instance, in 1.2, 1.3, 2.3, and cf. also 4.3), suggesting a degree of independence.

Within a century of Ḫalīl's death, however, the spoken language was replaced by writing as the dominant medium for religious, cultural and administrative discourse throughout the Islamic empire. The most prolific writer of the 3rd/9th century, Ǧāḥiẓ (d. 255/868–869) is praised for a book which, as the reigning Caliph Maʾmūn describes it, *yanūbu ʿan ḥuḍūri l-ṣāḥibi* "substitutes for the presence of the author",[35] indicating the social consequences of the great media shift. It did not put an end to oral delivery, far from it, but books came to replace memory as the repository of both knowledge and the power which went with it. The grammarians for their part had an interest in presenting Classical Arabic as a living mother tongue, so if there are any explicit statements about the written language it is likely that they will be scarce, at least before the Nahḍa. By that time scholarly interaction with the West might have led the grammarians to the recognition that their *naḥw* "correct way of speaking" had evolved spontaneously and independently into something resembling the Western science of "grammar", that is "correct way of writing", i.e. "literacy", but that is a topic which remains to be explored.

Bibliography

Primary Sources

ʾAbū Ḥayyān, *Irtišāf* = ʾAbū Ḥayyān Muḥammad b. Yūsuf al-Ġarnāṭī al-Naḥwī, *Irtišāf al-ḍarab fī lisān al-ʿArab*. Ed. by Muṣṭafā ʾAḥmad al-Nammās. Al-Qāhira: n.p., 2 vol., 1984–1987.

ʾAbū Tammām, *Dīwān* = ʾAbū Tammām Ḥabīb b. ʾAws b. al-Ḥāriṯ al-Ṭāʾī, *Dīwān ʾAbī Tammām*. Ed. by Ṣāhīn ʿAṭiyya, revised by Būlus al-Mawṣilī. Bayrūt: Maktabat al-ṭullāb wa-šarikat al-kitāb al-lubnānī, 1968.

Farrāʾ, *Maʿānī* = ʾAbū Zakariyyā Yaḥyā b. Ziyād b. ʿAbd Allāh b. Manẓūr al-Daylamī al-Farrāʾ, *Maʿānī al-Qurʾān*. Ed. by ʾAḥmad Yūsuf Naǧātī, Muḥammad ʿAlī al-Naǧǧār, and ʿAbd al-Fattāḥ ʾIsmāʿīl Šalabī. Al-Qāhira: al-Dār al-miṣriyya, 3 vol., 1955–1972.

Ḫalīl, *ʿAyn* = ʾAbū ʿAbd al-Raḥmān al-Ḫalīl b. ʾAḥmad b. ʿAmr b. Tamīm al-Farāhīdī al-ʾAzdī al-Yaḥmadī, *Kitāb al-ʿAyn*. Ed. by Mahdī al-Maḫzūmī & ʾIbrāhīm al-Sāmarrāʾī. Bayrūt: Muʾassasat al-ʾaʿlamī li-l-maṭbūʿāt, 8 vol., 1988.

Ibn Mālik, *ʾAlfiyya* = Ǧamāl al-Dīn ʾAbū ʿAbd Allāh Muḥammad b. ʿAbd Allāh b. Mālik al-Ṭāʾī al-Ǧayyānī al-ʾAndalusī, *Alfiyya, ou la quintessence de la grammaire arabe. Ouv-*

35 Cf. Pellat 1953:264 for details. The quotation is given in the paraphrase of Ibn al-Faqīh (d. 300/913?), with its suggestion of a link between *niyāba* and our notion of writing as a "medium", unlike Maʾmūn's prosaic original as reported by Ǧāḥiẓ himself, *huwa kitābun lā yaḥtāǧu ʾilā ḥuḍūri ṣāḥibihi*.

rage de Djémal-Eddin Mohammed connu sous le nom d'Ebn-Malec. Ed. by Antoine-Isaac Silvestre de Sacy. Paris: Printed for the Oriental Translation Fund of Great Britain and Ireland, 1833.

Ibn Mālik, *ʾAlfiyya*(2) = Ǧamāl al-Dīn ʾAbū ʿAbd Allāh Muḥammad b. ʿAbd Allāh b. Mālik al-Ṭāʾī al-Ǧayyānī al-ʾAndalusī, *La Alfiyyah d'Ibnu-Malik*. Ed. and translated by A. Goguyer. Bayrūt: Imprimerie des Belles-lettres, 1888.

Mubarrad, *Muqtaḍab* = ʾAbū al-ʿAbbās Muḥammad b. Yazīd b. ʿAbd al-ʾAkbar al-Ṯumālī al-ʾAzdī al-Mubarrad, *Kitāb al-Muqtaḍab*. Ed. by Muḥammad ʿAbd al-Ḫāliq ʿUḍayma. Al-Qāhira: Muʾassasat dār al-taḥrīr li-l-ṭabʿ wa-l-našr, 4 vol., 1965–1968.

Sībawayhi, *Kitāb* = ʾAbū Bišr ʿAmr b. ʿUṯmān b. Qanbar Sībawayhi. (1) *Le livre de Sîbawaihi. Traité de grammaire arabe par Sîboûya, dit Sîbawaihi*. Ed. by Hartwig Derenbourg. Paris: Imprimerie nationale, 2 vol., 1881–1889, reprint Hildesheim & New York, Georg Olms Verlag, 2 vol., 1970; (2) *Kitāb Sībawayhi*. Ed. Būlāq. Al-Qāhira: al-Maṭbaʿa al-kubrā al-ʾamīriyya, 2 vol., 1316–1317/1898–1900, reprint Baġdād, 2 vol., 1965; (3) *Kitāb Sībawayhi*. Ed. by ʿAbd al-Salām Muḥammad Hārūn. Al-Qāhira: Maktabat al-ḫānǧī, 2 vol., 1968–1970 and later eds.

Sīrāfī, *ŠKS* = ʾAbū Saʿīd al-Ḥasan b. ʿAbd Allāh b. al-Marzubān, *Šarḥ Kitāb Sībawayhi*, photo of MS Atef Efendi 2548.

Zamaḫšarī, *Mufaṣṣal* = Ǧār Allāh ʾAbū al-Qāsim Maḥmūd b. ʿUmar b. Muḥammad b. ʾAḥmad al-Ḫwārazmī al-Zamaḫšarī, *al-Mufaṣṣal. Opus de re grammatica arabicum, auctore Abu' l-Ḳâsim Maḥmûd Bin ʿOmar Zamaḫśario*. Ed. by Jens Peter Broch. Christianiae: Libraria P.T. Mallingli, 2nd ed., 1879, reprint [Baġdād] ND.

Secondary Sources

Ayoub, Georgine. 2018. "The theory of *mā yanṣarif wa-mā lā yanṣarif* in Sībawayhi's *Kitāb*". *The Foundations of Arabic Linguistics III. The Development of a Tradition: Continuity and Change*, ed. by Georgine Ayoub & Kees Versteegh, 11–49. Leiden & Boston: Brill, coll. "Studies in Semitic Languages and Linguistics" 94.

Baalbaki, Ramzi. 1982. "*Tawahhum*: an ambiguous concept in early Arabic grammar". *Bulletin of the School of Oriental and African Studies* 45/2. 233–244. [Reprint in *Grammarians and Grammatical Theory in the Medieval Arabic Tradition*, ed. by Ramzi Baalbaki, ch. XII. Aldershot/Burlington: Ashgate Variorum, coll. "Variorum Collected Studies Series", 2004.]

Baalbaki, Ramzi. 2000. "The Occurrence of *ʾinšāʾ* instead of *ḫabar*: the Gradual Formulation of a Grammatical Issue". *Langues et Littératures du Monde Arabe 1*. 193–211. [Reprint in *Grammarians and Grammatical Theory in the Medieval Arabic Tradition*, ed. by Ramzi Baalbaki, ch. XVI. Aldershot/Burlington: Ashgate Variorum, coll. "Variorum Collected Studies Series", 2004.]

Carter, Michael G. 2015. "The Grammar of Affective Language in the *Kitāb*". *The Foundations of Arabic Linguistics II. Kitāb Sībawayhi: Interpretation and Transmission*, ed.

by Amal E. Marogy & Kees Versteegh, 36–65. Leiden & Boston: Brill, coll. "Studies in Semitic Languages and Linguistics" 83.

Carter, Michael G. 2016. *Sībawayhi's Principles. Arabic Grammar and Law in Early Islamic Thought*. Atlanta, Ga.: Lockwood Press.

Fleischer, Heinrich Leberecht. 1885–1888. *Kleinere Schriften, gesammelt, durchgesehen und vermehrt*. Leipzig: S. Hirzel, 3 vol., reprint Osnabrück, Biblio Verlag, 1968.

Frolov, Dmitry. 2000. *Classical Arabic Verse: History and Theory of the* ʿArūḍ. Leiden & Boston: Brill, coll. "Studies in Arabic Literature" 21.

Ghersetti, Antonella. 2011. "'Word' in the linguistic thinking of ʿAbd al-Qāhir al-Ǧurǧānī". *The Word in Arabic*, ed. by Giuliano Lancioni & Lidia Bettini, 85–108. Leiden & Boston: Brill, coll. "Studies in Semitic Languages and Linguistics" 62.

Guillaume, Jean-Patrick. 2011. "Defining the Word within the Arabic Grammatical Tradition: ʾAstarābāḏī's Predicament". *The Word in Arabic*, ed. by Giuliano Lancioni & Lidia Bettini, 49–68. Leiden & Boston: Brill, coll. "Studies in Semitic Languages and Linguistics" 62.

Jahn, Gustav. 1895–1900. *Sîbawaihi's Buch über die Grammatik, übersetzt und erklärt*. Berlin: Reuther & Reichard, 2 vol., reprint Hildesheim: Georg Olms Verlag, 1969.

Kasher, Almog. 2013. "The Vocative as a 'Speech Act' in Early Arabic Grammatical Tradition". *Histoire Épistémologie Langage* 35/1. 143–159.

Kinberg, Naphtali. 1996. *A Lexicon of al-Farrāʾ's Terminology in his Qurʾān Commentary, with Full Definitions, English Summaries and Extensive Citations*. Leiden & New York: Brill, coll. "Handbook of Oriental Studies. Section 1, The Near and Middle East" 23.

Lancioni, Giuliani & Lidia Bettini (eds.). 2011. *The Word in Arabic*. Leiden & Boston: Brill, coll. "Studies in Semitic Languages and Linguistics" 62.

Larcher, Pierre. 2014. *Linguistique arabe et pragmatique*. Beyrouth: Presses de l'Ifpo.

Larcher, Pierre. 2017. *Syntaxe de l'arabe classique*. Aix-en-Provence: Presses Universitaires de Provence.

Marogy, Amal E. 2010. *Kitāb Sībawayhi. Syntax and Pragmatics*. Leiden & Boston: Brill, coll. "Studies in Semitic Languages and Linguistics" 56.

Marogy, Amal E. 2015. "The notion of *tanwīn* in the *Kitāb*: cognitive evaluation of function and meaning". *The Foundations of Arabic Linguistics II. Kitāb Sībawayhi: Interpretation and Transmission*, ed. by Amal E. Marogy & Kees Versteegh, 160–170. Leiden & Boston: Brill, coll. "Studies in Semitic Languages and Linguistics" 83.

Marogy, Amal E. & Kees Versteegh (eds.). 2015. *The Foundations of Arabic Linguistics II. Kitāb Sībawayhi: Interpretation and Transmission*. Leiden & Boston: Brill, coll. "Studies in Semitic Languages and Linguistics" 83.

Pellat, Charles. 1953. *Le milieu Baṣrien et la formation de Ǧāḥiẓ*. Paris: Librairie d'Amérique et d'Orient. Adrien-Maisonneuve.

Reuschel, Wolfgang. 1959. *Al-Ḫalīl Ibn-Aḥmad, der Lehrer Sībawaihs, als Grammatiker*. Berlin: Akademie Verlag, coll. "Deutsche Akademie der Wissenschaften zu Berlin, Institut für Orientforschung" 49.

Talmon, Rafael. 1993. "Ḥattā + Imperfect and Chapter 239 in Sībawayhī's *Kitāb*: A Study in the Early History of Arabic Grammar". *Journal of Semitic Studies* 38/1. 71–95.

Talmon, Rafael. 1997. *Arabic Grammar in its Formative Age. Kitāb al-ʿAyn & its Attribution to Ḫalīl b. Aḥmad*. Leiden & Boston: Brill, coll. "Studies in Semitic Languages and Linguistics" 25.

Talmon, Rafael. 2003. *Eighth-Century Iraqi Grammar: A Critical Exploration of Pre-Ḫalīlian Arabic Linguistics*. Winona Lake, In.: Eisenbrauns, coll. "Harvard Semitic Studies".

Troupeau, Gérard. 1976. *Lexique-index du* Kitāb *de Sībawayhi*. Paris: Klincksieck, coll. "Études arabes et islamiques".

CHAPTER 2

'A Little Yesterday': The "Canonical" Text of Sībawayhi's Teaching Confronted to Two Unedited Manuscripts of the *Kitāb*

Ilyass Amharar and Jean N. Druel

Introduction*

The two authors of this paper are currently working at the critical edition of two different manuscripts of Sībawayhi's (d. 180/796?) *Kitāb*: Milan, Ambrosiana X 56 *sup.* (first half of the 5th/11th century), to which also belongs Kazan, National Archives 10/5/822 (cf. Druel 2018 for the history of this split codex); and Paris, Bibliothèque nationale de France (BnF) ar. 6499 (dated 562/1166–1167). Discovered by Geneviève Humbert in the 1990s, the Milan-Kazan fragments contain readings that have never been studied. As for Paris, BnF ar. 6499, it is the personal copy of the Andalusian grammarian Ibn Ḫarūf (d. 609/1212) where he collated many variant readings from both the Andalusian and oriental manuscript tradition of the *Kitāb*, as well as many glosses, his own and that of other scholars.

Preparing this paper, we were looking for a grammatical issue that would, at the same time, be in the Milan-Kazan codex (which contains only one fourth of the *Kitāb*), in Ibn Ḫarūf's copy (which contains only two thirds of the *Kitāb*), and in the refutation of the *Kitāb* by Mubarrad (d. 285/898) (which contains 133 issues, transmitted and refuted by Ibn Wallād (d. 332/944) in his *Kitāb al-Intiṣār*). We were following a track suggested by Geneviève Humbert (1995: 190) that Ibn Wallād's judgment that Mubarrad had a poor version of the *Kitāb* could be proven to be true if we could find in the manuscripts variant readings that would explain Mubarrad's criticism.

We found a promising grammatical issue, thanks to an article by Monique Bernards (1989), in which she studies Ǧarmī's (d. 225/839) critical views on the

* We would like to express our gratitude to the reviewers of this article for their very relevant comments, as well as to Dr. Sulaymān b. ʿAbd al-ʿAzīz al-ʿUyūnī (Arabic Language Faculty, Imam Mohammad Ibn Saud Islamic University, Riyadh) whose expertise on the manuscripts of the *Kitāb* is invaluable. Dr. Sulaymān also introduced us to a second edition of Ibn Ḫarūf's *Tanqīḥ* that reshaped our initial assessment of his views on the *Kitāb*.

 | DOI:10.1163/9789004515895_004

Kitāb: is it permissible to form the diminutive of the names of the days of the week? Is there anything like a "little Monday", a "little Tuesday", etc.? What we found went beyond our expectations: we witnessed the progressive stabilisation of the text of the *Kitāb*, along with the tradition of its commentaries, and that of Sīrāfī (d. 368/979) in particular. In other words, Sīrāfī's commentary seems to have played an important role in the stabilisation and diffusion of the text of the *Kitāb*. In its older layers, elliptic and rough as they are, the Milan-Kazan codex is the witness of a text that has not yet been influenced by Sīrāfī's commentary (cf. Druel: 2020).

The other promising finding is the genuine criticism of the *Kitāb* found in Ibn Ḫarūf's glosses and commentary, which seems to be completely independent from Sīrāfī's commentary. We found nothing relevant in Mubarrad's *Radd* and *Muqtaḍab* for the issue discussed here, and Ibn Wallād's criticism of Mubarrad cannot be linked to the quality of his version of the *Kitāb* on this point, simply because Mubarrad's criticism is extremely simplistic and does not quote Sībawayhi's text.

We will first present the "canonical" teaching of Sībawayhi on this issue, as of Derenbourg's edition, before turning to the two unedited manuscripts mentioned above: the Milan-Kazan codex and Ibn Ḫarūf's copy. As for a detailed presentation of the grammatical tradition, it can be found in Druel (2020) where the following authors are discussed: Mubarrad, Ibn Wallād, Sīrāfī, ʾAbū ʿAlī al-Fārisī (d. 377/987), Ibn Sīda (d. 458/1066), al-ʾAʿlam al-Šantamarī (d. 476/1084), Zamaḫšarī (d. 538/1144), Ibn Ḫarūf, Ibn Yaʿīš (d. 643/1245) and Raḍī al-Dīn al-ʾAstarābāḏī (d. 688/1289?).

1 Formation of Diminutive Forms

Sībawayhi devotes quite a number of pages to the formation of diminutive forms (chapters 359–396: *Kitāb* II, 104–146), as a morphological testing tool (Lancioni 2011: 7–8). Many words in the language are not eligible to the formation of a diminutive, like verbs and their cognates, and particles. Examples of verbs include: *ḍarabat* "she hit", *kul* "eat!" or *yaḍaʿu* "he puts". Verbal cognates are the verbs' "proper names" (*ʾasmāʾ al-fiʿl*, *Kitāb* II, 137 l. 14, examples include *halumma* "bring close!" or *ʾilayka* "go away!", see Levin: 1991) and "nouns that have a verbal status" (*al-ism ʾiḏā kāna bi-manzilat al-fiʿl*, *Kitāb* II, 138 l. 16, example include *ḍārib*, if used in *ḍāribun zaydan* "hitting Zayd" but not in *ḍāribu zaydin* "the hitter of Zayd", see *Kitāb* I, 54 l. 7–13). However, if any of these words is used as a person's proper name, this impossibility is lifted (see Carter: 1981). It is thus possible (although probably very theoretical) to form the diminutive of the following words used as people's proper names: *kul* "eat!" or *ḫuḏ* "take!" (*Kitāb* II, 123 l. 7–8), *sal* "ask!" (*Kitāb* II, 123 l. 10–11), *ḍarabat* "she hit" (*Kitāb* II, 125 l. 20–126 l. 1), *yurī* "he shows" or *yaḍaʿu* "he puts" (*Kitāb* II, 126 l. 13–18), *sāra* "he walked" or *ġāba* "he was absent" (*Kitāb* II, 129 l. 4); *ʿan*, *ʾin* and *ʾan* (*Kitāb* II, 125 l. 1–3).

Let us now have a closer look at chapters 388 and 389 (*Kitāb* II, 137 l. 5–138 l. 20) where the issue at stake in this paper is presented.

At first glance, the title of chapter 389 is misleading: "This is the chapter in which a diminutive is formed to [express] its proximity to the thing [that is made diminutive], not its similarity with it" (*hāḏā bāb mā yuḥaqqaru li-dunuwwihi min al-šayʾ wa-laysa miṯlahu, Kitāb* II, 137 l. 5). Unlike the preceding chapters, 359 to 387, which explore the diminutive formation of all possible morphological shapes, chapters 388 and 389 deal with cases where the meaning is involved, not just the morphology.

In chapter 388, Sībawayhi discusses the case of words which have a diminutive shape and meaning but no corresponding "plain" form, such as *ǧumayl* and *kuʿayt* which both mean "nightingale" (*Kitāb* II, 136 l. 21). The proof that they are not diminutives lies in their plural: *ǧimlān* and *kiʿtān*, not **ǧumaylāt* (*Kitāb* II, 136 l. 22). It is not possible to form their diminutive because they already have a diminutive shape and meaning (*Kitāb* II, 136 l. 20–21). The same goes for *kumayt* "reddish-brown" (*Kitāb* II, 137 l. 1), which is not the diminutive of a "plain" form. According to Ḫalīl (d. 170/786?), its diminutive-like meaning lies in its proximity to both "red" and "black", which implies that no diminutive can be formed from it. What is "diminished" here is the distance between the two colours, not one of the two colours themselves, just like in *huwa duwayna ḏālika* "he is slightly below that" (*Kitāb* II, 137 l. 3–4). At this point, it is impossible to understand this last example and how it relates to the diminutive meaning of *kumayt*. This will be further explored in the next chapter.

Pushing his idea a step further in chapter 389, Sībawayhi gives more examples of cases where the diminutive meaning does not apply to the word that is made diminutive, rather to another element in the sentence. He says that it is not rare in Arabic for an expression to carry a meaning other than what is expected of it. Sībawayhi gives two such examples (*Kitāb* II, 137 l. 13): the expression *yaṭaʾuhum al-ṭarīqu* "the road treads upon them", which is an idiomatic expression meaning "the road is their guest", i.e. "they welcome as guest whoever passes on the road", and which stands for *yaṭaʾuhum ʾahlu al-ṭarīqi* "the passengers of the road tread upon them", i.e., "the passengers of the road are their guests" (cf. Lane 1863–1893: II, 2948). In the first expression, *al-ṭarīq* stands for *ʾahl al-ṭarīq*. Another example lies in the expression *ṣīda ʿalayhi yawmāni* "two days were mounted for the hunt", which stands for *ṣīda ʿalayhi al-ṣaydu fī yawmayni* "it was mounted for the hunt for two days" (cf. Dayyeh 2015: 69). The examples related to the diminutives given in this chapter include *huwa ʾuṣayġiru minka* "he is slightly younger than you", *huwa duwayna ḏāka* "he is slightly below that", *huwa fuwayqa ḏāka* "he is slightly above that", *ʾusayyidu* "slightly black", *huwa muṯaylu hāḏā* "he is slightly like this" (*Kitāb* II, 137 l. 5–8). Sībawayhi says that what is "diminished" in *huwa ʾuṣayġiru minka* is not the word itself (e. g., *ṣaġīr*) but the relation between the two words (e. g. *huwa* and *ʾanta*, *Kitāb* II, 137 l. 6).

The logic of Sībawayhi is slightly (!) puzzling since it is not clear why he would consider that these examples illustrate cases where an expression carries a meaning other than what is expected of it. However, at second glance, he is completely consistent in saying that what is actually made diminutive is not the meaning of the word itself (*ʾaṣġaru*, *dūna*, *fawqa*, *ʾaswadu*…), but rather the relation between the word and another element in the sentence. Strictly speaking, *ʾuṣayġiru* should refer to a "small smaller", *duwayna* to a "small below" and *ʾusayyidu* to a "small black". This is because diminutives apply only to nouns that can be "qualified" (*tūṣaf*, *Kitāb* II, 137 l. 10), or, more precisely, qualified as small or despicable, which is not the case with *ʾaṣġaru*, *dūna*, *fawqa*, *ʾaswadu*, although they are nouns. They cannot be qualified. If diminutives can be formed from these words, they can only express a proximal relationship to the original meaning ("close to blackness", for example, *qāraba al-sawāda*, *Kitāb* II, 137 l. 7), and not a similar, although diminutive, meaning (as in "small black"). This is exactly what the title of this chapter means: "This is the chapter in which a diminutive is formed to [express] its proximity to the thing [that is made diminutive], not its similarity with it" (*hāḏā bāb mā yuḥaqqaru li-dunuwwihi min al-šayʾ wa-laysa miṯlahu*, *Kitāb* II, 137 l. 5). The semantic reason behind this is that, although they are nouns, they cannot be qualified (unless they are used as people's proper names, of course).

We now better understand how the expression *huwa duwayna ḏālika* illustrates the diminutive-like meaning of *kumayt* (*Kitāb* II, 137 l. 1). Its diminutive-like meaning lies in its proximity to both "red" and "black", just like in *huwa duwayna ḏālika*, where it is not the word *dūna* itself that is made diminutive (a "small below"), but rather the relationship between the two elements *huwa* and *ḏālika* ("slightly below" and not just "below").

The rest of the chapter explores other nouns from which no diminutive can be formed, such as 'pronouns' (*ʿalāmat al-ʾiḍmār*), both independent and bound, particle-like nouns (*ʾayna* "where?", *matā* "when?", *kayfa* "how?", *ḥayṯu* "where"), and more generally nouns that lack 'strength' (*quwwa*) and 'flexibility' (*tamakkun*), such as *man* "who?", *mā* "what?", and *ʾayyuhum* "which of them?", or nouns from which it would mean nothing to form a diminutive, such as *siwā* and *ġayr*, both meaning "other than".

As for the names of times, Sībawayhi makes a distinction between words like *sāʿa* "hour", *yawm* "day", *šahr* "month", *sana* "year", and *layla* "night", on the one hand, for which it is possible to form a diminutive, and words like *ʾams* "yesterday" and *ġad* "tomorrow", for which it is not possible, because they can only mean "the day before your day" and "the day after your day" ([*al*]-*yawm allaḏī qabl yawmika wa-l-yawm allaḏī baʿd yawmika*, *Kitāb* II, 138 l. 8). In these expressions, *yawmuka* refers to the time when the speaker utters the words *ʾams* and *ġad*. Sībawayhi adds that *ʾams* and *ġad* do not have the same "flexibility" (*lam yatamakkanā*, *Kitāb* II, 138 l. 11) as *zayd*, *ʿamr*, *yawm*, *šahr* and the like. Whereas *hāḏā al-yawm* "this day" and *hāḏihi al-layla* "this night" can refer to present, future and past time (*li-mā ʾanta fīhi wa-li-mā lam yaʾti wa-li-mā maḍā*, *Kitāb* II, 138 l. 10), or just like *hāḏā zayd* "this is Zayd" and *ḏāka zayd* "that is Zayd" can refer to someone either present or absent (*mā yakūnu maʿaka wa-mā yatarāḫā ʿanka*, *Kitāb* II, 138 l. 11), *ʾams* and *ġad* can only refer to the day before and the day after whatever day is present when the speaker speaks. Nouns that behave like *ʾams* and *ġad* include: *ʾawwalu min ʾamsi*, *al-ṯalāṯāʾ* [1] "Tuesday", *al-ʾarbiʿāʾ* "Wednesday", *al-bāriḥa* "yesterday", or the names of the months of the year. In other words, *ʾams* and *ġad* contrast with *sāʿa*, *yawm*, *šahr*, and also with *zayd* and *ʿamr* in terms of deixis.

Sībawayhi further explains that only nouns that are not 'proper names' (*ʿalam*) and which refer to a whole 'category' (*ʾumma*), like *rağul* "man", *imraʾa* "woman" and the like, can have a diminutive form (*Kitāb* II, 138 l. 13–15). Later grammarians will argue on this very point: can *al-ṯalāṯāʾ*, as a proper name for the third day of the week, refer to the whole category of "Tuesdays", just like *zayd*, as a proper name, can refer to any man called "Zayd"? According to Sībawayhi, when one says "Tuesday", they can only refer a specific day, known to both the speaker and the hearer. There is not a category of "Tuesdays", in the past, in the present, and in the future that one could compare. The issue here is twofold: 1) the deictic meaning of these words (linked to the time when they are uttered), as opposed to their "generic" (*ğins*, *ʾumma*) meaning, and 2) their being "proper names" (*ʿalam*). As we will see below, the manuscript tradition casts a slightly different view than the canonical version of the *Kitāb* presented so far.

1 Cf. Druel (2012:118) on this vocalisation.

2 The Manuscript Testimony

Now that we have a better idea of the issue at stake, we can consider the manuscript tradition of this chapter of the *Kitāb* in order to try and understand how the text was transmitted. We will consider here two different unedited manuscript: Milan, Ambrosiana X 56 *sup.*[2] and Paris, BnF ar. 6499. We will refer to them respectively as M (for Milan) and P (for Paris). These two manuscripts are described by Humbert.[3] We had access to high definition images of M purchased from Ambrosiana and we had access to the physical copy in Milan on May 3, 2019. As for P, we accessed it online.[4] The edition of Hartwig Derenbourg (1844–1908), with which we will compare these manuscripts, is mainly based on three manuscripts, noted L, A and B.

Here is a chronological list of the manuscripts (and their different hands, in the case of M):

- M1: the first hand in Milan, Ambrosiana X 56 *sup.* It is not dated but has been estimated to be from the first half of the 5th/11th century (Humbert 1995: 172, 199, 201).
- M2: the second hand in Milan, Ambrosiana X 56 *sup.* It is either the same hand as M1, or the hand of someone very close to M1, belonging to the same scholarly milieu, and who corrects the text right after the book is bound (Bongianino, personal communication, December 19, 2018). M1 and M2 use a dark brown ink and write in an Old Western-Nasḫī style, also called semi-Maġribī (Bongianino 2015: 23).
- M3: the third hand in Milan, Ambrosiana X 56 *sup.* It is dated of the end of Raǧab 514/end of October 1120 and 517/1123–1124 (Bongianino 2015: 9). M3 uses a yellowish brown ink and writes in a rounded Maġribī style (Bongianino 2015: 9).
- P: Paris, Bibliothèque nationale de France ar. 6499. It is the personal copy of Ibn Ḫarūf and is dated 562/1166–1167 (Humbert 1994: 10–11; 1995: 234).
- L: Escorial, Real Biblioteca del Monasterio de San Lorenzo, árabe 1 (L in Derenbourg, 1881–1889: I, XXI–XXXV = 2O, in Humbert, 1995: 275–279). It is dated 27 Ḏū al-Qaʿda 629/September 14 (not 14–15), 1232 (Humbert 1995: 275).
- M4 is dated 714/1314–1315 (Bongianino 2015: 9). As for M4, it uses a dark black ink and writes in a rough Oriental style (Bongianino 2015: 9).

---

2 As stated above, the Milan fragments and the Kazan fragments belong the same codex. Since chapters 388 and 389 are found in the Milan fragments of this codex, we will refer here to them simply as "the Milan manuscript".

3 Cf. Humbert 1995:170–186 and 199–203 for Ambrosiana X 56 *sup.*, and Humbert 1995:145–154 and 234–239 for BnF ar. 6499. In Humbert, M is called 1A and P is called 2E.

4 https://gallica.bnf.fr/ark:/12148/btv1b84061824/f5.item (last accessed on September 29, 2020).

– B: Saint Petersburg, Institute of Oriental Manuscripts C 272 (B in Derenbourg, 1881–1889: I, IX–XI = 4G in Humbert: 1995: 361).[5] It is dated from late Ṣafar 1138/early November 1725 (not October, Derenbourg 1881–1889: I, XI; Humbert 1995: 29, 197).
– A: Paris, BnF ar. 3987 (A in Derenbourg, 1881–1889: I, III–IX = BnF, supplément arabe 1155 = Ça, in Humbert, 1995: 297–300). It is dated between 1140/1727 and 1151/1738 (Humbert 1995: 110). Derenbourg (1881–1889: I, V) estimated its date in the first half of the 8th/mid-14th century. Its mother (2Ç) is dated as follows: first volume, 26 Ṣafar 647/June 10 (not 31), 1249; second volume, 22 Ǧumādā I 647/September 2, 1249; third volume, 22 Šaʿbān 647/November 30, 1249; fourth volume 20 Ḏū al-Qaʿda 647/February (not March) 24, 1250 (Humbert 1995: 103).

In what follows, we will present only one locus found in M (four other loci are presented in Druel: 2020).

2.1 *Locus in M:* **li-ʾannahumā [laysa] smāni [smayni]**

There are many differences between the above mentioned manuscripts, regarding the issue that we are studying here, and we will only present one of them: instead of the reading *wa-ʾammā ʾamsi wa-ġadun fa-lā yuḥaqqarāni li-ʾannahumā laysā -smayni bi-manzilati zaydin*, which is found in all the manuscripts mentioned above (except that B has *yuḥaqqarna* and adds *wa-ʿamrin* after *zaydin*), M1 does not have the negation and reads *wa-ʾammā ʾamsi wa-ġadun fa-lā yuḥaqqarāni li-ʾannahumā -smāni bi-manzilati zaydin* (M 45^r l. 15, see fig. 2.1, the second line). M2 has then added the negation *laysā* but has left *ismāni* in the ungrammatical *marfūʿ* case. Lastly, M4 has corrected *ismāni* in *ismayni*, which is found in all the versions. The best evidence that the *ʾalif* in *ismān* was erased by M4 and replaced by a *yāʾ* is that the isolated form of the ending *nūn* is still visible. The rest of the sentence continues as follows: *wa-ʾinnamā humā li-l-yawmi llaḏī qabla yawmika wa-li-l-yawmi* (in M, but *wa-l-yawmi* in the other manuscripts) *allaḏī baʿda yawmika*.

---

5 According to Derenbourg, B is Saint Petersburg, Asiatic Museum of the Imperial Academy of Sciences 403. Humbert writes (1995:197) that 4G is Saint Petersburg, Institute of Oriental Languages of the Academy of Sciences (*"Inst. vostocnyx jazykov, Akad. Nauk"*) C-272, which is a bit confusing. In 1930, the Asiatic Museum was incorporated in the newly created Institute of Oriental Studies (Институт востоковедсния, not "Languages", as written by Humbert). In 1951, the institute was relocated in Moscow but the manuscript library remained in Saint Petersburg as a branch of the Institute of Oriental Studies. In 2007, it became independent and in 2009 it changed its name to thc Institute of Oriental Manuscripts (Институт восточных рукописей). By 1986, the call number of the manuscript had changed from 403 to C 272 (cf. Khalidov 1986:I, 302).

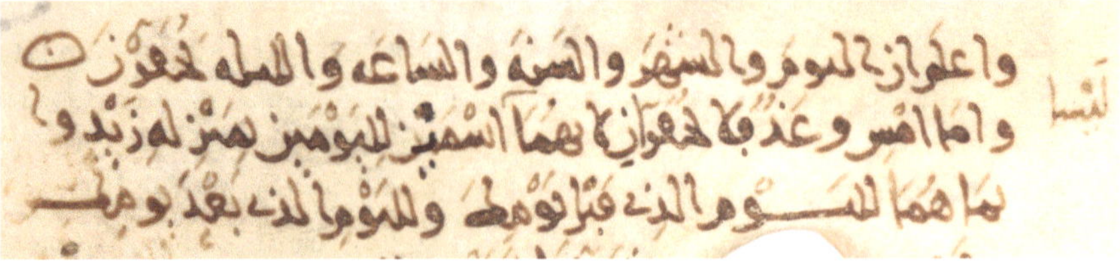

FIGURE 2.1 M 45^{r} l. 14–16

Our interpretation is that for M2 and the subsequent tradition it is not conceivable that Sībawayhi intended that *ʾams* and *ġad* could be proper names of "the day before your day" and "the day after your day". This is clear from the commentary tradition where none of the commentators envisions the possibility that *ʾams* and *ġad* could be proper names. The addition of a negation denotes the refusal—or the impossibility to conceive—that *ʾams* and *ġad* are proper names in the first place. Indeed, the commentators did not embark on the idea that *ʾams* and *ġad* are proper names but rather on the idea that their semantic referent is not flexible (cf. Druel: 2020 where some commentators compared *ʾams* and *ġad* to pronouns, like Sīrāfī, Šantamarī, and Ibn Yaʿīš; Fārisī compared *ʾams* to a particle; and ʾAstarābāḏī simply mentioned the semantic limitations of *ʾams* and *ġad*). It could then well be the case that the negation *laysa* in *li-ʾannahumā laysa -smayni* was introduced by commentators who would not see why Sībawayhi would call *ʾams* and *ġad* proper names.

If our interpretation is correct, the two versions of the text, with and without the negation can be paraphrased as follows (slightly forcing the translation in order to make it more explicit): according to M1, without the negation, "as for *ʾams* and *ġad*, one cannot form their diminutive because (although) they are (proper) names for the two days, (just) like *zayd* (is a proper name), they (only) refer to the day before your day and to the day after your day (and not to a whole category like the proper name *zayd*)"; and according to M2 and the following tradition, with the negation, "as for *ʾams* and *ġad*, one cannot form their diminutive because they are not (proper) names for the two days, like *zayd* (is a proper name), but they refer to the day before your day and to the day after your day." This second version carries the main information that it is not permissible to form the diminutive of *ʾams* and *ġad*, but it casts away the possibility that these two words are proper names and one does not understand the comparison with *zayd* anymore.

In conclusion, the reading of M1 is probably better. The commentary tradition, based on the reading with the negation, only kept Sībawayhi's conclusion about the impossibility to form the diminutive of *ʾams* and *ġad*, not his argumentation on different types of proper names, generic ones (like *zayd* that can refer to many Zayds) and specific ones (like *ʾams* and *ġad* that only refer to one specific day). To be sure, later grammarians understood that *ʾams* and *ġad* only referred to specific days, but not that they were the proper names of these two specific days.

2.2 *Marginal Glosses in P*

The Paris manuscript ar. 6499 (P), which is Ibn Ḫarūf's personal autograph copy of the *Kitāb*, contains both glosses and textual variants.[6] Most of these many glosses bear a small *ṭāʾ*, just like the glosses found in front of the passages that we are focusing on here. According to al-Ruʿaynī (d. 666/1268) in his *Barnāmaǧ* (81–82), Ibn Ḫarūf built his own commentary of the *Kitāb*, called *Tanqīḥ al-ʾalbāb fī šarḥ ġawāmiḍ al-Kitāb*, on the glosses of his Sevillian master ʾAbū Bakr Ibn Ṭāhir al-Ḫidabb (d. 580/1184), only adding commentaries of the poetic verses to them. And indeed, when we compare these *ṭāʾ*-glosses with the text of the *Tanqīḥ*, it appears clearly that most Ibn Ṭāhir's glosses are integrated verbatim in the *Tanqīḥ* although the authority of ʾAbū Bakr (Ibn Ṭāhir) is seldom mentioned. In the introduction to his partial edition of the *Tanqīḥ* (46–47), Ḫalīfa Badīrī writes that Ibn Ḫarūf did not sanctify the opinions of his master, and he gives many examples where he clearly criticised him (140–145). Our chapter 389 is not found in Badīrī's edition but in that of al-Ġāmidī (538–541).

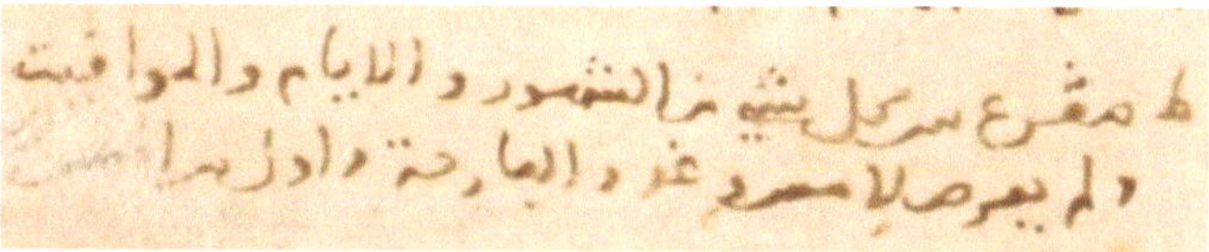

FIGURE 2.2 P 84r, first gloss

The first gloss is found in the right margin in front of the text *wa-kaḏālika ʾawwalu min ʾams wa-l-ṯalāṯāʾu…*, with a right-oriented footnote marker (see Gacek 2009: 250 for the signes de renvoi) above the word *ʾawwal*. The passage that is glossed mentions other words which, along with *ʾams* and *ġad*, cannot have diminutive forms, including *ʾawwal min ʾams*, the names of the days of the week, *al-bāriḥa* and the like. This first gloss reads: *mutafarriʿun*[7] *bayna kulli*

6 We do not understand why Humbert (1995:147) wrote that Ibn Ḫarūf did not add marginal glosses in his copy but only textual variants. The three cases we present here are clearly glosses, not variants of the *matn*.

7 Our first reading of this expression was *maqraʿun bayna*, of which we could not make much sense. Dr. Sulaymān b. ʿAbd al-ʿAzīz al-ʿUyūnī suggested the reading *mutafarriʿun min*. We finally opted for *mutafarriʿun bayna*.

šayʾin min al-šuhūri wa-l-ʾayyāmi wa-l-mawāqīti wa-lam yaʿriḍ li-ʾamsi wa-ġadin wa-l-bāriḥati wa-ʾawwali min ʾamsi "it applies to all [the names] of the months, days, and times, but not to *ʾams*, *ġad*, *al-bāriḥa* and *ʾawwal min ʾams*" (P 84^{r} l. 30, see fig. 2.2). It is not clear at this point what Ibn Ṭāhir's position is towards the names of the days and months

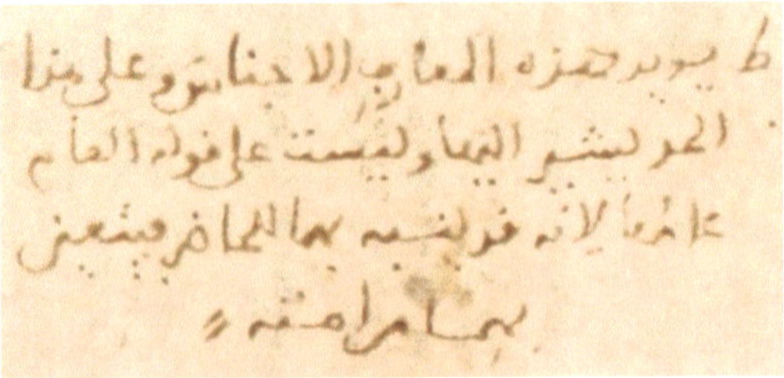

FIGURE 2.3 P 84r, second gloss

The next gloss (fig. 2.3) is found on the left side of the page and the marker is located above the word *fa-ʿalāmāt* (P 84^{r} l. 31). It comments the passage where the text says that the "time proper names" (*ʿalāmāt min al-dahr*) mentioned earlier cannot have a diminutive form. The term *ʿalāma* seems to have different meanings in the *Kitāb*, but we find once in the *Kitāb* this meaning of 'proper name'.[8] The gloss reads as follows: *yurīdu bi-hāḏihi l-maʿārifi l-ʾaǧnāsa wa-ʿalā hāḏā l-ḥaddi yušīru ʾilayhā wa-laysat ʿalā qawlihi l-ʿāmu ʿāmuhā li-ʾannahu qad yunabbahu bihimā li-l-ḥāḍiri fa-yataʿayyanu bihimā min ʾummatihi* "by these definite [expressions], he intends the categories and this is how he refers to them, not as in [the expression] *al-ʿāmu ʿāmuhā* ("this year is her year"), because one may refer to the present by the definite article (*bihimā*), specifying [it] by the article from its category". The expression *al-ʿāmu ʿāmuhā* is found once in the *Kitāb* (I, 177 l. 2) where it serves as an example of the definite article referring to the present in a time expression in the independent case, as opposed to the time complements (*ẓurūf*) in the dependent case, as in *al-hilālu al-laylata* ("the crescent is tonight"). As for the translation of *humā* by 'the definite article', we rely on Ibn Ḫarūf's commentary dealing with this issue (*Tanqīḥ* [Badīrī] 372 l. 19–373 l. 2), where he refers once to the definite article as *ʾalif wa-lām*, and then simply as *humā*.

Ibn Ṭāhir glosses here that the definite article can carry two meanings: it can refer to the whole category (*ǧins*), as in Sībawayhi's "time proper names" (*ʿalā-*

8 *fa-min ḏālika ʿabdu l-qaysi wa-mruʾu l-qaysi fa-hāḏihi l-ʾasmāʾu ʿalāmātun ka-zaydin wa-ʿamrin* ("the same goes for 'Abd al-Qays and Imru' al-Qays, these nouns are proper names like Zayd and 'Amr", *Kitāb* II, 85 l. 10–11).

māt min al-dahr) or to the present, as in *al-ʿāmu ʿāmuhā*. In his *Tanqīḥ* [Badīrī] (373 l. 1), Ibn Ḫarūf explains that the addition of the definite article to the word *iṯnayni* serves two opposite meanings: the whole category and the proper name. In this, he disagrees with Sībawayhi who teaches that the names of the days of the week do not refer to a whole category (cf. Druel: 2020).

Our interpretation of this gloss is that Ibn Ḫarūf's master, ʾAbū Bakr Ibn Ṭāhir, tries to reconcile his teaching with the text of the *Kitāb*. For Sībawayhi, the reason why these words do not have a diminutive form is because they do not refer to a whole category but only to specific times, and the definite article plays no role in this. For Ibn Ṭāhir, these words can both refer to categories and to definite times, linked to the present time when the speaker utters them. Both meaning are made possible by the definite article. If Sībawayhi, according to Ibn Ṭāhir's gloss, forbids their diminutive formation, it is only when they refer to a specific time, linked to the present, which is not what Sībawayhi intends…

In his *Tanqīḥ*, Ibn Ḫarūf does not hesitate to contradict Sībawayhi frontally on this issue, thus taking a step further than his master Ibn Ṭāhir. In his commentary of chapter 389 (*Tanqīḥ* [Ġāmidī], 538–541), Ibn Ḫarūf explains that *ʾams* and *ġad* can serve both meanings, the deictic one ("yesterday") and the generic one ("the day before"). This second meaning is usually expressed by the definite article. If the first meaning is intented, *ʾams* and *ġad* do not have a diminutive form whereas if the second meaning is intended, it is possible to form their diminutive. Ironically, Ibn Ḫarūf even quotes a poetic verse found in the *Kitāb* were *ʾams* has a generic meaning (*Tanqīḥ* [Ġāmidī], 539 l. 8; *Kitāb* I, 248 l. 13): *ʾa-min ʿamali al-Ǧarrāfi ʾamsi wa-ẓulmihi wa-ʿudwānihi ʾaʿtabtumūnā barāsimi* "Is it because of al-Ǧarrāf's deeds, iniquity and enemity, the day before, that you inflicted diseases on us?". It is not completely clear at this point what forbids to understand *ʾams* here are meaning "yesterday". Is it the past tense of the verb *ʾaʿtaba* that implies a narration in the past instead of a narration contemporaneous to the utterance? Ibn Ḫarūf also quotes the Qurʾān where *al-ʾams* has a generic meaning (*Tanqīḥ* [Ġāmidī], 539 l. 12–13; Q. 28 al-Qaṣaṣ, 82).

The last gloss (fig. 2.4) is also found on the left side of the page, and its signe-de-renvoi is located above the word *al-ism* in the sentence *ʾinnamā yuḥaqqaru l-ismu ġayru l-ʿalami* (P 84ʳ l. 31). Its texts reads: *ʾarā fī ʾasmāʾi al-šuhūri wa-ʾayyāmi l-ʾusbūʿi kamā ʾarāhu fī ʾamsi wa-ġadin wa-l-bāriḥati wa-ʾawwali min ʾamsi li-ʾannahā fī l-ʾaʿlāmi bi-manzilati zaydin wa-ʿamrin ʾa-lā tarā ʾannahā lā tantaqilu ʿan musammayātihā qarubat ʾaw tarāḫat wa-ʿalā ḏālika ṯunniyat wa-ǧumiʿat wa-ʾammā ʾamsi wa-ġadun wa-sāʾiru l-ʿalāmāti fa-tantaqilu l-ʿalāmatu ʿanhā li-tarāḫīhā* "my opinion about the names of the months and the days of the week is the same as for *ʾams, ġad, al-bāriḥa* and *ʾawwal min ʾams* because as

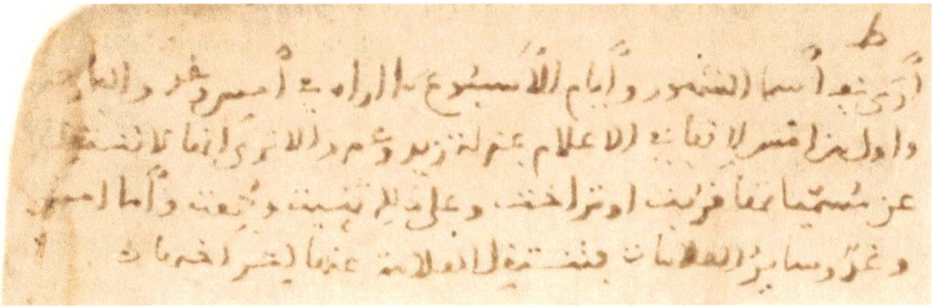

FIGURE 2.4 P 84[r], third gloss

proper names they have the same status as Zayd and ʿAmr. Don't you see that their referent does not change, whether they are close or far, and for this, they can be put in the dual and the plural. But *ʾams*, *ġad* and the other proper names, their referent changes when they are far".

The text of this gloss is very puzzling because there seems to be a contradiction in the comparison. On the one hand, Ibn Ṭāhir says that the names of the months and days compare to *ʾams* and the like, but then he says in great detail that, unlike them, their referent does not change when they are "far" (i.e., not present to the speaker).

This gloss of Ibn Ṭāhir is rephrased by Ibn Ḫarūf in his *Tanqīḥ* [Ġāmidī] (539) and there, a negation is found that gives the gloss a much clearer meaning: *wa-ʾammā ʾasmāʾu al-šuhūri wa-ʾasmāʾu al-ʾayyāmi ka-l-muḥarrami wa-ṣafara wa-l-sabti wa-l-ʾaḥadi wa-ʾaḫawātihā wa-ʾamsi wa-ġadun min yawmin bi-ʿaynihi wa-ʾawwalu min ʾamsi wa-l-bāriḥatu fa-hiya bi-manzilati zaydin wa-ʿamrin* ***ʾillā ʾannahā*** *lā tantaqilu ʿan musammayātihā wa-l-ʾaʿlāmu tantaqilu* "as for the names of the months and the days, like al-Muḥarram, Ṣafar, Saturday, Sunday and the like, and *ʾams* and *ġad* of a specific day, and *ʾawwal min ʾams* and *al-bāriḥa*, they have the same status as *zayd* and *ʿamr*, **except that** their referent does not change whereas that of the names does."

In the following lines (*Tanqīḥ* [Ġāmidī], 540), Ibn Ḫarūf explains that personal names do not apply (*mawqūfa*) to only one specific person but that "Zayd" can refer to many different Zayds, whereas not everyday can be called *al-sabt* or *al-ʾaḥad*.

It is thus very clear that for Ibn Ḫarūf although *ʾams* and *ġad* share the same status (*bi-manzilati*) as Zayd and ʿAmr (i.e., being proper names?), the former can have two meanings (deictic, if referring to a specific day, and generic, especially if carrying the definite article) whereas the latter only have a generic meaning (all the persons bearing this name). For Ibn Ḫarūf, it is possible to form the diminutive of *ʾams* and *ġad* only if their generic meaning is intended.

In the end, the difference between Sībawayhi and Ibn Ḫarūf is that Sībawayhi does not acknowledge a generic meaning to *ʾams* and *ġad* but only a deictic one.

3 Assessment of the Manuscript Tradition

As concluded by former research (Humbert 1995: 176; Druel 2019), M3 tends to align the text of M1 and M2 towards the "canonical" version, i.e, the version that is edited by Derenbourg (on L, A, and B) and which became the basis for the further, most widespread editions of the *Kitāb* (Būlāq and Hārūn, cf. Druel 2018: 23–24). The example in M (*li-ʾannahumā -smāni* → *laysa smāni* → *laysa -smayni*) is extremely interesting in this regard: the later tradition probably did not understand (or agree on) the teaching of Sībawayhi that *ʾams* and *ġad* are "proper names" and thus modified the text of the *Kitāb*. We argue that the successive hands in M are a witness of a process that led to the version we know today. A thorough study of all the variants found in M is obviously needed to evaluate the extent of this process.

The glosses found in P originate in the teaching of Ibn Ḫarūf's master, ʾAbū Bakr Ibn Ṭāhir. Ibn Ḫarūf later incorporated them in his *Tanqīḥ al-ʾalbāb fī šarḥ ġawāmiḍ al-Kitāb*. In this commentary, Ibn Ḫarūf pushes his master's criticism of Sībawayhi's text a step further by adding a distinction between two meanings for *ʾams* and *ġad*, deictic and generic, quoting poetry and the Qurʾān. He thus opens the possibility of forming a diminutive of these words, when their generic meaning is intended.

It is not possible to decide whether Ibn Ḫarūf would consider *ʾams* and *ġad* to be proper names but his commentary does not forbid this eventuality, especially when he quotes Sībawayhi's expression that they have the same "status" (*bi-manzilati*) as Zayd and ʿAmr. To be sure, however, Ibn Ḫarūf's version of the *Kitāb* does contain the negation *laysā -smayni* (P 84^r, l. 26).

Despite its limited scope, we hope that this article can encourage scholars to study Ibn Ḫarūf's *Tanqīḥ*, along with his master's glosses, that he patiently transcribed in his own copy of the *Kitāb*.

Bibliography

Primary Sources

Ibn Ḫarūf, *Tanqīḥ* [Badīrī] = ʾAbū al-Ḥasan ʿAlī b. Muḥammad Ibn Ḫarūf, *Šarḥ Kitāb Sībawayhi al-musammā Tanqīḥ al-ʾalbāb fī šarḥ ġawāmiḍ al-Kitāb*. Ed. by Ḫalīfa Muḥammad Ḫalīfa Badīrī. [Ṭarābulus]: Kulliyyat al-daʿwa al-ʾislāmiyya, [1425 (Lybian)/1995].

Ibn Ḫarūf, *Tanqīḥ* [Ġāmidī] = ʾAbū al-Ḥasan ʿAlī b. Muḥammad Ibn Ḫarūf, *Tanqīḥ al-ʾalbāb fī šarḥ ġawāmiḍ al-Kitāb*. Ed. by Ṣāliḥ b. ʾAḥmad al-Ġāmidī. PhD dissertation, Ǧāmiʿat ʿUmm al-Qurā, Makka al-Mukarrama, 2 vol., 1414/[1993–1994].

Ibn Wallād, *Intiṣār* = ʾAbū al-ʿAbbās ʾAḥmad b. Muḥammad Ibn Wallād, *al-Intiṣār li-Sībawayhi ʿalā al-Mubarrad*. Ed. by Zuhayr ʿAbd al-Muḥsin Sulṭān. Bayrūt: Muʾassasat al-risāla, 1996.

Mubarrad, *Muqtaḍab* = ʾAbū al-ʿAbbās Muḥammad b. Yazīd al-Mubarrad, *Kitāb al-Muqtaḍab*. Ed. by Muḥammad ʿAbd al-Ḫāliq ʿUḍayma. Al-Qāhira: Wizārat al-ʾawqāf, Laǧnat ʾiḥyāʾ al-turāṯ al-ʾislāmī, 2nd ed., 4 vol., 1966–1979.

Mubarrad, *Radd* = ʾAbū al-ʿAbbās Muḥammad b. Yazīd al-Mubarrad. Quoted extensively in Ibn Wallād's *Intiṣār* (see above).

Ruʿaynī, *Barnāmaǧ* = ʾAbū al-Ḥasan ʿAlī b. Muḥammad Ibn al-Faḫḫār al-Ruʿaynī, *Barnāmaǧ šuyūḫ al-Ruʿaynī*. Ed. by ʾIbrāhīm Šabbūḥ. Dimašq: Wizārat al-ṯaqāfa wa-l-iršād al-qawmī, 1 vol., 1962.

Sībawayhi, *Kitāb* = ʿAmr b. ʿUṯmān b. Qanbar ʾAbū Bišr Sībawayhi, *Le livre de Sîbawaihi. Traité de grammaire arabe par Sîboûya, dit Sîbawaihi*. Ed. by Hartwig Derenbourg. Paris: Imprimerie nationale, 2 vol., 1881–1889, reprint Hildesheim & New York: Georg Olms Verlag, 2 vol., 1970.

Sībawayhi, *Kitāb* [Būlāq] = *Kitāb Sībawayhi*. Al-Qāhira: al-Maṭbaʿa al-ʾamīriyya, 2 vol., 1316–1317/[1898–1900].

Sībawayhi, *Kitāb* [Hārūn] = *Kitāb Sībawayhi*. Ed. by ʿAbd al-Salām Muḥammad Hārūn. Vol. 1: al-Qāhira: Dār al-qalam, 1966. Vol. 2: al-Qāhira: Dār al-kitāb al-ʿarabī, 1968. Vol. 3–5: al-Qāhira: al-Hayʾa al-miṣriyya al-ʿāmma li-l-kitāb, 1973–1977.

Secondary Sources

Bernards, Monique. 1989. "The reception of the *Kitāb Sībawayh* among the early Arab grammarians". *Speculum historiographiae linguisticae. Kurzbeiträge der IV. Internationalen Konferenz zur Geschichte der Sprachwissenschaften (ICHoLS IV) Trier, 24.–27. August 1987*, 23–28. Münster: Nodus Publikationen.

Bongianino, Umberto. 2015. "Le manuscrit X 56 *sup*. (*Kitāb Sībawayh*) de la Bibliothèque Ambrosienne et les écritures de l'Occident arabe avant la diffusion du *maġribī* arrondi". *Paléographie des écritures arabes d'al-Andalus, du Maghreb et de l'Afrique subsaharienne. Journée d'étude tenue à Rabat le 28 novembre 2013 sous la direction de Mustapha Jaouhari*, 5–25, Rabat: coll. "Les Rencontres du Centre Jacques-Berque" 6.

Carter, Michael G. 1981. "The use of proper names as a testing device in Sībawayh's *Kitāb*". *The history of linguistics in the Near East,* ed. by Kees Versteegh, Konrad Koerner & Hans-Josef Niederehe. Amsterdam & Philadelphia: John Benjamins, 1983, 109–120. First published in *Historiographia linguistica* 8 (1981), 345–356.

Dayyeh, Hanadi. 2015. *"Ittisāʿ* in Sībawayhi's *Kitāb*: A Semantic *ʿilla* for Disorders in Meaning and Form". *The Foundations of Arabic Linguistics II. Kitāb Sībawayhi: Interpretation and Transmission*, ed. by Amal E. Marogy & Kees Versteegh, 66–80. Leiden & Boston: Brill, coll. "Studies in Semitic Languages and Linguistics" 83.

Derenbourg, Hartwig. 1881–1889. *Le livre de Sîbawaihi. Traité de grammaire arabe par Sîboûya dit Sîbawaihi.* Paris: Imprimerie nationale, 2 vol. reprint Hildesheim & New York: Georg Olms Verlag, 1970.

Druel, Jean N. 2012. "Numerals in Arabic grammatical theory. An impossible quest for consistency?". PhD dissertation, Radboud Universiteit (Nijmegen).

Druel, Jean N. 2018. "The Kazan parchment fragments of Sībawayh's *Kitāb*". *Гасырлар авазы* (= *Эхо веков*) 90/1. 14–26.

Druel, Jean N. 2019. "Can Ambrosiana X 56 Sup. improve our understanding of Sībawayhi's grammar?". *The Foundations of Arabic Linguistics IV. The Evolution of Theory*, ed. by Manuela E.B. Giolfo & Kees Versteegh, 133–156. Leiden & Boston: Brill, coll. "Studies in Semitic Languages and Linguistics" 97.

Druel, Jean N. 2020. "The *Kitāb Sībawayhi* of ʾAbū al-Ḥasan ʾAḥmad b. Naṣr: A non-Sīrāfian recension of the *Kitāb*". *Zeitschrift für Arabische Linguistik* 71. 29–56.

Gacek, Adam. 2009. *Arabic Manuscripts: A Vademecum for Readers*. Leiden & Boston: Brill, coll. "Handbook of Oriental Studies. Section 1, The Near and Middle East" 98.

Humbert, Geneviève. 1994. "Le *Kitāb* de Sībawayhi d'après l'autographe d'un grammairien andalou du XIIe siècle". *Al-Maḫṭūṭ al-ʿarabī wa-ʿilm al-maḫṭūṭāt*, ed. by ʾAḥmad Šawqī Binbīn, 9–20. Al-Ribāṭ: Kulliyyat al-ʾādāb, Ǧāmiʿat Muḥammad al-ḫāmis, coll. *"Nadawāt wa-munāẓarāt"* 33.

Humbert, Geneviève. 1995. *Les voies de la transmission du Kitāb de Sībawayhi.* Leiden & New York: Brill, coll. "Studies in Semitic Languages and Linguistics" 20.

Khalidov, A.B. 1986. *Арабские рукописи Института востоковедения*: *краткий каталог*. Moscow: Наука.

Lancioni, Giuliano. 2011. *Diminutives in Sībawayhi's* Kitāb. Roma: Edizioni Nuova Cultura, coll. "La Sapienza orientale—Ricerche" 7.

Lane, Edward William. 1863–1893. *An Arabic-English lexicon derived from the best and the most copious eastern sources*. London: Williams and Norgate, reprint Cambridge: The Islamic Text Society, 1984.

Levin, Aryeh. 1991. "The category of *ʾasmāʾ al-fiʿl* in Arabic grammar". *The Arabist*: Budapest studies in Arabic 3–4 (= *Proceedings of the colloquium on Arabic grammar*, Budapest, 1–7 September 1991, ed. by Kinga Dévényi & Tamás Iványi), 247–256.

CHAPTER 3

Arabic Grammar and Qurʾānic Scholarship in 2nd/8th Century's Basra: A Comparative Analysis of the Qurʾānic Material Found in the *Kitāb Sībawayhi* and in al-ʾAḫfaš al-ʾAwsaṭ's *Maʿānī al-Qurʾān*

Raoul Villano and Giuliano Lancioni

Introduction*

Sībawayhi's (d. 180/796?) actual reputation as a grammatical authority while still in life and in the first decades after his early death has been the subject of much scholarly debate, as well as the real nature of the relationship between Sībawayhi and the intellectual community of the time, notably his alleged most outstanding pupil al-ʾAḫfaš al-ʾAwsaṭ (d. 215/830, henceforth ʾAḫfaš).[1]

This is due, partly, to the lack and ambiguity of data found in Classical Arabic biographies, and partly, to a widespread, unduly, hypersceptical attitude in Western scholarship on early Arabic grammatical tradition.[2] The whole issue needs to be framed into the wider debate over the historical existence of grammatical schools in Basra and Kufa during 2nd/8th and early 3rd/9th centuries. According to the traditional account, early history of Arabic grammar was dominated by the opposition between the grammatical schools of Basra and Kufa: the schools were established in both Basra and Kufa already in early 2nd/8th century, and the historical existence of grammatical debates between leading

* Authors work at the same University and discussed at length the subjects treated in the chapter which is the result of joint work. As for authorship it can be attributed as follows: Raoul Villano wrote Introduction and sections 1, 2, 3, and 4; Giuliano Lancioni produced the graph in section 2.2 and the lists of section 5. Excel Index files were typed by Raoul Villano on the basis of ʿUḍayma 1975 for Sībawayhi, and Hudā Maḥmūd Qarrāʿa final indexes of ʾAḫfaš *Maʿānī* for ʾAḫfaš.

1 Cf., e.g., Humbert 1995:1–17, Bernards 1997:3–11, and Carter 2004:7–15.

2 On the lack and ambiguity of traditional data, cf. Humbert 1995:1–8; Bernards 1997:3–18 and Carter 2004:7–15. The case for the hypersceptical attitude of Western scholarship on the history of Arabic grammatical tradition can be seen, e.g., in Goldziher 1994 [1878]:3–9, Merx 1889:137–157, Weil 1913, Blachère 1950, Fleisch 1961–1979:I, 19–34, Rundgren 1976, Versteegh 1977, Owens 1990:1–5, Humbert 1995:1–17, Bernards 1997:3–18, and Sartori 2019.

 | DOI:10.1163/9789004515895_005

scholars of the two rival towns is attested, in Baghdad, at least starting from the caliphate of Hārūn al-Rašīd (r. 170/786–193/809).[3]

The traditional account has been seriously challenged by Gotthold Weil (1882–1960; cf. Weil 1913) who calls into question the existence of a real Kufan grammatical tradition and, based on the fact that no direct mention of the schools as such can be found in the works of Sībawayhi, Farrāʾ (d. 207/822), and Mubarrad (d. 285/898), argues that both grammatical debates and grammatical schools as proponents and advocates of points of controversy are a literary fiction forged by scholars of the generation after Mubarrad and Ṯaʿlab (d. 291/904) who projected, in Weil's hypothesis, their own oppositions back into a former situation that never existed in reality (cf. Weil 1913: 53 ff.). Although devoid of any objective evidence and based solely on an extensive application of the *argumentum e silentio*, Weil's hypothesis has dominated the scholarly debate until recent times.

Henri Fleisch (1904–1985) corroborates Weil's reconstruction and thinks that at the times of Sībawayhi real encounters between grammarians must have been a rare and very unlikely occurrence. He identifies Basra and Kufa as centers of grammatical studies, rather than real schools, emphasizing, thus, the geographical aspect over the methodological one (cf. Fleisch 1961–1979: I, 11–34).

Gérard Troupeau (1927–2010), on the contrary, accepts the traditional account, but speaks of methods (indeed a proper translation of the Arabic *maḏhab*) rather than schools, because, as he explains, already in 2nd/8th century, great Kufan masters like Kisāʾī (d. 189/805) and his pupil Farrāʾ used to live and teach in Baghdad and, by 4th/10th century, all Basran masters were established in Baghdad (cf. Troupeau 1962).

Weil's hypothesis is corroborated again by Carter (1973) who believes that the schools are a backward projection operated in 3rd/9th century and that the only real Arabic grammatical school is Basra. The two schools represent, in Carter's hypothesis, a specific reaction to the tensions occurred during the process of institutionalization of Islam, consistently with what happened in *fiqh*. The school of Basra would be, therefore, the result of a cultural process that is typical of early Islam and the *Kitāb* itself is not to be considered as Basran, firstly because at the times of Sībawayhi there were, according to Carter's reconstruction, no Basran nor Kufan schools, and secondly because later Basran approach to grammar proves to be didactic and prescriptive, while the *Kitāb* still shows a speculative and descriptivist approach tipycal of early Arabic

3 Cf., e.g., Ibn al-Nadīm *Fihrist* 45–97. Cf. also Flügel 1862, Ḍayf 1968, Sezgin 1984, and Ḥadīṯī 2001.

grammatical thinking. The school of Basra would be, therefore, the result of this process of legitimation that occurred later in 3rd/9th century's Baghdad while Kufa's school would have been built only in opposition with the principles of the new grammar elaborated in Baghdad.

An opposite point of view is to be found in Versteegh (1977: 107–112) who believes that the terminological divergence between the two schools needs to be framed in a dichotomic scheme. In his point of view, while it is true that real differences of opinion between the two schools were mainly related to points of detail and that from a methodological point of view the two schools were much more closer than what is depicted by later sources, it is still very unlikely that such a specific and developed terminology, like the one attributed by later sources to Kufan grammarians and found, as a matter of fact, in the works of Farrāʾ and Ṯaʿlab, could be the product of one single scholar "unless we are to assume that later grammarians not only invented the Kufan school, but a special terminology to go with it as well".

A real turning point is Baalbaki (1981) who admits that no mention of the schools as such is to be found in the works of Sībawayhi and Farrāʾ,[4] and recognizes that there is much more in common between the two schools than what is schematically represented in later sources, both in terms of method, terminology, sources, and subject-matter. Nonetheless, by comparing extant sources of 2nd/8th and 3rd/9th centuries, like Sībawayhi, Farrāʾ, Ibn al-Sikkīt (d. 244/858), Mubarrad and Ṯaʿlab, between each other and with the points of controversy found in the *Kitāb al-ʾInṣāf* of Ibn al-ʾAnbārī (d. 577/1181), he demonstrates the absurdity of Weil's hypothesis and proves the existence of a strict textual relation between early grammatical sources and late *ṭabaqāt*, *mağālis*, and *iḫtilāfāt*'s literature showing that at least one third of Ibn al-ʾAnbārī's *masāʾil* are actual points of disagreement between Farrāʾ on the one hand, and Sībawayhi and Mubarrad on the other (cf. Baalbaki 1981: 24).

Rafael Talmon (1948–2004) recognizes the existence of the schools, but believes that they were preceded by an earlier stage of grammatical teaching that he calls Old Iraqi School and that the reality of the schools in 2nd/8th cen-

4 No mention of Basrans as a group is to be found in the *Kitāb Sībawayhi* and only four mentions of Kufans are to be found in it, three of them referred to Qurʾānic *qirāʾāt*, but one of them clearly referred to a grammatical issue in which the opinion of Kufans is opposed by Sībawayhi to the view of his master Ḫalīl (cf. Baalbaki 1981:2–5, Talmon 1997:231). No mention of Basrans nor Kufans is to be found in Farrāʾ unless regarding *qirāʾāt* (cf. Baalbaki 1981:5–6). The first reference to Basrans as a group in a Kufan source is to be found in Ibn al-Sikkīt's *ʾIṣlāḥ al-manṭiq* (cf. Baalbaki 1981:6–7). The first reference to Kufans as a group in a Basran source, except the one found in Sībawayhi, is to be found in Mubarrad's *Muqtaḍab* (cf. Baalbaki 1981:7 ff.).

tury was not limited only to Basra and Kufa but was extended also to Medina and Hedjaz (cf. Talmon 1985, 1997, and 2003).

Owens (1990: 213–220, 1991) corroborates Weil's hypothesis again and suggests that the earliest stage of Arabic grammar was a period of linguistic heterogeneity in which scholars were free to mix ideas, methodologies, and terminologies. As for the dichotomic scheme that produced the opposition between Sībawayhi and Farrāʾ, or the grammatical schools of Basra and Kufa, it would be, in his point of view, only a late (4th/10th century) strategy for the organization and the understanding of this early heterogeneity.

Weil's hypothesis is revitalized once again by Humbert (1995: 1–17) who claims, on the one hand, that we don't know nothing about Sībawayhi and that all what we know about the author of the *Kitāb* is none other than a late forgery, and, on the other, that ʾAḫfaš was not a disciple of Sībawayhi, implicitly denying, by this way, the existence of anything like a grammatical school in Basra, at least at the times of Sībawayhi and ʾAḫfaš.

Later on, Bernards (1997: 3–18) questions even the reputation of Sībawayhi and the authority of the *Kitāb* during 2nd/8th and 3rd/9th centuries, claiming that most grammatical scholarship of the period would have been critical with the *Kitāb*, at least until Mubarrad's late retract, and thus corroborating, once again, Weil's hypothesis on grammatical debates and grammatical schools as a literary fiction forged by the generation after Mubarrad and Ṯaʿlab. While far from being demonstrated, Bernards' thesis is often taken for granted in academical circles (cf., e.g., Carter 2001; Ghersetti 2017: 881–882). In this context, very often, it is the same existence of a scholarly circle of *naḥwiyyūn* in Basra during 2nd/8th and early 3rd/9th centuries that is, more or less covertly, questioned.

The aim of this chapter is twofold. In the first part (section 1) an in-depth study of biographical, historiographical, and literary sources tries to demonstrate, on the one hand that the reputation of Sībawayhi was considerable, if not properly during his life, at least starting from the very first years after his early death, and, on the other, that ʾAḫfaš was perceived as the heir and successor of Sībawayhi's teaching at the very least already at the beginnings of 3rd/9th century. In the second part (sections 2 and 3) a comparative study of the Qurʾānic quotations found in Sībawayhi's *Kitāb* and in ʾAḫfaš's *Maʿānī al-Qurʾān* shows, on a textual basis, that both authors express a common scholarship that can only be explained by admitting the existence, in 2nd/8th century's Basra, of a scholarly circle of people concerned with the way of speech (*naḥwiyyūn*), if not exactly a grammatical school, of which both Sībawayhi and ʾAḫfaš were obviously part.

1 The Biography of Sībawayhi and the Relationship with ʾAḫfaš

1.1 *The Youth in Basra and the Case with Ḥammād b. Salama*

Practically all classical sources agree that Sībawayhi, who was Persian by birth, moved to Basra when he was very young and began to study Islamic law and *ḥadīṯ*-s' transmission in the scholarly circle of Ḥammād b. Salama (d. 167/784; cf. Zubaydī *Ṭabaqāt* 66; Tanūḫī *Taʾrīḫ* 92; Ibn al-ʾAnbārī *Nuzha* 54; Ibn Qutayba *Maʿārif* 503; Qifṭī *ʾInbāh* II, 354–355), a well-known and respected Basran traditionist and *faqīh* (cf. Yāqūt *ʾIršād* 1199), but also a poet, a Qurʾān scholar (cf. Marzubānī *Nūr* 32–33) and a pupil of Ḫalīl b. ʾAḥmad (d. 175/791?) and ʿĪsā b. ʿUmar al-Ṯaqafī (d. 149/766) in the field of *ʿarabiyya* (cf. Luġawī *Marātib* 74; Ibn al-ʾAnbārī *Nuzha* 42; Yāqūt *ʾIršād*, 1199), later on seen as a grammatical authority himself (cf. Ibn Qutayba *Maʿārif*, 503), having been the first master of none other than Yūnus b. Ḥabīb (d. 182/798?) (cf. Zubaydī *Ṭabaqāt* 51; Ibn al-ʾAnbārī *Nuzha* 42; Qifṭī *ʾInbāh* I, 364–365), one of the main and most quoted masters of Sībawayhi himself (cf. Troupeau 1961).

To the years of study with Ḥammād, who used to say that people who want to study the *ḥadīṯ* without knowing grammar are like a donkey carrying an empty fodder bag (*maṯal allaḏī yaṭlubu al-ḥadīṯ wa-lā yaʿrifu al-naḥw maṯal al-ḥimār ʿalayhi miḫlāt wa-lā šaʿīr fīhā*, Qifṭī *ʾInbāh* I, 364), dates the first public humiliation documented by classical biographies, by which, it seems, Sībawayhi's very interest in the study of grammar was actually generated.

The accident is described by sources in slightly different ways, all revolving around Sībawayhi's poor knowledge of *ʿarabiyya*, either because of his inability to spell like a native Arabic speaker, or because of his non-canonical ideas about Arabic grammar.

The oldest account of this accident is to be found in the *Maǧālis al-ʿulamāʾ* of ʾAbū al-Qāsim al-Zaǧǧāǧī (d. 337/949) who narrates two slightly different stories (cf. Zaǧǧāǧī *Maǧālis* 118). In both stories Sībawayhi is writing or reciting *ḥadīṯ*-s, under the dictation or in front of his master Ḥammād. In the first one, Ḥammād mentions the Prophet rising on the heights of Ṣafā and Sībawayhi spells it as *ṣafāʾ* (purity), being harshly criticized for that by Ḥammād who even calls him Persian (*yā fārisī*) to deplore his non-native spelling, whereupon Sībawayhi leaves the assembly in anger and frustration, breaking up his pen while saying: "I will not write anything, anymore, until I will perfectly master the *ʿarabiyya*" (*fa-lammā faraġa min maǧlisihi kasara al-qalam wa-qāla lā ʾaktubu šayʾan ḥattā ʾuḥkima al-ʿarabiyya*, Zaǧǧāǧī *Maǧālis* 118).

In the second story Ḥammād is dictating to Sībawayhi the very words of the Prophet: *laysa min ʾaṣḥābī ʾaḥadun ʾillā wa-law šiʾtu la-ʾaḫaḏtu ʿalayhi laysa ʾabā al-dardāʾ* ("there's no one, among my companions, to whom, if I wish, I could not make some remarks, except 'Abū al-Dardā'"). The text of the *ḥadīṯ* has an accusative case ending after the second *laysa*, but Sībawayhi reads it with a nominative case ending (*laysa 'abū al-dardā'*) and Ḥammād rebukes him saying: "you are wrong Sībawayhi, this is not correct in that way, because *laysa*, here, is just [a particle of] *istiṯnā'* (exception)" (*fa-ṣāḥa bihi ḥammād laḥanta yā sībawayhi laysa hāḏā ḥayṯu ḏahabta 'innamā huwa istiṯnā'*, Zaǧǧāǧī *Maǧālis* 118; cf. also Zubaydī *Ṭabaqāt* 66; Tanūḫī *Ta'rīḫ* 93; Ibn al-'Anbārī *Nuzha* 42; Yāqūt *'Iršād* 1199; Qifṭī *'Inbāh* II, 350; Suyūṭī *Buġya* I, 548), and, in Ḥammād's interpretation, being a particle of *istiṯnā'*, *laysa* needs here to be followed by an accusative case ending. Sībawayhi's reading was possibly defensible by assuming 'Abū al-Dardā' being the noun (*ism*) of *laysa* with ellipsis (*ḥaḏf*) of the *ḫabar*: *laysa 'Abū al-Dardā'* [*minhum*] ("'Abū al-Dardā' is not part of them", cf. Zubaydī *Ṭabaqāt* 66), but Sībawayhi did not actually stand up for his own reading and took the rebuke pretty bad: "Surely, but I swear, I am going to seek some kind of knowledge by which you will never be able to tell me I do not speak pure Arabic again" (*lā ǧaram wa-llāh la-'aṭlubanna 'ilman lā tulaḥḥinunī ma'ahu*, Zaǧǧāǧī *Maǧālis* 118; cf. also Zubaydī *Ṭabaqāt* 66; Tanūḫī *Ta'rīḫ* 93; Ibn al-'Anbārī *Nuzha* 42; Yāqūt *'Iršād* 1199; Qifṭī *'Inbāh* II, 350; Suyūṭī *Buġya* I, 548).

Thus, Sībawayhi definitely left Ḥammād and joined the scholarly circle of 'Aḫfaš, also frequented by the famous Qur'ānic canonical reader Ya'qūb al-Ḥaḍramī (d. 205/821), by Sībawayhi's principal master Ḫalīl b. 'Aḥmad and by other, anonymous, *naḥwiyyūn* (*fa-maḍā wa-lazima maǧlis al-'aḫfaš ma'a ya'qūb al-ḥaḍramī wa-l-ḫalīl wa-sā'ir al-naḥwiyyīn*, Zaǧǧāǧī *Maǧālis* 118).[5] The statement suggests a possible role of leader for 'Aḫfaš within the scholarly circle

5 The meaning of the term *naḥwiyyūn* in Sībawayhi's *Kitāb* has aroused some discussion in academical circles, notably after the publication of Carter 1972. For Ḥadīṯī (1967:100–102) they were Sībawayhi's teachers. Troupeau (1976:14, and s.v. N-Ḥ-W) translates it simply as *grammairiens*. Carter (1972) notices that most times Sībawayhi is critical towards those *naḥwiyyūn* and so, while he doesn't believe that the term designate the grammarians, nor some people dealing with a well established and recognized science, he speculates that they may have been just people concerned with the way of speech, consistently with the etymology of the term itself. Sībawayhi would have been, thus, the first Arab grammarian, and the term *naḥwiyyūn* would became the accepted technical term for grammarians only after him. Talmon (1982) questions Carter's interpretation according to which the *naḥwiyyūn* were anonymous, non-specialist, contemporaries of Sībawayhi and believes that also Yūnus b. Ḥabīb, 'Īsā b. 'Umar, Ḫalīl b. 'Aḥmad, and even Sībawayhi were part of the same group. In his point of view, the *naḥwiyyun* were indeed grammarians and, although Sībawayhi seems to reject the conclusions of the *naḥwiyyūn* in some specific instances, according to Talmon he never rejects their principles of grammatical analysis but, on the contrary, he founds his grammatical system on the ground of their advanced grammatical analysis. In my opinion, they were one out of many scholarly circles active in Basra and elsewhere in 2nd/8th century. They were not all strictly grammarians, as it is clear by the presence in the group of scholars like, e.g., the Qur'ānic

of the *naḥwiyyūn*, but in other accounts we are just told that Sībawayhi began to study grammar and followed Ḫalīl (*fa-ṭalaba al-naḥw wa-lazima al-ḫalīl*, Ibn al-ʾAnbārī *Nuzha* 42; cf. also Zubaydī *Ṭabaqāt* 66; Tanūḫī *Taʾrīḫ* 93; Yāqūt *ʾIršād* 1199; Qifṭī *ʾInbāh* II, 350, 354–355).

Be that as it may, it is true that some kind of public humiliation related to Sībawayhi's inability to speak pure or correct Arabic is a constant feature of all biographies: it's mentioned already by Ibn Qutayba (d. 270/889) in the oldest, preserved, biographical entry on Sībawayhi:

> He is ʿAmr b. ʿUṯmān and he was mainly concerned with grammar, he arrived once to Baghdad where he got involved in a public debate with other grammarians and was humiliated […]. (*huwa ʿamr b. ʿuṯmān wa-kāna al-naḥw ʾaġlaba ʿalayhi wa-kāna qadima baġdād fa-ǧumiʿa baynahu wa-bayna ʾaṣḥāb al-naḥw fa-ʾustuḏilla* […], Ibn Qutayba *Maʿārif* 544)[6]

and is found in all later sources, with the sole exceptions of the two biographical entries on Sībawayhi made by ʾAbū al-Ṭayyib al-Luġawī (d. 351/962; cf. Luġawī *Marātib* 73) and ʾAbū Saʿīd al-Sīrāfī (d. 368/979; cf. Sīrāfī *ʾAḫbār* 37–38).

The story of the public humiliation must be analyzed, here, in two different respects: the reputation of Sībawayhi as a grammatical authority, on the one hand, and, on the other, Sībawayhi's potential quarrelsomeness and the real nature of his relationship with the intellectual community of the time.

1.2 *Sībawayhi's Reputation*

As for Sībawayhi's reputation, it is true that classical biographies provide several clues to the hypothesis of a possible bad reputation for the author of the *Kitāb* while still in life, if not as a grammarian, at least as a speaker: rumors were circulating that he may even had some kind of speech defect.

Zubaydī (d. 379/989) relates the account of some ʾAḥmad b. Muʿāwiya b. Bakr al-ʿUlaymī who claimed once to have seen the young Sībawayhi speaking and debating about grammar and asserted that he had some speech impediment (*wa-kānat fī lisānihi ḥubsa*), nonetheless, after a look at the *Kitāb* he admitted that Sībawayhi's knowledge was actually much more effective than his elo-

reader Yaʿqūb al-Ḥaḍramī, but they were identified by the very fact to be concerned mainly with the way of speech. The term soon began to mean professional grammarians when being a grammarian became a paid profession (i.e. at least from the times of al-Mahdī [r. 158/775–169/785], who entrusted Kisāʾī with the education of his son Hārūn al-Rašīd, cf. Yāqūt *ʾIršād* 1738–1740).

6 Although, here, the author refers to the famous *masʾala zunbūriyya*, cf. *infra*.

quence (*a.l.* his knowledge was more eloquent than his speech), which is not very complimentary either (*fa-naẓartu fī kitābihi fa-ʿilmuhu ʾablaġ min lisānihi*, Zubaydī *Ṭabaqāt* 66–67; cf. Tanūḫī *Taʾrīḫ* 98; Yāqūt *ʾIršād* 2124; Qifṭī *ʾInbāh* II, 349; Ibn Ḫallikān *Wafayāt* III, 465; Suyūṭī *Buġya* II, 229).

According to Marzubānī (d. 384/994), his Kufan archrival Farrāʾ, commenting Sībawayhi's claim that a verse of the famous poet Baššār b. Burd (d. 167/783) was inconsistent with pure Bedouin speech, called him a real catastrophe (*kāna sībawayhi ʿuḍla min al-ʿuḍal*), a quite enigmatic, but certainly not flattering expression (cf. Marzubānī *Nūr* 68).

A late source like Qifṭī (d. 646/1248) records a discussion about the correct *ʾiʿrāb* of Sībawayhi's sobriquet. It seems, indeed, that Ṯaʿlab, who, according to Ibn al-Nadīm (d. 385/995), used to say that the *Kitāb* was actually composed by forty two scholars and that Sībawayhi was only one of them (*iğtamaʿa ʿalā ṣanʿat kitāb sībawayhi iṯnān wa-ʾarbaʿūn ʾinsānan minhum sībawayhi*, Ibn al-Nadīm *Fihrist* 57; cf. Qifṭī *ʾInbāh* II, 347), said once that Sībawayhi was wrong even about the *ʾiʿrāb* of his own name (*kāna sībawayhi yuḫṭiʾu fī ismihi*) because he used to say *sībawayhi wa-sībawayhin ʾāḫar* ("Sībawayhi and another Sībawayhi") treating therefore his name as a triptote when indefinite, while Kisāʾī would have said *sībawayhu wa-sībawayhu ʾāḫar*, treating it as a diptote, because, being a foreign name, it should not be trated as a triptote ever (*li-ʾannahu ʾaʿǧamī fa-lā yuǧrā*, Qifṭī *ʾInbāh* II, 352).

Another late source like Yāqūt (d. 626/1229) relates a story about Zaǧǧāǧ (d. 311/923) who finds himself involved, in the house of Ṯaʿlab, in a debate with ʾAbū Mūsā al-Ḥāmiḍ (d. 305/918), a fanatical Kufan supporter,[7] who openly tells, in order to insult Zaǧǧāǧ, that Sībawayhi was unable to speak correctly (*wa-llāh ʾinna ṣāḥibakum ʾalkan* [...] *fa-ʾaḥfaẓanī ḏālika*) and quotes the story of Farrāʾ who goes to Basra and visit Sībawayhi to find out that he was a stranger (*ʾaʿǧam*), unable to speak fluent Arabic (*fa-ʾataytuhu fa-ʾiḏā huwa ʾaʿǧam lā yufṣiḥu*, Yāqūt *ʾIršād* 55–56). As a proof of that, Farrāʾ declares to have heard him saying to his servant: *hāti ḏīka al-māʾ min ḏāka al-ǧarra* ("bring that water from that jar"), with both demonstratives mistaken (cf. Yāqūt *ʾIršād* 55–56).

This ʾAbū Mūsā, said al-Ḥāmiḍ (*a.l.* the quarrelsome one), is described by sources as a very nervous and irritable counterpart:[8] when his master Ṯaʿlab mentions the story of Farrāʾ who died with a copy of the *Kitāb* under his pillow

7 On ʾAbū Mūsā al-Ḥāmiḍ, cf. Zubaydī *Ṭabaqāt* 152–153; Ḫaṭīb *Taʾrīḫ* X, 85–86; Samʿānī *ʾAnsāb* IV, 29; Ibn al-ʾAnbārī *Nuzha* 181–182; Yāqūt *ʾIršād* 1400–1401; Ibn Ḫallikān *Wafayāt* II, 406.

8 "He has been called al-Ḥāmiḍ right because of his very cranky temper, from that comes the sobriquet al-Ḥāmiḍ" (*wa-ʾinnamā qīla lahu al-ḥāmiḍ li-ʾannahu kānat lahu ʾaḫlāq šarisa fa-luqqiba al-ḥāmiḍ li-ḏālika*, Ibn Ḫallikān *Wafayāt* II, 406).

(*māta al-farrā' wa-taḥta ra'sihi kitāb sībawayhi*), 'Abū Mūsā immediately replies that this happened just because Farrā' was chasing errors and grammatical mistakes in it (*'innamā kāna lā yufāriquhu li-'annahu kāna yatatabba'u ḫaṭa'ahu wa-luknatahu*, Luġawī *Marātib* 105), but the factiosity had already taken over his mind (*wa-kāna al-'aṣabiyya qad ḏahabat bi-'aql al-ḥāmiḍ*) and so, when Ibn Kaysān (d. 299/911 or 320/932), a pupil of both Mubarrad and Ṯa'lab who is said to have been acquainted with both Basran and Kufan *maḏāhib* (doctrines) (cf. Qifṭī *'Inbāh* III, 57–59), tells to Ṯa'lab his dream: "I was sleeping and I saw some jinns debating with each other on any possible kind of science and so I asked them which grammarian was their favorite one and they said Sībawayhi" (*ra'aytu fī al-manām al-ǧinn wa-hum yatanāẓarūna fī kull fann min al-'ulūm fa-qultu lahum 'ilā man tamīlūna fī al-naḥw fa-qālū 'ilā sībawayhi*), 'Abū Mūsā, who was there as Ṯa'lab's guest, loses his temper and bursts out: "Oh, this must be true, because Sībawayhi was nothing but an impostor and a devil and that's why jinns have a preference for him" (*qad ṣadaqa 'innamā sībawayhi daǧǧāl šayṭān fa-li-ḏālika tamīlu 'ilayhi al-ǧinn*, Luġawī *Marātib* 105–106; cf. also Ibn al-'Anbārī *Nuzha* 56; Qifṭī *'Inbāh* II, 356).

It must be said, however, that all this criticism, as well as rumors and hearsay, comes from Kufan sources. There is no real criticism of Sībawayhi coming from Basran sources.[9]

In Luġawī's *Marātib*, 'Aḫfaš is said to have pointed out to the Basrans any small flaw found in the *Kitāb* before leaving them (*nabbahahum 'alā 'uwar al-Kitāb wa-tarakahum*, Luġawī *Marātib* 80), but the information is reported on the authority of Kisā'ī, who is still, of course, a Kufan source.[10]

Bernards (1997: 3–9), in an attempt at demonstrate that late 2nd/8th and early 3rd/9th centuries' scholarship on Sībawayhi was mostly critical with the *Kitāb*, makes a list, albeit incomplete, of anything that might be, both in Kufan and in Basran sources, interpreted as potential criticism. Unfortunately, she regularly misunderstands practically all information given by Arabic tradition on behalf of Basran sources.[11]

9 The sole, possible, Basran criticism on the *Kitāb* is to be found in the manuscript glosses on the *Kitāb* written by 'Aḫfaš (cf. Humbert 1995:13–17, 58–64) and in Mubarrad's lost *Radd* (cf. Bernards 1997). On both see *infra* (sections 1.2 and 1.4).

10 Humbert, who has studied the manuscript glosses on the *Kitāb*, claims that there is some criticism to be found in the oldest layer of glosses ascribed to 'Aḫfaš (cf. Humbert 1995:15–16). It should be noted, however, that both Luġawī's account and 'Aḫfaš's glosses studied by Humbert seem much more a regular correction of a text that may well come from a student than a real criticism or refutation of the work of Sībawayhi. On that, see *infra* (section 1.4).

11 This is not the place to make a complete review of all evidence brought by Bernards,

According to her point of view, indeed, the very fact that ʾAbū Yaʿlā b. ʾAbī Zurʿa (d. 257/871) is said to have composed a commentary on the *Kitāb*, unfortunately lost, entitled *Nukat ʿalā Kitāb Sībawayhi* suggests, in her own words "that it was at the very least [*sic*] a critical commentary" (Bernards 1997: 3–4). It should be noted, however, that a correct translation for the title of Ibn ʾAbī Zurʿa's commentary should be *Selected problems found in Sībawayhi's* Kitāb: the modern meaning of *nukta* (i.e. witticism, wisecrack, joke), which probably Bernards supposes is at work here, is absolutely anachronistic and inappropriate in this case, as clearly suggested also by the only short account of the commentary given by a scholar who actually read it, Qifṭī, who is quoted, but apparently not taken seriously, by Bernards herself: "not bad in terms of usefulness" (*lā baʾs bi-fawāʾidihi*, Qifṭī *ʾInbāh* IV, 190).

Another such criticism coming from Basran sources would be, still according to Bernards (1997: 6), the opinion of Siǧistānī (d. 255/869) "that the *Kitāb* is remarkable for its elegance in metrics and poetry but whose author is otherwise of lesser quality than al-Māzinī [d. 249/863] as a grammarian [*sic*]".

It is unclear to me how Bernards gets to misunderstand in such a striking way the text of Sīrāfī which is, simply, a biographical account of Siǧistānī that mentions Sībawayhi just as the author of the *Kitāb* that Siǧistānī himself read twice in front of ʾAḫfaš.

Here's the complete text of Sīrāfī followed by a proper translation:

أخبار أبي حاتم السجستاني

هو سهل بن محمد. وكان كثير الرواية عن أبي زيد وأبي عبيدة والأصمعي، عالمًا باللغة والشعر. قال أبو العباس: وسمعته يقول: قرأت كتاب سيبويه على الأخفش مرتين، وكان حسن العلم بالعروض، وإخراج المعمى، ويقول الشعر الجيد، ويصيب المعنى، ولم يكن بالحاذق في النحو. قال أبو العباس: ولو قدم بغداد لم يقم له منهم أحد. وله كتاب في النحو. قال أبو العباس: وكان إذا التقى هو والمازني في دار عيسى بن جعفر الهاشمي، تشاغل أو بادر، خوفاً من أن يسأله المازني عن النحو، وكان جماعة للكتب يتجر فيها. وكان كثير تأليف الكتب في اللغة.

including Mubarrad's *Radd*. We are mainly concerned, here, with the analysis of biographical, historiographical, and literary sources on the life of Sībawayhi. One thing should be noted, anyway: Mubarrad's *Radd* is now lost and must be deduced, through a leap of faith in its author's accuracy, from Ibn Wallād's (d. 332/944) *Kitāb al-Intiṣār* that is also a 4th/10th century's source (as well as Ibn al-Nadīm, Sīrāfī, Zaǧǧāǧī, and so on). It is not clear, thus, why should we suspect of any sources on early Arabic grammatical tradition coming from 4th/10th century onward and trust solely the isolated account of Ibn Wallād?

قال أبو العباس: جئت السجستاني وأنا حدث، فرأيت بعض ما ينبغي أن تهجر حلقته له، فتركته مدة، ثم صرت إليه، وعميت له بيتاً لهارون الرشيد، وكان يجيد استخراج المعمى، فأجابني: [...]

Account of ʾAbū Ḥātim al-Siǧistānī

His name was Sahl b. Muḥammad and he transmitted on the authority of ʾAbū Zayd [al-ʾAnṣārī, d. 215/830?], ʾAbū ʿUbayda [d. 207/825] and ʾAṣmaʿī [d. 213/828]. He was learned in philology and in poetry. It has been related by Mubarrad that he heard Siǧistānī say: "I read Sībawayhi's *Kitāb* twice in front of ʾAḫfaš." And [Siǧistānī] was well-versed in metrics, able in the solution of enigmas and in the production of poems from both the formal and semantic point of view, but he was not so skilled in grammar. It has been said by Mubarrad that if Siǧistānī had gone to Baghdad none would have stood up out of respect for his authority. And he wrote a book on grammar. It has been related by Mubarrad that whenever Siǧistānī met Māzinī in the house of ʿĪsā b. Ǧaʿfar al-Hāšimī [dates unknown], he pretended like he was busy or he had to leave, fearing that Māzinī could ask him about some grammatical question. And he was a collector of books in which he loved to get lost. And he composed many books on philology.

It has been said by Mubarrad: "I went to Siǧistānī when I was young and I saw what was enough for me to leave his scholarly circle [i.e. things I didn't like], and so I dropped out of it for a while, but later I went back and I proposed him an enigma on a poetic verse of Hārūn al-Rašīd and [Siǧistānī] solved it perfectly and answered: [...]" (follows the poetic answer by which Siǧistānī solves the enigma, Sīrāfī *ʾAḫbār* 70–71).[12]

As it can easily be noticed by looking at the whole text, Mubarrad, in the text of Sīrāfī, did absolutely not say that for Siǧistānī Sībawayhi was not so skilled in grammar as Māzinī (as argued by Bernards), but that Siǧistānī himself was not so skilled in grammar and that whenever he met Māzinī he pretended to be busy or that he had to leave, fearing that Māzinī could ask him about grammar. And Siǧistānī (certainly not Sībawayhi) is the one who is able in the solution of enigmas and in the production of poems as it is clearly shown by the end of the text in which Siǧistānī's poetic solution of the enigma proposed by Mubarrad is reported.

12 Cf. also Ibn al-ʾAnbārī *Nuzha* 145–146; Suyūṭī *Buġya* I, 606 in which the two sentences are not even one after the other, being clearly two different short texts about the same scholar, i.e. Siǧistānī.

Finally, for Bernards (1997: 6), another element to be read as Basran criticism on the *Kitāb* is the account of 'Abū 'Isḥāq al-Ziyādī (d. 249/863) who "is said to have read parts of the *Kitāb Sībawayh* but never finished it; he wrote a short critical [*sic*] commentary in which he presented some points of disagreements with the *Kitāb*". Now, it is true that Ziyādī composed a commentary on selected problems (*nukat* doesn't mean critical) found in the *Kitāb* in which he is said to have expressed some points of disagreement with it (*wa-lahu nukat fī kitāb sībawayhi wa-ḫilāf lahu fī mawāḍiʿ*) which were already explained by Sīrāfī in his own commentary on the *Kitāb* (*qad ḏakarnāhā fī šarḥihi*), but the reason why he didn't actually finish it is most probably that he couldn't get to complete such a challenging and tricky reading (*fa-lam yutimmahu*, Sīrāfī *'Aḫbār* 67; cf. Ibn al-'Anbārī *Nuzha* 157),[13] not else.[14]

In Basran biographical and historiographical sources, indeed, Sībawayhi is always represented with rather enthusiastic statements.

For Luġawī, Sībawayhi was "the most learned of men in grammar after Ḫalīl and the Book he composed is called by people the Qur'ān of grammar" (*wa-huwa 'aʿlam al-nās fī al-naḥw baʿd al-ḫalīl wa-'allafa kitābahu allaḏī sammāhu al-nās qur'ān al-naḥw*, Luġawī *Marātib* 73).

For Ibn al-Nadīm, "nothing, either before it or afterwards, can outmatch or even just match the *Kitāb*" (*lam yasbiqhu 'ilā miṯlihi 'aḥad qablahu wa-lam yalḥaq bihi baʿdahu*, Ibn al-Nadīm *Fihrist* 57; cf. Ibn al-'Anbārī *Nuzha* 55; Qifṭī *'Inbāh* II, 347).

---

13 Cf. also Yāqūt *'Iršād* 67–68 where Ziyādī is said to have read the *Kitāb Sībawayhi* with Sībawayhi himself without having finished it (*qara'a kitāb sībawayhi ʿalā sībawayhi wa-lam yutimmahu*, Yāqūt *'Iršād* 67), and he is said to have composed a commentary on selected problems found in the *Kitāb Sībawayhi* (*Šarḥ nukat Kitāb Sībawayhi*) which, in another manuscript, is said to have been a commentary on a third of what is found in the *Kitāb Sībawayhi* (*Šarḥ ṯulṯ Kitāb Sībawayhi*, Yāqūt *'Iršād* 68, cf. fn. 2).

14 The point, here, is not to demonstrate that there never was any kind of criticism towards Sībawayhi coming from Basran, or Kufan, sources. Rather, it seems reasonable that if grammarians, during 2nd/8th and 3rd/9th centuries expressed some point of disagreement toward the *Kitāb*, this, far from being the sign of a bad reputation for the author of the *Kitāb*, demonstrate, on the contrary, that Sībawayhi became immediately the unavoidable point of reference for anyone wishing to debate about grammar. If the Arabic tradition relates the existence of no less than 20 between commentaries on full text (*šurūḥ, tafāsīr*), selected problems (*nukat, ʿuyūn*), introductory section alone (*risāla*), difficult words (*ġarā'ib*), commentaries and explanations of poetic *loci probantes* (*šawāhid, 'abyāt*), introductions (*mudḫalāt*), critical refutations (*rudūd*), and rebuttals of mentioned critical refutations (*iʿtirāḍāt*), all produced between the end of 2nd/8th and the end of 3rd/9th centuries (cf. Sezgin 1984:58–59), this means precisely that the work of Sībawayhi did arouse much interest already in the earliest period of its textual history.

Ibn Sallām al-Ǧumaḥī (d. 231/845?) is reported to have said once that Sībawayhi was the best of men (*ġāya fī al-ḫalq*) and his Book on grammar a guide for mankind (*wa-kitābuhu fī al-naḥw huwa al-ʾimām fīhi*, Ibn al-ʾAnbārī *Nuzha* 55; cf. Qifṭī *ʾInbāh* II, 355–356), and, according to Sīrāfī, it seems that in Basra, as soon as it was said that someone read "the Book", it was clear to anyone that the *Kitāb Sībawayhi* was intended with that (*wa-kāna yuqālu fī al-baṣra qaraʾa fulān al-kitāb fa-yuʿlamu ʾannahu kitāb sībawayhi*, Sīrāfī *ʾAḫbār* 39, cf. Ibn al-ʾAnbārī *Nuzha* 55; Qifṭī *ʾInbāh* II, 351).

When Ǧāḥiẓ (d. 255/868–869), who, according to Ibn Ḫallikān (d. 681/1282) used to say that "no one has ever written a book on grammar like the *Kitāb* and all subsequent books owe a debt with it" (*lam yaktub al-nās fī al-naḥw kitāban miṯlahu wa-ǧamīʿ kutub al-nās ʿalayhi ʿiyāl*, Ibn Ḫallikān *Wafayāt* III, 463; cf. Qifṭī *ʾInbāh* II, 351), wants to impress his host, the famous vizir Muḥammad b. ʿAbd al-Malik al-Zayyāt (d. 233/847) (cf. Ḫaṭīb *Taʾrīḫ* III, 593–596), with a unique gift, he doesn't find anything better than a copy of the *Kitāb* itself (*fa-lam ʾara ʾašraf min hāḏā al-kitāb*, Ibn al-ʾAnbārī *Nuzha* 55; cf. Yāqūt *ʾIršād* 2127; Qifṭī *ʾInbāh* II, 351; Ibn Ḫallikān *Wafayāt* III, 463).

Even Ḫalīl, the main master of Sībawayhi, unanimously seen as the genius and founder of most grammatical and linguistic sciences, according to the testimony of Ibn al-Naṭṭāḥ (d. 252/866), would have welcomed once Sībawayhi into his house with the greatest honors, saying: "greetings to a guest you never get bored with" (*marḥaban li-zāʾir lā yumallu*, Zubaydī *Ṭabaqāt* 67; cf. Tanūḫī *Taʾrīḫ* 94; Qifṭī *ʾInbāh* II, 352; Ibn Ḫallikān *Wafayāt* III, 463–464; Suyūṭī *Buġya* II, 229), and, in a discussion between Ḫalīl, Yūnus, Sībawayhi and Farrāʾ about Q. 19/69, Zaǧǧāǧī states that the most correct between Basran opinions is the one advocated by Sībawayhi (cf. Zaǧǧāǧī *Maǧālis* 231–232).

There is an interesting story narrated in the second part of Ibn Qutayba's oldest biographical account on Sībawayhi and reported on the authority of Siǧistānī. It seems that ʾAbū Zayd al-ʾAnṣārī said once that Sībawayhi used to frequent his scholarly circle when he was a young boy with two sidelocks in the hair and he assured that whenever Sībawayhi says "I was told that by someone whose Arabic I trust" he means with that ʾAbū Zayd himself (*kāna sībawayhi ġulāman yaʾtī maǧlisī wa-lahu ḏuʾābatān qāla wa-ʾiḏā samiʿtahu yaqūlu ʾaḫbaranī man ʾaṯiqu bi-ʿarabiyyatihi fa-ʾinnamā yurīdunī*, Ibn Qutayba *Maʿārif* 503; cf. Tanūḫī *Taʾrīḫ* 98; Qifṭī *ʾInbāh* II, 350). The same story is related, about one century later, by Sīrāfī and Marzubānī who add, very appositely, that ʾAbū Zayd used to say that in order to boast (*ka-l-muftaḫir*, Sīrāfī *ʾAḫbār* 37; cf. Marzubānī *Nūr* 68), which seems reasonable, but the story in itself must have been very old, being quoted already in Ibn Qutayba short entry on Sībawayhi.

Sometimes even the Kufan counterpart is involved in this process of glorification, and so, if Sībawayhi's archrival Kisāʾī is said to have hounded ʾAḫfaš to read him the *Kitāb* or teach him to read it (*ǧaʾanā al-kisāʾī ʾilā al-baṣra fa-saʾalanī ʾan ʾaqraʾa ʿalayhi ʾaw ʾuqriʾahu kitāb sībawayhi*) and have finally paid him fifty dinars to do it (*fa-faʿaltu fa-waǧǧaha ʾilayya ḫamsīn dīnāran*, Sīrāfī *ʾAḫbār* 40; cf. Zubaydī *Ṭabaqāt* 73; Marzubānī *Nūr* 68; Tanūḫī *Taʾrīḫ* 86; Yāqūt *ʾIršād* 1375, 2126–2127; Qifṭī *ʾInbāh* II, 40, 350), Kisāʾī's most outstanding pupil, as well as the other main rival of both Sībawayhi and ʾAḫfaš, the Kufan leader Farrāʾ, is said to have died with a copy of the *Kitāb* under his pillow (*māta al-farrāʾ wa-taḥta raʾsihi kitāb sībawayhi*, Luġawī *Marātib* 105).

Now, it could be said that most of these statements come from relatively late sources, but the admiration for the *Kitāb* and his author must have spread rather early if Ǧāḥiẓ (b. 160/776?), who was born in Basra some twenty years before the death of Sībawayhi, already mentions him as the symbol of grammatical knowledge in his *al-Bayān wa-l-tabyīn* when he tells the story of an aspirant teacher of the sons of ʿAttāb b. ʾAsīd (d. 23/644?) who finds one of ʿAttāb's descendants reading the *Kitāb Sībawayhi* and rebukes him courteously saying "Shame on you, this is a knowledge for preceptors and a concern for indigent people" (*wa-marra raǧul min qurayš bi-fatan min wuld ʿattāb b. ʾasīd wa-huwa yaqraʾu kitāb sībawayhi fa-qāla ʾuff lakum ʿilm al-muʾaddibīn wa-himmat al-muḥtāǧīn*, Ǧāḥiẓ *Bayān* I, 402–403, cf. Yāqūt *ʾIršād* 32), placing, therefore, grammatical studies out of princes' needs, but the *Kitāb Sībawayhi* right at the center of grammatical studies. Sībawayhi is mentioned twice also in Ǧāḥiẓ's *Kitāb al-Ḥayawān*, once as a transmitter of poetry (cf. Ǧāḥiẓ *Ḥayawān* III, 497), and once as a representative of Basran excellence "this book is not [...] on the supremacy of Basra over Kufa, nor on the supremacy of Sībawayhi over Kisāʾī" (*wa-laysa hāḏā al-kitāb* [...] *fī tafḍīl al-baṣra ʿalā al-kūfa* [...] *wa-lā fī tafḍīl sībawayhi ʿalā al-kisāʾī*, Ǧāḥiẓ *Ḥayawān* VII, 7), within an impressive list of names that represents very well the accepted canon of Arabic and Islamic civilization in late 2nd/8th and early 3rd/9th centuries, from ʿAlī b. ʾAbī Ṭālib (d. 40/661) and ʿUṯmān b. ʿAffān (d. 35/656) to Mālik b. ʾAnas (d. 179/795) and ʾAbū Ḥanīfa (d. 150/767), from Imruʾ al-Qays (d. 540? CE) and Nābiġa (d. 604 CE) to, indeed, Sībawayhi and Kisāʾī.

Even Ibn Sallām al-Ǧumaḥī (b. 139/756), who was a Basran contemporary of Sībawayhi, and whose father had studied with the pioneers of Arabic grammatical studies, quotes Sībawayhi directly in the introductory section of his *Kitāb Ṭabaqāt fuḥūl al-šuʿarāʾ* for having consulted him about the correct reading of Q. 6/27, without even feeling the need to introduce the reader to his personality (cf. Ibn Sallām *Ṭabaqāt* 19–20).[15]

Finally, Ibn Qutayba (b. 213/828), who was born in Kufa some thirty years after the death of Sībawayhi, devotes to him a full biographical entry in his *Maʿārif* (cf. Ibn Qutayba *Maʿārif* 544), thus including him among the greatest personalities of the previous century.

We can be quite sure that the author of the *Kitāb* was able, despite everything, to build a good reputation for himself, if not at all while still in life, at least in the first decades after his untimely death, as demonstrated also by some other anecdote related to his relationship with his most important pupil, ʾAḫfaš, to which I shall return later.

1.3 *Sībawayhi's Relationship with the Intellectual Community and the* mas'ala zunbūriyya

As for Sībawayhi's potential quarrelsomeness and his relationship with the intellectual community of the time we also have several indications that he may have had a very bad character. Clashes or discussions are reported between Sībawayhi and several grammarians of his generation and even of previous generations, including members of both Basran and Kufan sides.

According to extant sources, actually, it seems that the whole circle of Basran *naḥwiyyūn* was a very quarrelsome group. We are continuously told of discussions, debates, disputes and clashes, which often led to strong position statements, personal insults and furious outbursts in the public arena, involving the presence in turn of grammarians, philologists, poets, pure native Arabic speaker judges (i.e. Bedouins), theologians, traditionists, exegetes, *qāḍī*-s, *faqīh*-s, emirs and vizirs. The whole 2nd/8th and 3rd/9th centuries' Islamic society seems to have been living in a kind of great, all-embracing, and endless debate on any possible kind of science and theory, and grammar was, of course, one of the main issues at debate, and not only within the *naḥwiyyūn*'s circle, being fundamental in the interpretation of Qur'ān, *ḥadīṯ*, poetry, and law.

It is important not to underestimate, however, the role played in the shaping of this framework by the narrative needs of a literary genre particularly widespread in the Abbasid era, and through which lives of grammarians of 2nd/8th and 3rd/9th centuries are often narrated, the *iḫtilāfāt al-nuḥāt*, that is the disputes of grammarians.

The genre shall be placed, at a closer look, in a wider literary canon, that is the intellectual dispute (*munāẓara, muǧādala*), well attested in classical Arabic and Islamic culture, and probably part of a common Mediterranean substratum (cf. Capezzone 1998).

15 Cf. the full text and translation in Humbert (1995:3–4).

The most famous of those disputes is the well-known *masʾala zunbūriyya* ("the case of the scorpion") that took place at the court of the Barmekid vizir Yaḥyā b. Ḫālid (d. 190/806) in Baghdad.[16]

In the oldest, complete, extant account, related by Zaǧǧāǧī on the authority of both Ṯaʿlab and Mubarrad, who in turn transmitted it on the authority of Farrāʾ, we are told that when Sībawayhi arrived in Baghdad he had a first clash at the court of Yaḥyā b. Ḫālid with ʾAḥmar (d. 180/796 or 194/809)[17] and Farrāʾ, who are reported to have been very rude with him at the point that Sībawayhi refused to debate with anyone else but their leader Kisāʾī (*hāḏā sūʾ ʾadab* [...] *lastu ʾukallimukumā ʾaw yaḥḍura ṣāḥibukumā ḥattā ʾunāẓirahu*, Zaǧǧāǧī *Maǧālis* 9).

Unfortunately, the clash with Kisāʾī (a particularly sophisticated debate about the formal correctness of utterances with two nominative case endings or with a nominative case ending followed by an accusative case ending in some particular nominal sentences introduced by *ʾiḏā*) seems to have been particularly tough, up to the point that Bedouin judges were called to decide which position was the most correct one (i.e. the most correct according to pure Bedouin Arabic).[18] It seems that Bedouin judges corroborated Kisāʾī's position, but rumors began to circulate that Kisāʾī may have bribed Bedouin judges (*wa-ruwiya ʾannahum ʾuʿṭū ʿalā mutābaʿat al-kisāʾī ǧuʿlan*, Ibn al-ʾAnbārī *ʾInṣāf* 564; cf. Yāqūt *ʾIršād* 2123), and, in later versions, anecdotes of an alleged inability of Bedouin judges to even pronounce Kisāʾī's wrong utterance were added (*al-qawl qawl al-kisāʾī wa-lam yanṭuqū bi-l-naṣb*, Ibn Hišām al-ʾAnṣārī *Muġnī* I, 79; cf. Ibn Ḫallikān *Wafayāt* III, 464).

Be that as it may, it is difficult for us to know the reality of the situation, but the authenticity of the clash is out of doubt if the topos of the rivalry between Sībawayhi and Kisāʾī is already well established at the times of Ǧāḥiẓ (*wa-laysa hāḏā al-kitāb* [...] *fī tafḍīl sībawayhi ʿalā al-kisāʾī*, Ǧāḥiẓ *Ḥayawān* VII, 4; cf. Baalbaki 2008: 298) and if the clash itself is already related in its broad outlines by Ibn Qutayba (*wa-kāna qadima baġdād fa-ǧamaʿa baynahu wa-bayna ʾaṣḥāb al-naḥw fa-ʾustuḏilla*, Ibn Qutayba *Maʿārif* 544). The early account of Ibn Qutayba

16 The dispute is very well-known and has been widely discussed in scholarly literature. Cf., e.g., Fischer 1922; Blau 1963; Talmon 1986; Fiedler 2012; Edzard 2017.

17 It is unclear whether he was the famous Kufan grammarian Ḫalaf al-ʾAḥmar (d. 180/796), as asserted by Talmon (1986:136), or ʿAlī b. Ḥasan al-ʾAḥmar (d. 194/809), a friend of Kisāʾī, as asserted by Bernards (1997:6).

18 Cf. Zaǧǧāǧī *Maǧālis* 9–10; Zubaydī *Ṭabaqāt* 68–71; Ibn al-Nadīm *Fihrist* 57; Tanūḫī *Taʾrīḫ* 101–104; Ibn al-ʾAnbārī *Nuzha* 58; Ibn al-ʾAnbārī *ʾInṣāf* 562–566; Yāqūt *ʾIršād* 2123, 2125–2126; Qifṭī *ʾInbāh* II, 348, 358–359; Ibn Ḫallikān *Wafayāt* III, 464; Ibn Hišām al-ʾAnṣārī *Muġnī* I, 79–83; Suyūṭī *Buġya* II, 230.

seems to confirm the defeat of Sībawayhi, but the hypothesis that Kisāʾī may have bribed Bedouin judges cannot be totally ruled out if we think that Kisāʾī was very rich and powerful in Baghdad and that his position as the teacher of Hārūn al-Rašīd, later entrusted by the caliph also with the education of his two sons ʾAmīn and Maʾmūn, and finally promoted among Rašīd's personal companions and confidants (cf. Yāqūt *ʾIršād* 1738–1740), might probably have allowed him to have such an influence on judges.

Other sources relate that Sībawayhi had even other clashes and debates, with ʾAṣmaʿī (cf. Zubaydī *Ṭabaqāt* 68), with Ḫalīl, Yūnus, and Farrāʾ (cf. Zaǧǧāǧī *Maǧālis* 231–232), and, most interesting, even with his pupil ʾAḫfaš who, in the account of Ibn al-Nadīm, is mentioned along with Kisāʾī as one of the grammarians with whom Sībawayhi had clashes and by whom was defeated when he went to visit Yaḥyā b. Ḫālid in Baghdad (*kāna wurūduhu al-ʿirāq qāṣidan yaḥyā b. ḫālid fa-ǧumiʿa baynahu wa-bayna al-kisāʾī wa-l-ʾaḫfaš fa-nāẓarāhu wa-ḫaṭṭayāhu* [...], Ibn al-Nadīm *Fihrist* 57).

1.4 *Sībawayhi and ʾAḫfaš: A Controversial Relationship*

The role of ʾAḫfaš in the life of Sībawayhi and the real nature of the relationship between the two scholars is not obviously clear: classical biographical sources are inconsistent about that.

Most times, indeed, we are just told that ʾAḫfaš was a student of Sībawayhi (*ʾaḫaḏa ʿan sībawayhi*, Zubaydī *Ṭabaqāt* 72; Ibn al-Nadīm *Fihrist* 58; Ibn al-ʾAnbārī *Nuzha* 107; Qifṭī *ʾInbāh* II, 36; cf. Suyūṭī *Buġya* I, 590), or even his most outstanding pupil (*wa-ʾaḫaḏa al-naḥw ʿan sībawayhi ǧamāʿa baraʿa minhum* [...] *al-ʾaḫfaš*, Luġawī *Marātib* 80).

The role of transmitter of the *Kitāb* is consistently assigned to ʾAḫfaš by all sources. Moreover, ʾAḫfaš is said to have been the only extant access to the *Kitāb* of Sībawayhi, and this because nobody is known to have read the *Kitāb* in front of Sībawayhi or to have been taught it by him, nevertheless, when Sībawayhi died, the *Kitāb* was read at the presence of ʾAḫfaš, and between those who did so there would have been Ǧarmī (d. 225/839), Māzinī and even others, unnamed, scholars (*wa-l-ṭarīq ʾilā kitāb sībawayhi al-ʾaḫfaš wa-ḏālika ʾanna kitāb sībawayhi lā naʿlamu ʾaḥadan qaraʾahu ʿalā sībawayhi wa-lā qaraʾahu ʿalayhi sībawayhi wa-lākinnahu lammā māta sībawayhi quriʾa al-kitāb ʿalā* [...] *al-ʾaḫfaš wa-mimman qaraʾahu* [...] *al-ǧarmī* [...] *wa-l-māzinī* [...] *wa-ġayruhumā*, Sīrāfī *ʾAḫbār* 39; cf. Marzubānī *Nūr* 68; Ibn al-Nadīm *Fihrist* 58; Tanūḫī *Taʾrīḫ* 85; Ibn al-ʾAnbārī *Nuzha* 108; Yāqūt *ʾIršād* 1374; Qifṭī *ʾInbāh* II, 39). ʾAḫfaš is said to have been the one who actually used to spend time discussing, explaining, and clarifying the meanings of the *Kitāb* (*wa-huwa allaḏī takallama ʿalā kitāb sībawayhi wa-šaraḥahu wa-bayyanahu*, Sīrāfī *ʾAḫbār* 39; cf. Qifṭī *ʾInbāh* II, 39) but, in one source, ʾAḫfaš is also said to have been the one who pointed out to the Basran any small flaw found in the *Kitāb* before leaving them (*nabbahahum ʿalā ʿuwar al-kitāb wa-tarakahum*, Luġawī *Marātib* 80).

In other cases, however, the role of student, sole transmitter and commentator of the book of his master, gives way to more nuanced definitions, and so ʾAḫfaš is said to have been a companion, or a fellow scholar, of Sībawayhi (*al-ʾaḫfaš ṣāḥib sībawayhi*, Zaǧǧāǧī *Maǧālis* 124), still the most skilled one, as it is added in most cases (*wa-huwa ʾaḥḏaq ʾaṣḥāb sībawayhi*, Sīrāfī *ʾAḫbār* 38–39; Qifṭī *ʾInbāh* II, 354). We are told in some sources that they were studying together and, in some cases, even the very fact that ʾAḫfaš was older than Sībawayhi is emphasized (*kāna al-ʾaḫfaš ʾakbar sinnan min sībawayhi wa-kānā ǧamīʿan yaṭlubāni*, Sīrāfī *ʾAḫbār* 38–39; cf. Zubaydī *Ṭabaqāt* 73; Ibn al-Nadīm *Fihrist* 58; Tanūḫī *Taʾrīḫ* 86; Qifṭī *ʾInbāh* II, 36, 40; Suyūṭī *Buġya* I, 590).

Those scattered hints at ʾAḫfaš being older than Sībawayhi achieve perhaps their natural conclusion in the story of an alleged clash between Sībawayhi and ʾAḫfaš.

In the oldest preserved account, related by Sīrāfī on the authority of Mubarrad, when Sībawayhi became the most outstanding personality of their circle, ʾAḫfaš went to see him and challenged him to a public debate (*fa-ǧāʾahu al-ʾaḫfaš yunāẓiruhu baʿd ʾan baraʿa*, Sīrāfī *ʾAḫbār* 38; cf. Ibn al-ʾAnbārī *Nuzha* 57; Qifṭī *ʾInbāh* II, 40, 353). We are not told exactly how the clash ended up, but, in this case, it seems that a friendly solution was found: ʾAḫfaš told Sībawayhi that he had challenged him only to gain some knowledge, and Sībawayhi replied that no one could think that he had doubted of that (*fa-qāla lahu al-ʾaḫfaš ʾinnamā nāẓartuka li-ʾastafīda lā li-ġayrihi fa-qāla sībawayhi ʾa-turānī ʾašukku fī hāḏā*, Sīrāfī *ʾAḫbār* 38; cf. Ibn al-ʾAnbārī *Nuzha* 57; Qifṭī *ʾInbāh* II, 40, 353).

It is not totally clear if this one is the same clash referred to by Ibn al-Nadīm, but the context (the court of Yaḥyā b. Ḫālid in Baghdad and ʾAḫfaš mentioned immediately after Kisāʾī) in which is placed the story in the *Fihrist* seems to suggest that there might have been even a less friendly clash between the two scholars, once in Baghdad (cf. Ibn al-Nadīm *Fihrist* 57).

In some later sources, finally, we are even told that ʾAḫfaš may have tried to assume for himself the authorship of the *Kitāb*. In the accounts of Ibn al-ʾAnbārī and Yāqūt, related on the authority of Mubarrad, this would be the actual reason why Ǧarmī and Māzinī read the *Kitāb* in front of him (cf. Ibn al-ʾAnbārī *Nuzha* 108; Yāqūt *ʾIršād* 1374). It seems, indeed, that ʾAḫfaš was so fascinated by the *Kitāb* that Māzinī and Ǧarmī suspected that he might try to reclaim the authorship of the *Kitāb* for himself (*wa-kāna al-ʾaḫfaš yastaḥsinu kitāb sībawayhi kull al-istiḥsān fa-tawahhama al-ǧarmī wa-l-māzinī ʾanna al-ʾaḫfaš qad hamma ʾan yaddaʿiya al-kitāb li-nafsihi*) and so they attracted him by offering some money to read the *Kitāb* in his presence and he accepted (*fa-ʾarġabā al-ʾaḫfaš wa-badalā lahu šayʾan min al-māl ʿalā ʾan yaqraʾāhu ʿalayhi fa-ʾağāba*, Yāqūt *ʾIršād* 1374; cf. Ibn al-ʾAnbārī *Nuzha* 108). When they completed such reading with him, therefore, they were finally permitted to reveal to anyone that the book was the *Kitāb* of Sībawayhi (*wa-ʾaḫadā al-kitāb ʿanhu wa-ʾaẓharāhu li-l-nās*, Yāqūt *ʾIršād* 1374; cf. Ibn al-ʾAnbārī *Nuzha* 108).

Humbert, who has studied the manuscript transmission of the *Kitāb*, has already framed the inconsistence between the character of ʾAḫfaš and the role of the disciple and strict transmitter of the *Kitāb* that has been assigned to him by most sources (cf. Humbert 1995: 13–17). Moreover, according to her, what we are told by sources testifies only that if it is true, on the one hand, that ʾAḫfaš did transmit the *Kitāb*, it is also true, on the other, that this did not happen as a result of a deliberate choice of Sībawayhi, and this because of the untimely death of the author of the *Kitāb* that did not allow him to transmit his work through regular oral transmission from master to student (cf. Humbert 1995: 15). In her point of view, it is very likely that biographers switched, gradually, from the role of transmitter, clearly assigned to ʾAḫfaš by Sīrāfī, to the role of main pupil assigned to him by most later sources (cf. Humbert 1995: 14).

Although it should be observed that the role of Sībawayhi's most important pupil was already clearly assigned to ʾAḫfaš by ʾAbū al-Ṭayyib al-Luġawī (cf. *Marātib* 80), who was a contemporary of Sīrāfī, it is also true that ʾAḫfaš was a free scholar with an independent personality, and the transmission of the *Kitāb* does not encompass all his scholarship, as testified, by way of example, both by ʾAḫfaš's critical glosses preserved in the manuscript copies of the *Kitāb* and studied by Humbert (1995: 13–17 and 58–64) and by the peculiarity of his grammatical technical terminology as it appears in the *Maʿānī al-Qurʾān*.[19]

Now, the oldest extant reference to the relationship between Sībawayhi and ʾAḫfaš is the one that is found in the *Maʿārif* of Ibn Qutayba who relates, on the authority of Riyāšī (d. 257/871), that ʾAḫfaš used to say:

> whenever Sībawayhi was to write down something of his *Kitāb*, he used to read it first in front of me, because he believed that I was more learned than him, but actually he was more learned than me, although now I am more learned than he was. (*kāna sībawayhi ʾidā waḍaʿa šayʾan min kitābihi*

19 See the list of grammatical technical terms used by ʾAḫfaš made by Hudā Maḥmūd Qarrāʿa, the editor of the text of the *Maʿānī*, in ʾAḫfaš's *Maʿānī* 780–802. Cf. also Versteegh 1993:14–15.

> *ʿaraḍahu ʿalayya wa-huwa yarā ʾannī ʾaʿlam minhu wa-kāna ʾaʿlam minnī wa-ʾanā al-yawm ʾaʿlam minhu*, Ibn Qutayba *Maʿārif* 546; cf. Luġawī *Marātib* 81; Zubaydī *Ṭabaqāt* 67; Tanūḫī *Taʾrīḫ* 98; Yāqūt *ʾIršād* 1374–1375; Qifṭī *ʾInbāh* II, 350)

The text needs to be understood in the context of early Arabic scholarly tradition, in which it is normal that a later scholar who has learned previous scholarship should represent, on an ideal scale, a more complete degree of knowledge with respect to his predecessors.

This is clearly explained in Ibn Sallām's introduction to the *Kitāb Ṭabaqāt fuḥūl al-šuʿarāʾ*, through the very words of Yūnus b. Ḥabīb who, asked about ʿAbd Allāh b. ʾAbī ʾIsḥāq (d. 117/735) and his knowledge, replies at first that Ibn ʾAbī ʾIsḥāq and grammar were practically the very same thing, as to mean that he was the best grammarian ever (*huwa wa-l-naḥw sawāʾ ʾay huwa al-ġāya*, Ibn Sallām *Ṭabaqāt* 15). Asked again what exactly would be Ibn ʾAbī ʾIsḥāq's level if compared to the knowledge of Yūnus' day (*fa-ʾayna ʿilmuhu min ʿilm al-nās al-yawm*), he said:

> if someone today wouldn't know but what was already knew by Ibn ʾAbī ʾIsḥāq in his day, people would laugh at him, but, if someone between today's people had both his intellect and his acumen and was equipped with the critical tools of our day, he would be just the most learned of men. (*law kāna fī al-nās al-yawm man lā yaʿlamu ʾillā ʿilmahu yawmaʾiḏ la-ḍuḥika bihi wa-law kāna fīhim man lahu ḏihnuhu wa-nafāḏuhu wa-naẓara naẓarahum kāna ʾaʿlam al-nās*, Ibn Sallām *Ṭabaqāt* 15).

The text of Ibn Qutayba, if properly understood, therefore, clearly shows that ʾAḫfaš was felt, already in the first half of the 3rd/9th century, as the heir and successor of Sībawayhi, and the very words of ʾAḫfaš, as quoted by Ibn Qutayba, as well as Luġawī's account on ʾAḫfaš correcting the *Kitāb* before leaving the Basrans and ʾAḫfaš's own glosses on the *Kitāb*, far from being misunderstood as a sign of criticism or disrespect towards Sībawayhi, should, on the contrary, be read as a recognition of his grammatical authority, a sign of devotion and a declaration of total affiliation within the same school of thought and grammar of his master, consistently with the classical Islamic vision of the progression of knowledge perfectly explained by Ibn Sallām.

2 The Qur'ānic Material Found in the *Kitāb Sībawayhi* and in 'Aḫfaš's *Maʿānī al-Qur'ān*

2.1 *The* Kitāb Sībawayhi *and the* Maʿānī al Qur'ān*: A Formal Overview*

The two books are very different both in scope and methodology, as well as in the formal model adopted by respective authors. While the *Kitāb Sībawayhi* provides the earlier extant attempt at a complete grammar of Arabic language (including syntax, morphology and phonology), 'Aḫfaš's *Maʿānī al-Qur'ān* is placed at the boundary of Arabic grammar and Qur'ānic scholarship. It cannot be said to be a book on Qur'ānic exegesis, mostly if compared with the exegesis of the period that was mainly of the paraphrastic and/or narrative type (cf. Gilliot 2002: 104–108). 'Aḫfaš's book might be said to represent one of the oldest examples of philological commentary on the Qur'ān along with 'Abū ʿUbayda's *Maǧāz al-Qur'ān*, which is still more explanatory and semantically oriented than the *Maʿānī*. However, it still cannot be really said to represent an example of grammatical exegesis of the Qur'ān, as can be said for Farrā''s *Maʿānī al-Qur'ān*, and, at the very least, it could even be seen as the oldest attempt at this kind of exegesis. The book is a collection of Qur'ānic readings, philological observation on the language of the Qur'ān, with the addition of some grammatical explanation and even some short digressions on specific grammatical points.

Notoriously, Sībawayhi is never mentioned in the *Maʿānī* as well as 'Aḫfaš is never mentioned within the text of the *Kitāb*.[20]

2.2 *The Qur'ānic Material Found in the* Kitāb Sībawayhi *and in 'Aḫfaš's* Maʿānī al-Qur'ān*: A Quantitative Approach*

The inconsistency between 'Aḫfaš being the main pupil of Sībawayhi and Sībawayhi being not even quoted in 'Aḫfaš's *Maʿānī* and vice versa has puzzled scholars for some time (cf. section 1.4).

In the second part of this chapter (sections 2 and 3) the Qur'ānic material found in both books is compared in order to find traces, if not properly of a common grammatical school, at the very least of a common scholarly ground presumably originated in the same scholarly circle frequented by both authors as clearly stated by all biographical, doxographical, historiographical, and literary sources.

20 Being therefore the only contemporary of Sībawayhi who does not pretend to be quoted by him in the *Kitāb*, his name being only in the manuscript glosses on the text. (cf. Humbert 1995:14. Ibid., 13–17, and 58–64 about 'Aḫfaš's glosses on the *Kitāb*).

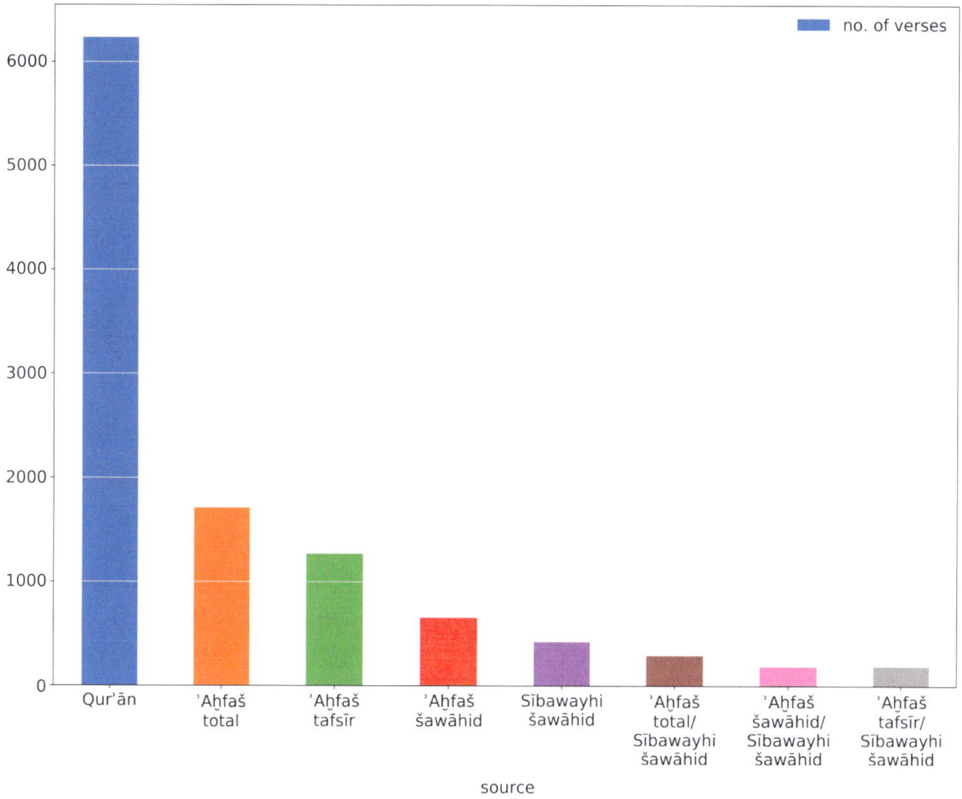

FIGURE 3.1 Total number of verses

As widely expected, the number of the Qur'ānic verses found in the *Ma'ānī* is far superior to the number of Qur'ānic verses found in the *Kitāb*. This because Sībawayhi only quotes Qur'ānic verses as *šawāhid* (*loci probantes*), while 'Aḫfaš has both Qur'ānic verses quoted as *šawāhid* and Qur'ānic verses commented as topic in the *tafsīr*. It may be noted, indeed, that the number of *šawāhid* found in both books is pretty close (657 in 'Aḫfaš vs 423 in Sībawayhi), and also that the number of intersections between them (187), if compared with the total number of *šawāhid* is not bad (i.e. the 44.21 % of Sībawayhi's total Qur'ānic *šawāhid* and the 28.46 % of 'Aḫfaš's total Qur'ānic *šawāhid*). This means that almost half (44.21 %) of Qur'ānic *šawāhid* found in Sībawayhi are also used (as grammatical *šawāhid*) by 'Aḫfaš.

This is the total number of verses found, as shown in the graph above:[21]

21 Full lists of verses are in section 5.

1. Total number of verses found in the Qurʾān (Qurʿān): 6236
2. Total number of verses found in the *Maʿānī* (ʾAḫfaš's total): 1709
3. Total number of verses commented in the *Maʿānī* (ʾAḫfaš's *tafsīr*): 1271
4. Total number of *šawāhid* found in the *Maʿānī* (ʾAḫfaš *šawāhid*): 657
5. Total number of *šawāhid* found in the *Kitāb* (Sībawayhi's *šawāhid*): 423
6. Total number of the intersection between 2 and 5 (ʾAḫfaš total/Sībawayhi *šawāhid*): 291
7. Total number of the intersection between 4 and 5 (ʾAḫfaš *šawāhid*/Sībawayhi *šawāhid*): 187
8. Total number of the intersection between 3 and 5 (ʾAḫfaš *tafsīr*/Sībawayhi *šawāhid*): 192

3 Two Practical Examples

3.1 *Sequences of Qurʾānic Quotations as a Sign of Common Scholarship*

In the chapter on the agent whose action passes beyond it towards two objects and you cannot restrict yourself to one object without the other (*bāb al-fāʿil allaḏī yataʿaddāhu fiʿluhu ʾilā mafʿūlayn wa-laysa laka ʾan taqtaṣira ʿalā ʾaḥad al-mafʿūlayn dūn al-ʾāḫar*, Sībawayhi *Kitāb* I, 39–41),[22] Sībawayhi explains that

> in such cases as *ḥasiba ʿabdu llāhi zaydan bakran* "ʿAbd Allāh reckoned Zayd [to be] Bakr", *ẓanna ʿamrun ḫālidan ʾabāka* "ʿAmr thought Ḫālid [to be] your father", *ḫāla ʿabdu llāhi zaydan ʾaḫāka* "ʿAbd Allāh believed Zayd [to be] your brother", *raʾā ʿabdu llāhi zaydan ṣāḥibanā* "ʿAbd Allāh regarded Zayd [to be] our companion", *waǧada ʿabdu llāhi zaydan ḏā l-ḥifāẓi* "ʿAbd Allāh found Zayd [to be] disdainful", and the similar, what prevents you from restricting to the first of the two [mandatory] objects is the fact that you just want to explain your conviction about the condition of the first object, be that in terms of certainty or doubt, and you mention the first [object] only to inform that what you assign to it [i.e. the second mandatory object] is your conviction on who is he, and you say I think (*ẓanantu*) and the similar only to make the predicate (*ḫabar*) assigned to the first object certain or doubtful, but you don't want to make doubtful or certain the first [object]. (*wa-ḏālika qawluka "ḥasiba ʿabdu llāhi zaydan bakiran", "ẓanna ʿamru ḫālidan ʾabāka", "ḫāla ʿabdu llāhi zaydan ʾaḫāka" wa-miṯl ḏālika: "raʾā ʿabdu llāhi zaydan ṣāḥibanā", wa-"waǧada ʿabdu llāhi zaydan ḏā l-ḥifāẓi" wa-ʾinnamā manaʿaka ʾan taqtaṣira ʿalā ʾaḥad al-mafʿūlayn hā-hunā ʾannaka ʾinnamā ʾaradta ʾan tubayy-*

22 For this translation, cf. Lancioni & Solimando 2015:144.

> *ina mā istaqarra ʿindaka min ḥāl al-mafʿūl al-ʾawwal, yaqīnan kāna ʾaw šakkan, wa-ḏakarta al-ʾawwal li-tuʿlima allaḏī tuḍīfu ʾilayhi mā istaqarra lahu ʿindaka [man huwa] fa-ʾinnamā ḏakarta "ẓanantu" wa-naḥwahu li-taǧʿala ḫabar al-mafʿūl al-ʾawwal yaqīnan ʾaw šakkan wa-lam turid ʾan taǧʿala al-ʾawwal fīhi al-šakk ʾaw tuqīma ʿalayhi fī al-yaqīn*, Sībawayhi *Kitāb* I, 39–40)

According to Sībawayhi, also sentences like

> *ʿalimtu zaydan al-ẓarīfa* "I knew Zayd [to be] the graceful" are of the same type […], (*wa-miṯl ḏālika "ʿalimtu zaydan al-ẓarīfa"* […]). Sometimes, however, *ʿalimtu* may have the status of *ʿaraftu* [i.e. of a verb that holds a single object] in which you don't mean anything else but the knowledge of the first object. It is of this type what is found in [Q. 2/65] *wa-laqad ʿalimtumu llaḏīna ʿtadaw minkum fī l-sabti* "And you knew those among you who broke the Sabbath" or in [Q 8/60] *wa-ʾāḫarīna min dūnihim lā taʿlamūnahumu llāhu yaʿlamuhum* "and others from besides them, you do not know them, but God knows them" they [i.e. derivatives of *ʿalima*] have, here, the same status of *ʿaraftu* [i.e. of a verb that holds a single object] (*wa-qad yakūnu "ʿalimtu" bi-manzilat "ʿaraftu" lā turīdu ʾillā ʿilm al-ʾawwal fa-min ḏālika qawluhu taʿālā "wa-la-qad ʿalimtumu llaḏīna ʿtadaw minkum fī l-sabti" wa-qāla subḥānahu "wa-ʾāḫarīna min dūnihim lā taʿlamūnahumu llāhu yaʿlamuhum" fa-hiya hā-hunā bi-manzilat "ʿaraftu"*, Sībawayhi, *Kitāb* I, 40)

A similar explanation of the two possible meanings of *ʿalima* (i.e. with one or two mandatory objects) can be found in ʾAḫfaš's comment on Q. 2/65. According to ʾAḫfaš *wa-laqad ʿalimtum* means here *wa-laqad ʿaraftum* "you knew", as you can say *laqad ʿalimtu zaydan* "I knew Zayd" or *wa-lam ʾakun ʾaʿlamuhu* "I didn't know him" [i.e. derivatives of *ʿalima* can hold a single object as in the examples given and as it is in the case of *ʿarafa*]. [Of the same type are also derivatives of *ʿalima* in] Q. 8/60, it means *yaʿrifuhum* "he knows them" (*wa-ʾammā qawluhu "wa-laqad ʿalimtumu llaḏīna ʿtadaw minkum fī l-sabt", yaqūlu "wa-laqad ʿaraftum"; kamā taqūlu "laqad ʿalimtu zaydan, wa lam ʾakun ʾaʿlamuhu" wa-qāla "wa-ʾāḫarīna min dūnihim lā taʿlamūnahumu llāhu yaʿlamuhum" yaqūlu "yaʿrifuhum"*, ʾAḫfaš *Maʿānī* 109).

And if you want the other meaning of *ʿalima* you [must] say *qad ʿalimtu zaydan ẓarīfan* "I knew Zayd [to be] graceful" [i.e. you need to add a second mandatory object], because [in this case] you are predicating his [i.e. Zayd's] grace, so, if you just said *qad ʿalimtu zaydan* "I knew Zayd [to be] […]", this would not be a complete sentence (*wa-ʾiḏā ʾaradta al-ʿilm al-ʾāḫar qulta "qad ʿalimtu zaydan ẓarīfan" li-ʾannaka tuḥaddiṯu ʿan ẓarfihi fa-law qulta "qad ʿalimtu zaydan" lam yakun kalāman*, ʾAḫfaš *Maʿānī* 109).

In ʾAḫfaš's comment on Q. 2/65 we find, thus, the same explanation of the two meaning of *ʿalima* already found in Sībawayhi (*ʿalima* that holds one single object is said by both scholars to have the same meaning of *ʿarafa*), the same order of Qurʾānic quotations (Q. 2/65 followed by Q. 8/60), and some similar wording and example too (Sībawayhi's *ʿalimtu zaydan al-ẓarīfa* becomes *ʿalimtu zaydan ẓarīfan* in ʾAḫfaš).

In Sībawayhi the Qurʾānic quotations are found at the end of the reasoning, while in ʾAḫfaš they are the starting point, and this accordingly to the difference in scope and genre between the two books.

Many other examples of that can be found by the reader if looking at the full list of intersection between Sībawayhi and ʾAḫfaš, particularly if looking for sequences of Qurʾānic *šawāhid* within the intersection between Sībawayhi and the whole *Maʿānī* (Section 5.3), and within the intersection between Sībawayhi and ʾAḫfaš's *šawāhid* (section 5.5).

These similarities may be said to be marginal, but, on the contrary, they're relevant in relation to the aim of this chapter because they demonstrate the existence of blocks of Qurʾānic quotations followed or preceded by grammatical explanation that circulated, most probably, within the scholarly circle of Basran *naḥwiyyūn* and that were shared already by both Sībawayhi and ʾAḫfaš.

3.2 *Basran Grammatical and Theological Issues*

In some cases, blocks, or sequences, of Qurʾānic quotations are found inside grammatical demonstrations by which a common theoretical background emerges.

It is such the case of Sībawayhi's chapter on command and prohibition (*bāb al-ʾamr wa-l-nahy*, Sībawayhi *Kitāb* I, 137–144) which has, towards its end, a sequence of three Qurʾānic quotations (Q. 24/2, Q. 5/38, and Q. 47/15) that is found also in ʾAḫfaš's comment on Q. 24/2 and Q. 5/38 (ʾAḫfaš *Maʿānī* 84–87).

In the chapter on command and prohibition [in *ištiġāl* constructions] (*bāb al-ʾamr wa-l-nahy*, Sībawayhi *Kitāb* I, 137–144), Sībawayhi explains that in command and prohibition accusative case ending should be choosed for the noun on which the verb is constructed and that is constructed on the verb (*al-ʾamr wa-l-nahy yuḫtāru fīhimā al-naṣb fī al-ism allaḏī yubnā ʿalayhi al-fiʿl wa-yubnā ʿalā al-fiʿl*), as it is choosed also in interrogative sentences, because command and prohibition need to have a verb in the sentence, as also for question markers it is preferable to be followed by a verb (*kamā uḫtīra ḏālika fī bāb al-istifhām li-ʾanna al-ʾamr wa-l-nahy ʾinnamā humā li-l-fiʿl kamā ʾanna ḥurūf al-istifhām bi-l-fiʿl ʾawlā*), and in both interrogative sentences and command and prohibition, the underlying [theoretical construct] should start with the verb before the noun (*wa-kāna al-ʾaṣl fīhā ʾan yabtadiʾa bi-l-fiʿl qabl al-ism fa-hākaḏā al-ʾamr wa-l-nahy*, Sībawayhi *Kitāb* I, 137).

Moreover, adds Sībawayhi, in command and prohibition this need [to choose accusative case ending for the noun] is stronger, because if you can still make an interrogative sentence without verbs, like when you say: *ʾa-zaydun ʾaḫūka* "Is Zayd your brother?", or *matā zaydun munṭaliqun* "When Zayd is leaving?" and so on (*wa-humā ʾaqwā fī hāḏā min al-istifhām li-ʾanna ḥurūf al-istifhām qad yustafhamu bihā wa-laysa baʿdahā ʾillā al-ʾasmāʾ naḥwa qawlika "ʾa-zaydun ʾaḫūka" wa "matā zaydun munṭaliqun"* [...]), in command and prohibition the verb is unavoidable, and this is like when you say: *zaydan iḍribhu* "Zayd (acc.) beat him!", or *ʿamran umrur bihi* "ʿAmr (acc.) pass by him!" (*wa-l-ʾamr wa-l-nahy lā yakūnāni ʾillā bi-fiʿl wa-ḏālika qawluka "zaydan iḍribhu" wa "ʿamran umrur bihi"*, Sībawayhi *Kitāb* I, 137–138).

Sometimes, explains Sībawayhi, in command and prohibition the verb may be constructed on the noun [that precedes it, i.e. it may be assigned to it as a verbal predicate], like when you say *ʿabdu llāhi ḍribhu* "ʿAbd Allāh (nom.), beat him!": you start the sentence with ʿAbd Allāh and you assign to it a nominative case ending because of the *ibtidāʾ* (*wa-qad yakūnu fī al-ʾamr wa-l-nahy ʾan yubnā al-fiʿl ʿalā al-ism wa-ḏālika qawluka "ʿabdu llāhi ḍribhu" ibtadaʾta ʿabd allāh fa-rafaʿtahu bi-l-ibtidāʾ*, Sībawayhi *Kitāb* I, 138).

Similarly, ʾAḫfaš states that nominative case endings in Q. 24/2 (*al-zāniyatu wa-l-zānī*), and Q. 5/38 (*al-sāriqu wa-l-sāriqatu*) are a consequence of their initial position: then the verb is given [in the text] after what already required nominative case ending for the first [elements of the sentence] because of the *ibtidāʾ* (*ṯumma ǧāʾa bi-l-fiʿl min baʿd mā ʾawǧaba al-rafʿ ʿalā al-ʾawwal ʿalā al-ibtidāʾ*, ʾAḫfaš *Maʿānī* 84).

According to Sībawayhi, if you say: *zaydun fa-ḍribhu* "Zayd (nom.), (*fa-*) beat him!", it wouldn't be correct to interpret it [i.e. Zayd] as a *mubtadaʾ* [i.e. it is not correct to introduce the predicate (*ḫabar*) assigned to a subject (*mubtadaʾ*) with *fa-*]: can't you see that if you said: *zaydun fa-munṭaliqun* "Zayd (nom.), (*fa-*) is leaving" this wouldn't be correct, and this is a proof that it cannot be a *mubtadaʾ* [in such cases] (*fa-ʾiḏā qulta "zaydun fa-ḍribhu" lam yastaqim ʾan taḥmilahu ʿalā al-ibtidāʾ ʾa lā tarā ʾannaka law qulta zaydun fa-munṭaliqun lam yastaqim fa-huwa dalīl ʿalā ʾannahu lā yaǧūzu ʾan yakūna mubtadaʾ* [...]), nevertheless, explains Sībawayhi, sometimes it is acceptable and correct to say: *ʿabdu llāhi fa-ḍribhu* "ʿAbd Allāh (nom.) (*fa-*) beat him!" if [ʿAbd Allāh] is constructed on a *mubtadaʾ*, be it explicit or implicit, as if it is explicit, it is like when you say: *hāḏā zaydun, fa-ḍribhu* "This is Zayd (nom.), (*fa-*) beat him!", and, if you want, you don't explicit *hāḏā*, but it governs it in the same way as if it was explicit, and this is when you say: *al-hilālu wa-llāhi fa-nẓur ʾilayhi* "the new moon (nom.), for God, so (*fa-*) look at it!", this is like if you said *hāḏā al-hilālu*, and then you give the command (*wa-qad yaḥsunu wa-yastaqīmu ʾan taqūla "ʿabdu llāhi fa-ḍribhu" ʾiḏā kāna mabniyyan ʿalā mubtadaʾ muẓhar ʾaw muḍmar fa-ʾammā fī al-muẓhar fa-qawluka "hāḏā zaydun fa-ḍribhu" wa-ʾin šiʾta lam tuẓhir hāḏā wa-yaʿmalu ka-ʿamalihi ʾiḏā ʾaẓhartahu wa-ḏālika qawluka "al-hilālu wa-llāhi fa-nẓur ʾilayhi" ka-ʾannaka qulta "hāḏā al-hilālu" ṯumma ǧiʾta bi-l-ʾamr*), and what shows you the acceptability of *fa-* in such cases is the fact that if you say: *hāḏā zaydun fa-ḥasanun ǧamīlun* "this is Zayd (nom.), and (*fa-*) is good and beautiful" this would be good speech, and it falls within that also the saying of the poet *wa-qāʾilatin ḫawlān fa-nkiḥ fatātahum* (and her who says "[those are the] Ḫawlān, so marry one of their daughters") (*wa-mimmā yadulluka ʿalā ḥusn al-fāʾ hā-hunā ʾannaka ʾiḏā qulta "hāḏā zaydun fa-ḥasanun ǧamīlun" kāna kalāman ǧayyīdan wa-min ḏālika qawl al-šāʿir "wa-qāʾilatin ḫawlān fa-nkiḥ fatātahum"* […]), Sībawayhi *Kitāb* I, 138–139).

Also for Aḫfaš, it is not possible, when speaking about [Q. 24/2] *al-zāniyatu wa-l-zānī fa-ǧlidū kulla wāḥidin minhumā miʾata ǧaldatin* "The adulteress and the adulterer, flog each one of them with one hundred lashes", and [Q. 5/38] *wa-l-sāriqu wa-l-sāriqatu fa-qṭaʿū ʾaydiyahumā* "The male thief and the female thief, cut off their hands", to consider God's words *fa-qṭaʿū* "cut off" and *fa-ǧlidū* "flog" as a predicate assigned to a subject (*ḫabar mubtadaʾ*), because the predicate assigned to a subject, in such cases, cannot be preceded by *fa-*, and if you said *ʿabdu llāhi fa-yanṭaliqu* "ʿAbd Allāh (nom.) (*fa-*) leaves" it would not be correct, and the predicate (*al-ḫabar*) [can only be deduced from] the implied [construction] explained already about [Q. 47/15] *mimmā naquṣṣu ʿalaykum* "between what we told you" [*maṯalu l-ǧannati*, see *infra* (i.e. a *mubtadaʾ* must be implied to let ʿAbd Allāh be its *ḫabar*)] (*laysa fī qawlihi fa-qṭaʿū wa-fa-ǧlidū ḫabar mubtadaʾ li-ʾanna ḫabar al-mubtadaʾ hākaḏā lā yakūnu bi-l-fāʾ law qulta ʿabdu llāhi fa-yanṭaliqu lam yaḥsun wa-ʾinnamā al-ḫabar huwa al-muḍmar allaḏī fassartu laka min qawlihi wa-mimmā naquṣṣu ʿalaykum* […]), [and the saying of the poet] *wa-qāʾilatin ḫawlān fa-nkiḥ fatātahum* (and her who says "[those are the] Ḫawlān, so marry one of their daughters"), it is like if he said "those are the Ḫawlān (*hāʾulāʾi ḫawlān*)", as when you say: *al-hilālu fa-nẓur ʾilayhi* "the new moon (nom.), so (*fa-*) look at it!",[23] it is like if you said *hāḏā al-hilālu fa-nẓur ʾilayhi* "this is the new moon (nom.), so (*fa-*) look at it!",

23 According to Qarrāʿa the meaning wanted may well be this one. In the edited manuscript, however, it is found *al-halāk* (the destruction).

and then the noun [i.e. *hāḏā*] was implied ([…] *wa-qā'ilatin ḫawlānu fa-nkiḥ fatātahum* […] *ka-'annahu qāla hā'ulā'i ḫawlānu kamā taqūlu al-hilālu fa-nẓur 'ilayhi ka-'annaka qulta hāḏā al-hilālu fa-nẓur 'ilayhi fa-'aḍmara al-ism*, 'Aḫfaš *Ma'ānī* 86–87).

Towards the end of the chapter, Sībawayhi proposes the same Qur'ānic quotations that are the starting point of 'Aḫfaš discussion: as for [Q. 24/2] *al-zāniyatu wa-l-zānī fa-ǧlidū kulla wāḥidin minhumā mi'ata ǧaldatin* "The adulteress and the adulterer, flog each one of them with one hundred lashes", and [Q. 5/38] *wa-l-sāriqu wa-l-sāriqatu fa-qṭa'ū 'aydiyahumā* "The male thief and the female thief, cut off their hands", surely this is not constructed on the verb [i.e. it doesn't take accusative case ending], but it goes like [Q. 47/15] *maṯalu l-ǧannati llatī wu'ida l-muttaqūn* "A similitude of the Garden which has been promised to the pious". He says shortly after: *fīhā 'anhārun min mā'in* "therein rivers of water", [that is] therein, so and so. The expression *maṯal* "similitude" occurs only to predicate on it what comes later […], and it is like if He had said *wa-min al-qaṣaṣ maṯal al-ǧanna 'aw mimmā yuqaṣṣu 'alaykum maṯal al-ǧanna* "between the stories there is the similitude of the Garden, or between what you are told about there is the similitude of the Garden", and it must be interpreted according to this implied sentence (*fa-'inna hāḏā lam yubna 'alā al-fi'l wa-lākinnahu ǧā'a 'alā miṯl qawlihi ta'ālā "maṯalu l-ǧannati llati wu'ida l-muttaqūn" ṯumma qāla ba'd "fīhā 'anhārun min mā'in" fīhā kaḏā wa-kaḏā fa-'innamā wuḍi'a al-maṯal li-l-ḥadīṯ allaḏī ba'dahu* […] *fa-ka-'annahu qāla wa-min al-qaṣaṣ maṯal al-ǧanna 'aw mimmā yuqaṣṣu 'alaykum maṯal al-ǧanna fa-huwa maḥmūl 'alā hāḏā 'al-'iḍmār* […], Sībawayhi *Kitāb* I, 142–143).

It is the same in the case of [Q. 24/2] *al-zāniyatu wa-l-zānī* "The adulteress and the adulterer": it is like if, when he said *sūratun 'anzalnāhā wa-faraḍnāhā* [Q. 24/1] "A sura we have sent down and made obligatory", He had said *fī al-farā'iḍ al-zāniyatu wa-l-zānī 'aw al-zāniyatu wa-l-zānī fī-l-farā'iḍ* "between what We have made obligatory there is the adulteress and the adulterer, or the adulteress and the adulterer are between what We have made obligatory", and then He says *fa-ǧlidū* "flog", but the verb is given when already had passed what gave them nominative case ending, as it is said [by the poet] *wa-qā'ilatin ḫawlān fa-nkiḥ fatātahum* (and her who says "[those are the] Ḫawlān, so marry one of their daughters"): the verb is given when the implied [i.e. *hā'ulā'i*] has already governed (*'amila*) it[24] (*wa-ka-ḏālika "al-zāniyatu wa-l-zānī", ka-'annahu lammā qāla* […] *"sūratun 'anzalnāhā wa-faraḍnāhā" qāla "fī l-farā'iḍi l-zāniyatu wa-*

24 Notice that it is exactly the same explanation given also by 'Aḫfaš about this poetic verse, see *supra*.

l-zānī, ʾaw al-zāniyatu wa-l-zānī fī l-farāʾiḍi" ṯumma qāla "fa-ǧlidū" fa-ǧāʾa bi-l-fiʿl baʿd ʾan maḍā fīhimā al-rafʿ kamā qāla wa-qāʾilatin ḫawlān fa-nkiḥ fatātahum fa-ǧāʾa bi-l-fiʿl baʿd ʾan ʿamila fīhi al-muḍmar). And the same it is also in the case of [Q. 5/38] *wa-l-sāriqu wa-l-sāriqatu* "The male thief and the female thief", it is like if He had said *fī-mā faraḍa llāhu ʿalaykum al-sāriqu wa-l-sāriqatu, ʿaw al-sāriqu wa-l-sāriqatu fī-mā faraḍa llāhu ʿalaykum* "between what God has made obligatory there is the male thief and the female thief, or the male thief and the female thief are between what you have been obliged to" (*wa-ka-ḏālika "wa-l-sāriqu wa-l-sāriqatu" ka-ʾannahu qāla "wa-fī-mā faraḍa llāhu ʿalaykum al-sāriqu wa-l-sāriqatu ʾaw al-sāriqu wa-l-sāriqatu fī-mā furiḍa ʿalaykum"* [...], Sībawayhi *Kitāb* I, 143).

ʾAḫfaš's explanation of Q. 24/2 and Q. 5/38 goes very similar: as for [Q. 24/2] *al-zāniyatu wa-l-zānī fa-ǧlidū kulla wāḥidin minhumā miʾata ǧaldatin* "The adulteress and the adulterer, flog each one of them with one hundred lashes", and [Q. 5/38] *wa-l-sāriqu wa-l-sāriqatu fa-qṭaʿū ʾaydiyahumā* "The male thief and the female thief, cut off their hands", it has been said [...] that it is [to be understood] as a communication [from God], as if [God] had said *wa-mimmā ʾaquṣṣu ʿalaykum al-zāniyatu wa-l-zānī wa-l-sāriqu wa-l-sāriqatu* "between what I tell you there is the adulteress and the adulterer, and the male thief and the female thief", then the verb is given after what already required nominative case ending in the first elements because of the *ibtidāʾ*, and this is permissible (*ʿalā al-maǧāz*), as if He had said: *ʾamr al-sāriqi wa-l-sāriqati wa-šaʾnuhumā mimmā naquṣṣu ʿalaykum* "the issue of male thief and female thief, as well as their affairs, are between what we are telling you" (*wa-ʾammā qawluhu "al-zāniyatu wa-l-zānī fa-ǧlidū kulla wāḥidin minhumā miʾata ǧaldatin", "wa-l-sāriqu wa-l-sāriqatu fa-qṭaʿū ʾaydiyahumā" fa-zaʿamū* [...] *ʾanna hāḏā ʿalā al-waḥy ka-ʾannahu yaqūlu "wa-mimmā ʾaquṣṣu ʿalaykum al-zāniyatu wa-l-zānī wa-l-sāriqu wa-l-sāriqatu" ṯumma ǧāʾa bi-l-fiʿl min baʿd mā ʾawǧaba al-rafʿ ʿalā al-ʾawwal ʿalā al-ibtidāʾ wa-hāḏā ʿalā al-maǧāz ka-ʾannahu qāla "ʾamr al-sāriqi wa-l-sāriqati wa-šaʾnuhumā mimmā naquṣṣu ʿalaykum"*, ʾAḫfaš *Maʿānī* 84).

And it is the same also in the case of [Q. 47/15] *maṯalu l-ǧannati llatī wuʿida l-muttaqūn* "A similitude of the Garden which has been promised to the pious", shortly after He says: *fīhā ʾanhārun min māʾin* "therein rivers of water", and it is like if He had said *wa-mimmā ʾaquṣṣu ʿalaykum maṯalu al-ǧanna* "between what I tell you there is the similitude of the Garden", then He begins to mention what is found in it, after what already required nominative case ending in the first element because of the *ibtidāʾ* (*wa-miṯluhu qawluhu "maṯalu l-ǧannati llatī wuʿida l-muttaqūna" ṯumma qāla "fīhā ʾanhārun min māʾin" ka-ʾannahu qāla "wa-mimmā ʾaquṣṣu ʿalaykum maṯalu al-ǧanna" ṯumma ʾaqbala yaḏkuru mā fīhā baʿd ʾan ʾawǧaba al-rafʿ fī al-ʾawwal ʿalā al-ibtidāʾ*, ʾAḫfaš *Maʿānī* 84).

Finally, Sībawayhi mentions the existence of alternative readings: there are also, for Q. 24/2 and Q. 5/38, readings with accusative case ending, and this is possible in Arabic language, for what I told you about the strength [of command and prohibition's need for verbs], but the majority approved only the reading with nominative case ending (*wa-qad qara'a 'unās al-sāriqa wa-l-sāriqata wa-l-zāniyata wa-l-zāniya wa-huwa fī al-ʿarabiyya ʿalā mā ḏakartu laka min al-quwwa wa-lākin 'abat al-ʿāmma 'illā al-qirā'a bi-l-rafʿ*, Sībawayhi *Kitāb* I, 144).

'Aḫfaš, too, mentions the existence [for Q. 24/2 and Q. 5/38] of readings with accusative case ending, [and this would be possible] because, he says, the verb is semantically linked with the first element, and may be a cause, for it, to take accusative case ending, and this is [always possible] in command and prohibition (*wa-qad qara'ahā qawm naṣban; 'iḏ kāna al-fiʿl yaqaʿu ʿalā mā huwa min sabab al-'awwal wa-huwa fī al-'amr wa-l-nahy*, 'Aḫfaš *Maʿānī* 84).

As can be seen, similarities between the two texts are striking in this second case: not only the sequence of Qur'ānic quotations, and of poetic *loci probantes* is the same, but also interpretation of Qur'ānic difficult passages, poetic verses, and important grammatical issues (command and prohibition in *ištiġāl* constructions) is consistent between the two scholars. Their approach is similar from both the terminological, methodological, and theoretical point of view.[25]

One particular thing deserves special attention here, the interpretation given by Sībawayhi to [Q. 47/15]: *maṯalu l-ğannati llatī wuʿida l-muttaqūn* "A similitude of the Garden which has been promised to the pious", He says shortly after: *fīhā 'anhārun min mā'in* "therein rivers of water", [that is] therein, so and so, the expression *maṯal* "similitude" occurs only to predicate on it what comes later [...], and it is like if He had said *wa-min al-qaṣaṣ maṯal al-ğanna 'aw mimmā yuqaṣṣu ʿalaykum maṯal al-ğanna* "between the stories there is the similitude of the Garden, or between what you are told about there is the similitude of the Garden", and it must be interpreted according to this implied sentence (*"maṯalu l-ğannati llati wuʿida l-muttaqūn" ṯumma qāla baʿd "fīhā 'anhārun min mā'in" fīhā kaḏā wa-kaḏā fa-'innamā wuḍiʿa al-maṯal li-l-ḥadīṯ allaḏī baʿdahu* [...] *fa-ka-'annahu qāla wa-min al-qaṣaṣ maṯal al-ğanna 'aw mimmā yuqaṣṣu ʿalaykum maṯal al-ğanna fa-huwa maḥmūl ʿalā hāḏā al-'iḍmār* [...], Sībawayhi *Kitāb* I, 143).

25 Other examples of this kind can be found by the reader if looking at the full list of intersection between Sībawayhi and 'Aḫfaš, particularly if looking for sequences of Qur'ānic *šawāhid* within the intersection between Sībawayhi and the whole *Maʿānī* (Section 5.3) and between Sībawayhi and 'Aḫfaš's *šawāhid* (Section 5.5).

The interpretation found in ʾAḫfaš, as already seen, is exactly the same yet given by Sībawayhi: [Q. 47/15] *maṯalu l-ǧannati llatī wuʿida l-muttaqūn* "A similitude of the Garden which has been promised to the pious", shortly after He says: *fīhā ʾanhārun min māʾin* "therein rivers of water", and it is like if He had said *wa-mimmā ʾaquṣṣu ʿalaykum maṯal al-ǧanna* "between what I tell you there is the similitude of the Garden", then He begins to mention what is found in it, after what already required nominative case ending in the first element because of the *ibtidāʾ* (*"maṯalu l-ǧannati llatī wuʿida l-muttaqūn" ṯumma qāla "fīhā ʾanhārun min māʾin" ka-ʾannahu qāla "wa-mimmā ʾaquṣṣu ʿalaykum maṯal al-ǧanna" ṯumma ʾaqbala yaḏkuru mā fīhā baʿd ʾan ʾawǧaba al-rafʿ fī al-ʾawwal ʿalā al-ibtidāʾ*, ʾAḫfaš *Maʿānī* 84).

Now, this early Basran interpretation of Q. 47/15 can be provenly opposed to an equally early Kufan interpretation of the same Qurʾānic passage that is found in Farrāʾ (*Maʿānī* II, 65) who explains the verse as meaning: qualities of the Garden (*ṣifāt al-ǧanna*) and reports, on the authority of ʾAbū ʿAbd al-Raḥmān al-Sulamī (d. 74/693), the *qirāʾa* of ʿAlī b. ʾAbī Ṭālib: *ʾamṯālu l-ǧannati* (similitudes of the Garden).

Interestingly enough, this controversy is related, about one century later by Mubarrad (*Muqtaḍab* III, 225) who states that the meaning (*taqdīr*) of Q. 47/15 is *fīmā yutlā ʿalaykum maṯal al-ǧanna* (between what is recited on you there is the similitude of the Garden) and explains that those who interpret it as meaning "quality of the Garden" are wrong because *maṯal* doesn't fit in the syntactical [and conceptual] position of *ṣifa*: it is said that the quality (*ṣifa*) of Zayd is that he is gracious and that he is intelligent, and it is said that the similitude (*maṯal*) of Zayd is like such a man, and this because *maṯal* is derived from model (*miṯāl*) and imitation (*ḥaḏw*), while *ṣifa* [means] attribute (*taḥliya*) and characteristic (*naʿt*) (*wa-man qāla ʾinnamā maʿnāhu ṣifat al-ǧanna fa-qad ʾaḫṭaʾa li-ʾanna maṯal lā yūḍaʿu fī mawḍiʿ ṣifat zayd ʾannahu ẓarīf wa-ʾannahu ʿāqil wa-yuqālu maṯal zayd maṯal fulān wa-ʾinnamā al-maṯal maʾḫūḏ min al-miṯāl wa-l-ḥaḏw wa-l-ṣifa taḥliya wa-naʿt*, Mubarrad *Muqtaḍab* III, 225).[26]

Now, if the texts of Sībawayhi, ʾAḫfaš, and Farrāʾ, read together prove the existence of a grammatical debate about the meaning of Q. 47/15 between Basran (as a group) and Kufan scholars already in late 2nd/8th century, which means that grammatical schools and grammatical debates existed in reality, at least starting from the generation of Sībawayhi, ʾAḫfaš, and Farrāʾ, the explanation given towards the end of 3rd/9th century by Mubarrad must be read,

26 Cf. Baalbaki (1981:12) who quotes Farrāʾ and Mubarrad, but fails to mention Sībawayhi and ʾAḫfaš.

here, from two different perspectives: on the one hand, indeed, it proves that late sources on early Arabic grammatical tradition are not necessarily inaccurate, not to say deliberately false, but most often accurate and reliable, when reporting debates and controversies between schools and scholars, while, on the other, it suggests also that grammatical debates might have been related not only to linguistic and philological issues, but to theological and exegetical issues as well, with the position advocated by Sībawayhi and ʾAḫfaš being apparently more close to Muʿtazilite theological principles and to the widespread opposition to *tašbīh* (anthropomorphism) in the descriptions of God, His attributes, and the Hereafter. This, finally, introduces us to a wider and more nuanced perception of schools and scholarly circles operating in the context of 2nd/8th century Basran intellectual milieu.

4 Conclusion: The Basran Intellectual Milieu and the Scholarly Circle of the *naḥwiyyūn*

Evidence from biographical, historiographical, and literary sources have demonstrated that the reputation of Sībawayhi and the authority of the *Kitāb*, far from being the object of criticism, as suggested by Bernards (1997: 3–18), was established already in late 2nd/8th and early 3rd/9th centuries (section 1.1), and that ʾAḫfaš was perceived, and most likely perceived himself, as the heir and successor of Sībawayhi's very teaching (sections 1.3 and 1.4), which proves also Humbert's thesis (1995: 1–17) to be doubtful.

Evidence from textual comparison between Sībawayhi's *Kitāb* and ʾAḫfaš's *Maʿānī* demonstrate, also, that Sībawayhi and ʾAḫfaš were indeed part of the same scholarly circle (section 3.1), and that terminological, methodological, theoretical, and even theological similarities can be found between the two books and opposed, as such, to different positions held by Farrāʾ, which proves the real existence of grammatical schools and grammatical debates between Basran and Kufan scholars already in late 2nd/8th century (section 3.2). Moreover, the account of Mubarrad proves also the reliability of late sources about early history of Arabic grammar (section 3.2).

A few last words may be spent about the scholarly circle of Basran *naḥwiyyūn*. It has been the merit of Carter (1972) to have shed light on the relationship between grammar and law. According to Carter it is important to keep in mind that Sībawayhi began to study at first Islamic law and *ḥadīṯ*-s transmission and only later switched to grammar "for the light it throws on Sībawayhi's role in the emergence of a science of grammar and for the nature of the grammatical system he created" (Carter 2004: 10). While this is perfectly true, it is also true that, for the same reasons, it would be important to fully understand the whole intellectual milieu in which Sībawayhi grew up.

We saw that, according to sources, when Sībawayhi left Ḥammād, he joined the scholarly circle of ʾAḫfaš, said to have been frequented also by the Qurʾānic scholar and canonical reader Yaʿqūb al-Ḥaḍramī, by Ḫalīl, who was the founder of both Arabic lexicography and metrics and by other, anonymous, *naḥwiyyūn* (*fa-maḍā wa-lazima maǧlis al-ʾaḫfaš maʿa yaʿqūb al-ḥaḍramī wa-l-ḫalīl wa-sāʾir al-naḥwiyyīn*, Zaǧǧāǧī *Maǧālis* 118; cf. Zubaydī *Ṭabaqāt* 66; Tanūḫī *Taʾrīḫ* 93; Ibn al-ʾAnbārī *Nuzha* 42; Yāqūt *ʾIršād* 1199; Qifṭī *ʾInbāh* II, 350, 354–355).

Now, if data collected by Talmon (1982) show that Sībawayhi's attitude towards the *naḥwiyyūn* was not so critical as suggested earlier by Carter (1972), data found in biographical and historiographical literature suggest that the *naḥwiyyūn* may well have been a mixed group of scholars with various scholarly interests, but particularly concerned with the way of speech, although not necessarily, and not all, *stricto sensu* grammarians. Even ʾAḫfaš, who is mostly known as a grammarian and a Qurʾānic philologist, is said, in some sources, to have been the most learned of men in theology (*ʾaʿlam al-nās bi-l-kalām*), the most skilled one at debating (*ʾaḥḏaqahum bi-l-ǧadal*) and to have also been a pupil of ʾAbū Šamir (fl. between 2nd/8th and 3rd/9th centuries) of whom he is said to have followed the theological *maḏhab* [being therefore a Qadarite, but not a Muʿtazilite] (cf. Luġawī *Marātib* 80; Ess 2017 [1991]: 99),[27] while Quṭrub (d. 206/821), the other main pupil of Sībawayhi, according to sources may have been the pupil of non-other than the famous Muʿtazilite theologian ʾIbrāhīm al-Naẓẓām (d. 221/836) (cf. Ess 2017 [1991]: 46, 100).

Even from a purely terminological point of view it is easy to perceive the interconnections between, not only grammar and law, as suggested by Carter (1972), or Qurʾānic exegesis and philology (cf. Versteegh 1993, and Shah 2003), but also theology (e.g. the term *manzila*, fundamental in the formation of Muʿtazilite theological approach), and *ḥadīṯ* transmission and logic (e.g. the term *musnad*, cf. Talmon 1987, Guillaume 2004, and Villano 2020). Not to say about metrics and lexicography, both founded by Sībawayhi's principal master Ḫalīl b. ʾAḥmad. The formation of this group of scholarly disciplines, as well as the very formation of Arabic grammatical tradition, thus, should be studied as a whole, and framed and explained in the context of the scientific and cultural blossoming of 2nd/8th century's Basra (cf. Pellat 1953).

The sophisticated Basran intellectual milieu of the 2nd/8th century, indeed, was a very stimulating scholarly environment in which not only Arabic gram-

27 Cf. also Suyūṭī *Buġya* I, 590 where he is openly said to have been a Muʿtazilite.

mar and Basran grammatical school originated, but also Basran schools of law (cf. Melchert 1997: 41–47) and theology (cf. Ess 2017 [1991]: 1–497), the Qur'ānic readings attributed to 'Abū 'Amr b. al-'Alā' (d. 154/771?) and Ya'qūb al-Ḥaḍramī, the Ḫāriǧism, the 'Azraqism, the 'Ibāḍism, the Naǧdāt and the Mu'tazila,[28] the Mirbad and the Poetic criticism of Ibn Sallām al-Ǧumaḥī, up to the Adab prose of Ǧāḥiẓ.

It is in this context that the scholarly group of Basran *naḥwiyyūn* must have operated to elaborate the terminology, the methodology, and the sophisticated principles of grammatical analysis that merged, finally, in the *Kitāb* of Sībawayhi and in the so-called Basran school of grammar, and it is in this context that the scholarly connections that were at work beyond the formation of both Arabic grammar and Qur'ānic philology in 2nd/8th century's Basra should be probably sought.

5 Full list of Qur'ānic Verses Found in Sībawayhi's *Kitāb* and in 'Aḫfaš's *Ma'ānī al-Qur'ān*

The following lists have been prepared from an automatic matching of a database of lists of quotations semiautomatically entered as a series of tab-separated value files. The matching has been performed by a Python script through database-manipulation functions in Pandas library.[29]

5.1 *Full List of Qur'ānic Verses Found in Sībawayhi's* Kitāb

1 (al-Fātiḥa), 2, 7;—2 (al-Baqara), 26, 34, 35, 42, 48, 54, 61, 65, 67, 72, 83, 85, 90, 100, 102, 112, 117, 126, 135, 145, 164, 165, 171, 177, 184, 198, 214, 217, 220, 222, 230, 237, 251, 271, 274, 275, 280, 282, 284;—3 ('Āl 'Imrān), 1, 2, 13, 45, 66, 79, 80, 81, 97, 105, 111, 142, 143, 154, 159, 180, 185;—4 (al-Nisā'), 4, 16, 23, 24, 29, 53, 58, 66, 78, 95, 119, 128, 155, 157, 159, 162, 171;—5 (al-Mā'ida), 1, 2, 24, 38, 69, 71, 73, 95, 115, 117, 119;—6 (al-'An'ām), 23, 27, 37, 54, 80, 91, 96, 109, 126, 137, 148, 152, 154, 160, 164;—7 (al-'A'rāf), 18, 23, 30, 32, 75, 77, 82, 97, 98, 99, 101, 102, 131, 155, 164, 176, 186, 193;—8 (al-'Anfāl), 7, 9, 14, 18, 37, 42, 60;—9 (al-Tawba), 3, 30, 40, 42, 54, 63, 117;—10 (Yūnus), 10, 42, 45, 62, 89, 98, 101;—11 (Hūd), 15, 25, 27, 43, 47, 60,

28 Denial, at least in theory, of the need for Imamate (i.e. for an established power) in all those groups led Patricia Crone (1945–2015; 2000) to speak openly of anarchism with reference to theological, philosophical and political speculations coming from 2nd/8th and 3rd/9th centuries' Basra.

29 Exceptionally, for the tables to come, the presentation of the Qur'ānic verses will be as {no. sura (name of the sura), no. verse, no. verse, etc.} instead of {sura/verse}.

72, 78, 108, 111, 116;—12 (Yūsuf), 4, 10, 18, 20, 30, 31, 32, 35, 82;—13 (al-Raʿd), 1, 9, 29, 43;—14 (ʾIbrāhīm), 31, 47;—15 (al-Ḥiǧr), 3, 30, 54;—16 (al-Naḥl), 24, 30, 62, 66, 124;—17 (al-ʾIsrāʾ), 28, 59, 67, 76, 96, 100, 106, 110;—18 (al-Kahf), 12, 19, 23, 39, 63, 98, 103, 110;—19 (Maryam), 1, 8, 26, 62, 69;—20 (Ṭāʾ Hāʾ), 44, 61, 74, 77, 89, 119;—21 (al-ʾAnbiyāʾ), 3, 22, 26, 34, 57, 92;—22 (al-Ḥaǧǧ), 5, 40, 48, 60, 63;—23 (al-Muʾminūn), 35, 52;—24 (al-Nūr), 1, 2, 6, 9, 37;—25 (al-Furqān), 20, 22, 38, 39, 63, 68, 69;—26 (al-Šuʿarāʾ), 15, 72, 73, 186;—27 (al-Naml), 18, 22, 25, 42, 47, 56, 87, 88;—28 (al-Qaṣaṣ), 23, 76, 81, 82;—29 (al-ʿAnkabūt), 24, 42;—30 (al-Rūm), 4, 36, 51;—31 (Luqmān), 27;—32 (al-Saǧda), 1, 2, 3, 7, 12, 16;—33 (al-ʾAḥzāb), 19, 31, 35;—34 (Sabaʾ), 6, 7, 10, 15, 24, 31, 33, 48;—35 (Fāṭir), 1, 31, 36, 41;—36 (Yāʾ Sīn), 1, 2, 15, 31, 32, 40, 41, 43, 44;—37 (al-Ṣāffāt), 8, 10, 16, 17, 47, 104, 105, 158, 167, 168;—38 (Ṣād), 3, 6, 21, 22, 41, 42, 73;—39 (al-Zumar), 3, 7, 12, 16, 46, 60, 64, 73;—40 (Ġāfir), 32;—41 (Fuṣṣilat), 10, 17, 30, 40;—42 (al-Šūrā), 51, 52, 53;—43 (al-Zuḫruf), 16, 51, 52, 76;—45 (al-Ǧāṯiya), 21, 25;—46 (al-ʾAḥqāf), 24, 35;—47 (Muḥammad), 4, 15, 18, 21, 38;—48 (al-Fatḥ), 16;—50 (Qāf), 1, 11, 23;—51 (al-Ḏāriyāt), 15, 16, 23;—52 (al-Ṭūr), 17, 18;—54 (al-Qamar), 6, 7, 10, 12, 15, 27, 49;—56 (al-Wāqiʿa), 21, 22, 90, 91;—57 (al-Ḥadīd), 29;—58 (al-Muǧādila), 9;—61 (al-Ṣaff), 10, 11, 12;—62 (al-Ǧumuʿa), 8;—63 (al-Munāfiqūn), 1, 4, 10;—66 (al-Taḥrīm), 4;—67 (al-Mulk), 20;—68 (al-Qalam), 9, 14;—69 (al-Ḥāqqa), 30;—70 (al-Maʿāriǧ), 15, 16;—71 (Nūḥ), 17;—72 (al-Ǧinn), 13, 18;—73 (al-Muzzammil), 3, 8, 18, 20;—74 (al-Muddaṯṯir), 35, 49;—75 (al-Qiyāma), 4, 10, 25, 26, 40;—76 (al-ʾInsān), 15, 16, 24, 31;—77 (al-Mursalāt), 15, 25, 35, 36;—78 (al-Nabaʾ), 11, 28;—83 (al-Muṭaffifīn), 1, 36;—84 (al-Inšiqāq), 2, 5;—85 (al-Burūǧ), 10;—86 (al-Ṭāriq), 4;—87 (al-ʾAʿlā), 16;—89 (al-Faǧr), 4, 15, 16;—90 (al-Balad), 6, 14;—91 (al-Šams), 9;—92 (al-Layl), 1, 2, 3;—96 (al-ʿAlaq), 15, 16;—97 (al-Qadr), 4;—106 (Qurayš), 1, 2, 3;—111 (al-Masad), 4;—112 (al-ʾIḫlāṣ), 1, 4.

5.2 *Full List of the Qurʾānic Verses Found in ʾAḫfaš's* Maʿānī al-Qurʾān

5.2.1 Full List of Qurʾānic Verses Commented by ʾAḫfaš (*tafsīr* List)

1 (al-Fātiḥa), 1, 2, 5, 6, 7;—2 (al-Baqara), 1, 2, 3, 6, 7, 8, 9, 10, 11, 13, 14, 15, 16, 17, 18, 20, 22, 24, 25, 26, 27, 28, 29, 30, 31, 32, 34, 35, 36, 37, 38, 40, 41, 42, 45, 46, 48, 49, 50, 51, 54, 55, 57, 58, 59, 60, 61, 63, 65, 66, 67, 68, 69, 70, 71, 72, 74, 78, 79, 83, 84, 88, 89, 90, 91, 96, 97, 98, 100, 102, 105, 106, 108, 111, 114, 115, 117, 119, 121, 124, 126, 127, 128, 130, 132, 133, 134, 135, 136, 137, 138, 139, 140, 143, 145, 147, 148, 150, 151, 152, 154, 158, 161, 162, 165, 173, 175, 176, 177, 178, 180, 183, 184, 185, 186, 188, 189, 192, 193, 194, 195, 196, 198, 203, 204, 207, 208, 210, 213, 216, 219, 222, 225, 226, 228, 232, 233, 234, 235, 237, 239, 240, 245, 246, 248, 251, 253, 255, 256, 257, 258, 259, 260, 264, 265, 266, 268, 270, 274, 279, 280, 282, 283, 285;—3 (ʾĀl ʿImrān), 3, 4, 7, 11, 12, 13, 14, 15, 18, 19, 28, 30, 34, 35, 37, 38, 39, 40, 41, 42, 44, 45, 46, 47, 51, 52, 59, 60, 64, 72, 73, 75, 77, 78, 79, 80, 81, 91, 93, 95, 96, 97, 103, 104, 106, 109, 110, 111, 112, 113, 118, 120, 121,

125, 127, 128, 140, 143, 144, 145, 146, 147, 153, 154, 156, 157, 158, 159, 161, 165, 166, 168, 173, 175, 187, 195, 180, 181, 188;—4 (al-Nisāʾ), 1, 2, 3, 4, 6, 7, 8, 9, 10, 12, 22, 25, 26, 29, 31, 32, 35, 36, 39, 42, 43, 46, 47, 55, 56, 65, 66, 69, 72, 74, 75, 79, 81, 83, 84, 88, 90, 92, 94, 95, 96, 97, 98, 104, 109, 114, 128, 131, 134, 135, 148, 155, 156, 157, 164, 170, 171, 176;—5 (al-Māʾida), 1, 2, 3, 4, 5, 9, 12, 14, 22, 26, 27, 30, 31, 32, 36, 41, 42, 45, 46, 48, 51, 60, 62, 63, 64, 67, 69, 71, 73, 94, 95, 97, 105, 106, 107, 112, 114;—6 (al-ʾAnʿām), 2, 6, 12, 14, 23, 25, 26, 27, 31, 33, 34, 35, 38, 40, 46, 52, 54, 55, 56, 59, 63, 65, 70, 71, 72, 73, 74, 76, 78, 84, 85, 86, 90, 92, 93, 96, 98, 99, 100, 105, 108, 109, 111, 113, 119, 123, 137, 138, 139, 141, 142, 143, 145, 146, 150, 159, 160, 161;—7 (al-ʾAʿrāf), 2, 6, 7, 10, 11, 12, 16, 18, 20, 22, 23, 26, 30, 35, 40, 41, 43, 44, 50, 53, 54, 56, 57, 63, 65, 66, 67, 68, 69, 70, 71, 72, 73, 85, 86, 92, 98, 100, 101, 105, 111, 126, 132, 133, 137, 143, 148, 149, 150, 154, 155, 156, 160, 168, 169, 176, 177, 179, 180, 189, 190, 201, 205;—8 (al-ʾAnfāl), 1, 7, 12, 14, 17, 18, 25, 32, 34, 35, 37, 42, 50, 61, 62, 72, 75;—9 (al-Tawba), 5, 6, 7, 8, 12, 13, 25, 28, 30, 32, 34, 35, 37, 38, 40, 41, 43, 46, 57, 58, 61, 62, 63, 81, 90, 98, 100, 102, 103, 106, 108, 109, 110, 113, 114, 117, 118, 123, 124, 127, 128;—10 (Yūnus), 2, 5, 9, 12, 19, 22, 23, 24, 26, 27, 28, 30, 31, 38, 50, 53, 58, 61, 71, 77, 78, 81, 83, 88, 92, 97, 99, 103, 105;—11 (Hūd), 5, 8, 10, 11, 15, 16, 17, 24, 27, 32, 40, 41, 43, 44, 46, 48, 54, 64, 66, 68, 70, 71, 72, 74, 78, 80, 81, 82, 83, 87, 100, 101, 105, 111, 112, 113, 114, 120, 123;—12 (Yūsuf), 3, 4, 5, 9, 14, 18, 19, 23, 24, 25, 32, 35, 44, 45, 51, 72, 76, 80, 83, 84, 85;—13 (al-Raʿd), 2, 3, 4, 5, 10, 11, 15, 16, 17, 23, 24, 29, 33;—14 (ʾIbrāhīm), 3, 17, 18, 22, 24, 25, 31, 34, 37, 43, 47, 49;—15 (al-Ḥiǧr), 2, 18, 22, 39, 41, 44, 53, 56, 58, 59, 66, 72, 91;—16 (al-Naḥl), 8, 9, 12, 13, 21, 30, 37, 48, 49, 53, 55, 67, 68, 69, 72, 73, 76, 81, 91, 92, 106, 111, 112, 116, 121;—17 (al-ʾIsrāʾ), 1, 5, 11, 23, 31, 35, 36, 37, 43, 45, 47, 53, 59, 64, 77, 78, 79, 80, 81, 82, 83, 84, 85, 86, 87, 110;—18 (al-Kahf), 1, 2, 5, 6, 11, 16, 17, 18, 19, 22, 25, 26, 28, 29, 30, 32, 33, 34, 50, 52, 55, 58, 59, 60, 62, 64, 74, 80, 94, 95, 97, 98, 102, 103, 107, 109;—19 (Maryam), 2, 3, 4, 10, 25, 28, 44, 50, 62, 64, 74, 78, 82, 90;—20 (Ṭāʾ Hāʾ), 1, 4, 5, 18, 22, 42, 44, 53, 63, 69, 72, 77, 81, 111, 129, 132;—21 (al-ʾAnbiyāʾ), 3, 30, 37, 63, 82, 87;—22 (al-Ḥaǧǧ), 2, 13, 15, 19, 25, 30, 36, 40, 45, 47, 72, 73, 78;—23 (al-Muʾminūn), 14, 20, 52, 61, 64, 66, 108, 114;—24 (al-Nūr), 17, 31, 32, 35;—25 (al-Furqān), 18, 19, 40, 49, 57, 62, 63, 74, 77;—26 (al-Šuʿarāʾ), 4, 16, 22, 72, 197, 198, 201, 202, 203;—27 (al-Naml), 7, 8, 11, 13, 16, 28, 40, 47, 48, 60, 61, 62, 63, 64, 65, 72, 82;—28 (al-Qaṣaṣ), 10, 11, 17, 27, 30, 32, 34, 46, 63, 76, 82, 86;—29 (al-ʿAnkabūt), 8, 12, 19, 20, 22, 33;—30 (al-Rūm), 1, 2, 4, 10, 24, 30, 34, 36, 49;—31 (Luqmān), 1, 2, 3, 12, 14, 15, 16, 21, 27, 34;—32 (al-Saǧda), 26;—33 (al-ʾAḥzāb), 4, 5, 6, 10, 16, 40, 52, 53, 56, 60;—34 (Sabaʾ), 7, 8, 15, 21, 22, 23, 24, 31, 33, 37, 45;—35 (Fāṭir), 1, 2, 18, 21, 27, 31, 36, 41, 42, 45;—36 (Yāʾ Sīn), 1, 2, 3, 6, 19, 40, 72;—37 (al-Ṣāffāt), 5, 6, 7, 103, 147;—38 (Ṣād), 1, 2, 3, 4, 5, 6, 7, 8, 9, 10, 11, 12, 13, 14, 33, 36;—39 (al-Zumar), 12, 17, 19, 22, 24, 33, 60, 64, 65, 67, 73, 75;—40 (Ġāfir), 1, 2, 5, 6, 7, 10, 15, 16, 18, 35, 36, 45, 46, 47, 48, 51, 55, 60, 79;—41 (Fuṣṣilat), 3, 4, 5, 9, 10, 12, 16, 21, 26, 28, 30, 34, 41, 42, 43, 44, 48;—42 (al-Šūrā), 13, 15, 23, 26,

43, 45, 53;—43 (al-Zuḫruf), 5, 26, 33, 35, 36, 53, 57;—44 (al-Duḫān), 4, 5, 54;—45 (al-Ǧāṯiya), 9, 10, 21, 31, 32;—46 (al-ʾAḥqāf), 9, 12, 33, 35;—47 (Muḥammad), 18, 22, 35, 38;—48 (al-Fatḥ), 25, 39;—49 (al-Ḥuǧurāt), 2, 13;—50 (Qāf), 1, 2, 3, 4, 15, 16, 17;—51 (al-Ḏāriyāt), 7, 12, 13, 59;—52 (al-Ṭūr), 9, 10, 30;—53 (al-Naǧm), 5, 19, 20, 37, 38;—54 (al-Qamar), 7, 19, 24, 44, 45, 48, 49, 53;—55 (al-Raḥmān), 5, 11, 48, 64;—56 (al-Wāqiʿa), 8, 9, 16, 26, 35, 36, 53, 54, 55, 73, 83, 84, 85, 86, 90, 91, 95;—57 (al-Ḥadīd), 11, 12, 13, 24, 29;—58 (al-Muǧādila), 3, 4;—59 (al-Ḥašr), 2, 5, 6, 7, 9, 12, 17;—60 (al-Mumtaḥana), 4;—61 (al-Ṣaff), 3, 13;—62 (al-Ǧumuʿa), 5, 9;—63 (al-Munāfiqūn), 4, 5;—64 (al-Taġābun), 6;—65 (al-Ṭalāq), 3, 6, 12;—66 (al-Taḥrīm), 4;—67 (al-Mulk), 4, 18, 19, 27, 30;—68 (al-Qalam), 6, 51;—69 (al-Ḥāqqa), 12, 13, 17, 36, 47;—70 (al-Maʿāriǧ), 15, 16, 19, 20, 21, 22, 36, 37;—71 (Nūḥ), 13, 14, 16, 17, 20, 24, 25, 26, 27, 28;—72 (al-Ǧinn), 1, 3, 8, 17;—73 (al-Muzzammil), 1, 2, 3, 8, 9, 14, 17, 20;—74 (al-Muddaṯṯir), 6, 16, 33, 35, 36, 54;—75 (al-Qiyāma), 4, 10, 14, 22, 23, 31, 40;—76 (al-ʾInsān), 2, 3, 9, 13, 14, 20;—77 (al-Mursalāt), 7, 8, 17, 25, 26, 27, 30, 31, 32, 33, 35, 36, 37, 38;—78 (al-Nabaʾ), 16, 26, 28, 29, 40;—79 (al-Nāziʿāt), 1, 2, 3, 4, 5, 6, 7, 8, 9, 10, 11, 12, 13, 14, 15, 16, 17, 18, 19, 20, 21, 22, 23, 24, 25, 26;—80 (ʿAbasa), 15, 16, 17, 20;—81 (al-Takwīr), 4, 6, 8, 9, 12, 16, 24;—82 (al-Infiṭār), 7, 8;—83 (al-Muṭaffifīn), 3, 5, 6, 14, 28, 36;—84 (al-Inšiqāq), 1, 2, 3, 4, 5, 6, 23;—85 (al-Burūǧ), 5, 15, 16, 17, 18, 19, 20, 21, 22;—88 (al-Ġāšiya), 11, 15;—89 (al-Faǧr), 6, 7, 16;—90 (al-Balad), 2, 11, 13, 14;—91 (al-Šams), 7, 8, 9, 13;—92 (al-Layl), 2, 3;—95 (al-Tīn), 2, 7;—96 (al-ʿAlaq), 5, 11, 12, 13, 17, 18;—99 (al-Zalzala), 5;—100 (al-ʿĀdiyāt), 5;—101 (al-Qāriʿa), 5, 10;—104 (al-Humaza), 2, 3, 4, 8;—107 (al-Māʿūn), 1, 2;—108 (al-Kawṯar), 3;—109 (al-Kāfirūn), 2, 3;—110 (al-Naṣr), 2, 3;—111 (al-Masad), 1, 4;—112 (al-ʾIḫlāṣ), 1, 4;—113 (al-Falaq), 3;—114 (al-Nās), 2, 3.

5.2.2 Full List of Qurʾānic Verses Quoted by ʾAḫfaš (*šawāhid* List)

1 (al-Fātiḥa), 2, 5, 6;—2 (al-Baqara), 4, 7, 10, 11, 14, 15, 16, 17, 19, 33, 40, 41, 47, 48, 51, 60, 62, 82, 87, 92, 107, 108, 112, 114, 120, 122, 123, 126, 127, 135, 139, 165, 167, 171, 173, 175, 177, 180, 185, 187, 197, 200, 202, 207, 213, 214, 217, 224, 230, 231, 233, 235, 246, 247, 249, 254, 257, 258, 259, 271, 283, 284;—3 (ʾĀl ʿImrān), 1, 2 21, 30, 35, 39, 41, 52, 54, 55, 64, 66, 75, 76, 86, 97, 112, 119, 142, 145, 152, 153, 154, 159, 169, 173, 180, 185, 188, 201;—4 (al-Nisāʾ), 3, 4, 8, 9, 12, 16, 22, 23, 24, 25, 26, 36, 46, 53, 56, 58, 66, 67, 91, 97, 102, 112, 122, 128, 142, 145, 158, 159, 162;—5 (al-Māʾida), 1, 9, 12, 23, 29, 38, 54, 60, 71, 73, 95, 115;—6 (al-ʾAnʿām), 1, 5, 28, 44, 54, 66, 78, 91, 93, 94, 96, 100, 103, 112, 113, 117, 126, 141, 152, 154, 158, 160;—7 (al-ʾAʿrāf), 1, 18, 22, 23, 38, 59, 60, 64, 75, 82, 86, 87, 104, 138, 144, 145, 150, 154, 164, 186, 189, 205;—8 (al-ʾAnfāl), 9, 14, 18, 37, 38, 45, 48, 53, 60;—9 (al-Tawba), 2, 14, 15, 20, 28, 37, 40, 57, 62, 63, 69, 100, 101, 111;—10 (Yūnus), 1, 10, 22, 35, 38, 42, 43, 45, 59, 62, 79, 87, 91, 93, 98;—11 (Hūd), 7, 15, 40, 68, 69, 72, 95, 116;—12 (Yūsuf), 4, 8, 11, 13, 17, 19, 29,

30, 31, 32, 43, 45, 48, 54, 77, 82, 87, 96, 99, 100, 101;—13 (al-Raʿd), 1, 4, 8, 12, 31, 35, 43;—14 (ʾIbrāhīm), 4, 26, 43;—15 (al-Ḥiğr), 3, 30, 41, 54, 68, 74, 78, 80, 94;—16 (al-Naḥl), 1, 24, 30, 40, 43, 44, 48, 51, 62, 66, 103;—17 (al-ʾIsrāʾ), 7, 52, 53, 67, 76, 80, 97;—18 (al-Kahf), 12, 18, 22, 28, 29, 55, 60, 62, 77, 79, 81, 82, 103, 109;—19 (Maryam), 1, 5, 6, 19, 26, 28, 45, 62, 69, 75;—20 (Ṭāʾ Hāʾ), 1, 10, 14, 15, 18, 30, 31, 61, 63, 69, 71, 89, 94, 118, 119, 128, 132;—21 (al-ʾAnbiyāʾ), 3, 22, 33, 34, 77, 95;—22 (al-Ḥağğ), 3, 5, 25, 35, 47, 65, 72;—23 (al-Muʾminūn), 20, 21, 22, 24, 33, 35, 36, 52, 68, 82, 93, 94, 99;—24 (al-Nūr), 2, 4, 7, 27, 40, 43;—25 (al-Furqān), 20, 22, 29, 49, 53, 63;—26 (al-Šuʿarāʾ), 1, 16, 45, 56, 61, 77, 102, 105, 119, 210;—27 (al-Naml), 1, 6, 18, 39, 40, 59, 67, 88, 90;—28 (al-Qaṣaṣ), 8, 26, 46, 70, 73, 76;—29 (al-ʿAnkabūt), 8, 29, 33;—30 (al-Rūm), 4, 51;—31 (Luqmān), 6;—32 (al-Sağda), 2, 3, 26;—33 (al-ʾAḥzāb), 10, 16, 30, 31, 35, 37, 51, 67;—34 (Sabaʾ), 8, 10, 13, 14, 24, 33, 46;—35 (Fāṭir), 1, 36, 41, 43;—36 (Yā Sīn), 1, 2, 14, 23, 25, 29, 43, 44, 45, 46, 49, 53, 77;—37 (al-Ṣāffāt), 7, 8, 16, 17, 21, 38, 47, 49, 62, 63, 143, 144, 147, 153;—38 (Ṣād), 1, 2, 6, 8, 16, 17, 23, 41, 42, 45, 49, 50, 62, 63;—39 (al-Zumar), 3, 16, 33, 56, 59, 73;—40 (Ġāfir), 1, 36, 48, 60, 64, 66, 67, 83;—41 (Fuṣṣilat), 6, 11, 17, 37;—42 (al-Šūrā), 2, 5, 11, 15, 20, 33, 34, 35, 45, 52, 53;—43 (al-Zuḫruf), 33, 51, 52, 57, 76, 81, 83, 89;—44 (al-Duḫān), 15, 16, 51;—45 (al-Ğāṯiya), 14, 21,25;—46 (al-ʾAḥqāf), 15, 17, 24, 26, 33;—47 (Muḥammad), 4, 8, 13, 15, 18, 20, 21, 34, 35, 38;—48 (al-Fatḥ), 11, 15, 29;—49 (al-Ḥuğurāt), 2, 9;—50 (Qāf), 1, 10, 17, 23;—51 (al-Ḏāriyāt), 13, 14, 23, 25, 49, 50, 51;—52 (al-Ṭūr), 6, 22, 29, 30, 37;—53 (al-Nağm), 12, 19;—54 (al-Qamar), 15, 24, 27, 45, 49, 50;—55 (al-Raḥmān), 1, 2, 3, 4, 5, 7, 46, 70;—56 (al-Wāqiʿa), 65;—57 (al-Ḥadīd), 10, 13, 15, 22, 23, 29;—58 (al-Muğādila), 7, 9, 12;—59 (al-Ḥašr), 7, 9, 10;—62 (al-Ğumuʿa), 8, 9, 11;—63 (al-Munāfiqūn), 1, 6, 10;—64 (al-Taġābun), 14;—65 (al-Ṭalāq), 12;—66 (al-Taḥrīm), 4, 6, 8;—67 (al-Mulk), 3, 20;—68 (al-Qalam), 1, 9, 43;—69 (al-Ḥāqqa), 12;—71 (Nūḥ), 6, 17, 28;—72 (al-Ğinn), 3, 15, 18, 19;—73 (al-Muzzammil), 6, 8, 16, 18, 20;—74 (al-Muddaṯṯir), 1; 5, 30, 35;—75 (al-Qiyāma), 1, 4, 22, 23, 24, 25, 31;—76 (al-ʾInsān), 3, 21, 24, 30, 31;—77 (al-Mursalāt), 6, 15, 35;—78 (al-Nabaʾ), 24, 25, 40;—79 (al-Nāziʿāt), 27, 30, 43;—80 (ʿAbasa), 17;—81 (al-Takwīr), 12;—84 (al-Inšiqāq), 14;—86 (al-Ṭāriq), 4;—87 (al-ʾAʿlā), 14, 16;—88 (al-Ġāšiya), 22, 25;—89 (al-Fağr), 5, 22;—91 (al-Šams), 1, 2, 4, 6, 9, 10;—92 (al-Layl), 2, 19, 20;—93 (al-Ḍuḥā), 9, 10;—94 (al-Šarḥ), 5, 6;—96 (al-ʿAlaq), 11, 15, 16;—98 (al-Bayyina), 5, 6;—100 (al-ʿĀdiyāt), 9, 10, 11;—102 (al-Takāṯur), 6;—105 (al-Fīl), 3;—106 (Qurayš), 3;—107 (al-Māʿūn), 1;—109 (al-Kāfirūn), 5;—110 (al-Naṣr), 3;—111 (al-Masad), 4.

5.3 *Full List of the Intersection between Sībawayhi and the Whole* Maʿānī

1 (al-Fātiḥa), 2, 7;—2 (al-Baqara), 26, 34, 35, 42, 48, 54, 61, 65, 67, 72, 83, 90, 100, 102, 112, 117, 126, 135, 145, 165, 171, 177, 177, 184, 198, 214, 217, 222, 230, 237, 251, 271, 274, 280, 282, 284;—3 (ʾĀl ʿImrān), 1, 2, 13, 45, 66, 79, 80, 81, 97, 111, 142, 143, 154,

159, 180, 185;—4 (al-Nisāʾ), 4, 16, 23, 24, 29, 53, 58, 66, 95, 128, 155, 157, 159, 162, 162, 171;—5 (al-Māʾida), 1, 2, 38, 69, 71, 73, 95, 95, 115;—6 (al-ʾAnʿām), 23, 27, 54, 91, 96, 109, 126, 1376, 152, 154, 160;—7 (al-ʾAʿrāf), 18, 23, 30, 75, 82, 98, 101, 155, 164, 176, 186;—8 (al-ʾAnfāl), 7, 9, 14, 18, 37, 42, 42, 60;—9 (al-Tawba), 30, 40, 63, 117;—10 (Yūnus), 10, 42, 4510, 62, 98;—11 (Hūd), 15, 27, 43, 72, 72, 78, 111, 116;—12 (Yūsuf), 4, 18, 30, 31, 31, 32, 35, 82;—13 (al-Raʿd), 1, 29, 43;—14 (ʾIbrāhīm), 31, 47;—15 (al-Ḥiğr), 3, 30, 54;—16 (al-Naḥl), 24, 30, 62, 66;—17 (al-ʾIsrāʾ), 59, 67, 76, 110;—18 (al-Kahf), 12, 19, 103;—19 (Maryam), 1, 26, 62, 69;—20 (Ṭāʾ Hāʾ), 44, 61, 77, 89, 119;—21 (al-ʾAnbiyāʾ), 3, 22, 34;—22 (al-Ḥağğ), 5, 40, 40;—23 (al-Muʾminūn), 35, 52;—24 (al-Nūr), 2;—25 (al-Furqān), 20, 22, 63;—26 (al-Šuʿarāʾ), 72;—27 (al-Naml), 18, 47, 88;—28 (al-Qaṣaṣ), 76, 82;—30 (al-Rūm), 4, 36, 51;—31 (Luqmān), 27;—32 (al-Sağda), 2, 3;—33 (al-ʾAḥzāb), 31, 35;—34 (Sabaʾ), 7, 10, 15, 24, 33;—35 (Fāṭir), 1, 31, 36, 41;—36 (Yāʾ Sīn), 1, 2, 40, 43, 44;—37 (al-Ṣāffāt), 8, 16, 17, 47;—38 (Ṣād), 3, 6, 41, 42;—39 (al-Zumar), 3, 12, 16, 60, 64, 73;—41 (Fuṣṣilat), 10, 17, 30;—42 (al-Šūrā), 52, 53;—43 (al-Zuḫruf), 51, 52, 76;—45 (al-Ğāṯiya), 21, 25;—46 (al-ʾAḥqāf), 24, 35;—47 (Muḥammad), 4, 4, 15, 18, 21, 38;—50 (Qāf), 1, 23;—51 (al-Ḏāriyāt), 23;—54 (al-Qamar), 7, 15, 27, 49;—56 (al-Wāqiʿa), 90, 91;—57 (al-Ḥadīd), 29;—58 (al-Muğādila), 9;—62 (al-Ğumuʿa), 8;—63 (al-Munāfiqūn), 1, 4, 10;—66 (al-Taḥrīm), 4, 20;—68 (al-Qalam), 9;—70 (al-Maʿāriğ), 15, 16;—71 (Nūḥ), 17;—72 (al-Ğinn), 18;—73 (al-Muzzammil), 3, 8, 18, 20, 20;—74 (al-Muddaṯṯir), 35;—75 (al-Qiyāma), 4, 10, 25, 40;—76 (al-ʾInsān), 24, 31;—77 (al-Mursalāt), 15, 25, 35, 36;—78 (al-Nabaʾ), 28;—83 (al-Muṭaffifīn), 36;—84 (al-Inšiqāq), 2, 5;—86 (al-Ṭāriq), 4;—87 (al-ʾAʿlā), 16;—89 (al-Fağr), 16;—90 (al-Balad), 14;—91 (al-Šams), 9;—92 (al-Layl), 2, 3;—96 (al-ʿAlaq), 15, 15, 16;—106 (Qurayš), 3;—111 (al-Masad), 4;—112 (al-ʾIḫlāṣ), 1, 4.

5.4 *Full List of the Intersection between Sībawayhi and ʾAḫfaš's* tafsīr

1 (al-Fātiḥa), 2;—2 (al-Baqara), 48, 112, 126, 135, 165, 171, 177, 177, 214, 217, 230, 271, 284;—3 (ʾĀl ʿImrān), 1, 2, 66, 97, 142, 154, 159, 180, 185;—4 (al-Nisāʾ), 4, 16, 23, 24, 53, 58, 66, 128, 159, 162, 162;—5 (al-Māʾida), 1, 38, 71, 73, 95, 115;—6 (al-ʾAnʿām), 54, 91, 96, 126, 152, 154, 160;—7 (al-ʾAʿrāf), 18, 23, 75, 82, 164, 186;—8 (al-ʾAnfāl), 9, 14, 18, 37, 60;—9 (al-Tawba), 40, 63;—10 (Yūnus), 10, 42, 45, 62, 98;—11 (Hūd), 15, 72, 72, 116;—12 (Yūsuf), 4, 30, 31, 31, 32, 82;—13 (al-Raʿd), 1, 43;—15 (al-Ḥiğr), 3, 30, 54;—16 (al-Naḥl), 24, 30, 62, 66;—17 (al-ʾIsrāʾ), 67, 76;—18 (al-Kahf), 12, 103;—19 (Maryam), 1, 26, 62, 69;—20 (Ṭāʾ Hāʾ), 61, 89, 119;—21 (al-ʾAnbiyāʾ), 3, 22, 34;—22 (al-Ḥağğ), 5;—23 (al-Muʾminūn), 35, 52;—24 (al-Nūr), 2;—25 (al-Furqān), 20, 22, 63;—27 (al-Naml), 18, 88;—28 (al-Qaṣaṣ), 76;—30 (al-Rūm), 4, 51;—32 (al-Sağda), 2, 3;—33 (al-ʾAḥzāb), 31, 35;—34 (Sabaʾ), 10, 24, 33;—35 (Fāṭir), 1, 36, 41;—36 (Yāʾ Sīn), 1, 2, 43, 44;—37 (al-Ṣāffāt), 8, 16, 17, 47;—38 (Ṣād), 6, 41, 42;—39 (al-Zumar), 3, 16, 73;—41 (Fuṣṣilat), 17;—42 (al-Šūrā), 52,

53;—43 (al-Zuḫruf), 51, 52; 76;—45 (al-Ǧāṯiya), 21, 25;—46 (al-ʾAḥqāf), 24;—47 (Muḥammad), 4, 15, 18, 21, 38;—50 (Qāf), 1, 23;—51 (al-Ḏāriyāt), 23;—54 (al-Qamar), 15, 27, 49;—57 (al-Ḥadīd), 29;—58 (al-Muǧādila), 9;—62 (al-Ǧumuʿa), 8;—63 (al-Munāfiqūn), 1, 10;—66 (al-Taḥrīm), 4;—67 (al-Mulk), 20;—68 (al-Qalam), 9;—71 (Nūḥ), 17;—72 (al-Ǧinn), 18;—73 (al-Muzzammil), 8, 18, 20, 20;—74 (al-Muddaṯṯir), 35;—75 (al-Qiyāma), 4, 25;—76 (al-ʾInsān), 24, 31;—77 (al-Mursalāt), 15, 35;—86 (al-Ṭāriq), 4;—87 (al-ʾAʿlā), 16;—91 (al-Šams), 9;—92 (al-Layl), 2;—96 (al-ʿAlaq), 15, 15, 16;—106 (Qurayš), 3;—111 (al-Masad), 4.

5.5 *Full List of the Intersection between Sībawayhi and ʾAḫfaš's* šawāhid

1 (al-Fātiḥa), 2;—2 (al-Baqara), 48, 112, 126, 135, 165, 171, 177, 177, 214, 217, 230, 271, 284;—3 (ʾĀl ʿImrān), 1, 2, 66, 97, 142, 154, 159, 180, 185;—4 (al-Nisāʾ), 4, 16, 23, 24, 53, 58, 66, 128, 159, 162, 162;—5 (al-Māʾida), 1, 38, 71, 73, 95, 115;—6 (al-ʾAnʿām), 54, 91, 96, 126, 152, 154, 160;—7 (al-ʾAʿrāf), 18, 23, 75, 82, 164, 186;—8 (al-ʾAnfāl), 9, 14, 18, 37, 60;—9 (al-Tawba), 40, 63;—10 (Yūnus), 10, 42, 45, 62, 98;—11 (Hūd), 15, 72, 72, 116;—12 (Yūsuf), 4, 30, 31, 31, 32, 82;—13 (al-Raʿd), 1, 43;—15 (al-Ḥiǧr), 3, 30, 54;—16 (al-Naḥl), 24, 30, 62, 66;—17 (al-ʾIsrāʾ), 67, 76;—18 (al-Kahf), 12, 103;—19 (Maryam), 1, 26, 62, 69;—20 (Ṭāʾ Hāʾ), 61, 89, 119;—21 (al-ʾAnbiyāʾ), 3, 22, 34;—22 (al-Ḥaǧǧ), 5;—23 (al-Muʾminūn), 35, 52;—24 (al-Nūr), 2;—25 (al-Furqān), 20, 22, 63;—27 (al-Naml), 18, 88;—28 (al-Qaṣaṣ), 76;—30 (al-Rūm), 4, 51;—32 (al-Saǧda), 2, 3;—33 (al-ʾAḥzāb), 31, 35;—34 (Sabaʾ), 10, 24, 33;—35 (Fāṭir), 1, 36, 41;—36 (Yāʾ Sīn), 1, 2, 43, 44;—37 (al-Ṣāffāt), 8, 16, 17, 47;—38 (Ṣād), 6, 41, 42;—39 (al-Zumar), 3, 16, 73;—41 (Fuṣṣilat), 17;—42 (al-Šūrā), 52, 53;—43 (al-Zuḫruf), 51, 52, 76;—45 (al-Ǧāṯiya), 21, 25;—46 (al-ʾAḥqāf), 24;—47 (Muḥammad), 4, 4, 15, 18, 21, 38;—50 (Qāf), 1, 23;—51 (al-Ḏāriyāt), 23;—54 (al-Qamar), 15, 27, 49;—57 (al-Ḥadīd), 29;—58 (al-Muǧādila), 9;—62 (al-Ǧumuʿa), 8;—63 (al-Munāfiqūn), 1, 10;—66 (al-Taḥrīm), 4;—67 (al-Mulk), 20;—68 (al-Qalam), 9;—71 (Nūḥ), 17;—72 (al-Ǧinn), 18;—73 (al-Muzzammil), 8, 18, 20, 20;—74 (al-Muddaṯṯir), 35;—75 (al-Qiyāma), 4, 25;—76 (al-ʾInsān), 24, 31;—77 (al-Mursalāt), 15, 35;—86 (al-Ṭāriq), 4;—87 (al-ʾAʿlā), 16;—91 (al-Šams), 9;—92 (al-Layl), 2;—96 (al-ʿAlaq), 15, 16;—106 (Qurayš), 3;—111 (al-Masad), 4.

Bibliography

Primary Sources

ʾAbū ʿUbayda, *Maǧāz* = ʾAbū ʿUbayda Maʿmar b. al-Muṯannā, *Maǧāz al-Qurʾān*. Ed. by Muḥammad Fuʾād Sazkīn (Fuat Sezgin). Al-Qāhira: Maktabat al-ḫānǧī, 2 vol., 1962.

ʾAḫfaš, *Maʿānī* = ʾAbū al-Ḥasan Saʿīd b. Masʿada al-ʾAḫfaš al-ʾAwsaṭ, *Maʿānī al-Qurʾān*. Ed. by Hudā Maḥmūd Qarrāʿa. Al-Qāhira: Maktabat al-ḫānǧī, 2 vol. in 1, 1990.

Farrāʾ, *Maʿānī* = ʾAbū Zakariyyā Yaḥyā b. Ziyād b. ʿAbd Allāh b. Manẓūr al-Daylamī al-Farrāʾ, *Maʿānī al-Qurʾān*. Ed. by ʾAḥmad Yūsuf Naǧātī, Muḥammad ʿAlī al-Naǧǧār, and ʿAbd al-Fattāḥ ʾIsmāʿīl Šalabī. Al-Qāhira: al-Dār al-miṣriyya, 3 vol., 1955–1972.

Ǧāḥiẓ, *Bayān* = ʾAbū ʿUṯmān ʿAmr b. Bakr b. Maḥbūb al-Ǧāḥiẓ al-Kinānī al-Layṯī, *al-Bayān wa-l-tabyīn*. Ed. by ʿAbd al-Salām Muḥammad Hārūn. Bayrūt & al-Qāhira: Dār wa-maktabat al-hilāl & Maktabat al-ḫānǧī, 3 vol., 1968.

Ǧāḥiẓ, *Ḥayawān* = ʾAbū ʿUṯmān ʿAmr b. Bakr b. Maḥbūb al-Ǧāḥiẓ al-Kinānī al-Layṯī, *Kitāb al-Ḥayawān*. Ed. by ʿAbd al-Salām Muḥammad Hārūn. Miṣr: Muṣṭafā al-Bābī al-Ḥalabī, 2nd ed., 8 vol., 1965.

Ḫaṭīb, *Taʾrīḫ* = ʾAbū Bakr ʾAḥmad b. ʿAlī b. Ṯābit al-Ḫaṭīb al-Baġdādī, *Taʾrīḫ Madīnat al-salām wa-ʾaḫbār muḥaddiṯīhā wa-ḏikr quṭṭānihā al-ʿulamāʾ min ġayr ʾahlihā wa-wāridīhā*. Ed. by Baššār ʿAwwār Maʿrūf. Bayrūt: Dār al-ġarb al-ʾislāmī, 17 vol., 2001.

Ibn al-ʾAnbārī, *ʾInṣāf* = Kamāl al-Dīn ʾAbū al-Barakāt ʿAbd al-Raḥmān b. Muḥammad b. ʾAbī ʿUbayd Allāh b. ʾAbī Saʿīd al-ʾAnbārī, *al-ʾInṣāf fī masāʾil al-ḫilāf bayna al-naḥwiyyīn al-baṣriyyīn wa-l-kūfiyyīn*. Ed. by Ǧawda Mabrūk Muḥammad Mabrūk. Al-Qāhira: Maktabat al-ḫānǧī, 2002.

Ibn al-ʾAnbārī, *Nuzha* = Kamāl al-Dīn ʾAbū al-Barakāt ʿAbd al-Raḥmān b. Muḥammad b. ʾAbī ʿUbayd Allāh b. ʾAbī Saʿīd al-ʾAnbārī, *Nuzhat al-ʾalibbāʾ fī ṭabaqāt al-ʾudabāʾ*. Ed. by ʾIbrāhīm al-Sāmarrāʾī. Al-Zarqāʾ (al-ʾUrdunn): Maktabat al-manār, 1980.

Ibn al-Nadīm, *Fihrist* = ʾAbū al-Faraǧ Muḥammad b. ʾAbī Yaʿqūb ʾIsḥāq al-Warrāq, *Kitāb al-Fihrist li-l-Nadīm*. Ed. by Riḍā Taǧaddud. Bayrūt: Dār al-masīra, 3rd ed., 1988.

Ibn Ḫallikān, *Wafayāt* = Šams al-Dīn ʾAbū al-ʿAbbās ʾAḥmad b. Muḥammad b. ʾIbrāhīm b. ʾAbī Bakr al-Barmakī al-ʾIrbilī Ibn Ḫallikān, *Wafayāt al-ʾaʿyān wa-ʾanbāʾ ʾabnāʾ al-zamān*. Ed. ʾIḥsān ʿAbbās. Bayrūt: Dār ṣādir, 8 vol., 1968.

Ibn Hišām, *Muġnī* = Ǧamāl al-Dīn ʾAbū Muḥammad ʿAbd Allāh b. Yūsuf b. ʾAḥmad b. ʿAbd Allāh b. Hišām al-ʾAnṣārī al-Miṣrī, *Muġnī al-labīb ʿan kutub al-ʾaʿārīb*. Ed. by ʾAbū ʿAbd Allāh ʿAlī ʿĀšūr al-Ǧanūbī. Bayrūt: Dār ʾiḥyāʾ al-turāṯ al-ʿarabī, 2 vol., 2001.

Ibn Qutayba, *Maʿārif* = ʾAbū Muḥammad ʿAbd Allāh b. Muslim b. Qutayba, *al-Maʿārif*. Ed. by Ṯarwat ʿUkāša. Al-Qāhira: Dār al-maʿārif, 4th ed., 1969.

Ibn Sallām, *Ṭabaqāt* = Muḥammad b. Sallām al-Ǧumaḥī, *Ṭabaqāt fuḥūl al-šuʿarāʾ*. Ed. Maḥmūd Muḥammad Šākir. Ǧudda: Dār al-madanī, 1997.

Luġawī, *Marātib* = ʾAbū al-Ṭayyib ʿAbd al-Wāḥid b. ʿAlī al-Luġawī, *Marātib al-naḥwiyyīn*. Ed. by Muḥammad ʾAbū al-Faḍl ʾIbrāhīm. Ṣaydā (Bayrūt): al-Maktaba al-ʿaṣriyya, 2009.

Marzubānī, *Nūr* = ʾAbū ʿUbayd Allāh Muḥammad b. ʿImrān al-Marzubānī, *Kitāb Nūr al-qabas al-muḫtaṣar min al-Muqtabas fī 'aḫbār al-nuḥāt wa-l-'udabā' wa-l-šu'arā' wa-l-'ulamā'*. Ed. by Rudolph Sellheim. Wiesbaden: F. Steiner, 1964.

Mubarrad, *Muqtaḍab* = 'Abū al-'Abbās Muḥammad b. Yazīd al-'Akbar al-Ṯumālī al-'Azdī al-Mubarrad, *Kitāb al-Muqtaḍab*. Ed. by Muḥammad 'Abd al-Ḫāliq 'Uḍayma. Al-Qāhira: Lağnat 'Iḥyā' al-turāṯ al-'Islāmī, 4 vol., 1994.

Qifṭī, *'Inbāh* = Ğamāl al-Dīn 'Abū al-Ḥasan 'Alī b. Yūsuf al-Qifṭī, *'Inbāh al-ruwāt 'alā 'anbāh al-nuḥāt*. Ed. by Muḥammad 'Abū al-Faḍl 'Ibrāhīm. Al-Qāhira & Bayrūt: Dār al-fikr al-'arabī & Mu'assasat al-kutub al-ṯaqāfiyya, 4 vol., 1986.

Sam'ānī, *'Ansāb* = 'Abū Sa'd 'Abd al-Karīm b. Muḥammad al-Sam'ānī al-Tamīmī, *al-'Ansāb*. Ed. by 'Abd al-Raḥmān b. Yaḥyā al-Mu'allimī al-Yamānī. Ḥaydarābād al-Dakkan: Mağlis dā'irat al-ma'ārif al-'uṯmāniyya, 13 vol., 1977.

Šantamarī, *Nukat* = 'Abū al-Ḥağğāğ Yūsuf b. Sulaymān b. 'Īsā al-'A'lam al-Šantamarī, *al-Nukat fī tafsīr Kitāb Sībawayhi wa-tabyīn al-ḫafī min lafẓihi wa-šarḥ 'abyātihi wa-ġarībihi*. Ed. by Rašīd Bi-l-Ḥabīb. Ribāṭ: Wizārat al-'awqāf wa-l-šu'ūn al-'islāmiyya, 3 vol. 1999.

Sībawayhi, *Kitāb* = 'Abū Bišr 'Amr b. 'Uṯmān b. Qanbar Sībawayhi, *al-Kitāb*. Ed. by 'Abd al-Salām Muḥammad Hārūn. Al-Qāhira: Maktabat al-ḫānğī, 3rd ed., 5 vol., 1988.

Sīrāfī, *'Aḫbār* = 'Abū Sa'īd al-Ḥasan b. 'Abd Allāh b. al-Marzubān, *'Aḫbār al-naḥwiyyīn al-baṣriyyīn*. Ed. by Ṭaha Muḥammad al-Zaytī & Muḥammad 'Abd al-Mun'im Ḫafāğī. Al-Qāhira: Muṣṭafā al-Bābī al-Ḥalabī, 1955.

Sīrāfī, *Šarḥ* = 'Abū Sa'īd al-Ḥasan b. 'Abd Allāh b. al-Marzubān, *Šarḥ Kitāb Sībawayhi*. Ed. by Ramaḍān 'Abd al-Tawwāb, Maḥmūd Fahmī Ḥiğāzī, and Muḥammad Hāšim 'Abd al-Dāyim. Al-Qāhira: Dār al-kutub wa-l-waṯā'iq al-qawmiyya, 2 vol. 1986–1990.

Suyūṭī, *Buġya* = Ğalāl al-Dīn 'Abd al-Raḥmān b. 'Abī Bakr b. Muḥammad b. Sābiq al-Dīn al-Ḫuḍayrī al-Šāfi'ī al-Suyūṭī, *Buġyat al-wu'āt fī ṭabaqāt al-luġawiyyīn wa-l-nuḥāt*. Ed. by Muḥammad 'Abū al-Faḍl 'Ibrāhīm. Al-Qāhira: 'Īsā al-Bābī al-Ḥalabī, 2 vol., 1964–1965.

Tanūḫī, *Ta'rīḫ* = 'Abū al-Maḥāsin al-Mufaḍḍal b. Muḥammad b. Mis'ar al-Tanūḫī al-Ma'arrī. *Ta'rīḫ al-'ulamā' al-naḥwiyyīn min al-baṣriyyīn wa-l-kūfiyyīn wa-ġayrihim*. Ed. by 'Abd al-Fattāḥ Muḥammad al-Ḥulw. Al-Qāhira: Dār hağar, 1992.

Yāqūt, *'Iršād* = Šihāb al-Dīn 'Abū 'Abd Allāh Ya'qūb b. 'Abd Allāh Yāqūt al-Ḥamawī al-Rūmī, *Mu'ğam al-'udabā' 'iršād al-'arīb 'ilā ma'rifat al-'adīb*. Ed. by 'Iḥsān 'Abbās. Bayrūt: Dār al-ġarb al-'islāmī, 7 vol. in 1, 1993.

Zağğāğī, *Mağālis* = 'Abū al-Qāsim 'Abd al-Raḥmān b. 'Isḥāq al-Zağğāğī, *Mağālis al-'ulamā'*. Ed. by 'Abd al-Salām Muḥammad Hārūn. Al-Qāhira: Maktabat al-ḫānğī, 1983.

Zubaydī, *Ṭabaqāt* = 'Abū Bakr Muḥammad b. al-Ḥasan b. 'Ubayd Allāh b. Muḏaḥḥiğ al-Zubaydī al-'Andalusī al-'Išbīlī, *Ṭabaqāt al-naḥwiyyīn wa-l-luġawiyyīn*. Ed. by Muḥammad 'Abū al-Faḍl 'Ibrāhīm. Al-Qāhira: Dār al-ma'ārif, 2nd ed., 1973.

Secondary Sources

Baalbaki, Ramzi. 1981. "Arab grammatical controversies and the extant sources of the second and third centuries A.H.". *Studia Arabica et Islamica: Festschrift for Iḥṣān ʿAbbās*, ed. by Wadād al-Qāḍī, 1–26. Beirut: American University of Beirut.

Baalbaki, Ramzi. 2008. *The Legacy of the* Kitāb: *Sībawayhi's Analytical Methods within the Context of the Arabic Grammatical Theory*. Leiden & Boston: Brill, coll. "Studies in Semitic Languages and Linguistics" 51.

Bernards, Monique. 1997. *Changing Traditions: Al-Mubarrad's Refutation of Sībawayh and the Subsequent Reception of the* Kitāb. Leiden & Boston: Brill, coll. "Studies in Semitic Languages and Linguistics" 23.

Blachère, Régis. 1950. "Les savants iraqiens et leurs informateurs bédouins aux IIe–IVe siècles de l'Hégire". *Mélanges William Marçais*, 37–48. Paris: Maisonneuve.

Blau, Joshua. 1963. "The Role of the Bedouins as Arbiters in Linguistic Questions and the *Masʾala az-Zunburiyya*". *Journal of Semitic Studies* 8/1. 42–51.

Capezzone, Leonardo. 1998. "La politica ecumenica califfale: pluriconfessionalismo, dispute interreligiose e trasmissione del patrimonio greco nei secoli VIII–IX". *Oriente Moderno* N.S. 17 (78). 1–62.

Carter, Michael G. 1972. "Les origines de la grammaire arabe". *Revue des études islamiques* 40. 69–97.

Carter, Michael G. 1973. "Ṣarf et ḫilāf, contribution à l'histoire de la grammaire arabe". *Arabica* 20/3. 292–304.

Carter, Michael G. 2001. "A Missing Link between Law and Grammar, the *Intiṣār* of Ibn Wallād". *Arabica* 48/1. 51–65.

Carter, Michael G. 2004. *Sībawayhi*. Oxford: Oxford University Press, coll. "Makers of Islamic Civilization".

Crone, Patricia. 2000. "Ninth-Century Muslim Anarchists". *Past & Present* 167. 3–28.

Ḍayf, Šawqī. 1968. *Al-Madāris al-naḥwiyya*. Al-Qāhira: Dār al-maʿārif.

Edzard, Lutz. 2017. "The *masʾala zunbūriyya* in a Semitic and Afroasiatic Perspective". *Approaches to the History and Dialectology of Arabic in Honor of Pierre Larcher*, ed. by Manuel Sartori et al., 102–116. Leiden—Boston: E.J. Brill, coll. "Studies in Semitic Languages and Linguistics" 88.

Ess, Joseph van. 2017 [1991]. *Theology and Society in the Second and Third Centuries of the Hijra: a History of Religious Thought in Early Islam*, 2. Leiden & Boston: Brill, coll. "Handbook of Oriental Studies. Section 1, The Near and Middle East" 116/2 [Trans. by Gwendolin Goldbloom of *Theologie und Gesellschaft im 2. und 3. Jahrhundert Hidschra. Eine Geschichte des religiösen Denkens im frühen Islam*. Berlin & New York: Walter de Gruyter].

Fiedler, Katalyn. 2012. "*Iyyāka wa-l-masʾala z-zunbūriyya*: On a Widely Debated Mediaeval Grammatical Issue". *Papers Presented to Alexander Fodor on His Seventieth Birthday by his disciples*, ed. by Kinga Dévényi, 79–90. Budapest: Eötvös Loránd

University & Csoma de Kőrös Society, coll. "The Arabist: Budapest Studies in Arabic" 31.

Fischer, August. 1922. "Die Mas'ala Zunbūrīja". *A Volume of Oriental Studies Presented to Edward G. Browne on his 60th Birthday* (*7 February 1922*), ed. by Thomas Walker Arnold & Reynold Alleyne Nicholson, 150–156. Cambridge: Cambridge University Press.

Fleisch, Henri. 1961–1979. *Traité de philologie arabe*. Beyrouth: Imprimerie catholique, 2 vol.

Flügel, Gustav. 1862. *Die grammatischen Schulen der Araber. Nach den Quellen bearbeitet*. Leiden: Brill.

Ghersetti, Antonella. 2017. "Systematizing the Description of Arabic: The Case of Ibn al-Sarrāj". *Asiatische Studien—Études Asiatiques* 71/3. 879–906.

Gilliot, Claude. 2002. "Exegesis of the Qurʾān: Classical and Medieval". *Encyclopaedia of the Qurʾān*, II, ed. by Jane Dammen McAuliffe. Leiden & Boston: Brill.

Goldziher, Ignaz. 1994 [1878]. *On the History of Grammar Among the Arabs: An essay in literary history*. Amsterdam & Philadelphia: John Benjamins, coll. "Studies in the History of Language Sciences" 73 [Trans. and ed. by Kinga Dévényi and Tamás Iványi of "Anyelvtudomány történetéröl az araboknál". *Nyelvtudomány Közlemények* 14. 309–375].

Guillaume, Jean-Patrick. 2004. "Nouvelles élucubrations sur l'apport et le support". *Langues et littératures du monde arabe* 5. 69–79.

Ḥadīṯī (al-), Ḫadīǧa. 2001. *Al-Madāris al-naḥwiyya*. Irbid: Dār al-ʾamal (3rd ed.).

Humbert, Geneviève. 1995. *Les voies de la transmission du Kitāb de Sībawayhi*. Leiden & Boston: Brill, coll. "Studies in Semitic Languages and Linguistics" 20.

Lancioni, Giuliano & Cristina Solimando. 2015. "The Analysis of Valency in Sībawayhi's *Kitāb*". *The Foundations of Arabic Linguistics II. Kitāb Sībawayhi: Interpretation and Transmission*, ed. by Amal Elesha Marogy & Kees Versteegh. Leiden & Boston: Brill, coll. "Studies in Semitic Languages and Linguistics" 83. 138–159.

Melchert, Christopher. 1997. *The Formation of the Sunni Schools of Law: 9th–10th Centuries C.E.* Leiden & Boston: Brill, coll. "Studies in Islamic Law and Society" 4.

Merx, Adalbertus. 1889. *Historia artis grammaticae apud Syros*. Leipzig: F.A. Brockhaus, coll. "Abhandlungen für die Kunde des Morgenlandes".

Owens, Jonathan. 1990. *Early Arabic Grammatical Theory: Heterogeneity and Standardization*. Amsterdam & Philadelphia: John Benjamins.

Owens, Jonathan. 1991. "Models for Interpreting the Development of Medieval Arabic Grammatical Theory". *Journal of the American Oriental Society* 111/2. 225–238.

Rundgren, Frithiof. 1976. "Über den griechischen Einfluß auf die arabische Nationalgrammatik". *Acta Societatis Linguisticae Upsaliensis* Nova Series 2/5. 119–144.

Sartori, Manuel. 2019. "Entre influence et coïncidence : la réminiscence du grec dans l'arabe. Contribution à l'histoire de la grammaire arabe". *Historiographia Linguistica* 46/3. 219–249.

Sezgin, Fuat. 1984. *Geschichte des Arabischen Schrifttums (Band IX—Grammatik bis ca. 430 h.)*. Leiden: E.J. Brill.

Shah, Mustapha. 2003. "Exploring the Genesis of Early Arabic Linguistic Thought: Qur'anic Readers and Grammarians of the Baṣran Tradition (Part II)". *Journal of Qur'anic Studies* 5/2. 1–47.

Talmon, Rafael. 1982. "*Naḥwiyyūn* in Sībawayhi's *Kitāb*". *Zeitschrift für Arabische Linguistik* 8. 12–38.

Talmon, Rafael. 1985. "An Eighth Century Grammatical School in Medina: the Collection and Evaluation of the Available Material". *BSOAS* 48. 224–236.

Talmon, Rafael. 1986. "*al-Mas'ala al-zunbūriyya. Dirāsa fī māhīya iḫtilāf al-maḏhabayn al-naḥwiyyayn*". *al-Karmil* 7. 131–163.

Talmon, Rafael. 1987. "*Musnad, Musnad Ilayhi* and the Early History of Arabic Grammar: A Reconsideration". *The Journal of the Royal Asiatic Society of Great Britain and Ireland* 2. 208-222.

Talmon, Rafael. 1997. *Arabic grammar in its formative age: Kitāb al-ʿAyn and its attribution to Ḫalīl b. Aḥmad*. Leiden—New York—Köln: Brill, coll. "Studies in Semitic Languages and Linguistics" 25.

Talmon, Rafael. 2003. *Eighth-century Iraqi grammar: a critical exploration of pre-Ḫalīlian Arabic linguistics*. Winona Lake, Indiana: Eisenbrauns.

Troupeau, Gérard. 1961. "À Propos des Grammairiens cités par Sībawayhi dans le *Kitāb*". *Arabica* 8/3. 309–312.

Troupeau, Gérard. 1962. "La grammaire à Baġdād du IXe au XIIIe siècle". *Arabica* 9/3. 397–405.

ʿUḍayma, Maḥmūd ʿAbd al-Ḫāliq. 1975. *Fahāris Kitāb Sībawayhi wa-dirāsa lahu*. Al-Qāhira: Maṭbaʿat al-saʿāda.

Versteegh, Kees. 1977. *Greek Elements in Arabic Linguistic Thinking*. Leiden & Boston: Brill, coll. "Studies in Semitic Languages and Linguistics" 7.

Versteegh, Kees. 1993. *Arabic Grammar and Qur'ānic Exegesis in Early Islam*. Leiden & Boston: Brill, coll. "Studies in Semitic Languages and Linguistics" 19.

Villano, Raoul. 2020. "*Musnad, Musnad 'ilayhi* and Commentaries on the *Kitāb* of Sībawayhi: Transmission and Development of Grammatical Knowledge between 2nd/8th and 5th/11th Centuries". *The International Journal of Arabic Linguistics* 6/1&2. 1–44.

Weil, Gotthold. 1913. *Die grammatischen Streitfragen der Basrer und Kufer*. Leiden: Brill.

CHAPTER 4

The Arabic Linguistic Tradition after Sībawayhi: A Study in the Profile of the Speaker

Hanadi Dayyeh

Introduction

The opening scene for this study is set in the city of Basra in the mid of the 2nd/8th century, where a young *mawlā* (client) named ʾAbū Bišr ʿAmr b. ʿUṯmān Sībawayhi (d. 180/796?) decides to collate, study and analyze the speech of Arabs in a book that becomes famously known as *al-Kitāb* "The Book"—the oldest book of Arabic grammar that we know about.[1] The reasons behind Sībawayhi's decision to write this book are neither stated by the writer nor by his later commentators and biographers (cf. Luġawī *Marātib* 65; Zubaydī *Ṭabaqāt* 66–74; Ibn al-ʾAnbārī *Nuzha* 54–58; Qifṭī *ʾInbāh* II, 346–360; Suyūṭī *Buġya* II, 229–230). What we know from Sībawayhi's biography is that he moved from his hometown al-Bayḍāʾ in Shiraz to the city of Basra to study Islamic law. There he joined the *maǧlis* (circle) of Ḥammād b. Salama where he was ridiculed for making a grammar mistake (cf. Zubaydī *Ṭabaqāt* 66–67; Ibn al-ʾAnbārī *Nuzha* 54–55; Suyūṭī *Buġya* II, 350). His embarrassment made him vow to study the language of Arabs, and so he did. In the absence of any mention in the resources as to when or why he decides to compile his book, one may speculate that Sībawayhi intended for *al-Kitāb* to be a manifestation of his acquired mastery of the Arabic language, either to show his rivals or simply to share this mastery with learners of Arabic like himself. Whatever the reason is, Sībawayhi's mastery of the Arabic language, unfortunately, did not gain the acknowledgment of his rivals who continued to doubt his language abilities and ridicule him for his Persian accent (cf. Zubaydī *Ṭabaqāt* 67). In fact, the stories around the causes of his death—in what is famously known as *al-masʾala al-zunbūriyya* "the hornet problem" (cf. Zubaydī *Ṭabaqāt* 69–73)—reveal that his rivals never spared a chance to prove him wrong. It is only after Sībawayhi's death, and thanks to his student al-ʾAḫfaš al-ʾAwsaṭ

1 On early grammatical activity before Sībawayhi and works contemporary to *al-Kitāb*, cf. Baalbaki 2013:95–97.

 | DOI:10.1163/9789004515895_006

(d. 215/830), that *al-Kitāb* gains its fame and status in the Arabic Linguistic Tradition (Luġawī *Marātib* 68; Ibn al-ʾAnbārī *Nuzha* 108; Qifṭī *ʾInbāh* II, 358–359).[2] Studies in the development of this tradition after Sībawayhi generally speak of the legacy of *al-Kitāb* which was never challenged by any of the later grammar works (cf. Versteegh 1997: 51; Carter 2004: 132–133; Baalbaki 2008: 1–2).

Sībawayhi's voluminous and comprehensive content became the main source for the works of later grammarians. The approach to analyzing this content, however, developed in a different direction than Sībawayhi's. Studies in the development of the Arabic Linguistic Tradition after *al-Kitāb* often speak of the attention that Sībawayhi gives to the meaning and form of the utterance in his analysis as compared to the attention paid only to form by his successors (cf. Baalbaki 2008: 170–195). Few studies speak of Sībawayhi's enunciative approach to linguistic analysis (cf. Bohas et al. 1990: 38–47). Some others focus on the pragmatic role he gives to the speaker to highlight his unique method of analysis (cf. Carter 2007; Marogy 2010). Quite often, the history of the Arabic Linguistic Tradition is looked at in phases where Sībawayhi represents the beginning phase and the era of innovation while the phase of later grammarians represents the era of rigidity and standardization (cf. Owens 1990: 54; Baalbaki 2013: 102–105). Generally speaking, all these studies speak of Sībawayhi's unique approach to linguistic analysis and agree that a shift in this approach happened after him. In this paper, I will look into the development of the Arabic Linguistic Tradition after Sībawayhi using the lens of the profile of the speaker, the source of the corpus of his book. I will show that Sībawayhi's speaker is the originator and the arbiter of the utterance, a profile that was not maintained in the writings of Sībawayhi's successors. The study will trace the profile of the speaker in selected works of the 3rd/9th and 4th/10th centuries to show how the profile of the speaker as a learner emerged, and how later it was established in the tradition. The study will pause at a unique reappearance of the profile of the speaker as an originator in the 4th/10th century, only to show that in spite of this reappearance, Sībawayhi's speaker never shows up again in the tradition and that the speaker's profile as a learner prevails in the Arabic Linguistic Tradition.

2 Also cf. Carter 2004:136–137; and Bernards 1997:5.

1 The Speaker as an Originator and Arbiter in Sībawayhi's *Kitāb*

The speaker, "the trusted Arab speaker" (*al-ʿarabī al-mawṯūqu bi-kalāmihi*) to be specific, is the main source of the *Kitāb*'s corpus.[3] Sībawayhi collates in his book an enormous body of the speech of Arabs which he describes, analyzes and explains.[4] His approach to linguistic analysis starts with an utterance where he begins by addressing the speaker of this utterance either directly (*ʾin qulta* "if you say" / *wa-ʿlam* "know (that)" / *ʾin ʾaradta ʾan taqūla* "if you want to say") or indirectly (*ka-ʾannahu qāla*, "as if he said" / *samiʿtu ʾaʿrābiyyan yaqūlu* "I heard an Arab saying" / *samiʿtu man yūṯaqu fī kalāmihim* "I heard those whose language is trusted"). Sībawayhi's discourse across his book consistently alternates between speaking to or about a speaker. He says, for example, explaining *al-nidāʾ* (vocative):

> And among what becomes dependent due to verbs that remain covert other than commanding and prohibiting [verbs] you saying *yā ʿabda llāhi* and all the vocative, as to *yā zaydu*, its cause will be seen in the chapter on vocative if God's willing, they [Arabs] deleted the verb because this [calling] is frequently used in speech and *yā* substituted for the utterance of the verb as if he [the speaker] says "*yā* I want *ʿabda llāhi*" so he deleted "I want" and *yā* substituted for it because if you say "*yā* someone" it is known that you want him. (*wa-mimmā yantaṣibu fī ġayri al-ʾamr wa-l-nahy ʿalā al-fiʿl al-matrūk ʾiẓhāruhu* ***qawluka*** *yā ʿabda llāhi wa-****l-nidāʾ kulluhu*** *wa-ʾammā yā zaydu fa-lahu ʿilla* ***satarāha fī bāb al-nidāʾ ʾin šāʾa allāh haḏafū*** *al-fiʿl li-kaṯrat istiʿmālihim hāḏā fī al-kalām wa-ṣāra yā badalan min al-lafẓ bi-l-fiʿl* ***ka-ʾannahu qāla*** *"yā ʾurīdu ʿabda llāhi" fa-ḥuḏifa "ʾurīdu" wa-ṣārat yā badalan minhā* ***li-ʾannaka ʾiḏā qulta*** *"yā fulān" ʿulima ʾannaka turīduhu*, Sībawayhi *Kitāb* I, 147 l. 8)

In this excerpt, Sībawayhi starts with a speaker's utterance (*qawluka*) *yā ʿabda llāhi* where *ʿabda llāhi* is dependent due to a deleted verb. To explain this utterance, Sībawayhi engages in a conversation with a 'hypothetically' present

3 Carter studies the sources of the corpus of *al-Kitāb* and identifies six categories of data that range from naturalness to normativeness: "The natural language of Bedouins, the artificial language of Arabic poetry, the inherently different language of the Qurʾān, the Traditions of the Prophet (hadith), made-up words and sentences" (Carter 2004:39). Whether the data is natural or made up, the speaker remains the main source of the corpus of *al-Kitāb* in any of the above-mentioned categories.

4 Cf. Levin 1994:204–208.

speaker. He first states to the speaker that the utterance is an example of the whole notion of *nidāʾ* (*al-nidāʾ kulluhu*). Then, he provides an example of the other forms of *nidāʾ*, mainly the form where the noun is independent. Sībawayhi promises to explain all these forms to the speaker in the coming chapter on *nidāʾ* (*sa-tarāha fī bāb al-nidāʾ ʾin šāʾa allāh*). He then starts analyzing the utterance and why *ʿabda llāhi* is dependent so he references the Arabs who delete (*ḥaḏafū*) the verb due to frequency of usage. He also calls on another "hypothetical" speaker (*ka-ʾannahu qāl*) to simulate saying the utterance without deleting the verb (*yā ʾurīdu ʿabda llāhi*). To further explain the utterance, Sībawayhi turns back to the first speaker (*li-ʾannaka ʾiḏā qulta*) and clarifies that the deleted verb is known by the recipient.

This excerpt is only one example of the style that Sībawayhi follows consistently across his book. He is in constant conversation with a "hypothetical" speaker who originates an utterance in a form that best conveys the intended meaning. In the above example, the speaker says *yā ʿabda llāhi* instead of saying *yā ʾurīdu ʿabda llāhi*. To explain the speaker's choice not to utter the verb *ʾurīdu*, Sībawayhi engages in a direct conversation with the speaker of the utterance as if the latter is present. He calls on another speaker (*ka-ʾannahu qāl*), who is not present, to simulate saying the utterance in its original form. Both speakers are originators of *al-nidāʾ* utterance: one of them originates the utterance in its primary form where the verb is overt, while the other, although aware of this "primary" form, decides to originate the *nidāʾ* utterance without the verb *ʾurīdu*. According to Sībawayhi, the speaker's choice to delete the verb stems from his awareness that *yā* is enough clue for the recipient to know that the speaker is calling *ʿabda llāhi*.[5] In many other cases of deletion across the book, the speaker chooses to omit a word or more from the utterance due to frequency of usage (*al-kaṯra fī al-istiʿmāl*)[6] or for the sake of brevity (*al-iḫtiṣār wa-l-ʾīǧāz*),[7] lightness (*taḫfīf*)[8] and/or sufficiency (*istiġnāʾ*).[9] Sībawayhi's speaker

5 In a study on this speaker's awareness, Baalbaki discusses the impact of the speaker's choices on the form of the utterance as in the use of the word *māḏā* ("what") (cf. Baalbaki 2007). If the speaker chooses to use *māḏā* as one word as in *māḏā raʾayta* ("what did you see"), then the answer would be in the dependent form *matāʿan ḥasanan* ("nice things"). While if the speaker chooses to separate *mā ḏā* as in *mā ḏā raʾayta*, then the answer would be in the independent *matāʿun ḥasanun* ("nice things") (cf. Baalbaki 2007:5).

6 For a detailed study on deletion in the *Kitāb* and its relation to the notions of frequency of usage, cf. Dayyeh 2012:75–87.

7 For examples of deletion due to brevity, cf. Sībawayhi *Kitāb* I, 105, 108–109, 117.

8 For examples of deletion due to lightness, cf. Sībawayhi *Kitāb* I, 84, 171, 211, 226–227, 231.

9 For examples of deletion due to sufficiency, cf. Sībawayhi *Kitāb* I, 33, 137–138, 171, 309–310.

appears in dealing with all of these notions as an originator of the form of the utterance that best conveys the intended meaning.

The speaker's profile as an originator also appears in Sībawayhi's treatment of the notion of *taqdīm wa-taʾḫīr* (hysteron-proteron) and *ittisāʿ* (latitude). I have studied these notions in previous articles and showed that they are linked to a speaker who is an originator of the utterance and thus enjoys an ability to change the form of the utterance to best convey the intended meaning (cf. Dayyeh 2019). Sībawayhi's speaker, for example, despite knowing that the norm for the subject is to precede the object as in saying *ḍaraba ʿabdu llāhi zaydan*, chooses to change the word order and says *ḍaraba zaydan ʿabdu llāhi* instead (cf. Sībawayhi *Kitāb* I, 14 l. 16). Sībawayhi explains that advancing a word in the utterance is due to the speaker's interest in uttering first what is important for the intended meaning:

> As if they [the Arabs] antepose that which is of more importance for them to show and that which they are more interested to show, even though both together are of importance and interest to them [the Arabs]. (*ka-ʾannahum ʾinnamā yuqaddimūna allaḏī bayānuhu ʾahammu lahum wa-hum bi-bayānihi ʾaʿnā wa-ʾin kānā ǧamīʿan yuhimmānihim wa-yaʿniyānihim*, Sībawayhi *Kitāb* I, 15 l. 1)

Sībawayhi's speaker may also decide to disrupt the norm and originate an utterance that unveils a disorder between its form and meaning as in saying "Ask the village" (*wa-sʾali l-qaryata*, Sībawayhi *Kitāb* I, 108 l. 14) where one does not ask the village but the people of the village or "I entered the cap in my head" (*ʾadḫaltu fī raʾsī l-qalansuwata*, Sībawayhi *Kitāb* I, 92 l. 10) where one enters the head in the cap and not the cap in the head. Sībawayhi clarifies that it is the speaker's drive for brevity (*al-ʾīǧāz wa-l-iḫtiṣār*) and his intent to expand the language (*li-ittisāʿihim fī al-kalām*, cf. Sībawayhi *Kitāb* I, 108 l. 6) that justifies originating such utterances.[10] Sībawayhi's speaker is clearly the sole originator and arbiter of the utterance and is revealed as such in Sībawayhi's approach to dealing with linguistic notions such as *ḥaḏf* (deletion), *taqdīm wa-taʾḫīr* (hysteron-proteron) and *ittisāʿ* (latitude). Such an approach to linguistic analysis, however, is not maintained by Sībawayhi's successors as will the next section show.

10 For a detailed study on the notion of *ittisāʿ* in Sībawayhi's *Kitāb*, cf. Dayyeh 2015.

2 The Emergence of the Speaker as a Learner in Mubarrad's *Muqtaḍab*

The scene in this section is set almost a century after Sībawayhi. Although the main player in this scene, ʾAbū al-ʿAbbās Muḥammad b. Yazīd al-Mubarrad, is of Basran origin, the scene itself is set in Baghdad where he resided, built a career as a grammarian and teacher, wrote his books—among which his famous *Muqtaḍab*—and died in 285/898 or 286/899 (cf. Zubaydī *Ṭabaqāt* 108–120; Ibn al-ʾAnbārī *Nuzha* 164–173). Baghdad, at the time, was growing as a center of intellectual and scholarly activity; and in this milieu, Mubarrad gained his reputation as an authority in the field of Arabic grammar (cf. Bernards 1997: 32–37). His grammar book *al-Muqtaḍab* stands out among the grammar works that we know about from the 3rd/9th century not only for its comprehensiveness since it includes almost all of the *Kitāb*'s corpus but also for its approach to linguistic analysis. Although Mubarrad adopts the *Kitāb*'s content, his approach reveals a more direct focus on *qiyās* (analogy) and *taʿlīl* (cause) and less attention to *samāʿ* (attested data). This shift in focus marks what Baalbaki refers to as a "transitory stage" in the development of the Arabic grammatical tradition between Sībawayhi and later grammarians (cf. Baalbaki 2008: 248). Mubarrad thus plays a major role in the development of the tradition after Sībawayhi.[11] Bernards explains that it is Mubarrad's approach to the *Kitāb* that contributes to its reception in the tradition and sets the trend that was followed by later grammarians (cf. Bernards 1997: 37).

In this section of the study, Mubarrad's approach to the *Kitāb* will be examined not from the perspective of his focus on *qiyās* (analogy) and *taʿlīl* (cause) but from the profile of the speaker as it appears in his *Muqtaḍab*. We have seen above that Sībawayhi's speaker is the sole arbiter and originator of the utterance. The question of whether a speaker of a similar profile continued to exist in Mubarrad's *Muqtaḍab* will now be examined.

It is evident to the reader of *Muqtaḍab* that Mubarrad follows a pattern in addressing the linguistic concepts and issues. He starts first by stating the grammatical concept that he intends to explain, then he offers examples of this concept to exhaust all related possibilities. To take the example of *nidāʾ*—which is discussed above and thus offers a good opportunity for comparing Sībawayhi's and Mubarrad's approaches to the same notion—Mubarrad starts by presenting *al-nidāʾ* "and know that if you called an annexed [noun] you

11 On the implications of this focus on the Arabic grammatical tradition, cf. Bohas et al. 1990:6–8, and Baalbaki 2008:235–244.

make it dependent due to a verb that is covert" (*wa-ʿlam ʾannaka ʾiḏā daʿawta muḍāfan naṣabtahu ʿalā al-fiʿl al-matrūk ʾiẓhāruhu*, Mubarrad *Muqtaḍab* IV, 202), then he gives an example of *nidāʾ* "like you saying *yā ʿabda llāhi*" (*wa-ḏālika qawluka yā ʿabda llāhi*), and explains this example "because *yā* substitutes for you saying 'I call *ʿabda llāhi* and I want [him]'" (*li-ʾanna yā badal min qawlika ʾadʿū ʿabda llāhi wa-ʾurīdu*, Mubarrad *Muqtaḍab* IV, 202), then he continues to explain why the noun is dependent:

> So if you say ʿAbd Allāh then the calling falls on ʿAbd Allāh so it is dependent because it is an object governed by your verb. (*fa-ʾiḏā qulta yā ʿabda llāhi fa-qad waqaʿa duʿāʾuka bi-ʿabdi llahi fa-ntaṣaba ʿalā ʾannahu mafʿūl taʿaddā ʾilayhi fiʿluka*, Mubarrad *Muqtaḍab* IV, 202)

Comparing this excerpt with Sībawayhi's excerpt on *nidāʾ*, one clearly finds that the content is very similar and that Mubarrad adopts Sībawayhi's explanation, examples, and terms. One will also notice an emerging interest in stating the *ʿāmil* (government) "so it is dependent because it is an object governed by your verb" (*fa-ntaṣaba ʿalā ʾannahu mafʿūl taʿadda ʾilayhi fiʿluka*, Mubarrad *Muqtaḍab* IV, 202) and no interest in justifying the deletion of the verb in a *nidāʾ* structure—the main focus of Sībawayhi's analysis—and thus the absence of notions such as frequency of usage and knowledge of the recipient which Sībawayhi uses in justifying the deletion of the verb of *nidāʾ*. More importantly, there is an absence of the speaker as the originator of the utterance. Mubarrad addresses a hypothetical speaker whose role is to receive the explanation and learn about *nidāʾ*. Unlike Sībawayhi's speaker who is active and has a role as an originator of the utterance, Mubarrad's speaker is passive and his role is restricted to learning from Mubarrad all about *nidāʾ*.

To further study the role of the speaker in *Muqtaḍab*, the notion of *taqdīm* and *taʾḫīr* (hysteron-proteron)—also discussed above—is worth examining for it offers another opportunity for comparing the profile of the speaker as used by Sībawayhi and Mubarrad (cf. Dayyeh 2019: 116–119). While changing of the word order in an utterance is in the hands of Sībawayhi's speaker (cf. above Sībawayhi *Kitāb* I, 15 l. 1), Mubarrad restricts the speaker's choice of changing the word order to when such a change does not affect the meaning of the utterance. In a chapter on bi-transitive verbs, Mubarrad addresses the advancing of the objects of the verbs of doubt and certainty and makes it clear that this change is only allowed if the meaning of the utterance remains clear "anteposing and postposing are appropriate when the utterance clarifies the meaning" (*wa ʾinnamā yaṣluḥu al-taqdīm wa-l-taʾḫīr ʾiḏā kāna al-kalām muwaḍḍiḥan ʿan al-maʿnā*, Mubarrad *Muqtaḍab* III, 95–96). In this chapter, Mubarrad engages the speaker in an exercise to train him on forming utterances using the verbs of doubt and certainty:

> If you say I believe Zayd [is] your brother and he [a speaker] tells you: turn yourself into a predicate you say the one who believes Zayd [is] your brother [is] yourself, and if he [a speaker] says: turn Zayd into a predicate, you say Zayd is the one I believe is your brother. (*fa-ʾiḏā qulta "ẓanantu zaydan ʾaḫāka" fa-qāla laka "ʾaḫbir ʿan nafsika" qulta "al-ẓānnu zaydan ʾaḫāka nafsuka" fa-ʾiḏā qāla "ʾaḫbir ʿan zayd" qulta "al-ẓānnuhu ʾanā ʾaḫāka zayd"*, cf. Mubarrad *Muqtaḍab* III, 95)

The exercise goes on and on challenging the speaker to construct more variations of the same utterance. Mubarrad uses this hypothetical dialogue to offer an exhaustive list of all the possible structures of the utterance and to train the speaker on forming the various possibilities.

Such exercises where Mubarrad is training the speaker or listing all the possible forms of the utterances that the speaker may or may not use are frequent in *Muqtaḍab*. One may look at any excerpt to find that Mubarrad is adamant at relaying to the speaker every detail related to the linguistic concept he is explaining. The speaker's profile as a learner emerges in *Muqtaḍab* and its profile as an originator fades away. In fact, the term 'learner' is used explicitly by Mubarrad in the heading of some chapters which he dedicates to assessing the speaker/learner "lengthy [linguistic] issues for assessing the learner" (*masāʾil ṭiwāl yumtaḥanu fīhā al-mutaʿallim*, Mubarrad *Muqtaḍab* II, 62–64 and IV, 59–71). In these chapters, Mubarrad fabricates a very complicated sentence and asks the speaker to find the operant in every word in it to test his ability and learning of grammar. The emergence of the speaker as a learner marks a shift in the development of the grammatical tradition after Sībawayhi to a more didactic approach. Sībawayhi's speaker who is an originator disappears with Mubarrad and the speaker/learner emerges. As mentioned before, Mubarrad's approach to *Kitāb* sets the trend that was followed by later grammarians. The emergence of the profile of the speaker as a learner indeed sets the trend and the speaker only appears as a learner in the works of later grammarians.

3 The Establishing of the Role of the Speaker as a Learner in Ibn al-Sarrāǧ's *ʾUṣūl*

The scene in this section continues in Baghdad; towards the end of the 3rd/9th century and at the beginning of the 4th/10th. The player in this scene is Mubarrad's student ʾAbū Bakr Muḥammad b. Sahl Ibn al-Sarrāǧ (d. 316/929), the writer of *al-ʾUṣūl fī al-naḥw*, a book on the foundations (*ʾuṣūl*) of Arabic grammar. Biographers speak to the importance of *ʾUṣūl*, mainly because of its systematic arrangement of Sībawayhi's grammar (cf. Zubaydī *Ṭabaqāt* 122–125; Ibn al-ʾAnbārī *Nuzha* 186–187). Ibn al Sarrāǧ was able to capture the foundations of grammar from *Kitāb* and collate them in an organized and systematic way. In fact, he was able to consolidate and standardize the grammar activity of the previous years (cf. Owens 1990: 54). Owens considers Ibn al-Sarrāǧ's *ʾUṣūl* the culmination of the previous diverse linguistic ideas and the beginning of a new direction in the development of the Arabic grammatical tradition (cf. Owens 1990: 243).

ʾUṣūl indeed represents the start of a new phase in the Arabic grammatical tradition. Apart from setting the trend for the study of *ʾuṣūl* (foundations, cf. Baalbaki 2013: 103), it is in *ʾUṣūl* that the speaker's role as a learner is established. Ibn al-Sarrāǧ introduces his book with a definition of grammar in which he explicitly differentiates between two profiles of speakers: the originator and the learner "It is a discipline that the later [speakers] deduced by examining the speech of Arabs in order to grasp the purposes intended by the originators of the language" (*wa-huwa ʿilm istaḫrağahu al-mutaqaddimūn fīhi min istiqrāʾ kalām al-ʿarab ḥattā waqafū minhu ʿalā al-ġaraḍ allaḏī qaṣadahu al-mubtadiʾūn bi-hāḏihi al-luġa*, Ibn al-Sarrāǧ *ʾUṣūl* I, 35). There are thus two speakers: a speaker who originates the language and a speaker who learns the language of this originator. To further elaborate, Ibn al-Sarrāǧ explains that there are two types of *ʿilla* (cause) in *ʿilm al-naḥw* (science of grammar): a 'direct *ʿilla*' that is needed to acquire the language, like saying "every subject is nominative" (*kullu fāʿilin marfūʿ*) and *ʿillat al-ʿilla* (the cause of cause), that is meant to unveil the wisdom of the Arabic language, like explaining why the subject is nominative (cf. Ibn al-Sarrāǧ *ʾUṣūl* I, 35). Ibn al-Sarrāǧ states that in his book he will focus on the *ʿilla* that helps the speaker learn the language only:

> And my intent for this book is only to mention the *ʿilla* (cause) that, if followed, their [the Arab's] speech can be accessed, and to mention what is foundational and common because it is a book that is [intended to be] brief. (*wa-ġaraḍī min hāḏā al-kitāb ḏikr al-ʿilla allatī ʾiḏā iṭṭaradat wuṣila bihā ʾilā kalāmihim faqaṭ wa-ḏikr al-ʾuṣūl wa-l-šaʾiʿ li-ʾannahu kitāb ʾīǧāz*, Ibn al-Sarrāǧ *ʾUṣūl* I, 36)

After all, to him grammar is intended for the speaker to learn the speech of Arabs: "Grammar is intended for the speaker to imitate, if he learns it [Grammar], the speech of Arabs" (*al-naḥw ʾinnamā ʾurīda bihi ʾan yanḥuwa al-*

mutakallim ʾiḏā taʿallamahu kalām al-ʿarab, Ibn al Sarrāǧ *ʾUṣūl* I, 35), and for that he chose a style of writing that is comprehensible by the speaker/learner "and since I did not create this book for the expert to the exclusion of the learner, I had to mention what is handy to the learner" (*wa-lammā kuntu lam ʾaʿmal hāḏā al-kitāb li-l-ʿālim dūn al-mutaʿallim iḥtaǧtu ʾan ʾaḏkura mā yuqarribu ʿalā al-mutaʿallim*, Ibn al Sarrāǧ *ʾUṣūl* I, 37).

The speaker/learner is thus the target of Ibn al-Sarrāǧ's book on the foundations of grammar. Consequently, the speaker appears throughout the book as a learner who is told what is permissible and not permissible in forming the utterance. In dealing with the notion of *taqdīm wa-taʾḫīr* for example, Ibn al-Sarrāǧ lists thirteen cases where the speaker is not allowed to change the word order of the utterance (cf. Ibn al-Sarrāǧ *ʾUṣūl* II, 222–223 and Dayyeh 2019: 119–121). In explaining *ittisāʿ*, he completely ignores the relation between the notion and the speakers' ability to originate an utterance that disrupts the norm and simply presents *ittisāʿ* as a type of deletion (cf. Ibn al-Sarrāǧ *ʾUṣūl* II, 255–256 and Dayyeh 2015: 74–75). Even when Ibn al-Sarrāǧ adopts Sībawayhi's content and *šawāhid* (examples) verbatim, as the case in his chapter on *ʾiḍmār* (suppression), the speaker is present not as an originator but as a learner who is offered an exhaustive list of all the *ʾiḍmār* cases to learn them (cf. Ibn al-Sarrāǧ *ʾUṣūl* II, 247–254).[12] The same can be said about his approach to the linguistic concepts in his *ʾUṣūl*. After establishing the speaker as a learner in his introduction, Ibn al-Sarrāǧ follows a didactic approach that offers the speaker a comprehensive explanation of the foundations of grammar and exhaustive lists of what is permissible and not permissible within these foundations.

Addressing the speaker as a learner and following a didactic approach to linguistic analysis became the trend in the Arabic grammatical tradition from the time of Ibn al-Sarrāǧ onwards. A quick survey of the grammarians' work in the following centuries shows that they produced books for teaching grammar (cf. Baalbaki 2013: 105). These books were intended to provide the learner with *šurūḥ* (commentaries), *ʾīḍāḥāt* (clarifications), and *muḫtaṣarāt* or *mūǧazāt* (summaries) of the Arabic grammar. Some of the books were dedicated to *taqrīb al-naḥw* ("making it accessible/comprehensible") to the learner, and some to help memorize its rules. Ibn Mālik's (d. 672/1274) *ʾAlfiyya*, a poem that presents the grammar rules in rhyming verses, is an example of the many innovative ways that the grammarians came up with to make it easy for the learner to study and remember the grammar rules. The speaker's profile as a learner

12 On the relation between *ʾiḍmār* and the notion of frequency of usage in *ʾUṣūl*, cf. Dayyeh 2012:89–90.

becomes the target and focus of what constitutes the Arabic grammatical tradition. The speaker as an originator never appears again in this mainstream tradition.

It is worth noting that it does not appear in the "*taʿlīl* track" of the tradition either. This track is believed to have started with Zağğāğī (d. 337/949), and particularly with his book *al-ʾĪḍāḥ fī ʿilal al-naḥw*, a book that is dedicated to unearthing the causes of certain grammatical concepts and issues. In the introduction, Zağğāğī claims that his book is the first of its kind because it focuses—unlike the numerous books on the 'foundations' of grammar (*al-ʾuṣūl*)—on the 'causes' (*ʿilal*) and the 'secrets of grammar' (*ʾasrār al-naḥw*) (cf. Zağğāğī *ʾĪḍāḥ* 38; cf. Suleiman 1999: 43–45). Regardless whether Zağğağī's claim is true or not, *ʾĪḍāḥ* marks the beginning of the development of a series of books on *taʿlīl* in the centuries to come, thus establishing a branch in the Arabic Linguistic Tradition concerned with revealing the causes and secrets of grammar. In the introduction of *ʾĪḍāḥ*, Zağğāğī states that his book is intended for the learner, however a higher level of learners "and whose level in this discipline is up to it" (*wa-kānat martabatuhu min hāḏā al-ʿilm qad tanāhat bihi ʾilayhi*, Zağğāğī *ʾĪḍāḥ* 39). The learner, the advanced learner, is thus the target of Zağğāğī's *ʾĪḍāḥ*.[13] In fact, the advanced learner becomes the target of later works on *taʿlīl*. A glance at some of these works, such as Ibn al-ʾAnbārī's (d. 577/1181) *ʾAsrār al-ʿarabiyya* and *Lumaʿ al-ʾadilla*, and Suyūṭī's (d. 911/1505) *al-Iqtirāḥ fī ʿilm ʾuṣūl al-naḥw*, confirms that these books are intended for the learner, particularly one who has acquired the foundations of grammar and is ready for receiving a higher level of knowledge. After all, using *taʿlīl* in the process of teaching, as Suleiman suggests, "was seen as a kind of mental training, whose aim was, among other things, to develop the learner's ability to think logically and in abstract fashion" (Suleiman 1999: 210).

It is worth mentioning in this context that this level of abstraction in the teaching and learning of the language contributed to the complexity of grammar, a fact that caused Ibn Maḍāʾ al-Qurṭubī (d. 592/1196) to write his *al-Radd ʿalā al-nuḥāt* in which he refutes the grammarians' approach to teaching the language that is based on *taʿlīl* and *qiyās*. The level of abstraction and complexity resulting from such an approach is, according to Ibn Maḍāʾ, not necessary for the learning of the language. For that, his book is intended to discard all that

13 Suleiman highlights the interaction between the *taʿlīl* discipline and pedagogy. He suggests that Zağğāğī's three types of *ʿilla*—*ʿilla taʿlīmiyya* (pedagogical), *qiyāsiyya* (analogical) and *ğadaliyya-naẓariyya* (argumentational-theoretical)—reflect three levels of language learning: a beginner level with the *ʿilla taʿlīmiyya*, an intermediate level with *ʿilla qiyāsiyya* and an advanced level with *ʿilla ğadaliyya-naẓariyya* (cf. Suleiman 1999:210).

is not necessary for the grammarians to the sake of simplifying the learning of Arabic grammar (cf. Ibn Maḍāʾ *Radd* 76).

It is clear that the focus of the Arabic Linguistic Tradition from the 4th/10th century onwards is the speaker learner. The establishing of this profile in Ibn al-Sarrāǧ's *ʾUṣūl* seems to have had a huge impact on the development of the tradition. After Ibn al-Sarrāǧ, the speaker's profile as a learner dominates the tradition whereas the speaker's profile as an originator or arbiter fades away. An attempt at presenting the speaker as originator, however, appears in Ibn Ǧinnī's (d. 392/1002) *Ḫaṣāʾiṣ* as will be discussed in the following section.

4 The Appearance of the Wise, Courageous Speaker in Ibn Ǧinnī's *Ḫaṣāʾiṣ*

The scene in this section is set in the city of Mosul in the 4th/10th century. The player in this scene is ʾAbū al-Fatḥ ʿUṯmān b. Ǧinnī, a grammarian of a unique style and approach (cf. Ibn al-ʾAnbārī *Nuzha* 244–246; Qifṭī *ʾInbāh* II, 385–386; Suyūṭī *Buġya* II, 132). His most famous book, *Ḫaṣāʾiṣ*, stands out in the tradition for it is not a conventional book of grammar but rather an encyclopedia of language topics intended to prove "the nobility of the language of Arabs and its distinguished features of wisdom" (*šaraf luġat al-ʿarab wa-tamāyuzuha bi-ḫaṣāʾiṣ al-ḥikma*, Ibn Ǧinnī *Ḫaṣāʾiṣ* I, 1). The book thus does not focus on grammar, yet employs the study of grammatical notions and concepts to unveil the special features (*ḫaṣāʾiṣ*) of the Arabic language.

The first and most important feature is "wisdom" (*ḥikma*). As mentioned earlier, Ibn Ǧinnī dedicates his book to proving this distinguished feature of the Arabic language (cf. Ibn Ǧinnī *Ḫaṣāʾiṣ* I, 1). To him, the wisdom of the Arabic language goes back to the wisdom of its originators. In a scene on the creation of the language, Ibn Ǧinnī refers to a first group of wise speakers who came together and named the things around them:

> And this is as if two or three and more wise men come together and the need arises to identify the known things so they create a feature and a name for each one when it [the name] is mentioned the named thing is known so that it is differentiated from others. (*wa-ḏālika ka-ʾan yaǧtamiʿa ḥakīmān ʾaw ṯalāṯa fa-ṣāʿidan fa-yaḥtāǧū ʾilā al-ʾibāna ʿan al-ʾašyāʾ al-maʿlūmāt fa-yaḍaʿū li-kulli wāḥid minhā simatan wa-lafẓan ʾiḏā ḏukira ʿurifa bihi musamman li-yamtāza ʿan ġayrihi*, Ibn Ǧinnī *Ḫaṣāʾiṣ* I, 44)

The scene continues and shows the process by which the wise speakers have created these names: when they see a human being, for example, the first speakers point their fingers towards him and say *ʾinsān ʾinsān ʾinsān* ("human human human"), other speakers hear the word, learn it and every time the word *ʾinsān* is used the speakers would know that it means a human being (cf. Ibn Ǧinnī *Ḫaṣāʾiṣ* I, 44).

The scene is surely hypothetical and Ibn Ǧinnī fabricates it for the sake of proving that 'Arabic' is a wise language created by wise speakers. A close look at the scene, however, shows that there are two groups of speakers: the originators of the language and the learners of that language. According to Ibn Ǧinnī, both groups are wise and he never loses a chance throughout his book to prove their wisdom. To him, the originators' wisdom is evident in their awareness of the notions of 'lightness' (*ḫiffa*) and 'heaviness' (*ṯiqal*) and consequently in their creation of a language that is 'light' for the speaker to utter (cf. Ibn Ǧinnī *Ḫaṣāʾiṣ* I, 64 and Suleiman 1999: 98–103). It is also evident in the fact that they invented verbs made up of letters whose sounds reflect the intended actions like saying *qaḍama* "chew" for dry food and *ḫaḍama* "chew" for soft food:

> And that is for the strength of the letter *qāf* and the weakness of the letter *ḫāʾ* so they [the originators] gave the stronger sound to the stronger action and the weaker sound to the weaker action. (*wa-ḏālika li-quwwat al-qāf wa-ḍuʿf al-ḫāʾ fa-ǧaʿalū al-ṣawt al-ʾaqwā li-l-fiʿl al-ʾaqwā wa-l-ṣawt al-ʾaḍʿaf li-l-fiʿl al-ʾaḍʿaf*, Ibn Ǧinnī *Ḫaṣāʾiṣ* I, 65)

Like the originators, the speakers who learn from them are also wise. They enjoy an intuitive ability to learn the language from the originators (cf. Ibn Ǧinnī *Ḫaṣāʾiṣ* I, 239). Ibn Ǧinnī narrates many stories which show that the Arab speakers know their language intuitively (cf. Ibn Ǧinnī *Ḫaṣāʾiṣ* I, 239–241). In some of these stories Ibn Ǧinnī intentionally tries to lead the speaker to make a mistake in order to test his knowledge of the language. He asks a Bedouin, for example, to give him the plural of *dukkān* "shop", and the Bedouin says *dakākīn* "shops", then he asks for the plural of *qurṭān* and *sirḥān* and the Bedouin answers *qarāṭīn* and *sarāḥīn*, then he asks about the plural of *ʿuṯmān* and the Bedouin replies *ʿuṯmānūn*. Ibn Ǧinnī asks him why he does not say *ʿaṯāmīn* and the Bedouin immediately replies "what is this ʿAṯāmīn, have you seen anyone saying something not belonging to his language, by God I will never say this word [ʿAṯāmīn]" (*ʾayšin ʿaṯāmīn, ʾa-raʾayta ʾinsānan yatakallamu bimā laysa min luġatihi, wa-llāhi lā ʾaqūluhā ʾabadan*, Ibn Ǧinnī *Ḫaṣāʾiṣ* I, 242).

The speakers/learners thus know their language as set by the originators and follow its rules faithfully (Ibn Ǧinnī *Ḫaṣāʾiṣ* I, 238–242). They are, however, originators too and allowed to go by what is frequently used even if it does not follow the *qiyās* (analogy). Ibn Ǧinnī distinguishes in his book between four types of *kalām* (speech): that which is frequently used and follows *qiyās*, that which is frequently used but does not follow *qiyās*, that which is not frequently used but follows *qiyās*, and lastly that which is neither frequently used nor follows *qiyās* (cf. Ibn Ǧinnī *Ḫaṣāʾiṣ* I, 97–99). He states that the first type of speech is what the speaker should utter. However, in the three other cases, he favors the speech that is frequently used even if it does not follow *qiyās* (cf. Ibn Ǧinnī *Ḫaṣāʾiṣ* I, 97–99). Ibn Ǧinnī clarifies that the speaker can change that which is frequently used (cf. Ibn Ǧinnī *Ḫaṣāʾiṣ* I, 124). In fact, he believes that the Arab speakers visualize the language in their minds before uttering it and know ahead of time that a certain utterance will be frequently used so they change it even before it is uttered (cf. Ibn Ǧinnī *Ḫaṣāʾiṣ* II, 31–32). In short, Arab speakers, whether originators or learners, are wise and their wisdom is evident in the wisdom of the language they originate.

Arab speakers are also courageous and brave. In a chapter titled "*šaǧāʿat al-ʿarabiyya*", Ibn Ǧinnī discusses five notions that prove the courageous feature of the language: *ḥaḏf* (deletion), *ziyāda* (augment), *taqdīm wa-taʾḫīr* (hysteron-proteron), *al-ḥaml ʿalā al-maʿnā* (semantic approximation), and *taḥrīf* (morphological changes) (cf. Ibn Ǧinnī *Ḫaṣāʾiṣ* II, 360). In explaining each notion, the Arab speaker is presented as courageously changing the utterance either by deleting parts of it, changing its word order, adding prefixes and suffixes to certain words, changing the morphological structure of some words or even not following the syntactical rules for the sake of meaning. Ibn Ǧinnī explains these notions and shows the boundaries within which the speakers' courage may be exercised. Speakers may not delete a word if there are no contextual clues that would help the listener understand the utterance (cf. Ibn Ǧinnī *Ḫaṣāʾiṣ* II, 371). They may not change the word order or the form of a word or a certain utterance either if the change is not accepted by *qiyās* or justified by frequent usage (cf. Ibn Ǧinnī *Ḫaṣāʾiṣ* II, 382). Ibn Ǧinnī's explanation of the boundaries is not, however, intended to restrict the speakers' courage but to provide further evidence of their wisdom. These explanations show that the courage of the Arab speaker is not irrational and that it is governed by a wisdom that ensures the wisdom of the Arabic language and maintains it.

The wise, courageous speaker also entertains the ability to expand the language. In various chapters in *Ḫaṣāʾiṣ*, the speaker's contribution to expanding the Arabic language is present in the ability to change the form and/or the meaning of the utterance (cf. Ibn Ǧinnī *Ḫaṣāʾiṣ* I, 18, 23, 274–275, 330, 395). Ibn Ǧinnī speaks about a certain power in the Arab speakers' emotions and imagination which allows them to change the form of an utterance to create new meanings (cf. Ibn Ǧinnī *Ḫaṣāʾiṣ* I, 213–215). He also links this power to the courage of the speaker (cf. Ibn Ǧinnī *Ḫaṣāʾiṣ* II, 447). The courage of the speaker combined with wisdom constantly originates new forms and meanings and contributes to *saʿat al-ʿarabiyya* (latitude), another unique feature of the Arabic language.

Al-ḥikma "wisdom", *al-šaǧāʿa* "courage" and *al-saʿa* "latitude" are three features of the Arabic language that Ibn Ǧinnī presents in his *Ḫaṣāʾiṣ*. A closer look at these features shows that they are in fact features of the speaker of Arabic. Across his book, Ibn Ǧinnī attempts to show that the Arab speaker is a wise, courageous speaker who contributes to the expansion of the Arabic language. The profile of the speaker as an originator thus appears across the *Ḫaṣāʾiṣ*. This profile emerges in Sībawayhi's *Kitāb* and fades away, but later reappears in Ibn Ǧinnī's *Ḫaṣāʾiṣ* in the form of a wise, courageous speaker. While Sībawayhi's speaker appears in the *Kitāb* to explain and analyze the linguistic concepts and issues, Ibn Ǧinnī's speaker appears in his *Ḫaṣāʾiṣ* to prove the nobility and wisdom of the Arabic language. After all, the two books serve two different purposes. It is worth mentioning here that the profile of the speaker as an originator in the *Ḫaṣāʾiṣ* faces the same fate as Sībawayhi's speaker, in ultimately not being taken up by the tradition. Despite the reappearance of the speaker originator in the *Ḫaṣāʾiṣ*, the speaker learner profile which emerges in the *Muqtaḍab* and is established in the *ʾUṣūl* continues to be the target and focus of the Arabic Linguistic Tradition afterwards. It is still the target and focus of present-day language books!

Bibliography

Primary Sources

Ibn al-ʾAnbārī, *Nuzha* = ʾAbū al-Barakāt ʿAbd al-Raḥmān b. Muḥammad al-ʾAnbārī, *Nuzhat al-ʾalibbāʾ fī ṭabaqāt al-ʾudabāʾ*. Ed. by ʾIbrāhīm al-Sāmarrāʾī. Baġdād: Maktabat al-ʾAndalus, 1970.

Ibn Ǧinnī, *Ḫaṣāʾiṣ* = ʾAbū al-Fatḥ ʿUṯmān b. Ǧinnī, *al-Ḫaṣāʾiṣ*. Ed. by ʿAbd al-Ḥamīd Hindāwī. Bayrūt: Dār al-kutub al-ʿilmiyya, 3 vol., 2013.

Ibn Maḍāʾ, *Radd* = ʾAbū al-ʿAbbās ʾAḥmad b. ʿAbd al-Raḥmān Ibn Maḍāʾ al-Laḫmī, *al-Radd ʿalā al-nuḥāt*. Ed. by Šawqī Ḍayf. Al-Qāhira: Dār al-maʿārif, 3rd ed., 1988.

Ibn al-Sarrāǧ, *ʾUṣūl* = ʾAbū Bakr Muḥammad b. Sahl, *al-ʾUṣūl fī al-naḥw*. Ed. by ʿAbd al-Ḥusayn al-Fatlī. Bayrūt: Muʾassasat al-risāla, 3 vol., 2015.

Luġawī, *Marātib* = ʾAbū al-Ṭayyib ʿAbd al-Raḥmān b. ʿAlī al-Luġawī, *Marātib al-naḥwiyyīn*. Ed. by Muḥammad ʾAbū al-Faḍl ʾIbrāhīm. Al-Qāhira: Maṭbaʿat nahḍat Miṣr, 1955.

Mubarrad, *Muqtaḍab* = Muḥammad b. Yazīd, *al-Muqtaḍab*. Bayrūt: ʿĀlam al-kutub, 4 vol., 2010.

Qifṭī, *ʾInbāh* = Ǧamāl al-Dīn ʾAbū al-Ḥasan ʿAlī b. Yūsuf al-Qifṭī, *ʾInbāh al-ruwāt ʿalā ʾanbāh al-nuḥāt*. Ed. by Muḥammad ʾAbū al-Faḍl ʾIbrāhīm. Al-Qāhira & Bayrūt: Dār al-fikr al-ʿarabī & Muʾassasat al-kutub al-ṯaqāfiyya, 4 vol., 1986.

Sībawayhi, *Kitāb* = ʾAbū Bišr ʿAmr b. ʿUṯmān Sībawayhi, *Kitāb Sībawayhi*. Ed. Būlāq. Al-Qāhira: al-Maṭbaʿat al-kubrā al-ʾamīriyya, 2 vol., 1316–1317/1898–1900.

Suyūṭī, *Buġya* = Ǧalāl al-Dīn ʾAbū al-Faḍl ʿAbd al-Raḥmān b. ʾAbī Bakr al-Suyūṭī, *Buġyat al-wuʿāt fī ṭabaqāt al-luġawiyyīn wa-l-nuḥāt*. Ed. by Muḥammad ʾAbū al-Faḍl ʾIbrāhīm. Al-Qāhira: ʿĪsā al-Bābī al-Ḥalabī, 2 vol., 1964–1965.

Zaǧǧāǧī, *ʾĪḍāḥ* = ʾAbū al-Qāsim ʿAbd al-Raḥmān b. ʾIsḥāq al-Zaǧǧāǧī, *al-ʾĪḍāḥ fī ʿilal al-naḥw*. Ed. by Māzin Mubārak. Bayrūt: Dār al-nafāʾis, 1974.

Zubaydī, *Ṭabaqāt* = ʾAbū Bakr Muḥammad b. al-Ḥasan al-Zubaydī al-ʾAndalusī, *Ṭabaqāt al-naḥwiyyīn wa-l-luġawiyyīn*. Ed. by Muḥammad ʾAbū al-Faḍl ʾIbrāhīm. Al-Qāhira: Maṭbaʿat al-ḫānǧī, 1954.

Secondary Sources

Baalbaki, Ramzi. 2007. "Inside the Speaker's Mind: Speaker's Awareness as Arbiter of Usage in the Arab Grammatical Theory". *Approaches to Arabic Linguistics: Presented to Kees Versteegh on the Occasion of His Sixtieth Birthday*, ed. by Everhard Ditters & Harold Motzki, 3–23. Leiden & Boston: Brill, coll. "Studies in Semitic Languages and Linguistics" 49.

Baalbaki, Ramzi. 2008. *The Legacy of the* Kitāb: *Sībawayhi's Analytical Methods within the Context of the Arabic Grammatical Tradition*. Leiden & Boston: Brill, coll. "Studies in Semitic Languages and Linguistics" 51.

Baalbaki, Ramzi. 2013. "Arabic Linguistic Tradition I: *Naḥw* and *ṣarf*". *The Oxford Handbook of Arabic Linguistics*, ed. by Jonathan Owens, 92–114. New York: Oxford University Press.

Bernards, Monique. 1997. *Changing Traditions: Al-Mubarrad's Refutation of Sībawayh and Subsequent Reception of the* Kitāb. Leiden & Boston: Brill, coll. "Studies in Semitic Languages and Linguistics" 23.

Bohas, Georges, Jean-Patrick Guillaume, and Djamel Eddine Kouloughli. 1990. *The Arabic Linguistic Tradition*. London & New York: Routledge, coll. "Arabic Thought and Culture".

Carter, Michael G. 2004. *Sībawayhi*. Oxford: Oxford University Press, coll. "Makers of Islamic Civilization".

Carter, Michael G. 2007. "Pragmatics and Contractual Language in Early Arabic Grammar and Legal Theory". *Approaches to Arabic Linguistics: Presented to Kees Versteegh on the Occasion of His Sixtieth Birthday*, ed. by Everhard Ditters & Harold Motzki, 25–44. Leiden & Boston: Brill, coll. "Studies in Semitic Languages and Linguistics" 49.

Dayyeh, Hanadi. 2012. "The Relation between Frequency of Usage and Deletion in Sībawayhi's *Kitāb*". *The Foundations of Arabic Linguistics. Sībawayhi and Early Arabic Grammatical Theory*, ed. by Amal E. Marogy, 75–98. Leiden & Boston: Brill, coll. "Studies in Semitic Languages and Linguistics" 65.

Dayyeh, Hanadi. 2015. "*Ittisāʿ* in Sībawayhi's *Kitāb*: A Semantic *ʿilla* for Disorders in Meaning and Form". *The Foundations of Arabic Linguistics II. Kitāb Sībawayhi: Interpretation and Transmission*, ed. by Amal E. Marogy & Kees Versteegh, 66–80. Leiden & Boston: Brill, coll. "Studies in Semitic Languages and Linguistics" 83.

Dayyeh, Hanadi. 2019. "The Notion of *taqdīm wa-taʾḫīr* in *al-Kitāb* and Its Development in the Arabic Grammatical Tradition until the 4th/10th Century". *The Foundations of Arabic Linguistics IV. The Evolution of Theory*, ed. by Manuela E.B. Giolfo & Kees Versteegh, 106–122. Leiden & Boston: Brill, coll. "Studies in Semitic Languages and Linguistics" 97.

Levin, Aryeh. 1981. "The Grammatical Terms *Al-Musnad, Al-Musnad ʾIlayhi* and *Al-ʾIsnād*". *Journal of the American Oriental Society* 101/2. 145–165.

Levin, Aryeh. 1994. "Sībawayhi's Attitude to Spoken Language". *Jerusalem Studies in Arabic and Islam* 17. 204–243.

Marogy, Amal E. 2010. *Kitāb Sībawayhi: Syntax and Pragmatics*. Leiden & Boston: Brill, coll. "Studies in Semitic Languages and Linguistics" 56.

Owens, Jonathan. 1990. *Early Arabic Grammatical Theory: Heterogeneity and Standardization*. Amsterdam & Philadelphia: John Benjamins.

Suleiman, Yasir. 1999. *The Arabic Grammatical Tradition: A Study in Taʿlīl*. Edinburgh: Edinburgh University Press.

Versteegh, Kees. 1997. *Landmarks in Linguistic Thought III: The Arabic Linguistic Tradition*. London & New York: Routledge.

CHAPTER 5

Referencing Sībawayhi: The Reception of the *Kitāb* as a Source

Simona Olivieri

Introduction

In the Arabic linguistic tradition, there is perhaps no other book equal to the *Kitāb Sībawayhi*. This work, dated to the 2nd/8th century, rendered a systematized presentation of the grammatical structure of the Arabic language, and most—if not all—we know of the linguistic theorizations on Classical Arabic is summarily presented therein.

Nonetheless, it is not only the accurate description of the language or the level of linguistic speculation achieved that make this work fundamental for the tradition, but it is also the noticeable impact it had on the Arabic linguistic sciences that must be measured.

Considering the data and methods accounted for in his work, Sībawayhi's (d. 180/796?) approach is primarily descriptivist (Carter 1973: 146), and rather different from the prescriptivist methods that we may find in later traditions. Furthermore, the data presented in the *Kitāb* together with the discussions thereupon laid the foundations for the upcoming tradition of grammatical and linguistic studies that developed in the following centuries.

The *Kitāb* and its data are ultimately important for a number of reasons. To begin with, the *Kitāb* is in itself an exceptional result of scholarly efforts to describe the linguistic system of Arabic, accomplished by means of a meticulous collection of data, which come alongside the author's reasoning. Secondly, the *Kitāb* represents a precious witness of 2nd/8th century grammatical literature and allows us to consider how the matter would be approached by Arabic scholars of the time. But despite Sībawayhi's invaluable contribution to the discipline, his *Kitāb* is not a major specimen of "organization and clarity of style" (Owens 2006: 87), due, for instance, to the fact that technical terms do not come along with an explanation, and that fundamental issues are oftentimes distributed throughout the text, mostly lacking clear elucidation.

Sībawayhi's work is in fact rather obscure especially in certain passages, and this consequently led to the production of a number of works aimed to further elucidate the author's theorization. Nevertheless, the lack of exhaustive

 | DOI:10.1163/9789004515895_007

explanation of certain matters, as well as the ambiguity that accompanies the presentation of others, eventually produced a number of readings of the arguments in the *Kitāb*. Such an issue is of ultimate interest insofar as Sībawayhi's words have been received as the foundations of most of the linguistic arguments in the Arabic tradition, but ambiguity in the text may have also led to peculiar misinterpretations.

This contribution finally aims to provide an overview of the matter, presenting the grounds for the text's transmission as well as for the credit bestowed on both Sībawayhi and his *Kitāb*.

1 The Background

Sībawayhi's contribution to the development of the grammatical theories is of invaluable importance, despite the fact that the theorizations in the *Kitāb* did not merge into a fully-fledged model, which we instead find at a later stage. It is in fact in the 4th/10th century, with the *Kitāb al-ʾUṣūl* by Ibn al-Sarrāǧ (d. 316/929), that grammatical theories find their systematization in a categorical model (cf. Ghersetti 2017). As argued by Bohas, Guillaume, and Kouloughli:

> Sībawayhi had, in fact, laid down the basic rules and methods of grammar, while the later grammarians' contribution consisted only in expounding his theory in a more explicit and systematic form, or in finding new applications for it. Such a linear conception of the history of the grammatical tradition led, in fact, to many misrepresentations and false problems.
>
> BOHAS et al. 1990: 5

The systematization of a model was evidently not the main outcome of the *Kitāb*. Sībawayhi worked instead toward a thorough description of the language, the systematization of which would be accomplished only later on. However, his description remains a major asset for coeval as well as non-coeval studies, for the *Kitāb*, with its descriptive approach and aim, returns a fairly accurate picture of both sources and data deployed (cf. Carter 2004). The *Kitāb*, in fact, does not present Sībawayhi's theorizations only, but rather returns the outcomes of the linguistic discussions of the first and second centuries of the Islamic era, and thus represents a precious witness of linguistic arguments, presented alongside Sībawayhi's interpretations and explanations.

Both its contents and structure finally make it a substantial milestone in the whole tradition, for its being representative of a wider linguistic debate. Besides the evident importance in terms of linguistic description of the classical language, the *Kitāb* is then also an invaluable specimen from a historical viewpoint, for it allows us to obtain some little information on the stages of the Arabic linguistic tradition before Sībawayhi (cf. Carter 2004). Interestingly enough, it is, in fact, the *Kitāb* itself that enables us to gather notice of the grammatical activities prior to it: through the direct and indirect references that Sībawayhi reports, we may eventually infer some details of the activities taking place before and alongside Sībawayhi.

The environment in which Sībawayhi's work is grounded is in fact not quite clear in terms of composition. Nevertheless, the Iraqi context (cf. Talmon 2000) in which the Islamic sciences developed was surely the homeland of terrifically intense intellectual activities. The cultural mosaic that characterized the area, with the different cultural and religious groups that populated it, historically favored the rise of a number of disciplines developed within the Islamic context but that also drew inspiration from other traditions.[1]

However, we do not find a clear mention to this multifaceted context neither in the *Kitāb* nor in other texts, and no evident connections between the *Kitāb* and previous works are available either. Consequently, the task of attributing a certain opinion to one or another figure is particularly challenging. The number of scholars and readers mentioned in the *Kitāb*, according to Troupeau's *Lexique-Index* (1976) amounts to 16. Apart from these references, Sībawayhi quotes several other scholars, to whom he refers as *naḥwiyyūn* (cf. Talmon 1982).

In modern Western scholarship, the discussion on whether these belonged to some kind of "institutional" grammatical school was mainly triggered by Carter and Talmon's works, with several works revolving around the question about whether there were systematized groups of scholars before Sībawayhi. Carter (1972) recognizes Sībawayhi and his teachers as the first Arabic grammarians. With regard to the other *naḥwiyyūn*, these would have been a group of skilled but yet "non-professional" grammarians. Conversely, Talmon (1982) argues that the twenty-two mentions to the *naḥwiyyūn* in the *Kitāb* should be read as a reference to a homogenous group of grammarians who would be working in different centers (cf. Talmon 1985; 2000).

The discussion on the subject includes, despite the brevity of our description, other important observations, which we cannot properly discuss here. The short outline sketched, however, aims to outline the composite environ-

1 Cf. Carter 1972, and Versteegh 1977.

ment in which the *Kitāb* finds grounds, and describe how the identification of the actors who played a role before and in the *Kitāb* is surely not an easy task. Nevertheless, despite the difficulty of tracing the actual profiles, we do know that these data and arguments were somewhat accepted by Sībawayhi, and thus blended in the *Kitāb*, at least to a certain extent.[2] The issue is thus of absolute relevance, nevertheless. In fact, assuming that it was not Sībawayhi only who devised the sophisticated linguistic reasoning presented in the *Kitāb*, there must have been something that prompted or contributed to his theorizations, and this might have been firstly integrated into the *Kitāb* and then transmitted alongside Sībawayhi's teaching.

2 Linguistic Data

Sībawayhi's linguistic description revolves around several primary sources. Those deployed in the *Kitāb* consist of a wide range of data from: "1. the natural language of the Bedouin; 2. the artificial language of Arabic poetry; 3. the inherently different language of the Qur'ān; 4. the Traditions of the Prophet (Hadith); 5. proverbs and idiomatic phrases; 6. made-up words and sentences" (Carter 2004: 39).

Grammarians faced the issue of how to tackle linguistic data way before dealing with their model set-up, and this holds especially true in the case of the *language of the Arabs*:

> The grammatical tradition was confronted by two distinct kinds of problem relating to linguistic data. The first was to distinguish on clear, explicit criteria what could and could not be considered as 'authoritative' (*ḥuǧǧa*) data, i.e. authentically representative of the actual use of the original Arabs. The second was concerned with classifying data according to their degree of relevance to linguistic analysis, or (but from the Arabic grammarians' point of view it amounts to the same thing) their status within the general system of the language.
>
> BOHAS et al. 1990: 17

Data validity, and thus their admissibility as an authoritative linguistic proof, was surely of primary importance. Of the six sources listed above, Carter (2004:

2 For instance, Carter argues that the possible influence of these *naḥwiyyūn* on Sībawayhi is recognizable in the seven introductory chapters of the *Kitāb* known as *al-Risāla* (*Kitāb* I, 12–33), and that the use of the *qiyās* is the distinctive feature of their approach (cf. Carter 1972:76).

39) gives an introductory description remarking that the first and the last, namely the speech of the Arabs and the made-up expressions, are to be considered the two poles of authenticity, whereas the others rather represent different level of artificiality, although none of which productive. The Qurʾān, as well as the *ḥadīṯ*-s as per they are presented in the *Kitāb*, are mostly referred to not because of their being religious sources but rather as a piece of linguistic evidence. Also, the *ḥadīṯ*-s are not widely employed in the *Kitāb*, but are found in larger extent in later works. In the *Kitāb* the number of *ḥadīṯ*-s quoted is rather small,[3] and they would not be introduced by the more traditional formulas, which we rather find in later literature, e.g., *wa-fī al-ḥadīṯ* or *kamā qāla al-nabī*. One of the readings of such formulations could be that quotations of this kind are not considered an important linguistic proof because of their religious nature, but are rather recognized as part of the wider language and thus presented as correct expressions.

Data collected from Bedouin informants play perhaps the most important role in the overall description of the language. The Arabs represent a varied group in which different elements are combined. In the *Kitāb*, we find several tribal groups mentioned, and the variants and varieties accounted for portray the kind of compromise reached by Arabic grammarians who were confronted with the possible inconsistencies of the language they would speak. According to the description available in grammatical sources, the image of the Bedouins, as well as of their role as authoritative linguistic sources, is finally a combination of different factors. On the one hand, we are held up to the historical tribal idea of the Arabs coming from the central peninsula; on the other hand, the new value attributed to the tribes from the Mekkan area, native land of the Prophet, is also particularly relevant. These tribal groups, in fact, had in the meantime acquired a higher status since the Qurʾān would reflect instances of the Mekkan variety.[4]

Linguistic data gathered from direct linguistic inquiries represent the founding elements Sībawayhi refers to, for both authority and amount, insofar as the *kalām al-ʿarab* ultimately constitutes the widest corpus of data available in the *Kitāb*. This mainly holds idiomatic expressions, proverbs, locutions, and more importantly spontaneous realizations of random utterances in Arabic as a result of direct inquiries. The linguistic data are, in fact, gathered from the answers that the Bedouins would give with regard to how to utter something

3 For a wider discussion on this, cf. Sadan 2015.

4 Cf. Bohas et al. 1990. For an examination of the relation between pre-Islamic, Qurʾānic and Classical Arabic, see Larcher 2005; more specifically on the Qurʾānic matter, see Larcher 2008b; 2013; 2014.

properly, either directly collected by Sībawayhi himself or borrowed from other authoritative sources, for example Ḫalīl (d. 175/791?). Variants from different tribal varieties, manifestly referred to, are registered and listed by the grammarians when differences would be relevant. Sometimes Arabs would not be correct in their uttering, which Sībawayhi well declares in his work.[5]

The composition of the data in the *Kitāb*, alongside the data collected in the *Kitāb al-ʿAyn*, does represent an invaluable testimony of the different earliest varieties. The fact that such data were being transmitted is finally of particular relevance if we consider that, being the language evidently subject to inevitable changes, these data could be transmitted to later traditions of scholars.

Finally, the collected corpus of data is of major importance for its being representative of a specific variety. If the process of standardization was to be accomplished on what it is called the "clear variety" of the Arabic language, as per the definition that the Qurʾān provides for itself,[6] the data to base the arguments on could not be other than those constituting such variety. The transmission and description of the linguistic features of this language, at risk because of the inevitable process of language corruption of which Arabic scholars were surely aware,[7] was important also concerning the perception of the variety to standardize itself. Being the linguistic description the ultimate aim and manifested intention of grammarians, data needed to be collected and transmitted in their purest form.

3 The *Kitāb* as a Source in Later Traditions

3.1 *Data Transmission and Reuse*

In the process of language description, linguistic data constitute the basic vocabulary, meaning the collection of lexical items, that needs to appear alongside a descriptive grammar based on the very same data, that is to say, a set of formal rules as to how those elements should be organized into larger and logical units.

5 See, for instance, *Kitāb* II, 34; III, 555; IV, 197. As described by Carter "Not every item was accepted merely because it came from a Bedouin Arab: now and then Sībawayhi actually points out errors in speech, calling one particular usage 'very bad' (*radīʾ jiddan*), and referring to one set of incorrect speakers as *ʾahl al-jafāʾ* 'coarse people'." (Carter 2004:40).

6 *lisān ʿarabī mubīn*, Q. 16/103; 26/195.

7 The topic is widely addressed by Arabic scholars themselves. Cf. for instance the *Muqaddima* by Ibn Ḫaldūn (d. 808/1406), who discusses the fact that the distortion in language may be traced in the interaction of native speakers of Arabic and those who acquired Arabic as a consequence of their inclusion in the Islamic empire (cf. Ibn Ḫaldūn *Muqaddima* III, 343).

In the case of the Arabic tradition, this vocabulary holds a particularly significant legacy, due to the nature of the elements it is composed of. The Qurʾān, the pre-Islamic poetry, and the data gathered from the Bedouins' varieties do play a substantial role because of their cultural significance, and the descriptive aim striven for by grammarians provides grounds for and supplies the materials with which the grammatical arrangement operates.

As we have discussed above, a major portion of the founding vocabulary for linguistic theorizations on Arabic grammar comes from the "speakers with an innate knowledge of grammar", as Zaǧǧāǧī (d. 337/949) refers to Bedouins (*ʾĪḍāḥ* 66). Their speech was a fundamental building block to record and make available through linguistic collections, and the availability of informants' data in the earliest grammatical as well as lexicographical treatises is significant because they are meant to portray the linguistic reality of the 1st/7th century.

The fact that these data would be made available in the *Kitāb* contributes to the establishment of the role of this work across the tradition. In fact, a noticeable point in the contents and structures of—especially later—grammatical treatises is that they seem to find foundations in the *Kitāb* and in the data discussed therein. The *Kitāb* was in fact not only *the* authoritative source, but also a container of information, and gained such a significant status that it finally became a corpus in itself. Its data were clearly not only pieces of evidence for linguistic arguments to be utilized once, but an actual collection to be transmitted.

A major issue in the process of transmission of data in the linguistic tradition pertains to the shortage of first-hand data. Sībawayhi had inquired the Bedouins directly and had thus the opportunity to collect some expressions that he could well deploy for linguistic arguments. But even in the cases in which he would not have data collected by himself, he could still rely on data collected by other reliable scholars, first and foremost Ḫalīl. His master is in fact mentioned several times with respect to data collection, and included in the anecdotes in which we are told that they had "asked the Arabs and found that they agree".[8]

Arabs, as well as their speech, played such a central role because informants of the Arabic varieties at issue mastered the language, and were thus trusted because of their natural instinct toward the appropriateness of speech. Such a role is praised rather decidedly in grammarians' works, for it is presented as the manifest evidence for the correctness of an argument. Bedouins would thus be inquired by Sībawayhi and other scholars, all driven by the ambition to collect

8 E.g., *wa-saʾalnā al-ʿarab fa-waǧadnāhum yuwafiqūnahu* (*Kitāb* III, 390).

information and translate into words their innate sense of linguistic correctness. The "fieldwork", if we may use this term to refer to the kind of linguistic investigation carried out by grammarians, is introduced in grammatical texts alongside statements that avoid suspicion, and hint at the unquestionable reliability of the data deployed. We thus find expressions such as "we heard it from whom whose Arabic can be trusted", and several other variations on the theme that set forth the grammarians' judgment on the substantiality of the data.[9]

Grammarians were also confronted with the sometimes-attested lack of proficiency of some Arabs. In the case of Sībawayhi, he would well depreciate some of their expressions. Analogous circumstances are recounted much later by Ibn Ǧinnī (d. 392/1002) who discusses (*Ḫaṣāʾiṣ* II, 5) the linguistic errors made by Bedouins who seem to be unable to speak proper Arabic, which would affect the linguistic research based on a preliminary description of discrete data.

Despite the narration in the *Ḫaṣāʾiṣ*, an interesting point in Ibn Ǧinnī's approach to teaching is that data collection would still be a central element in linguistic investigation. For first-hand data description was then so fundamental, Ibn Ǧinnī would still encourage his students to check on linguistic facts by inquiring Bedouin informants to formulate linguistic analyses. The question finally remains on how disciples, and grammarians themselves, would relate to data knowing that these would not be representative of the pure Arabic they strove for.

Shortage in (or perhaps also lack of) availability of first-hand data directly collected from innate grammarians gives then a further explanation to the fact that the earliest collections would be transmitted as a whole corpus, alongside their status of reference texts. If data could no longer be collected, and professional grammarians together with their disciples were inevitably confronted with the issue of language change, data reliability from other sources was finally the way forward. Sībawayhi's corpus of data, partly also based on Ḫalīl's collection as we have mentioned above, is hence of major importance for many factors. On the one hand, it is representative of several attestations of the language, as the grammarian would collect variants from different varieties and list them together while providing an overall categorization; on the other hand, the data included in the *Kitāb* as well as in the earliest grammatical treatises were to become an inventory of linguistic information, a memoir of the Arabic linguistic identity.

9 The declination of the expression mostly follows the same patterns in all anecdotes, with formulations such as *samiʿnāhu mi-man yūṯaqu bi-ʿarabiyyatihi, yūṯaqu bi-ʿarabiyyatihi min al-ʿarab*, or that even point at specific groups of informants: *wa-samiʿnā baʿḍ man yūṯaqu bi-ʿarabiyyatihim yaqūlu*.

Furthermore, Sībawayhi laid the foundations of a hierarchy of variants and varieties, by discussing the appropriateness of the speech construction. For instance, even though the elements at the basis of the pursued *fuṣḥā*[10] were mostly from the Tamīmī variety, he would still praise the high-level of the Ḥiǧāzī speech[11] (*Kitāb* IV, 473) defined as *al-luġa al-ʿarabiyya al-qadīma al-ǧayyida* ("the good old Arabic language"). Conversely, there are instances in which Sībawayhi returns a severe judgment on certain expressions, labeled as 'bad' or only 'partly appropriate'. We thus find in the *Kitāb* expressions such as *wa-hāḏihi luġa radīʾa* (*Kitāb* II, 34), *wa-ʾammā ʾahl al-luġa al-radīʾa* (*Kitāb* IV, 197), *wa-ḏālika qalīl radīʾ* (*Kitāb* III, 555) that provide us with Sībawayhi's appraisal of the data presented but that also surely served later grammarians in further selecting them.

Finally, the collection and consequent systematization of the data, as far as their status of reliability is concerned, is of twofold importance for the upcoming traditions. On the one hand, the shortage of first-hand data did play a substantial role in approaching the sources, and data collected directly were at some point inevitably supplanted by referred data. Scholars who were not able—for whatever reason—to collect data themselves, clearly relied on the established sources (or excerpts of these) on which there was already a scholarly agreement, enough for making their use legitimate. It is thus the scholarly transmission that provided the data their legitimacy and validity to be used for linguistic theorizations.

On the other hand, we should also consider that sometimes linguistic arguments are not supported by data at all, for grammarians would discuss hypothetical structures that could not get a match or be grounded in the corpus at their disposal. Finally, many of the examples used for describing a certain argument were often made up and designed for that specific purpose and had no direct relation with the corpus. This would be the case, for instance, of the number of examples containing the words *zayd*, *ʿamr*, *ḍaraba*, *qāʾim*, and all possible shuffled options with these and other wild card words.

This being the case, linguistic description eventually turned into theorizations grounded in a closed corpus.[12] Legitimacy on linguistic arguments thus

---

10 The term *fuṣḥā* does not appear in Sībawayhi's *Kitāb*. Nevertheless, as described by Larcher, "Tous les arabisants savent que l'expression d'*al-lugha al-fuṣḥâ* désigne la variété d'arabe qu'ils appellent eux-mêmes « arabe classique »" (Larcher 2008a:263). Thus, that being the case, we have opted for using the term regardless of its absence in the *Kitāb*. As the matter would surely need to be discussed at much length, which unfortunately we cannot properly do here, cf. on this Larcher 2008a.

11 On the topic of dialect variation, see Larcher 2010.

12 With regard to this matter, Carter's assertions are ultimately explicative: "More disturb-

resulted from a common agreement among scholars, and the reliability of the conclusions was accepted as long as these were framed within a consistent linguistic theorization based on the *ʾuṣūl al-naḥw*, the foundations of grammar.

3.2 *Author's Significance*

The reliability of the *Kitāb* is undisputed across the grammatical schools, and its significance was evidently not only a matter of data collected. By laying the foundations of the discipline, Sībawayhi's became beyond doubt the most prominent figure of the tradition. His influence was also not only limited to the Basran grammatical school that developed out of his teaching,[13] but was well established all throughout the Arabic linguistic tradition.

The internal conflict among the professional grammarians was sparked off by the question of authority.[14] They had learned from the logicians that rules depend for their validity on the data from which they are inductively derived and that only a closed corpus could guarantee that these rules could never be overturned by new data. The controversy, which would result into the Basran (closed corpus)/Kufan (open corpus) division, was long and acrimonious; nevertheless, grammarians never lost sight of the fact that the grammatical science must draw its authority objectively from its logical structure and not, as had formerly been the case, subjectively from the personal prestige and strength of character of its leading practitioners.

Notwithstanding, no other grammarians, whatever the school, ever proposed a completely different approach from Sībawayhi's. Despite some differences in the formulation and slightly dissimilar features, the general remarks, as well as the more specific elucidations provided by Sībawayhi on the linguistic structure of the *fuṣḥā*, are traceable in any later theorization. Just as an example, no other Arabic scholar ever proposed an alternative theory for the parts of speech (*ʾaqsām al-kalām*), up to modern times almost undisputed in its original formulation: *fa-l-kalim ism wa-fiʿl wa-ḥarf* (*Kitāb* I, 1)[15] Only in

---

ing still is the difference in attitude to data. The traditional Arab grammarians, after an initial and relatively short phase of truly descriptive grammar, were left with a corpus of data which was no longer the product of direct observation but had acquired the nature of legal evidence whose authenticity was guaranteed by the reliability of its transmitters. This material legitimized a self-consciously prescriptive grammar whose purpose was to perpetuate an ideal form of Arabic for reasons that are well known" (Carter 1987/1988:213).

13 For a discussion on the development of the grammatical schools after Sībawayhi, cf., among others, Carter 2000.

14 Cf. on this Carter 1999.

15 There have been some further propositions but none of them accomplished the task of reformulating this completely or went as far as proposing a new theory.

a few cases the need for a more specific classification is registered, namely in Suyūṭī (d. 911/1505; *ʾAšbāh* III, 2) who mentions the fourth category *ḫālifa*,[16] and in Fārābī (d. 350/961), who proposes the category *ḫawālif* among others. But regardless of the propositions, the only fully accepted formulation is the one proposed in the *Kitāb* and all further assertions are based on this.

The respect paid to Sībawayhi's figure entails a certain adherence to his propositions also when it comes to providing linguistic arguments. In the grammatical schools' tradition and the *ḫilāfāt* tradition as well,[17] Sībawayhi's statements are often used both when providing argumentations and when confuting other grammarians' theories. As Carter put it: "the history of Arabic grammar is the history of what happened to the *Kitāb*" (Carter 2004: 138), thus pointing at the undisputed significance and impact of the *Kitāb* all across the Arabic linguistic tradition.

Arabic grammarians would acknowledge the relevance of Sībawayhi's propositions as early as in the 3rd/9th century. We thus find claims such as Māzinī's (d. 249/863) who argues that anyone who aimed at writing a large book on grammar after the *Kitāb* should be ashamed (*man ʾarāda ʾan yaʿmala kitāban kabīran fī al-naḥw baʿd Sībawayhi fa-l-yastaḥyi*).[18]

The prestige attributed to Sībawayhi, as in the case of data reliability discussed in the previous section, comes from a scholarly agreement and transmission. By the end of the 3rd/9th century, and thanks to the credit bestowed by al-ʾAḫfaš al-ʾAwsaṭ (d. 215/830), Māzinī, and Mubarrad (d. 285/898), the *Kitāb* had reached the status of founding text of Arabic grammar.

The importance of the figure is evident also in that, when presenting their data, grammarians would claim their consistency with Sībawayhi's theories as much as they would do with the *kalām al-ʿarab* or other substantial sources. The respect is paid through fixed formulas widely deployed in literature:

> What demonstrates the correctness of what we have affirmed is that Sībawayhi himself confirms it, by saying that […]. (*wa-llaḏī yadullu ʿalā ṣiḥḥati mā ḏahabnā ʾilayhi ʾanna sībawayhi yusāʿidunā ʿalā ʾanna* […]);

16 Further information on the category *ḫālifa* can be resumed by the studies of ʾAḥmad Makkī al-ʾAnṣārī (notably ʾAnṣārī 1964) who investigates Farrāʾ's (d. 207/822) role in the Arabic linguistic tradition as the leading figure of the grammatical school of Kufa. The author states that Farrāʾ was the first who investigated and proposed a fourth lexical category between the noun and the verb.

17 *Ḫilāfāt* refers to the tradition of grammatical works such as the *Tabyīn* of ʿUkbarī (d. 616/1219) or the *Kitāb al-ʾInṣāf* by Ibn al-ʾAnbārī (d. 577/1181), structured as to present the different opinions adduced by grammarians and grammatical schools for each linguistic issue debated.

18 Quote attributed to Māzinī, reported in Sīrāfī *ʾAḫbār* 50; Ibn al-ʾAnbārī *Nuzha* 56.

What demonstrates the correctness of what we have affirmed is that a similar expression exists in the variety of the Arabs (*wa-llaḏī yadullu ʿalā ṣiḥḥat mā ḏahabnā ʾilayhi lahu naẓīr fī kalām al-ʿarab*).[19]

What can be immediately inferred by the examples above, and that is self-evident considering the congruence in phrasing, is the perception of coincidence between the two elements, the *Kitāb*, and the *kalām al-ʿarab*. Thus, the comparative relation of the two sources illustrates how, in linguistic literature, Sībawayhi's conclusions represent a source as authoritative as Bedouins' speech.

However, the *Kitāb* was never easy to approach and was certainly thorny to interpret. Its complexity, even obscurity at times, are acknowledged in many instances. For example, in the *Ṭabaqāt* by Zubaydī (d. 379/989) we are told of Ibn Kaysān (d. 299/911 or 320/932), a Basran disciple of Ṯaʿlab (d. 291/904) and Mubarrad (cf. *Ṭabaqāt* 153) who did not read the *Kitāb* to Mabramān (d. 326/938). In addition to this, we are also told of Ibn Kaysān relying on Zağğāğ (d. 311/923) for the transmission on the text (cf. *Ṭabaqāt* 153).

One of the reasons that would explain Ibn Kaysān's approach to the text, which is not dissimilar from other authors', is perhaps the major difficulties with which scholars were confronted when endeavoring to interpret the text. The *Kitāb* is in fact acknowledged as the hardest Arabic grammar to read,[20] and Sībawayhi's arguing style is often far from being clear. This eventually led, on the one hand, to the production of many works that aimed at further clarifying his propositions, and, on the other hand, to the rise of a new literary genre, more pedagogical,[21] that could be more easily approached by disciples.

The tendency of reading the *Kitāb* through the lens of the scholars who devoted their works to further explaining Sībawayhi's *Kitāb* is consistent up to modern times, since even modern translations of the text—like the one by Jahn (1895–1900)—are not so much a translation but rather re-interpretation of Sībawayhi through the medium of Sīrāfī (d. 368/979), his major commentator (cf. Sīrāfī *Šarḥ*).

19 Such formulas are widely used in e.g., the *Kitāb al-ʾInṣāf*.

20 For instance, we are told by Mubarrad that the *Kitāb* was as hard as "how to ride the sea" (Carter 2004:133).

21 For further discussion on this, cf., among others, Baalbaki 2019.

4 The Legacy of the *Kitāb*[22]

Major issue in the kind of mosaic portrayed so far is the lack of transparency when it comes to distinguishing the distinctiveness of the text itself from interpretations set forth by later grammarians and commentators.

The problem is twofold: on the one hand, the issue of pinpointing what is distinctive of the *Kitāb* is substantial in that further elucidations of similar matters may have returned results far from their original formulation; on the other hand, there is an issue that arises from re-interpretations that may have been intentionally diverging from the original message.

The first aspect mentioned regards the transmission of the text. As we have already discussed above, the *Kitāb* was never easy to approach, and coeval as well as later traditions were confronted with such difficulties. Grammarians then put an effort in elucidating it, producing many works that would serve the purpose of making Sībawayhi's theorizations more widely available.

The second issue, instead, concerns interpretations of the text that may have been somewhat altered. Of this second aspect, we will briefly mention a few illustrative instances in the next sections.

4.1 *Examples of Ambiguous Reference*

As we have seen in the previous paragraphs, Sībawayhi clearly represents a well-grounded authority and recipient of an across-the-board acknowledgment by all branches of the Arabic linguistic tradition. Hence, excerpts from the *Kitāb* are widely found in other Arabic grammarians' arguments.

It is thus clear that arguments finding justification in one substantial source, i.e. the *kalām al-ʿarab*, the Qurʾān, the *ḥadīṯ*-s, as well as authoritative sources like the *Kitāb*, are provided with an indisputable legitimacy that is hard to challenge. As far as the *Kitāb* is concerned, what may happen is that not only actual references are mentioned, but also arguments that are either inferred from a more general viewpoint or only ascribed to Sībawayhi, without providing an exact reference. But given the importance of the actor, claiming a direct attribution of a statement seemed to be enough for purporting the same consensus one would gain with an exact phrasing or reference.

In many instances, finally, Sībawayhi's words might have been misinterpreted. Whether this was intentionally done or simply an issue of transmission or interpretation, it is not known. Nevertheless, we do find few references to

22 For a wider examination of the legacy of the *Kitāb*, see in particular Bernards 1997, and Baalbaki 2008.

Sībawayhi's theorizations that were referred to or re-proposed in a formulation distant from their original version.

One case of misinterpretation is reported for instance by Marogy (2010: 151ff.) who, addressing the issue of the structure of *ʾinna*, aims to demonstrate:

> That Sībawayhi's discussion of *ʾinna*'s operation has been misinterpreted. By analogy with the operation of *ʿišrūna* 'twenty' on *dirhaman*, *ʾinna*'s operation consists of assigning the dependent form to the *mubtadaʾ* 'subject/topic' while leaving the *ḫabar* independent, i.e. unaffected by *ʾinna*'s operation.
>
> MAROGY 2010: 152

Another example is presented in Kasher (2015) who discusses the identity of the operator of the independent mood of the verb. One remark provided by Kasher is the discussion on how earlier writers:

> Do not ascribe this view to Ṯaʿlab, but rather state that Ṯaʿlab misinterpreted Sībawayhi as if the *latter* had regarded this resemblance as the operator assigning the independent mood to the verb [...]. The later grammarians' ascription of this view to Ṯaʿlab might thus be due to their misinterpretation of earlier sources.
>
> KASHER 2015: 124, fn. 21

Kasher provides then a possible source for Ṯaʿlab's misinterpretation, referring to the *Muqtaḍab* (IV, 84) by Mubarrad, "where the text reads: *fa-hāḏihi l-ʾafʿālu marfūʿatun li-muḍāraʿatihā l-ʾasmāʾa wa-wuqūʿihā mawāqiʿahā*... (cf. ibid. IV, 80–81)" (Kasher 2015: 124), and thus suggesting a reading of where the misinterpretation might have stemmed from.

4.1.1 *Haǧar*

Ambiguous references are also found[23] in the case of *haǧar*. The case is presented in the *Kitāb* in the chapter on the *ʾasmāʾ al-ʾarāḍī* (*Kitāb* III, 242–246) ('city names'), in which Sībawayhi addresses the matter about the treatment of *haǧar* as either masculine or feminine (*wa-kaḏālika haǧar yuʾannāṯu wa-yuḏakkaru*, *Kitāb* III, 243).

---

23 The two cases reported here, about *haǧar* and *laysa*, are presented also in Baalbaki (2008:233–235). With regard to the former, cf. also Baalbaki 1999.

Sībawayhi's argument is based on the discussion on two quotes; one is from Farazdaq (d. 114/732?):

> *qāla al-farazdaq: minhunna ʾayyām ṣidq qad ʿuriftu bihā ʾayyām fāris wa-l-ʾayyām min hağarā.*
>
> *Kitāb* III, 243

and the other is the proverb:

> *wa-samiʿnā man yaqūlu ka-ğalibi al-tamr ʾilā hağar yā fatā.*
>
> *Kitāb* III, 244

These same examples have later been reused for addressing diverse matters. Thus, both the quote of Farazdaq and the proverb have been presented in the same formulation to discuss the treatment of *hağar* concerning a different aspect. What we find in following traditions is in fact a wider discussion revolving around the treatment of the term as either diptotic or triptotic, an aspect not discussed by Sībawayhi. The argument, though, is triggered by the same elements as presented in the *Kitāb*, regarding the data reported therein, and with distinct mentions to Sībawayhi, who—as we mentioned above—never discussed the matter from this perspective.

In its further formulation, the discussion on the subject parts: on the one hand, grammarians consider *hağar* diptotic; on the other hand, lexicographers treat *hağar* as a triptotic noun.

Needless to say, legitimacy is claimed by both sides, also by directly quoting Sībawayhi as a supporting argument: in the grammatical tradition, we find Zağğāğī who reports the quote from Farazdaq, as per it is presented in the *Kitāb*, and associates *hağar* and its morphological features with those of the *ʾasmāʾ al-mudun* (*Ğumal* 231).

In the lexicographical tradition, instead, we find Ibn Sīda (d. 458/1066) quoting Sībawayhi and the proverb *wa-samiʿnā man yaqūlu ka-ğalibi al-tamr ʾilā hağar yā fatā* (*Muḥkam* IV, 159). In this latter case, the lexicographer argues for a triptotic declension of *hağar* due to the presence of *yā fatā* at the end. The placement of *yā fatā* as a closing element of the sentence would in fact be a device to force an ending on the preceding word, preventing it from taking on a pausal form; if *hağar* were triptotic, *yā fatā* could not be used for the sentence, that instead would have to end with a noun carrying a *tanwīn*.

4.1.2 *Laysa*

Another case of ambiguous reference, again concerning the way Sībawayhi's position is reported, regards *laysa* and the position of its *ḫabar* (comment). The cornerstone of the discussion is the anticipation of its predicate, within a structure like the following:

comment–*kāna*/its sisters–topic

The wider discussion on this kind of construction is generally rather controversial in grammatical literature and includes several opposing arguments on its admissibility.

The case we want to address here refers specifically to *laysa*. The discussion is presented with the made-up expression *qāʾiman laysa zaydun*, with the *ḫabar* of *laysa* preceding *laysa* and its noun following it.

Among the grammarians who allow the comment–*laysa*–topic construction at issue, we find the grammatical school of Basra, Suyūṭī, Zamaḫšarī (d. 538/1144), and Ibn Barhān al-ʿUkbarī (d. 456/1064); on the other hand, those who do not allow such formulation belong to the grammatical school of Kufa, Mubarrad, Ǧurǧānī (d. 471/1078), Zaǧǧāǧ, Ibn al-Sarrāǧ, and Sīrāfī.[24]

To briefly recall two of the arguments from both sides, we here mention al-Suyūṭī's proposition in which he assimilates *laysa* with *kāna*, conferring it the same characteristics of its bigger sister. Hence, since *kāna* may be placed after its *ḫabar*, the same should hold true for *laysa*. The assertion is thus based on the wider characteristics of the whole group (*kāna* and its sisters), as confronted with the group of *ʿasā*, which is weaker than the former, and for which a selfsame construction should not be allowed (*Hamʿ* I, 373).

Such construction is also reported in Ibn al-Nāẓim's (d. 686/1287) *Šarḥ* (p. 135) in which the author claims that additional support to such thesis is provided by Sībawayhi's acceptance of similar constructions, e.g., *ʾa-zaydan lasta miṯlahu*.

Conversely, a major weakness in this argument is alleged by Ǧurǧānī who claims that being *laysa* weaker than *kāna*—that is fully declinable—it should not be assigned those characteristics belonging to *kāna* only, because of its full conjugation (*Muqtaṣid* I, 408–409).

Nevertheless, the most interesting point is Ǧurǧānī's argument regarding the fact that, despite the diverse claims of his contestants, Sībawayhi never really mentioned the issue (cf. *Muqtaṣid* I, 409).

24 One later recounting on the discussion on the subject is, for instance, available in the *Kitāb al-ʾInṣāf*, in the chapter on *taqdīr ḫabar laysa* (Ibn al-ʾAnbārī *ʾInṣāf* 138).

5 Conclusion

In this paper, the role of Sībawayhi and his *Kitāb* as a source for Arabic grammarians' theorizations was presented.

Starting with the data contained in the *Kitāb* and the reasons why these became so fundamental, we discussed Sībawayhi's role in the Arabic linguistic tradition. The main objective of this paper was to provide an overview of the role played by Sībawayhi's figure in the development of the linguistic sciences by discussing the way his work was received by coeval and later traditions as well as what impact it had on them.

What comes from this outline is the picture of a particular source, whose legacy remains uttermost relevant throughout the Arabic linguistic tradition, conceptually connected to Sībawayhi to a noticeable extent and all across its branches.

The reasons why the *Kitāb* played such a significant role and had a huge impact on Arabic scholars are various. As we have discussed in this paper, Sībawayhi's role in the linguistic tradition is of absolute relevance first and foremost due to the credit bestowed on him by grammarians even from opposed traditions. The respect paid, in fact, exceedingly contributed to the circulation and study of the text, with a noticeable impact on the traditions to come. The circulation of the *Kitāb* ensured the circulation of the data contained therein as well; data which later provided for a major issue for the coming generations of scholars, who were confronted with the shortage of first-hand data.

Thus, if the figure of the author were not relevant enough, this second aspect would surely contribute to the substantiation of the *Kitāb* as a corpus. It was not only Sībawayhi's arguments that circulated, but they came along the data he had collected, which later served as a core corpus for the traditions to come. As Carter asserted, "by the tenth century *laysa fī kalām al-ʿarab* was virtually the same as *laysa fī Kitāb Sībawayhi*" (Carter 1999: 64): the relevance of the source was by that time well established, and its reliability for both reasoning and data was incontrovertible.

Hence, considering the relevance of the figure, Sībawayhi's words—whether attested or inferred—evidently provided legitimacy to linguistic arguments, whatever the line of thoughts of the scholar at issue. The *Kitāb* had, in fact, such a noticeable impact all across the Arabic linguistic tradition that it shortly became a reference work for all grammarians. Consequently, claims in this direction, namely the claim to be in line with Sībawayhi's view on a certain matter, somehow would prevent scholars from being challenged by their contestants, as would happen by proving consistency with other fundamental sources.

The *Kitāb* was, in conclusion, a substantial source for the coming generations of Arabic scholars, who could not but relate to the founder of the linguistic disciplines, despite the widely acknowledged difficulties in approaching Sībawayhi's work:

> The ever rich potential for controversy and interpretation which the *Kitāb* offers makes it by far the most inspiring treatise in the Arabic linguistic tradition, if one chooses not to mention several other fields of Arabic studies.
>
> BAALBAKI 1999: 12

Bibliography

Primary Sources

Ǧurǧānī, *Muqtaṣid* = ʿAbd al-Qāhir b. ʿAbd al-Raḥmān b. Muḥammad ʾAbū Bakr al-Ǧurǧānī, *Kitāb al-Muqtaṣid fī šarḥ al-ʾĪḍāḥ*. Ed. by Kāẓim Baḥr al-Marǧān. Baġdād: Manšūrāt wizārat al-ṯaqāfa wa-l-ʾiʿlām, 2 vol., 1982.

Ibn al-ʾAnbārī, *ʾInṣāf* = ʿAbd al-Raḥmān b. Muḥammad b. ʿUbayd Allāh ʾAbū al-Barakāt Kamāl al-Dīn al-ʾAnṣārī al-ʾAnbārī, *al-ʾInṣāf fī masāʾil al-ḫilāf bayn al-naḥwiyyīn al-baṣriyyīn wa-l-kūfiyyīn*. Ed. by Gotthold Weil. Leiden: E.J. Brill, 1913.

Ibn al-ʾAnbārī, *Nuzha* = ʿAbd al-Raḥmān b. Muḥammad b. ʿUbayd Allāh ʾAbū al-Barakāt Kamāl al-Dīn al-ʾAnṣārī al-ʾAnbārī, *Nuzhat al-ʾalibbāʾ fī ṭabaqāt al-ʾudabāʾ*. Baġdād: Maktabat al-ʾAndalus, 1970, 2nd ed.

Ibn al-Nāẓim, *Šarḥ* = ʾAbū ʿAbd Allāh Badr al-Dīn Muḥammad Ibn al-Nāẓim, *Šarḥ Ibn al-Nāẓim ʿalā ʾAlfiyyat Ibn Mālik*. Ed. by Muḥammad Bāsil ʿUyūn al-Sūd. Bayrūt: Dār al-kutub al-ʿilmiyya, 2000.

Ibn al-Sarrāǧ, *ʾUṣūl* = Muḥammad b. al-Sarī b. Sahl ʾAbū Bakr Ibn al-Sarrāǧ al-Baġdādī, *al-ʾUṣūl fī al-naḥw*. Ed. by ʿAbd al-Ḥusayn al-Fatlī. Dimašq & Bayrūt: Muʾassasat al-risāla, 3 vol., 1988.

Ibn Ǧinnī, *Ḫaṣāʾiṣ* = ʿUṯmān b. Ǧinnī ʾAbū al-Fatḥ al-Mawṣilī, *al-Ḫaṣāʾiṣ*. Ed. by Muḥammad ʿAlī al-Naǧǧār. Al-Qāhira: Dār al-kutub al-miṣriyya, 3 vol., 1952.

Ibn Ḫaldūn, *Muqaddima* = Walī al-Dīn ʿAbd al-Raḥmān b. Muḥammad b. Muḥammad b. ʾAbī Bakr Muḥammad b. al-Ḥasan Ibn Ḫaldūn, *al-Muqaddima*. Ed. by. N.J. Dawood. Trans. by Franz Rosenthal [*The Muqaddimah, an Introduction to History*]. Princeton, N.J.: Princeton University Press, 1969.

Ibn Sīda, *Muḥkam* = ʾAbū al-Ḥasan ʿAlī b. ʾIsmāʿīl Ibn Sīda al-Mursī, *al-Muḥkam wa-l-muḥīṭ al-ʾaʿẓam*. Ed. by ʿAbd al-Ḥamīd Hindāwī. Bayrūt: Dār al-kutub al-ʿilmiyya, 11 vol., 2000.

Sībawayhi, *Kitāb* = ʿAmr b. ʿUṯmān b. Qanbar ʾAbū Bišr Sībawayhi, *al-Kitāb*. Ed. by ʿAbd al-Salām Muḥammad Hārūn. Al-Qāhira: Maktabat al-ḫānǧī, 5 vol., 1966.

Sīrāfī, *ʾAḫbār* = ʾAbū Saʿīd al-Ḥasan b. ʿAbd Allāh b. al-Marzubān, *Kitāb ʾAḫbār al-naḥwiyyīn al-baṣriyyīn*. Ed. by Fritz Krenkow. Paris & Bayrūt: Geuthner & al-Maṭbaʿa al-kāṯūlīkiyya. 1936.

Sīrāfī, *Šarḥ* = ʾAbū Saʿīd al-Ḥasan b. ʿAbd Allāh b. al-Marzubān, *Šarḥ Kitāb Sībawayhi*. Ed. by Muḥammad Hāšim ʿAbd al-Dāyim. Al-Qāhira: al-Hayʾa al-miṣriyya al-ʿāmma li-l-kitāb, 1986.

Suyūṭī, *ʾAšbāh* = ʿAbd al-Raḥmān b. ʾAbī Bakr b. Muḥammad b. Sābiq al-Dīn Ǧalāl al-Dīn al-Ḫuḍayrī al-Šāfiʿī al-Suyūṭī, *al-ʾAšbāh wa-l-naẓāʾir fī al-naḥw*. Hyderabad: Maṭbaʿat dāʾirat al-maʿārif al-ʿuṯmāniyya, 2nd ed., 4 vol., 1940.

Suyūṭī, *Hamʿ* = ʿAbd al-Raḥmān b. ʾAbī Bakr b. Muḥammad b. Sābiq al-Dīn Ǧalāl al-Dīn al-Ḫuḍayrī al-Šāfiʿī al-Suyūṭī, *Hamʿ al-hawāmiʿ fī šarḥ Ǧamʿ al-ǧawāmiʿ*. Ed. by ʿAbd al-ʿĀl Sālim Mukarram. Bayrūt: Muʾassasat al-risāla, 6 vol., 1992.

Zaǧǧāǧī, *Ǧumal* = ʾAbū al-Qāsim ʿAbd al-Raḥmān b. ʾIsḥāq al-Zaǧǧāǧī, *Kitāb al-Ǧumal fī al-naḥw*. Ed. by ʿAlī Tawfīq al-Ḥamad. Bayrūt & ʾIrbid: Muʾassasat al-risāla & Dār al-ʾamal, 1984.

Zaǧǧāǧī, *ʾĪḍāḥ* = ʾAbū al-Qāsim ʿAbd al-Raḥmān b. ʾIsḥāq al-Zaǧǧāǧī, *al-ʾĪḍāḥ fī ʿilal al-naḥw*. Ed. by Māzin al-Mubārak. Al-Qāhira: Dār al-ʿurūba, 1959.

Zubaydī, *Ṭabaqāt* = ʾAbū Bakr Muḥammad b. al-Ḥasan b. ʿUbayd Allāh b. Muḏaḥḥiǧ al-Zubaydī al-ʾAndalusī al-ʾIšbīlī, *Ṭabaqāt al-naḥwiyyīn wa-l-luġawiyyīn*. Ed. by Muḥammad ʾAbū al-Faḍl ʾIbrāhīm. Al-Qāhira: Maktabat al-ḫānǧī, 1954.

Secondary Sources

ʾAnṣārī (al-), ʾAḥmad Makkī. 1964. *ʾAbū Zakariyyā al-Farrāʾ wa-maḏhabuhu fī al-naḥw wa-l-luġa*. Al-Qāhira: al-Maǧlis al-ʾaʿlā li-riʿāyat al-funūn wa-l-ʾādāb wa-l-ʿulūm al-iǧtimāʿiyya.

Baalbaki, Ramzi. 1999. "A Note on a Controversial Passage in Sībawayhi's *Kitāb*". *Zeitschrift für Arabische Linguistik* 37. 9–12.

Baalbaki, Ramzi. 2008. *The Legacy of the* Kitāb: *Sībawayhi's Analytical Methods within the Context of the Arabic Grammatical Theory*. Leiden & Boston: Brill, coll. "Studies in Semitic Languages and Linguistics" 51.

Baalbaki, Ramzi. 2019. "Grammar for Beginners and Ibn Hišām's Approach to Issues of *ʾiʿrāb*". *The Foundations of Arabic Linguistics IV. The Evolution of Theory*, ed. by Manuela E.B. Giolfo & Kees Versteegh, 61–88. Leiden & Boston: Brill, coll. "Studies in Semitic Languages and Linguistics" 97.

Bernards, Monique. 1997. *Changing Traditions: Al-Mubarrad's Refutation of Sībawayh and the Subsequent Reception of the Kitāb*. Studies in Semitic Languages and Linguistics 23. Leiden; New York: E.J. Brill.

Bohas, Georges, Jean-Patrick Guillaume, and Djamel Eddine Kouloughli. 1990. *The Arabic Linguistic Tradition*. London & New York: Routledge, coll. "Arabic Thought and Culture".

Carter, Michael G. 1972. "Les origines de la grammaire arabe". *Revue des Études Islamiques* 40/1. 69–97.

Carter, Michael G. 1973. "An Arab Grammarian of the Eighth Century A.D.: A Contribution to the History of Linguistics". *Journal of the American Oriental Society* 93/2. 146–157.

Carter, Michael G. 1987/1988. "Arab Linguistics and Arabic Linguistics". *Zeitschrift für Geschichte der arabisch-islamischen Wissenschaften* 4. 205–218.

Carter, Michael G. 1999. "The Struggle for Authority. A Re-Examination of the Basran and Kufan Debate". *Tradition and Innovation. Norm and Deviation in Arabic and Semitic Linguistics*, ed. by Lutz Edzard & Mohammed Nekroumi, 55–70. Wiesbaden: Harrassowitz.

Carter, Michael G. 2000. "The Development of Arabic Linguistics after Sībawayhi: Basra, Kufa and Baghdad". *History of the Language Sciences. An International Handbook on the Evolution of the Study of Language from the Beginnings to the Present*, 1, ed. by Sylvain Auroux, E.F.K. Koerner, Hans-Josef Niederehe, Kees Versteegh, and Sören Philipps, 263–272. Berlin & New York: Walter de Gruyter.

Carter, Michael G. 2004. *Sībawayhi*. London & New York: I.B. Tauris, coll. "Makers of Islamic Civilization".

Ghersetti, Antonella. 2017. "Systematizing the Description of Arabic: The Case of Ibn Al-Sarrāj". *Asiatische Studien—Études Asiatiques* 71/3. 879–906.

Jahn, Gustav. 1895–1900. *Sîbawaihi's Buch über die Grammatik: nach der Ausgabe von H. Derenbourg und dem Commentar des Sîrâfî: Übersetzt und Erklärt und mit Auszügen aus Sîrâfî und anderen Commentaren*. Berlin: Reuther & Reichard, 2 vol.

Kasher, Almog. 2015. "Abstract Principles in Arabic Grammatical Theory: The Operator Assigning the Independent Mood". *The Foundations of Arabic Linguistics II. Kitāb Sībawayhi: Interpretation and Transmission*, ed. by Amal E. Marogy & Kees Versteegh, 120–137. Leiden & Boston: Brill, coll. "Studies in Semitic Languages and Linguistics" 83.

Larcher, Pierre. 2005. "Arabe Préislamique—Arabe Coranique—Arabe Classique. Un *continuum* ?". *Die dunklen Anfänge: neue Forschungen zur Entstehung und frühen Geschichte des Islam*, ed. by Karl-Heinz Ohlig and Gerd-Rüdiger Puin, 248–265. Berlin: Verlag Hans Schiler.

Larcher, Pierre. 2008a. "Al-lugha al-fuṣḥâ: *archéologie d'un concept « idéolinguistique »*". *Revue des mondes musulmans et de la Méditerranée* 124. 263–278.

Larcher, Pierre. 2008b. "Qu' est-ce que l' arabe du Coran? Réflexions d' un linguiste". *Linguistique arabe*, ed. by Georgine Ayoub and Jérôme Lentin, *Cahiers de linguistique de l'INALCO* 5 [2003–2005, années de tomaison]. 27–47.

Larcher, Pierre. 2010. "In search of a standard: dialect variation and New Arabic features in the oldest Arabic written documents". *The development of Arabic as a written language*, (Supplement to the Proceedings of the Seminar for Arabian Studies 40), ed. by M.C.A. Macdonald, 103–112. Oxford: Archaeopress.

Larcher, Pierre. 2013. "Le Coran : l'écrit, le lu, le récité". *Le Coran. Nouvelles approches*, Actes de la Journée d'étude *Les études coraniques aujourd'hui. Méthodes, enjeux, débats*, Paris, IISMM, 26 et 27 novembre 2009, ed. by Mehdi Azaiez and avec la collaboration de Sabrina Mervin, 243–255. Paris: CNRS Éditions.

Larcher, Pierre. 2014. "Le Coran : le dit et l'écrit". *Oralité et Écriture dans la Bible et le Coran*, ed. By Philippe Cassuto and Pierre Larcher, 53–67. Aix-en-Provence: Presses Universitaires de Provence.

Marogy, Amal E. 2010. *Kitāb Sībawayhi: Syntax and Pragmatics*. Leiden & Boston: Brill, coll. "Studies in Semitic Languages and Linguistics" 56.

Owens, Jonathan. 2006. *A Linguistic History of Arabic*. Oxford & New York: Oxford University Press, coll. "Oxford Linguistics".

Sadan, Arik. 2015. "Sībawayhi's and Later Grammarians' Usage of *ḥadīṯ*s as a Grammatical Tool". *The Foundations of Arabic Linguistics II. Kitāb Sībawayhi: Interpretation and Transmission*, ed. by Amal E. Marogy and Kees Versteegh, 171–183. Leiden & Boston: Brill, coll. "Studies in Semitic Languages and Linguistics" 83.

Talmon, Rafael. 1982. "*Naḥwiyyūn* in Sībawayhi's *Kitāb*". *Zeitschrift für Arabische Linguistik* 8. 12–38.

Talmon, Rafael. 1985. "An Eighth-Century Grammatical School in Medina: The Collection and Evaluation of the Available Material". *Bulletin of the School of Oriental and African Studies* 48/2. 224–236.

Talmon, Rafael. 2000. "The first beginnings of Arabic linguistics: The era of the Old Iraqi School". *History of the Language Sciences. An International Handbook on the Evolution of the Study of Language from the Beginnings to the Present*, 1, ed. by Sylvain Auroux, E.F.K. Koerner, Hans-Josef Niederehe, Kees Versteegh, and Sören Philipps, 245–252. Berlin & New York: Walter de Gruyter.

Troupeau, Gérard. 1976. *Lexique-index du "Kitāb" de Sībawayhi*. Paris: Klincksieck, "Études arabes et islamiques : série 3, Études et documents" 7.

Versteegh, Kees. 1977. *Greek Elements in Arabic Linguistic Thinking*. Leiden: Brill, "Studies in Semitic Languages and Linguistics" 7.

CHAPTER 6

Grammar and the *radd* Genre in al-Andalus

Francesco Binaghi

Introduction

Written refutations, in both forms of short epistles and longer treatises, have represented common scholarly productions in the Islamicate world since its earliest times. Typically known under the title of *Kitāb* (*al-Radd*) *ʿalā…*, these compilations were particularly abundant in all fields of profane and religious literature between the 2nd/8th and the 4th/10th centuries, when they might have contributed to the development of the different sciences. The importance of these works can easily be attested by the number of such titles included in Ibn al-Nadīm's (d. 385/995) *Fihrist*.[1]

This trend can also be observed in the field of language studies. As far as Arabic grammar is concerned, two very well-known refutations are *al-Radd ʿalā Sībawayhi* by Mubarrad (d. 285/898) and *al-Radd ʿalā al-Mubarrad*, also known as *al-Intiṣār li-Sībawayhi*, by Ibn Wallād (d. 332/944). Similar works were also ascribed to other important grammarians like Ḫalīl (d. 175/791?), Farrāʾ (d. 207/822), Ṯaʿlab (d. 291/904) and Ibn Ḫālawayhi (d. 370/980). After this period, however, the importance of such compilations seems to have faded, since a significantly smaller number of *Radd*-s were attributed to later grammarians. As a matter of fact, an inclination for the intellectual debate certainly lived through to later authors (personal attacks and scholarly criticisms can for instance be found in bigger commentaries and compendia), but biobibliographical dictionaries recorded a small number of such titles, which entails that autonomous refutations were deemed to be less important for the intellectual life of their period.

Once more, the situation appeared to be different in the Western periphery of the Islamicate world, namely al-Andalus, where many aspects of the intellectual life tended to be characterized by archaic features that had meanwhile disappeared or evolved in the heart of the Islamicate world.[2]

1 Cf. Ibn al-Nadīm *Fihrist* index, 109–111. Cf. also *EI2*, art. "Radd" (D. Gimaret).

2 In the field of grammar, this is exemplified by the dominant role played by earlier treatises—notably, but not exclusively, Sībawayhi's (d. 180/796?) *Kitāb*, Zaǧǧāǧī's (d. 337/949) *Ǧumal* and Fārisī's (d. 377/987) *ʾĪḍāḥ*—in the development of grammatical studies at least until the 7th/13th century (cf. Binaghi 2015: notably 6–18).

 | DOI:10.1163/9789004515895_008

1 Grammatical *Radd*-s in al-Andalus

In the studies on the history of the Arabic grammatical tradition, one of the most cited references is undoubtedly the "Refutation of the grammarians", *Kitāb al-Radd ʿalā al-nuḥāt*, by the Andalusi Ibn Maḍāʾ (d. 592/1196). Even though its author was a Ẓāhirī jurist, who became *qāḍī al-quḍāt* under the Almohades, and its core message should be taken as coming from a religious polemist, not a grammarian strictly speaking, this treatise directly tackled some of the grammarians' pillars, such as the theory of *ʿamal* (case and mood allocation, hence linked to *ʾiʿrāb*) and grammatical justifications (*ʿilal*), on which they had built their theory. Therefore, it must be taken as a contribution intervening in the field of grammatical discussions, and its anticonformist and revolutionary approach has attracted the attention of many authors and researchers especially in the last century.

However extreme Ibn Maḍāʾ's work was in its conceptual stance, it is far from being the only case of grammatical *radd* in al-Andalus; quite on the contrary, it could be seen as a prototypical example of an Andalusi inclination towards intellectual debate and polemics. Biobibliographical sources record a great number of *radd* works composed by Andalusi authors (some 71 titles according to *BA*: B, 305–306),[3] a good amount of which discussed grammatical matters. Unfortunately, just a few of all the works related to linguistic issues have been transmitted up until today, therefore it is not always easy to clearly define the specific topic in which lost refutations intervened. For the purpose of this research, I have only retained those *radd*-s dealing—certainly or most likely—with the grammatical theory.[4] The criteria adopted for the selection of works are as follows: (a) an explicit mention, in the title, of a grammatical treatise or issue; (b) indirect reference of their content in other sources, especially biobibliographical dictionaries; (c) the author and the target of the refutation are both grammarians, or one of them has expressed views related to language

3 This figure only includes treatises whose title starts with *Radd*, therefore it does not encompass other refutations bearing original titles or starting with a different word.

4 Some refutations were addressing issues of language use and "applied grammar", such as *al-Radd ʿalā al-ʾaʾimma fī-mā yaqaʿu fī al-ṣalāt min al-ḫaṭaʾ wa-l-laḥn fī šahr ramaḍān wa-ġayrihi* by Makkī b. ʾAbī Ṭālib (d. 437/1045), rather than dealing with the grammatical theory in broader terms.

I have not considered as refutations the treatises presenting a systematic analysis of another text (*matn*), e.g. the *al-Ḥulal fī ʾiṣlāḥ al-ḫalal al-wāqiʿ fī al-Ǧumal* by Ibn al-Sīd al-Baṭalyawsī or the *Risālat al-ʾIfṣāḥ bi-baʿḍ mā ǧāʾa min al-ḫaṭaʾ fī al-ʾĪḍāḥ* by Ibn al-Ṭarāwa: even though some of them can prove quite critical, as discussed below, I would rather categorize them as commentaries because they provide a chapter-by-chapter discussion of the *matn*.

and grammar. A list of 25 titles, ordered chronologically according to the date of death of its author, can be drawn:

1) *al-Radd ʿalā ʾAbī Ǧaʿfar al-Naḥḥās fī kitāb al-Kāfī* by Ibn al-ʿArīf (d. 390/1000)
2) *Radd ʿalā Ibn Sirāǧ bi-risāla farīda* by al-ʾAʿlam al-Šantamarī (d. 476/1084)[5]
3) *Risāla ʾilā ʾAbī ʿAbd Allāh Muḥammad Ibn Ḫalaṣa* by Ibn al-Sīd al-Baṭalyawsī (d. 521/1127)[6]
4) *Radd ʿalā ʾAbī Muḥammad Ibn al-Sīd al-Baṭalyawsī* by Ibn Ḫalaṣa (d. 519/1125 or 521/1127)
5) *Risāla fī-mā ǧarā baynahu wa-bayna ʾAbī al-Ḥasan [Ibn] al-Bāḏiš fī masʾala naḥwiyya* by Ibn al-Ṭarāwa (d. 526/1132 or 528/1134)[7]
6) *Risāla fī iḫtilāfihi ʾilā ʾAbī ʿAbd Allāh Ibn Ḫalaṣa* by Ibn al-Ǧazzār (d. 540/1145)[8]
7) *al-Radd ʿalā al-nuḥāt* by Ibn Maḍāʾ[9]
8) *Radd ʿalā Ibn Ḥazm fī baʿḍ maqālātihi* by Ibn Ḫarūf al-ʾIšbīlī (d. 609/1212)[10]

---

5 This "refutation against Ibn Sirāǧ through a unique epistle" is mentioned by Kalāʿī (fl. 6th/12th century; *ʾIḥkām* 68), who also provides us with information on its topic. The debate between Ibn Sirāǧ (d. 489/1096) and al-ʾAʿlam al-Šantamarī originated in this latter's *al-Masʾala al-rašīdiyya*, and more precisely in his etymological and morphological analysis of the name *Allāh*. Such an analysis, mixing divine and profane elements, drew Ibn Sirāǧ's severe theology-based criticism—even though we ignore under which form and in which context this was expressed: was it an autonomous *radd* compilation as well?—, to which al-ʾAʿlam al-Šantamarī responded with a *risāla farīda*. This latter's refutation must have been conveyed in an independent, written pamphlet.

6 Ibn Ḫayr (d. 575/1179; *Fahrasa* 515, no. 1228) mentions this epistle, as well as "Ibn Ḫalāṣa's [*sic*] answer" (cf. *radd* no. 4), among the works he had studied. It is to be noted that Ibn al-Sīd al-Baṭalyawsī's name is directly followed by the title *al-naḥwī* (the grammarian), which must point to the fact that these debates concerned grammatical issues.

7 According to Bannā (1980:50–51), this controversy between Ibn al-Ṭarāwa and Ibn al-Bāḏiš (d. 528/1133) concerned the particle *ʾillā* in exceptive constructions.

8 According to Ibn al-ʾAbbār (d. 658/1260; *Takmila* II, 134), this *risāla* recorded the debates between Ibn al-Ǧazzār and Ibn Ḫalaṣa on several issues relating to the grammatical analysis (*ʾiʿrāb*) of Qurʾānic verses.

9 This is the title under which the text was published and by which it is commonly referred to today. However, Wolfe (1984:27–39 and 1990) argues that this text is actually the result of the merger of two different works on grammar that Ibn Maḍāʾ had originally written, *Tanzīh al-Qurʾān ʿammā lā yalīqu bi-l-bayān* (to which the preamble and sections one, five and six of the published *Radd* would belong) and *al-Mušriq fī al-naḥw* (for the remaining sections two, three and four).

10 We have no information about the content of this refutation. However, given that Ibn Ḫarūf was a renowned grammarian in al-Andalus, the author of grammatical commentaries and many *radd*-s against other grammarians (cf. below), and that Ibn Ḥazm's (d. 456/1064) thought reveals many connections with linguistic concepts and ideas (cf. for in-

9) *Radd ʿalā al-ʾAʿlam fī risālatihi al-Rašīdiyya wa-ġayrihā* by Ibn Ḫarūf al-ʾIšbīlī[11]
10) *Radd ʿalā Ibn al-Ṭarāwa fī Muqaddimātihi ʿalā ʾabwāb al-Kitāb* by Ibn Ḫarūf al-ʾIšbīlī
11) *Radd ʿalā Ibn Malkūn* by Ibn Ḫarūf al-ʾIšbīlī[12]
12) *Radd ʿalā ʾAbī Zayd al-Suhaylī* by Ibn Ḫarūf al-ʾIšbīlī[13]
13) *Tanzīh ʾaʾimmat al-naḥw ʿammā nusiba ʾilayhim min al-ḫaṭaʾ wa-l-sahw* by Ibn Ḫarūf al-ʾIšbīlī[14]
14) *Radd ʿalā ʾAbī al-Walīd Ibn Rušd* by Ibn Ḫarūf al-ʾIšbīlī[15]
15) *Radd ʿalā ʾAbī ʿAlī al-Rundī* by Ibn Ḫarūf al-ʾIšbīlī[16]
16) *Radd ʿalā Ibn Ḫarūf muntaṣiran li-šayḫihi al-Suhaylī* by ʾAbū ʿAlī al-Rundī (d. 616/1219)
17) *al-Tanbīh ʿalā ʾaġlāṭ al-Zamaḫšarī fī al-Mufaṣṣal wa-mā ḫālafa fīhi Sībawayhi* by Ibn Maʿzūz (d. 625/1227)[17]

---

stance Asín Palacios 1939, Arnaldez 1956 or, more recently, Peña 2013), we can suppose that this refutation might also have dealt with some kind of grammatical or language-related issue. Also, in the list of Ibn Ḫarūf's *radd*-s given by Ibn ʿAbd al-Malik (d. 703/1303; *Ḏayl* V, 320), this title is immediately preceded and immediately followed by other titles clearly dealing with grammar (refutations against Ibn al-Ṭarāwa and al-ʾAʿlam al-Šantamarī before it, and against Ibn Malkūn after it), which means that probably this author considered it to be a grammatical *radd* as well.

11 Another refutation of al-ʾAʿlam al-Šantamarī's *al-Masʾala al-rašīdiyya* (cf. *radd* no. 2).

12 Ibn al-ʾAbbār (*Takmila* III, 383) informs us that this *radd* against Ibn Malkūn (d. 581/1185 or 584/1188) was about "the Arabic language" (*fī al-ʿarabiyya*), probably meaning grammar.

13 This refutation is also included by Ibn al-ʾAbbār (*Takmila* III, 383) among those dealing with "the Arabic language" (*fī al-ʿarabiyya*), i.e. likely grammar.

14 Ḫwānsārī (d. 1313/1895; *Rawḍāt* V, 246), who provides this title (previous biobibliographical sources had only mentioned a *Radd ʿalā Ibn Maḍāʾ*, adding however that it concerned linguistic matters; cf. for instance Ibn al-ʾAbbār *Takmila* III, 383), also informs us that this refutation targeted Ibn Maḍāʾ's *Tanzīh al-Qurʾān ʿammā lā yalīqu bi-l-bayān*. Ibn Ḫarūf's title attests an evident polemical attitude towards it.

15 We have no concrete information about the content of this *radd*. However, two elements drive us to believe that it might be included in this list: the fact that Ibn Rušd (d. 595/1198) was also the author of a grammatical treatise, *al-Ḍarūrī fī ṣināʿat al-naḥw* (cf. Hamzé 2002); and the fact that Ibn ʿAbd al-Malik (*Ḏayl* V, 320) mentions it after the *Radd ʿalā Ibn Malkūn*, and before the two refutations against Suhaylī (d. 581/1185) and Ibn Maḍāʾ, all of which dealt with grammatical issues.

16 Ruʿaynī (d. 666/1268; *Barnāmaǧ* 82) informs us that Ibn Ḫarūf and Rundī had some disagreements on different issues relating to the Arabic language (*munāqaḍāt fī masāʾil min al-ʿarabiyya*, i.e. grammar). We deduce that probably, following Ibn Ḫarūf's refutation against Suhaylī (cf. *radd* no. 11), Rundī intervened to defend his teacher (cf. *radd* no. 16), so Ibn Ḫarūf also addressed a counter-refutation to this latter.

17 This refutation was also known in some sources as *al-Radd ʿalā al-Zamaḫšarī fī Mufaṣṣalihi*.

18) *Talḫīṣ radd al-Mubarrad ʿalā Sībawayhi wa-ntiṣār Ibn Wallād lahu* by Ibn al-Ḥāǧǧ al-ʾAzdī (d. 647/1249 or 651/1253)[18]
19) *Radd iʿtirāḍāt Ibn al-Ṭarāwa ʿalā Sībawayhi* by Ibn al-Ḍāʾiʿ (d. 680/1281)[19]
20) *Radd iʿtirāḍāt Ibn al-Ṭarāwa ʿalā al-Fārisī* by Ibn al-Ḍāʾiʿ[20]
21) *Radd iʿtirāḍāt Ibn al-Sīd al-Baṭalyawsī ʿalā al-Zaǧǧāǧī* by Ibn al-Ḍāʾiʿ[21]
22) *Radd ʿalā Muqarrib Ibn ʿUṣfūr* by Ibn al-Ḍāʾiʿ
23) *Šadd al-ziyār ʿalā ǧaḥfalat al-ḥimār* by Ḥāzim al-Qarṭāǧannī (d. 684/1285)[22]
24) *Iḫtiṣār al-intiṣār li-kitāb al-ʾĪḍāḥ min risālat al-ʾIfṣāḥ* by Ibn al-Faḫḫār al-ʾArkušī al-Ǧuḏāmī (d. 723/1323)[23]
25) *al-Ǧawāb al-lāʾiḥ al-muʿtamad ʿalayhi fī al-radd ʿalā man nasaba rafʿ al-ḫabar bi-lā ʾilā Sībawayhi* by Ibn al-Faḫḫār al-ʾArkušī al-Ǧuḏāmī.

A quick look at the list enables us to remark that almost all of the refutations simply bear a generic, descriptive title including the name of the author and/or the title of the treatise which constitute the target. Only four refutations (no. 13, 17, 23 and 24) have a proper, specific title, even though two of them (no. 13 and 17) are also known in some sources with the more generic *al-Radd ʿalā*.

A more interesting clue for a typological analysis of *radd* writing in al-Andalus could be underlying in the opposition between the terms *radd* and

18 The title suggests a summary of the dispute that opposed Ibn Wallād to Mubarrad, which was related to Sībawayhi's heritage and played a central role in the textual history of the *Kitāb*. We cannot exclude that Ibn al-Ḥāǧǧ intervened himself in these debates and expressed his own criticisms. According to *BA* (III, 331), a manuscript dated as of 623 H (= 1226 CE) would have been preserved in the Maktaba ʾAḥmadiyya (Tunis) under no. 3966. The manuscripts of the Maktaba ʾAḥmadiyya have now been integrated in the collection of the National Library of Tunisia, and manuscripts have been recatalogued with new code numbers. During my research at the National Library of Tunisia in August–September 2013, I was unable to find this text.

19 Probably another refutation of *al-Muqaddimāt ʾilā ʿilm al-Kitāb* (cf. *radd* no. 10).

20 The target of this refutation must have been the *Risālat al-ʾIfṣāḥ bi-baʿḍ mā ǧāʾa min al-ḫaṭaʾ fī al-ʾĪḍāḥ* (cf. Ibn al-Faḫḫār al-ʾArkušī al-Ǧuḏāmī's *Iḫtiṣār al-intiṣār li-kitāb al-ʾĪḍāḥ min risālat al-ʾIfṣāḥ*, no. 24).

21 Ibn al-Sīd al-Baṭalyawsī is the author of two (complementary) commentaries on Zaǧǧāǧī's *Ǧumal*: *al-Ḥulal fī ʾiṣlāḥ al-ḫalal al-wāqiʿ fī al-Ǧumal* on grammar, and *al-Ḥulal fī šarḥ ʾabyāt al-Ǧumal* on its poetic quotes. This refutation must have targeted the former.

22 Mentioned by Maqqarī (d. 1041/1632; *Nafḥ* IV, 148) within a rather long list of authors who criticized (*intaqada*) Ibn ʿUṣfūr's (d. 669/1271) treatise *al-Muqarrib fī al-naḥw*, alongside Ibn al-Ḍāʾiʿ's *Radd* (cf. no. 22) and others written by learned men from the Maghrib (e.g. *al-Minhaǧ al-muʿarrib fī al-radd ʿalā al-Muqarrib* by ʾAbū ʾIsḥāq ʾIbrāhīm b. ʾAḥmad b. Muḥammad al-Ǧazarī al-Ḫazraǧī al-ʾAnṣārī al-Maǧribī, d. 709/1309).

23 It was presumably an abridged version of the *Radd* by Ibn al-Ḍāʾiʿ, who had been his teacher.

risāla that appear in the titles, as they might have been used for two different forms of refutation. The term *risāla* seems to have been used for writings either outlining the debates between two contemporary grammarians (no. 5 and 6), or expressing the author's views in a dispute opposing him to a peer (no. 2 and 3). Treatises called *radd*, on the contrary, seem to identify works targeting a specific treatise (no. 1, 9, 10, 13, 17 and 22) or an earlier grammarian, this latter being identified in either an explicit way (no. 8, 11, 12, 14, 18, 19, 20 and 21) or in more general and anonymous terms (no. 7 and 25). Three exceptions should be accounted for, nevertheless, in such a typological division: Ibn Ḫalaṣa's answer to Ibn al-Sīd al-Baṭalyawsī (no. 4) and, one century later, Rundī's response to Ibn Ḫarūf and Ibn Ḫarūf's subsequent answer to Rundī (respectively no. 16 and 15). A possible, partial explanation of these exceptions—I would hypothesize—lies in a more archaic use of the term *risāla* to identify grammatical debates between contemporary authors. Both the term and the practice might have been abandoned around the mid-6th/12th century, when data shows that a greater number of refutations of earlier grammarians and grammatical treatises started to be composed, in parallel with the decline of epistolary disputes.

As grammatical *radd* writing spanned over three centuries and a half in al-Andalus, from the end of the 4th/10th century to the first half of the 8th/14th century, two common characteristics can be found in all of these titles: (1) they were written works, some of which even studied and transmitted as any other literary or scientific text;[24] and (2) they were compiled as autonomous works. We can likely identify this production as pertaining to a specific literary genre, related to but at the same time independent from a more general and common attitude towards intellectual debate, which was expressed either in oral form[25] or within other treatises as an argumentative tool for theoretical elaboration.

Regrettably, only one out of the twenty-five titles listed previously has been preserved and is presently available to us: the aforementioned *Kitāb al-Radd ʿalā al-nuḥāt* by Ibn Maḍāʾ.[26] Apart from this work, which has already been studied extensively,[27] it is therefore impossible to analyze the content of the Andalusi grammatical *radd*-s in order to better define their extension, the

24 Cf. for instance Ibn Ḫayr's (*Fahrasa* 515, no. 1228) and Ruʿaynī's (*Barnāmaǧ* 82) testimonies about *radd*-s no. 3 and 16.

25 Some of which, especially in earlier periods, were recorded in the *maǧālis* and *ʾaḫbār* literature.

26 A second title might have been preserved in manuscript, but I was unfortunately unable to locate it (cf. fn. 17).

27 Among the quite abundant literature on this treatise, cf. for instance Wolfe 1984, Versteegh 2013, and Campanelli 2016.

authors' methodology and the impact that they might have had on the grammatical theory. Nonetheless, the analysis of their title could be very enriching for a better understanding of the kind of relations linking some of the most important figures in the field of Andalusi Arabic grammar, and more generally of the scholarly networks in which they evolved.

2 Grammatical Debates and Scholarly Affiliations

Among the peculiar features of this production—as I have already pointed out—is also the fact that the titles usually include the name of the grammarian who is the target of the refutation and, sometimes, the title of the specific work that is refuted.[28] This data has been gathered in the following table:[29]

TABLE 6.1 List of *radd*-s with respective targets

Author	Target *Grammarian*	*Treatise*	*Radd no.*
1. Ibn al-ʿArīf	Naḥḥās (d. 338/950)	*al-Kāfī fī al-naḥw*	(1)
2. al-ʾAʿlam al-Šantamarī	Ibn Sirāǧ		(2)
3. Ibn al-Sīd al-Baṭalyawsī	Ibn Ḫalaṣa		(3)
4. Ibn Ḫalaṣa	Ibn al-Sīd al-Baṭalyawsī		(4)
5. Ibn al-Ṭarāwa	Ibn al-Bāḏiš		(5)
6. Ibn al-Ǧazzār	Ibn Ḫalaṣa		(6)
7. Ibn Maḍāʾ	*nuḥāt* (grammarians generally speaking)		(7)
8. Ibn Ḫarūf	Ibn Ḥazm	*maqālāt* (not better identified)	(8)
	al-ʾAʿlam al-Šantamarī	*al-Masʾala al-rašīdiyya* (and other undefined treatises)	(9)

28 For some *radd*-s, this information can be found in other sources or deduced from the other elements in our possession. Elements that are not mentioned explicitly in the title of the refutation, but that can be inferred, will be mentioned into brackets in table 6.1.

29 Numbers on the left are associated with different authors and aim at counting them; numbers into parentheses on the right of the table refer to the list of *radd*-s given above.

TABLE 6.1 List of *radd*-s with respective targets (*cont.*)

Author	Target Grammarian	Treatise	*Radd* no.
8. Ibn Ḫarūf (*cont.*)	Ibn al-Ṭarāwa	*al-Muqaddimāt ʾilā ʿilm al-Kitāb*[30]	(10)
	Ibn Malkūn		(11)
	Suhaylī		(12)
	[Ibn Maḍāʾ]	[*Tanzīh al-Qurʾān ʿammā lā yalīqu bi-l-bayān*]	(13)
	Ibn Rušd		(14)
	Rundī		(15)
9. Rundī	Ibn Ḫarūf		(16)
10. Ibn Maʿzūz	Zamaḫšarī (d. 538/1144)	*Mufaṣṣal*	(17)
11. Ibn al-Ḥāǧǧ al-ʾAzdī	Mubarrad?	*Radd al-Mubarrad ʿalā Sībawayhi?*[31]	(18)
12. Ibn al-Ḍāʾiʿ	Ibn al-Ṭarāwa	[*al-Muqaddimāt ʾilā ʿilm al-Kitāb*]	(19)
	Ibn al-Ṭarāwa	[*al-ʾIfṣāḥ bi-baʿḍ mā ǧāʾa min al-ḫaṭaʾ fī al-ʾĪḍāḥ*]	(20)
	Ibn al-Sīd al-Baṭalyawsī	[*al-Ḥulal fī ʾiṣlāḥ al-ḫalal al-wāqiʿ fī al-Ǧumal*]	(21)
	Ibn ʿUṣfūr	*Muqarrib*	(22)
13. Ḥāzim al-Qarṭāǧannī	[Ibn ʿUṣfūr]	[*Muqarrib*]	(23)
14. Ibn al-Faḫḫār al-ʾArkušī al-Ǧuḏāmī	[Ibn al-Ṭarāwa]	*al-ʾIfṣāḥ bi-baʿḍ mā ǧāʾa min al-ḫaṭaʾ fī al-ʾĪḍāḥ*	(24)
	man nasaba rafʿ al-ḫabar bi-lā ʾilā Sībawayhi (undefined grammarians)		(25)

30 Its full title is *al-Muqaddimāt ʾilā ʿilm al-Kitāb wa-šarḥ al-muškilāt ʿalā tawālī al-ʾabwāb*.

31 The phrasing of the title of this *radd* (*Talḫīṣ radd al-Mubarrad ʿalā Sībawayhi wa-ntiṣār*

Table 6.1 shows even more clearly that three grammarians (Ibn Ḫarūf, Ibn al-Ḍāʾiʿ and Ibn al-Faḫḫār al-ʾArkušī al-Ǧuḏāmī) composed more than half of the titles of the list. Their polemical disposition might be explained as an idiosyncratic feature, especially in the case of Ibn Ḫarūf, whose contribution amounts to no less than eight refutations. Nevertheless, it might also be a sign of the evolution of the Andalusi grammarians' interest for this genre. Whereas in the Islamicate world as a whole *radd*-s had been particularly abundant in the earlier period, namely between the 2nd/8th and the 4th/10th centuries, this practice seems to have developed later—at least among grammarians—in al-Andalus: among the fourteen different authors, five lived in(to) the 6th/12th century (five titles out of twenty-five), and seven in(to) the 7th/13th and early 8th/14th centuries (eighteen titles).

More important, table 6.1 highlights the geographical "endogamy" of such debates. Only a few treatises (no. 1, 17 and 18, at least explicitly) targeted grammarians or treatises from outside al-Andalus. This does not necessarily mean that the evolution of the grammatical theory in this area was completely independent of the contemporary contribution of Eastern grammarians. However, this does imply that Andalusi grammarians perceived themselves as an autonomous community. They did not oppose their Eastern colleagues altogether as a single block, which suggests that they did not perceive their identity as being shaped exclusively by an East-West opposition. They mainly targeted grammarians within their geographical and cultural environment in an effort to compete for intellectual supremacy, therefore proving their in fine total independence in scholarly debates vis-à-vis Eastern grammarians.

The identification of the grammarians involved in this process, both as authors and as targets, proves useful for the analysis of Andalusi scholarly networks, since some figures occur more than once and so they enable us to look for some regular patterns. In figure 6.1 below, I have reorganized the elements emerging from the *Radd*-s and then cross-referenced them with data available on master-pupil teaching relations. A division between two groups can be drawn.

Such a reconstruction certainly has its limits, notably because some grammarians only appear once in the corpus and, at the same time, the significant number of refutations written by Ibn Ḫarūf and Ibn al-Ḍāʾiʿ has driven me to place all of their targets in the opposite column. Had the texts of the *Radd*-s

Ibn Wallād lahu) suggests that Ibn al-Ḥāǧǧ al-ʾAzdī was rather leaning towards Ibn Wallād's position, even though we unfortunately have no elements to confirm it.

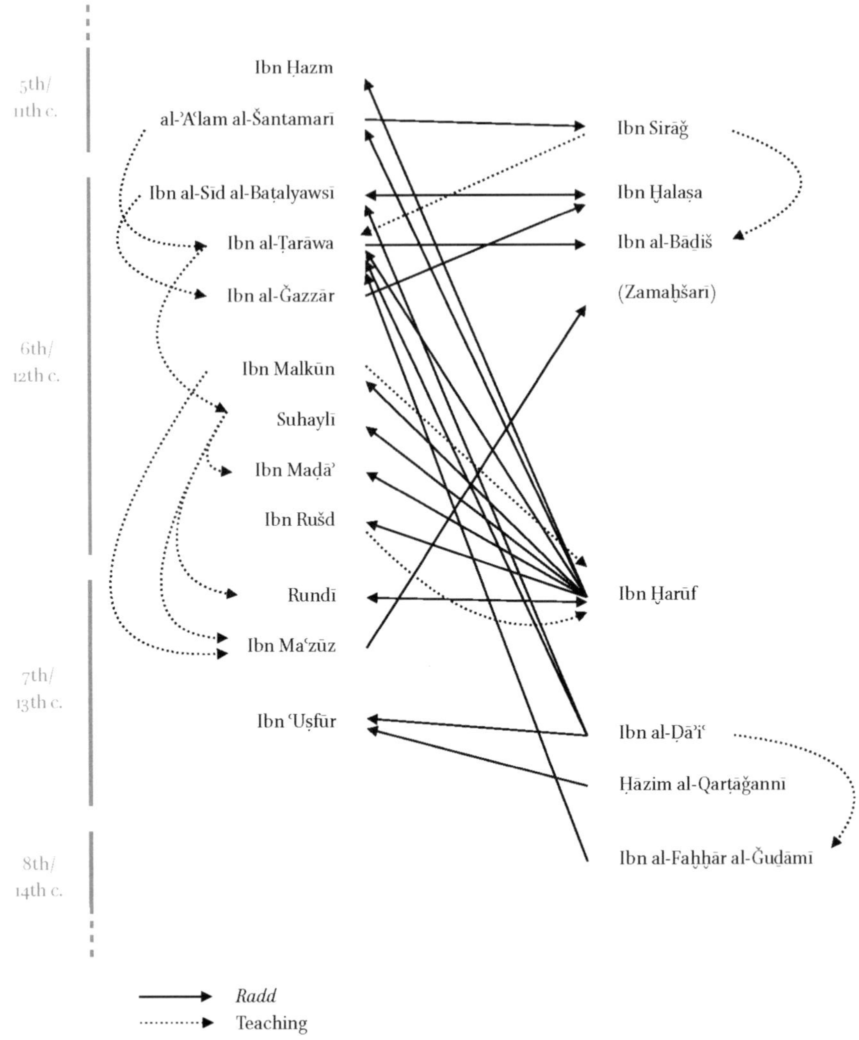

FIGURE 6.1 *Radd*-s and teaching relations

been preserved, they might have revealed a more nuanced picture, especially with regard to the scope of the criticism and the extent of the opposition. However, master-pupil relations support this pattern considerably, since they allow us to identify some regularities. Foremost, it confirms the importance of direct scholarly ties in shaping intellectual legacies and loyalties, which take the form of either a pupil defending his master (Ibn al-Ǧazzār defending Ibn al-Sīd al-Baṭalyawsī following Ibn Ḫalaṣa's refutation; Rundī endorsing Suhaylī against Ibn Ḫarūf's attack), or a pupil targeting the same author/treatise as his master (Ibn al-Ḍāʾiʿ and Ibn al-Faḫḫār al-ʾArkušī al-Ǧuḏāmī both refuting

Ibn al-Ṭarāwa's *Risālat al-ʾIfṣāḥ*). At the same time, a long, uninterrupted, direct teaching line starting from al-ʾAʿlam al-Šantamarī, passing through Ibn al-Ṭarāwa and Suhaylī, and arriving at Ibn Maḍāʾ, Rundī and Ibn Maʿzūz could strengthen the architecture of such a sketch. Clearly, we should not minimize the (sometimes strong) differences between these authors, nor underestimate the imprint other teachers (even from other disciplines) might have left. Notably so in a region characterized by a high number of scholars and of learning centers, where studying with several learned men and—at least as much as the political situation allowed it—in different cities was rather the norm until later periods. We should not think either, more generally speaking, that all of the grammarians in the left column of figure 6.1 subscribed to the same theoretical framework. Nevertheless, despite all of this, it is still worth questioning whether authors in each one of the two groups share any common features.

3 Of Sources and Epistemology

The most criticized author in our list is Ibn al-Ṭarāwa: he will thus be the starting point of our inquiry. The main books he wrote on grammar were both equally criticized by some Andalusi grammarians: *al-Muqaddimāt ʾilā ʿilm al-Kitāb wa-šarḥ al-muškilāt ʿalā tawālī al-ʾabwāb* (targeted by Ibn Ḫarūf and Ibn al-Ḍāʾiʿ) and *Risālat al-ʾIfṣāḥ bi-baʿḍ mā ǧāʾa min al-ḫaṭaʾ fī al-ʾĪḍāḥ* (refuted by Ibn al-Ḍāʾiʿ and Ibn al-Faḫḫār al-ʾArkušī al-Ǧuḏāmī). These two treatises reveal Ibn al-Ṭarāwa's conception of what grammar should be: a prelude to the study of Sībawayhi's *Kitāb*. Such a conception is revealed not exclusively through the title of the first work (*al-Muqaddimāt ʾilā ʿilm al-Kitāb*), but also in the introduction to the second one, when he alludes to "transmitted compendia" (*al-muḫtaṣarāt al-marwiyya*) as "authoritative treatises" (*al-tawālīf al-musnada*, Ibn al-Ṭarāwa *ʾIfṣāḥ* 16), and later identifies such "authoritative treatises" with Zaǧǧāǧī's *Ǧumal*, Naḥḥās' *Kāfī* and finally Sībawayhi's *Kitāb* (Ibn al-Ṭarāwa *ʾIfṣāḥ* 35).[32] Ibn al-Ṭarāwa clearly exhibits his preference for these works, and all throughout the *Risālat al-ʾIfṣāḥ* he criticizes Fārisī's *ʾĪḍāḥ*. The opposition between the *Ǧumal* and the *ʾĪḍāḥ* reflects their divergent taxonomic organization and, in fine, their theoretical framework: Fārisī's volume presents a highly systematized theory that reorganizes Sībawayhi's material in a rational

32 On Ibn al-Ṭarāwa's *Risālat al-ʾIfṣāḥ*, and notably on his conception of grammar, cf. Guillaume 2018:56–58.

way; Zaǧǧāǧī's compendium, on the contrary, has no particular theoretical pretension[33] and simply presents the grammatical material in a pragmatic way which particularly suits the beginner.[34] It is no surprise that Zaǧǧāǧī's approach would particularly suit Ibn al-Ṭarāwa's conception and needs.

It is this criticism of Fārisī's *ʾĪḍāḥ* that sparked reactions and refutations from other grammarians. His contemporary Ibn al-Bāḏiš was the first one to overtly attack Ibn al-Ṭarāwa's stance (Bannā 1980: 18), but later grammarians Ibn Ḫarūf, Ibn al-Ḍāʾiʿ and Ibn al-Faḫḫār al-ʾArkušī al-Ǧuḏāmī also intervened to endorse Fārisī's work (all of these grammarians are in the right column in figure 6.1). Regrettably, the only treatises at our disposal among those composed by these authors are Ibn Ḫarūf's commentaries on the *Kitāb* and on the *Ǧumal*, thus we have little proof to definitely confirm their predilection for Fārisī over Zaǧǧāǧī. However, Ibn Ḫarūf provides us with some interesting comments in the introduction to his *Šarḥ al-Ǧumal*:

> He [i.e. Zaǧǧāǧī] compiled it [i.e. the *Kitāb al-Ǧumal*] for the beginners, but depended on the teachers to elucidate it, and he aimed at conciseness like the Bedouins used to do with metonymical and figurative expressions; working with this is a loss of time in more than one respect. (*ʾiḏ waḍaʿahu li-l-mubtadiʾīn wa-ttakala fī bayānihi ʿalā al-muʿallimīn wa-qaṣada al-ʾīǧāz ʿalā maḏhab al-ʿarab fī al-ittisāʿ wa-l-maǧāz fa-l-ištiġāl bi-ḏālika taḍyīʿ li-l-zamān fī ġayr šaʾn*, Ibn Ḫarūf *Šarḥ al-Ǧumal* I, 243).

Here, the pronoun "this" (*ḏālika*) could refer to either the *Ǧumal* or its conciseness (*ʾīǧāz*): in both readings, however, the final sentence sounds like a negative assessment. We infer that Ibn Ḫarūf was unsatisfied with Zaǧǧāǧī's treatise, which he considered globally inadequate both as a handbook for grammar teaching (it requires teachers to elucidate it) and for its approach to the grammatical theory (its conciseness with the use of metonymical and figurative expressions).

On the other side, Ibn al-Ṭarāwa's positive opinion about Zaǧǧāǧī's *Ǧumal* was also shared by Ibn al-Sīd al-Baṭalyawsī. In the introduction to his *al-Ḥulal fī ʾiṣlāḥ al-ḫalal al-wāqiʿ fī al-Ǧumal*, he states:

33 Despite that, some principles of its taxonomic organization—notably the primacy of the verbal sentence over the nominal sentence, and hence the centrality of the verb and of the theory of *ʿamal*—would be retained by most Andalusi grammarians and would become a distinctive feature of the Andalusi and Maghribi grammatical approach (cf. Larcher 2018).

34 On the structure and content of Zaǧǧāǧī's *Ǧumal*, cf. Binaghi 2015:164–171. For a comparative study of different taxonomic approaches in the Arabic grammatical tradition, including both Zaǧǧāǧī's *Ǧumal* and Fārisī's *ʾĪḍāḥ*, cf. Viain 2014.

> [...] that he is one of the most important of this art. With his book we have begun the study of this science, and he is the one who trained our insights for the understanding that he bestowed upon us. Others have preceded us in raising objections to him and finding mistakes in some of his instructions, but the imperfection of part of his phrasing is not something that is detrimental to his standing within this science and to his prestige. ([...] *wa-ʾannahu min ʾaʾimmat hāḏihi al-ṣināʿa fa-ʾinnanā bi-kitābihi iftataḥnā al-naẓar fī hāḏā al-ʿilm wa-huwa allaḏī raššaḥa baṣāʾiranā li-mā manaḥanāhu min al-fahm wa-qad sabaqanā ġayrunā ʾilā al-iʿtirāḍ ʿalayhi wa-taḫṭiʾatihi fī baʿḍ mā naḥā ʾilayhi wa-laysa iḫtilāl baʿḍ ʿibāratihi mim-mā yuḫillu bi-maḥallihi fī al-ʿilm wa-makānatihi,* Baṭalyawsī *Ḥulal* 19)

Despite pointing to some imperfections, which Ibn al-Sīd al-Baṭalyawsī attributes to an excessive abridgement and condensation of the grammatical matter (*ʾafraṭa fī al-ʾīǧāz wa-l-iḫtiṣār*), he nevertheless recognizes its central role for the discipline and its importance as a propaedeutical introductory text.

Ibn al-Sīd al-Baṭalyawsī and Ibn al-Ṭarāwa actually diverge in the development of their grammatical analysis, as the latter keeps a more textualist stance, whereas the former betrays a deep influence of philosophy. Yet, they share their appreciation for Zaǧǧāǧī's *Ǧumal* and the idea that grammar should be considered as an introductory discipline, where the value of a text lies not in its intrinsic qualities, but rather in its propaedeutical potential. These elements are also shared by other grammarians listed in the left column of figure 6.1.

From the point of view of intertextual relations, sources indirectly link Ibn ʿUṣfūr's *Muqarrib* to Zaǧǧāǧī's *Ǧumal*. Ibn al-Zubayr (d. 708/1308) reports a common opinion that all of the *Muqarrib*'s definitions had been taken from Ǧazūlī's (d. 607/1211) *al-Muqaddima al-ǧazūliyya*.[35] As for this latter treatise, all of the sources, starting from Qifṭī (d. 646/1248), underline the fact that its origin lay in a series of glosses on Zaǧǧāǧī's *Ǧumal* written by Ǧazūlī himself while studying this text in Egypt with the grammarian Ibn Barrī (d. 582/1187), glosses which were subsequently re-elaborated to serve as the basis of the text of the *Muqaddima ǧazūliyya* (Qifṭī *ʾInbāh* II, 378). Even though the grammatical theory had evolved between Zaǧǧāǧī and Ibn ʿUṣfūr, and this latter distanced himself from some elements and principles of the former's work, sources recorded the trace of this link and (at least some) grammarians kept perceiving this

35 *wa-kitāb al-Muqarrib fī al-naḥw yuqālu ʾinna ḥudūdahu kullahā maʾḫūḏa min al-Ǧazūliyya*, cited in Kutubī *Fawāt* III, 110.

legacy. Ibn ʿUṣfūr's *Muqarrib* was targeted by two refutations, notably by Ibn al-Ḍāʾiʿ who had also refuted Ibn al-Ṭarāwa's works.

Following Ibn al-Ṭarāwa's textualist stance, other grammarians seemed to oppose the predominance of formal considerations and excessive theorization over basic principles and common sense. It is first of all the case of Suhaylī, who "advances views which imply that the theory [of *ʿamal*] should be amended in ways which would reveal the importance of *maʿnā* as an essential criterion in interpreting usage" (Baalbaki 2008: 290, and following pages for the analysis of Suhaylī's views). His opposition against arbitrariness and unnecessarily far-fetched theoretical explanations is also revealed in his treatment of the question of *mamnūʿ min al-ṣarf*, especially with regard to proper names. While the mainstream theory saw such proper names as the exception (*ʾiʿrāb* being the central principle of Arabic grammar) that needed to be explained through a complex system of underlying traits, Suhaylī considered that it was proper names taking *tanwīn* that represented the deviation from common sense. In his view, proper and common nouns represent two different classes (hence not sharing the same grammatical requirements), and proper names behaving as common nouns (i.e. taking *ʾiʿrāb*) could simply be explained as having their origin in the latter's class.[36]

Further down this way went Ibn Maḍāʾ, who—as we have already mentioned—wanted to abolish the method developed by Arab grammarians by challenging some of their central notions: he postulated the priority of *samāʿ* (oral attestation) over *qiyās* (analogical reasoning); he argued against secondary and tertiary justifications (*ʿilal*), which he deemed to be far too speculative and abstract; he asserted the insanity of the theory of *ʿamal* (and of its subsidiary principle of *taqdīr*), as it contradicted the Ẓāhirī principle that Allāh is the only true "governor" in this world. However, Ibn Maḍāʾ wanted to preserve almost all of the normative content of grammar, and from this viewpoint—despite the considerable differences that I have just mentioned[37]—he seemed to link with Ibn al-Ṭarāwa's conception of grammar as an introductory, propaedeutical discipline for the study of "sacred" texts: the Qurʾān and other religious texts in the case of Ibn Maḍāʾ; *Kitāb Sībawayhi*, the *qurʾān al-naḥw*, in the case of Ibn al-Ṭarāwa.

---

36 For an in-depth study of *mamnūʿ min al-ṣarf* in the Arabic grammatical tradition, and more details on Suhaylī's criticism of the mainstream theory, cf. Druel & Kasher 2019.

37 Baalbaki (2008:279), however, also points out that "[b]y frequently referring to the speaker's intention (cf. his use of *yanwī* and *yurīd*), Ibn Maḍāʾ is in broad agreement with authors who do take meaning into consideration in their syntactical analysis", as it was the case with Suhaylī.

4 Conclusions

As the genre of *radd* in al-Andalus will always be identified with today's famous *Kitāb al-Radd ʿalā al-nuḥāt* by Ibn Maḍāʾ, it actually accounted for a rather abundant production that attests to Andalusi grammarians' intellectual activity and polemical disposition.[38] This article aimed at collecting, systemizing and presenting this production in order to enlarge our knowledge of the Arabic grammatical tradition that flourished in al-Andalus. As no other treatise than Ibn Maḍāʾ's seems to have been preserved, preventing us from a direct investigation into their content, the analysis had to be based on the scarce information provided directly by their title or by other sources, and on the theories that the grammarians involved in these debates had exposed in other treatises. As a result, the conclusions could only be of a speculative and somehow impressionistic nature given the fragmented data available, especially on some grammarians.

After a presentation of the corpus, the relations between the grammarians involved in the debates have been schematized, also taking into account the broader intellectual networks and master-pupil ties (figure 6.1). The result presents a general division into two groups, whose coherence and pertinence have subsequently been evaluated.

Two elements seem to characterize each one of the two groups. The first one is the source which represents the most prestigious reference (in addition to Sībawayhi's *Kitāb*) in their theory. Most authors (those in the left column of figure 6.1) considered Zaǧǧāǧī's *Ǧumal* to be the most prestigious and appropriate handbook for the study of grammar (e.g. Ibn al-Sīd al-Baṭalyawsī and Ibn al-Ṭarāwa); or they linked up with it in the genesis of their treatises (e.g. Ibn ʿUṣfūr and his *Muqarrib*) and in the basic principles adopted for the elaboration of their theory: Suhaylī's and Ibn Maḍāʾ's proposals for a simplification of the general theory and for a wider application of common sense in grammatical analysis could reflect the *Ǧumal*'s taxonomy, devoid of any speculative theorization and based, on the contrary, on pragmatic considerations. On the other side of the divide, Ibn al-Bāḏiš, Ibn Ḫarūf, Ibn al-Ḍāʾiʿ and Ibn al-Faḫḫār al-ʾArkušī al-Ǧuḏāmī (right column in figure 6.1) seemed to lean in favor of Fārisī's *ʾĪḍāḥ*, defending this treatise notably from the criticisms of Ibn al-Ṭarāwa. Ibn

38 An anonymous reviewer has drawn my attention to the fact that the West Mediterranean witnessed many polemics also among grammarians of Hebrew. An evaluation of whether there was a common denominator for such a fertile ground for polemical writing among both Arabic and Hebrew grammarians would deserve further research.

Ḫarūf's very sharp judgements on the *Ǧumal*, in the introduction to his *Šarḥ Ǧumal al-Zaǧǧāǧī*, point to this same direction.

This battle for legitimacy and predominance among two of the most important sources for grammatical studies in al-Andalus—the third one being Sībawayhi's *Kitāb*—probably underlies an epistemological opposition with regard to the purpose of grammar. Authors adopting Zaǧǧāǧī's *Ǧumal* as the main reference seem to consider grammar as an instrumental, auxiliary science for the study of founding texts of the Arabo-Islamic civilization, be it the Qur'ān and other religious texts (Ibn Maḍā'), or the first and foremost treatise of the Arabic grammatical tradition, Sībawayhi's *Kitāb*, the *qur'ān al-naḥw* (Ibn al-Ṭarāwa). Taking into consideration the *Ǧumal*'s internal structure and the particular sociolinguistic situation of al-Andalus, we might infer that their primary objective was language teaching and pedagogical efficacy. The authors preaching for the superiority of Fārisī's *'Īḍāḥ*, on the contrary, might have been more interested in the rational construction, systematization and general coherence of the theory; in other terms, they would have been more prone to perceive grammar as a speculative science. I argue that this opposition is of an epistemological nature because the conception of grammar either as an instrumental/auxiliary or as a speculative science clearly has an influence on the grammarians' theoretical approach to grammatical knowledge: Suhaylī's stance on the role of *maʿnā*, for instance, challenges one of the basic methods of grammatical analysis (i.e. *ʿamal*), while Ibn Maḍā''s radical opposition to several principles of the grammatical theory builds up as a clear disagreement about the scope of this science, as he also tries to reassess the distinction between justified belief (i.e. grammatical rules) and unjustified opinion (i.e. grammatical argumentation). In view of the fact that the study of the *'Īḍāḥ* in al-Andalus started at a later period if compared to the *Ǧumal*'s,[39] we might suppose an Eastern (i.e. from the *mašriq*) influence on such a development.

An important remark, however: what I tried to define as the primary purpose for grammar would not have prevented authors from developing their analysis in different directions, so we should not consider the two groups as constituting monolithic entities. When we look at the first group of grammarians, for instance, we could immediately notice at least three different approaches: grammarians moved by common sense and textual considerations (Ibn al-Ṭarāwa and Suhaylī); grammarians more influenced by philosophical

39 The first commentary on the *Ǧumal* was compiled by Ibn al-ʿArīf in the second half of the 4th/10th century, i.e. roughly half a century after Zaǧǧāǧī's death. In comparison, the first commentary on Fārisī's treatise, the *Ṭurar ʿalā al-'Īḍāḥ* by Ibn al-'Aḫḍar (d. 514/1120), only saw the light of day more than a century later.

questioning and principles (Ibn al-Sīd al-Baṭalyawsī and Ibn Rušd); and authors abiding by religious tenets and inflecting their linguistic thinking accordingly (Ibn Ḥazm and Ibn Maḍāʾ).

Finally, we should query whether these fraction lines, in addition to the aforementioned questions of sources and epistemology, also developed alongside the evolution of the textual history of Sībawayhi's *Kitāb*: thanks to Humbert (1995), we know that Fārisī and Zaǧǧāǧ (d. 311/923)—Zaǧǧāǧī's main teacher, from whom he took his *šuhra*—were key figures in the establishment of, respectively, the Eastern and the Western recensions of the *Kitāb*. Was the interest for any of the two books (the *ʾĪḍāḥ* and the *Ǧumal*) possibly linked to the history of these two recensions? Further research might provide us with an answer.[40]

Bibliography

Primary Sources

Baṭalyawsī, *Ḥulal* = ʾAbū Muḥammad ʿAbd Allāh b. Muḥammad Ibn al-Sīd al-Baṭalyawsī, *ʾIṣlāḥ al-ḫalal al-wāqiʿ fī al-Ǧumal li-l-Zaǧǧāǧī*. Ed. by Ḥamza ʿAbd Allāh al-Našratī. Bayrūt: Dār al-kutub al-ʿilmiyya, 1424/2003.

Ḫwānsārī, *Rawḍāt* = Muḥammad Bāqir al-Mūsawī al-Ḫwānsārī al-ʾIṣbahānī, *Rawḍāt al-ǧannāt fī ʾaḥwāl al-ʿulamāʾ wa-l-sādāt*. Bayrūt: al-Dār al-ʾislāmiyya, 8 vol., 1411/1991.

Ibn al-ʾAbbār, *Takmila* = ʾAbū ʿAbd Allāh Muḥammad b. ʿAbd Allāh b. ʾAbī Bakr al-Quḍāʿī Ibn al-ʾAbbār al-Balansī, *al-Takmila li-kitāb al-Ṣila*. Ed. by Baššār ʿAwwād Maʿrūf. Tūnis: Dār al-ġarb al-ʾislāmī, coll. "Silsilat al-tarāǧim al-ʾandalusiyya" 7, 4 vol., 2011.

Ibn ʿAbd al-Malik, *Ḏayl* = ʾAbū ʿAbd Allāh Muḥammad b. Muḥammad Ibn ʿAbd al-Malik al-ʾAnṣārī al-ʾAwsī al-Marrākušī, *al-Ḏayl wa-l-takmila li-kitābay al-mawṣūl wa-l-ṣila*. Vol. 5: ed. by ʾIḥsān ʿAbbās. Bayrūt: Dār al-ṯaqāfa, 1965.

Ibn Ḫarūf, *Šarḥ al-Ǧumal* = ʾAbū al-Ḥasan ʿAlī b. Muḥammad b. ʿAlī Ibn Ḫarūf al-ʾIšbīlī, *Šarḥ Ǧumal al-Zaǧǧāǧī*. Ed. by Salwā Muḥammad ʿUmar ʿArab. Makka: Ǧāmiʿat ʾUmm al-Qurā, coll. "Silsilat al-rasāʾil al-ʿilmiyya al-mūṣā bi-ṭabʿihā" 22, 2 vol., 1419 H.

Ibn Ḫayr, *Fahrasa* = Ibn Ḫayr al-ʾIšbīlī, *Fahrasat Ibn Ḫayr al-ʾIšbīlī*. Ed. by Baššār ʿAwwād Maʿrūf & Maḥmūd Baššār ʿAwwād. Tūnis: Dār al-ġarb al-ʾislāmī, coll. "Silsilat al-tarāǧim al-ʾandalusiyya" 4, 2009.

Ibn al-Nadīm, *Fihrist* = ʾAbū al-Faraǧ Muḥammad b. ʾAbī Yaʿqūb ʾIsḥāq al-Warrāq, *Kitāb al-Fihrist li-l-Nadīm*. Ed. by Riḍā Taǧaddud. Bayrūt: Dār al-masīra, 3rd ed., 1988.

40 For some initial elements on this question, cf. already Amharar & Druel (ch. 2 in this volume).

Ibn al-Ṭarāwa, *ʾIfṣāḥ* = Ibn al-Ṭarāwa al-Naḥwī, *Risālat al-ʾIfṣāḥ bi-baʿḍ mā ǧāʾa min al-ḫaṭaʾ fī al-ʾĪḍāḥ*. Ed. by Ḥātim Ṣāliḥ al-Ḍāmin. Bayrūt: ʿĀlam al-kutub, 1432/2011.

Kalāʿī, *ʾIḥkām* = ʾAbū al-Qāsim Muḥammad b. ʿAbd al-Ġafūr al-Kalāʿī al-ʾIšbīlī al-ʾAndalusī, *ʾIḥkām ṣanʿat al-kalām*. Ed. by Muḥammad Riḍwān al-Dāya. Bayrūt: Dār al-ṯaqāfa, coll. "al-Maktaba al-ʾandalusiyya" 16, 1966.

Kutubī, *Fawāt* = Muḥammad b. Šākir al-Kutubī, *Fawāt al-Wafayāt wa-l-ḏayl ʿalayhā*. Ed. by ʾIḥsān ʿAbbās. Bayrūt: Dār ṣādir, 5 vol., 1973–1974.

Maqqarī, *Nafḥ* = Šihāb al-Dīn ʾAḥmad b. Muḥammad al-Maqqarī al-Tilmisānī, *Nafḥ al-ṭīb min ġuṣn al-ʾAndalus al-raṭīb*. Ed. by ʾIḥsān ʿAbbās. Bayrūt: Dār ṣādir, 8 vol., 1408/1988.

Qifṭī, *ʾInbāh* = Ǧamāl al-Dīn ʾAbū al-Ḥasan ʿAlī b. Yūsuf al-Qifṭī, *ʾInbāh al-ruwāt ʿalā ʾanbāh al-nuḥāt*. Ed. by Muḥammad ʾAbū al-Faḍl ʾIbrāhīm. Al-Qāhira & Bayrūt: Dār al-fikr al-ʿarabī & Muʾassasat al-kutub al-ṯaqāfiyya, 4 vol., 1406/1986.

Ruʿaynī, *Barnāmaǧ* = ʾAbū al-Ḥasan ʿAlī b. Muḥammad b. ʿAlī al-Ruʿaynī al-ʾIšbīlī, *Barnāmaǧ šuyūḫ al-Ruʿaynī*. Ed. by ʾIbrāhīm Šabbūḥ. Dimašq: Wizārat al-ṯaqāfa wa-l-ʾiršād al-qawmī, coll. "Maṭbūʿāt mudīriyyat ʾiḥyāʾ al-turāṯ al-qadīm" 4, 1381/1962.

Secondary Sources

Arnaldez, Roger. 1956. *Grammaire et théologie chez Ibn Ḥazm de Cordoue : essai sur la structure et les conditions de la pensée musulmane*. Paris: Librairie Philosophique J. Vrin, coll. "Études musulmanes" 3.

Asín Palacios, Miguel. 1939. "El origen del lenguaje y problemas conexos, en Algazel, Ibn Sīda e Ibn Ḥazm". *Al-Andalus* 4/2. 253–281.

BA = Lirola Delgado, Jorge & José Miguel Puerta Vílchez (eds.). 2004–2012. *Biblioteca de al-Andalus*. Almería: Fundación Ibn Tufayl de Estudios Árabes, coll. "Enciclopedia de la cultura andalusí" 1, 7 vol. + A[péndice] + B[alance de resultados e índices].

Baalbaki, Ramzi. 2008. *The Legacy of the* Kitāb: *Sībawayhi's Analytical Methods within the Context of the Arabic Grammatical Theory*. Leiden & Boston: Brill, coll. "Studies in Semitic Languages and Linguistics" 51.

Bannā (al-), Muḥammad ʾIbrāhīm. 1980. *ʾAbū al-Ḥusayn Ibn al-Ṭarāwa wa-ʾaṯaruhu fī al-naḥw*. Tūnis: Dār Bū Salāma li-l-ṭibāʿa wa-l-našr wa-l-tawzīʿ.

Binaghi, Francesco. 2015. "La postérité andalouse du *Ǧumal* d'al-Zaǧǧāǧī". PhD dissertation, Aix-Marseille Université.

Campanelli, Marta. 2016. "Complessità e Astrattezza della Tradizione Linguistica Araba: la Teoria della Reggenza e la Contestazione di Ibn Maḍāʾ al-Qurṭubī". PhD dissertation, Università degli Studi di Roma 'La Sapienza'.

Druel, Jean N. & Almog Kasher. 2019. "'Though This Be Madness, Yet There Is Method In't': The *mamnūʿ min al-ṣarf* (Diptotes) in Arabic Grammatical Tradition". *Arabica* 66/1–2. 98–136.

EI2 = *Encyclopaedia of Islam*. Leiden: Brill, 2nd ed., 13 vol., 1960–2009.

Guillaume, Jean-Patrick. 2018. "Un critique andalou d'al-Fārisī : la *Risālat al-ʾIfṣāḥ* d'Ibn al-Ṭarāwa". *Histoire Épistémologie Langage* 40/2. 55–65.

Hamzé, Hassan. 2002. "Logique et grammaire arabe dans l'œuvre d'Averroès". *Averroes (1126–1198): oder der Triumph des Rationalismus. Internationales Symposium anlässlich des 800. Todestages des islamischen Philosophen. Heidelberg, 7.–11. Oktober 1998*, ed. by Raif Georges Khoury, 157–174. Heidelberg: Universitätsverlag C. Winter.

Humbert, Geneviève. 1995. *Les voies de la transmission du Kitāb de Sībawayhi*. Leiden & New York: Brill, coll. "Studies in Semitic Languages and Linguistics" 20.

Larcher, Pierre. 2018. "Un grammairien 'oublié' : Ibn Muʿṭī. Note sur son ouvrage en prose *al-Fuṣūl al-ḫamsūn*". *Histoire Épistémologie Langage* 40/2. 87–100.

Peña, Salvador. 2013. "Which Curiosity? Ibn Ḥazm's Suspicion of Grammarians". *Ibn Ḥazm of Cordoba: The Life and Works of a Controversial Thinker*, ed. by Camilla Adang, Maribel Fierro & Sabine Schmidtke, 233–250. Leiden & Boston: Brill, coll. "Handbook of Oriental Studies. Section 1, The Near and Middle East" 103.

Versteegh, Kees. 2013. "Ibn Maḍāʾ as a Ẓāhirī Grammarian". *Ibn Ḥazm of Cordoba: The Life and Works of a Controversial Thinker*, ed. by Camilla Adang, Maribel Fierro & Sabine Schmidtke, 205–231. Leiden & Boston: Brill, coll. "Handbook of Oriental Studies. Section 1, The Near and Middle East" 103.

Viain, Marie. 2014. "La taxinomie des traités de grammaire arabe médiévaux (IVᵉ/Xᵉ–VIIIᵉ/ XIVᵉ siècle), entre représentation de l'articulation conceptuelle de la théorie et visée pratique : Enjeux théoriques, polémiques et pédagogiques des modélisations formelles et sémantiques du marquage casuel". PhD dissertation, Université Sorbonne Nouvelle – Paris 3.

Wolfe, Ronald Gary. 1984. "Ibn Maḍāʾ al-Qurṭubī and the 'Book in refutation of the Grammarians' ". PhD dissertation, Indiana University.

Wolfe, Ronald Gary. 1990. "Ibn Maḍāʾ al-Qurṭubī's *Kitāb ar-Radd ʿalā n-Nuḥāt*: An Historical Misnomer". *Studies in the History of Arabic Grammar II: Proceedings of the 2nd Symposium on the History of Arabic Grammar, Nijmegen, 27 April–1 May 1987*, ed. by Kees Versteegh & Michael G. Carter, 295–304. Amsterdam & Philadelphia: John Benjamins, coll. "Studies in the History of the Language Sciences" 56.

PART 2

Further Developments of the Critical Theory

CHAPTER 7

Fārābī against the Grammarians??

Wilfrid Hodges and Manuela E.B. Giolfo

Introduction*

The two present authors have a joint project to compare the views of Sīrāfī (d. 368/979) and Ibn Sīnā (d. 427/1037) on language, and in particular on the role of meaning and its interaction with syntax. They contributed some of this work to *The Foundations of Arabic Linguistics* III, IV (cf. Giolfo and Hodges 2018, 2019). For conference V in this series, Amal Marogy invited the contributors to "focus on the challenges to the *Kitāb*'s status during the formative and medieval periods of Arabic grammatical activities". Neither Sīrāfī nor Ibn Sīnā can be regarded as posing a challenge to the status of the *Kitāb*, and so we decided to break away from our joint project and look elsewhere.

Since one of us has recently been closely involved with the linguistic and logical views of Fārābī (d. 339/950), we wondered if he could be regarded as posing a challenge to Sībawayhi (d. 180/796?). There are hints that he could. For example Cornelia Schöck (2006: 427) describes Fārābī as holding views on language which were "in direct confrontation to the Arab grammarians". Also Kees Versteegh (2000: 304) comments that

(1) [Fārābī's] open admission of a lacuna in Arabic compared to all other languages is quite unusual in Arabic writings; it would certainly be unthinkable in a grammatical treatise.

Fritz Zimmermann (1981: CXXXV) illustrates Fārābī's attitude to Arabic grammar as follows:

(2) If the Greek grammarians say that there are five cases of the noun, then our world must be such that for something to be a noun is to have five cases, even if the Arabic noun has no more than three and the Syriac does not inflect at all.

* The writing of this paper was hindered by a spell in hospital for one of the authors following a stroke. We warmly thank Manuel Sartori and Francesco Binaghi for their support and patience under these difficult circumstances.

 | DOI:10.1163/9789004515895_009

Could Fārābī be considered as a kind of accidental *radd* author? We will argue No, in three steps.

First we will examine the evidence for Fārābī's relationships with the linguists among his contemporaries, and we will find them to be entirely cordial and productive.

Secondly we will extract from his writings a description of grammar as he sees it. His description is complementary to that of the Arabic linguists, in the following sense. He is concerned to describe language in general, the needs that create language, and the extent to which Arabic meets these needs; while the Arabic linguists take the Arabic language as a fact and aim to give an accurate and evidence-based account of its structures.

Thirdly we will ask whether Versteegh, Zimmermann and Schöck have uncovered any conflict between Fārābī's grammar and that of the linguists. Versteegh's remark quoted above is correct but it reflects the complementary relation between the grammatical theories, not a conflict. Zimmermann has briefly allowed a vivid imagination to get the better of him. Schöck has raised questions about early Islamic theologians and their relationship to notions from Aristotle (d. 322 BC). These questions deserve to be studied, but Schöck herself fails to engage in a meaningful way with the basic notions of either logic or linguistics.

1 Fārābī Himself

Fārābī lived from ca. 870 to ca. 950 CE. He was fluent in Arabic and can be presumed to have known some Persian, not necessarily fluent. He also mentions Greek, Syriac and Sogdian (an Indo-Iranian language of the Silk Road). But it's clear he didn't know Greek. There is no good evidence that he knew Syriac or Sogdian either, since his brief references to them are mainly lexicographic. He never mentions Turkic languages. His origins are unknown, but his interest in Sogdian might be a clue to them.[1]

He spent most of his life in Baghdad. He reports (quoted in ʾUṣaybiʿa's [d. 668/1270] *ʿUyūn* 604–606) that he was a student of the Syrian Yūḥannā b. Ḥaylān. In the context of his report, the implication is that Yūḥannā introduced him to the Aristotelian part of the syllabus of the old Neoplatonic School

1 For general information on Fārābī, see Druart 2019. Zimmermann (1981:XLVIIf) discusses evidence of his lack of knowledge of several languages. Note 9 below illustrates why it is hard to believe he could read Greek.

in Alexandria (5th–6th ca.), translated via Syriac from the Greek originals. Fārābī devoted the rest of his life to expounding this material in Arabic, with added commentary of his own, for the benefit of educated readers of Arabic.

His teaching on language is mainly scattered between four books. First, his *Catalogue of the Sciences* (*'Iḥṣā'*) begins at pages 45.1 to 52.1 with a section on 'the science of language' (*'ilm al-lisān*). Then he describes the 'art of logic', and a key ingredient of his description is an extended comparison of the art of logic to the 'art of grammar' (*ṣinā'at al-naḥw*) at 54 l. 2–63 l. 12. Secondly his *Ḥurūf* has various comments on language, including a theory of how languages came to be created, the development of technical terms in the sciences, and a sense in which the structure of language imitates the structure of concepts. Thirdly his *Šarḥ 'Ibāra* on Aristotle's *De Interpretatione* tackles some particular questions of grammar and semantics, mostly in relation to time and tense. The work also repeats the theme of language imitating the structure of concepts. And fourthly his book *'Alfāẓ* introduces the technical vocabulary of logic, with a number of linguistic comments along the way.

A feature of Fārābī's writing is that what he says about a topic varies with the context in which he is discussing it.[2] As a result, the accounts of grammar in the four works just mentioned are by no means variants of a single account, though in Section 3 below we will aim to find a single account that will accommodate all four. In the case of *'Iḥṣā'* we know that the variation depends partly on his use of sources. His account of the science of logic there is based on an earlier essay of the Neoplatonist scholar Paul the Persian (6th century CE), and thanks to Miskawayhi's (d. 421/1030) *Tartīb* (19 l. 13ff.) we have a more direct Arabic translation of this essay.[3] It will be important to note places where Fārābī says something different from his Neoplatonist template.

Given that Fārābī used a template for his description of logic in *'Iḥṣā'*, we may wonder if he used another template for his description of language. A recent paper of Vidro (2020) describes a genre of descriptions of Arabic grammar which could have served this purpose; they report Arabic grammar using notions from Greek grammar. Vidro considers one fragmentary example and gives reasons for ascribing it to the translator Ḥunayn b. 'Isḥāq (d. 260/873).[4]

---

2 Contrast Ibn Sīnā, who on any topic will give his current view. These current views tend to change slowly through Ibn Sīnā's career, preserving their main points.

3 Gutas (1983) analyzes the relationship between the versions of Paul's essay in al-Fārābī's *'Iḥṣā'* and Miskawayhi's *Tartīb*. See also Perkams 2019. We have used the edition of Miskawayhi currently in print; we regret that we have not seen earlier editions which agree with the paginations used by Gutas and Perkams.

4 We became aware of Vidro's paper very recently, and we regret that we have not had an oppor-

The change from 'language' in pages 45 to 52 of *ʾIḥṣāʾ* to 'grammar' in pages 54 to 63 of *ʾIḥṣāʾ* probably reflects the terminology in Fārābī's templates, since the earlier section is hardly less grammatical than the later.[5]

Besides the four works *ʾIḥṣāʾ*, *Ḥurūf*, *Šarḥ ʿIbāra* and *ʾAlfāẓ*, we can draw information from Fārābī's own linguistic practice, particularly where it brings him alongside linguists of his time. One of these linguists was Ibn al-Sarrāǧ, known to us chiefly for his *ʾUṣūl*; he died in 316/929. Another was Sīrāfī (cf. Pingree 2002), from whom we have a detailed commentary (referred to below as *Šarḥ*) on the *Kitāb* of Sībawayhi. Ibn al-Sarrāǧ is named as one of Sīrāfī's teachers in linguistics.[6]

2 Fārābī's Relations with Grammarians

According to the historian Ibn ʾAbī ʾUṣaybiʿa:

(3) History has it that Fārābī used to meet ʾAbū Bakr b. al-Sarrāǧ in order to learn from him grammar and to teach him logic. (*wa-fī al-tārīḫ ʾanna al-fārābī kāna yaǧtamiʿu bi-ʾabī bakr b. al-sarrāǧ fa-yaqraʾu ʿalayhi ṣināʿat al-naḥw wa-ibn al-sarrāǧ yaqraʾu ʿalayhi ṣināʿat al-manṭiq*, *ʿUyūn* 606 l. 8 f.)

Not everything that the medieval historians tell us about Fārābī is believable. But Zimmermann on pages CXVIII–CXX in the learned introduction to his (1981) assembles some evidence in support of (3). The chief items are a statement by Ibn al-Nadīm (d. 385/995) in his *Fihrist* that "Ibn al-Sarrāǧ had for a time allowed himself to be distracted from grammar by the study of logic and music" (Ibn al-Nadīm *Fihrist* 98 l. 14 f.);[7] and the fact that both Ibn al-Sarrāǧ and Fārābī describe parts of speech using Peripatetic terminology.

---

tunity to study it fully. Vidro notes in particular that the paper under study agrees with Fārābī at *ʾIḥṣāʾ* 48.10 in referring to the persons of a verb as *wuǧūh*, translating Greek *prósōpa* (cf. Versteegh 1977:62 note 53).

5 Miskawayhi (*Tartīb* 51 l. 15; 54 l. 2) does talk of the 'art of grammar' (*ṣināʿat al-naḥw*).

6 Sīrāfī is also known for his public debate with Mattā b. Yūnus (d. 328/939) on Greek logic versus Arabic linguistics, at the court of the vizier Ibn al-Furāt (d. 327/939) in 320/932. Elamrani-Jamal (1983) translates into French the text of the debate on his pages 149–163, with discussion on his pages 61–67. The absence of any mention of Fārābī in the report of this debate suggests that even in his sixties Fārābī was still not widely recognized as the major logician that we now know him to be.

7 Bear in mind Fārābī's prowess as a musical theorist (cf. Druart 2020).

Zimmermann then observes that to prove the truth of Ibn ʾAbī ʾUṣaybiʿa's account it would be necessary

(4) (a) to show that both men's knowledge of the other's subject was not obtained from random sources, but from each other; and (b) to explain why neither man ever seems to refer to the other, and why the biographical tradition is virtually mute on the subject of their connexion.

ZIMMERMANN 1981: CXX

We will return to (b) in Section 4.1 below. As to (a), we can certainly point to more agreements between Fārābī's terminology and that of Ibn al-Sarrāǧ than Zimmermann mentions. The most likely explanation for these agreements is that Fārābī adapted to logic some linguistic terminology that he learned from Ibn al-Sarrāǧ or from Sīrāfī. Chatti and Hodges (2020) give as likely examples *fāʾida* (Chatti and Hodges 2020: 92), *istiṯnāʾ* (56 f.) and possibly *ḍamīr* (35).

There is a pertinent passage in Sīrāfī's *Šarḥ*:

(5) Know that these verbs which make up this section […] give information on the definite time or negation or transition or permanence. One such is *kāna*, which has three meanings, of which the first is the one we have [just] mentioned, as when you say 'Zayd was knowledgeable', where the original [sentence] is 'Zayd [is] knowledgeable', and *kāna* is inserted so as to indicate that that holds in time past. Similarly with 'Zayd will be leaving'. (*ʾiʿlam ʾanna hāḏihi al-ʾafʿāla allatī ḍammanahā hāḏā l-bābu ʾafʿāla* […] *wa-ḫabar fa-tufīdu fīhā zamānan muḥaṣṣalan ʾaw nafyan ʾaw intiqālan ʾaw dawāman, fa-min ḏālika: "kāna" wa-lahā ṯalāṯatu maʿānin, ʾaḥaduhā: mā ḏakarnāhu, ka-qawlika: "kāna zaydun ʿāliman", wa-kāna l-ʾaṣlu "zaydun ʿālimun" fa-daḫalat "kāna" li-tūǧiba ʾanna ḏālika fī zamānin māḍin, wa-ka-ḏālika: "yakūnu zaydun munṭaliqan"*, Sīrāfī's *Šarḥ* I, 296 l. 1–4)

Sīrāfī's argument here is remarkably similar to one that Fārābī adopts at *Šarḥ ʿIbāra* (42 l. 1–18).

Both Sīrāfī and Fārābī are showing that the word *kāna* has one usage in which it does no more than express past time. They both show this by exhibiting a sentence about the past which is construed by adding *kāna* to a sentence that is already complete although it does not contain reference to time past. Fārābī's example is the sentence *zaydun kāna yamšī*, which adds *kāna* to the complete sentence *zaydun yamšī*.

Fārābī makes two further points. First, in this usage *kāna* is not a copula, since the sentence *zaydun yamšī* already has a copula in *yamšī*. (This fact would not have interested Sīrāfī, who makes no use of the logicians' notion of copula.) And second, only Arabic needs a word expressing pure past tense, since in "other languages" past tense is expressed by linking a particle (*yuqranu bihā ḥarfun*, 42 l. 10f.) to the present-tense form. Hasnawi (1985: 31) rightly comments on this "remarkable" application of linguistic tools simultaneously to two languages with contrasting properties.[8]

So here we find the Peripatetic logician Fārābī in the role of linguist, while the linguist Sīrāfī invokes Peripatetic terminology (*muḥaṣṣal* for 'definite'). Note that Sīrāfī, for whom this argument is on his home ground, gives his conclusion in a slightly more general form than Fārābī, by allowing the verb or participle to be inflected when *kāna* is introduced. But the differences in approach by the two authors are relatively minor; it is very easy to read the two forms of the argument as reports of the same conversation by two people who come at it from different angles. If so then we are watching Fārābī doing serious business with his younger contemporary.[9]

Chatti and Hodges (2020: 25f., 92) give several examples of innovations in logical terminology that appear simultaneously in the treatises of Fārābī and in translations from the Greek by ʾAbū ʿUṯmān al-Dimašqī (d. 302/914). The most natural explanation is that al-Fārābī and Dimašqī quietly put their heads together and made some joint decisions. Dimašqī was not a grammarian; he was employed as a doctor, and he also translated several philosophical works from Greek into Arabic. But this evidence of conversations between him and Fārābī, though it is hardly decisive, tends to confirm the picture of Fārābī as a scholar who was happy to discuss linguistic points with his contemporaries in other fields.

8 But Fārābī is wrong here, even about classical Greek. Many of its past tenses are not formed by linking a particle to present-tense forms. Thus present *lambánō*, aorist *élabon*, perfect *eílēpha*. Also Hasnawi may not be right in suggesting that the "other language" is introduced to show that *kāna* expresses nothing but time; Sīrāfī's form of the argument already shows that without mentioning another language. An alternative suggestion is that Fārābī introduces the "other language" to show that Arabic is a defective language.

9 Zimmermann (1981:CXIXf) observes that Ibn al-Sarrāǧ uses the Peripatetic notion of a *muḥaṣṣal* (i.e. definite) time at *ʾUṣūl* 37 l. 3. But we have not found an argument like (5) in *ʾUṣūl*.

3 A Language in the Abstract

3.1 *What is in Our Minds before Language?*

We will find within Fārābī's descriptions of grammar a general account that can serve as a framework for his various views of grammar. Happily the description in his *Ḥurūf* (134 l. 16–142 l. 4) seems written for just this purpose. Fārābī believes that language first arises in communities. So he imagines a community that has no language but is ripe to acquire a language. He asks what needs in this community will cause it to create a language, and how these needs influence the form of the language.

Fārābī begins his account by examining how a community in this initial state comes to adopt an alphabet. But it soon becomes clear that he is making strong assumptions about the community before it develops a language; we need to draw out these assumptions. Thus he assumes the people in the community are individually able to act and plan rationally, for example so as to acquire skills, though without language (135 l. 14). They are also able to make each other aware of their present basic needs, by pointing (*ʾišāra*, 135 l. 16), again without language. The notion of things that are 'pointable at' (*mušār ʾilayhi*) is fundamental in Fārābī's epistemology. Being pointable at makes a thing accessible to our minds, and is the basic source of the concepts that Fārābī elsewhere in *Ḥurūf* (64 l. 4; 65 l. 11) calls the "first intellecteds" or the "primary intellecteds".[10]

Fārābī speaks of how the contents of our minds increase. Unfortunately it is not always clear whether he is talking about what is available already before language; some of his sources of new concepts may depend on our having language. The one clear case is the concepts of the things that are pointable at; these are available before language. Since you and I can point at the same things, these concepts provide a starting-point shared by all members of the same community. But Fārābī goes on to speak of processes that might require language. For example meanings can be combined into compound meanings, in a way that is 'similar' (*šabīh*, 140 l. 20) to the compounding of expressions in a language. Another process is that we come to realize that our concepts can be grouped, for example into those that are genera and those that are not genera; this allows us to introduce the concept 'genus', which is not acquired by pointing. Fārābī describes concepts acquired in this secondary way as 'secondary intellecteds' (64 l. 19). He emphasizes that the process can be iterated

10 By assuming that the community can communicate with each other by pointing, al-Fārābī assumes that they already know how to *mean* or *signify* things and concepts. (He seems to include both individual and universal concepts here; e.g. [*Ḥurūf* 137 l. 7].) So his account of the origin of language sidesteps the question of the origin of semantics.

to infinity: 'genus', 'genus of genera', 'genus of genera of genera' etc. (65 l. 5) So it seems that the concepts available to any of us even before language are a potentially infinite collection, even if in practice language may be needed for realizing the potential.

3.2 *Communicating from One Mind to Another*

Language begins when a member of the community forms a habit of using a particular sound to represent a particular concept, instead of pointing to instances of the concept, and other members of the community agree to adopt this same habit (135 l. 17–136 l. 4). The people who first correlated a sound with a concept are said to have 'imposed' it (*waḍaʿa*, 142 l. 2). The potential infinity of concepts will cause a problem here, because in practice the number of distinguishable sounds that we can make is severely limited. But the community will soon realize that this problem can be overcome by using finite successions of sounds instead of single sounds (137 l. 36). The finite successions of sounds accepted by the community form the expressions of the language of the community.

But it will be hopelessly inefficient for the community to rely on a fresh act of imposition for each expression. We would like Fārābī to say at this point—especially if we have read our Chomsky—that:

(6) just as one can't use newly-invented single words, so one can't invent constructions. [...] The difference between grammar (*naḥw*) and lexicography is that grammar studies universal [rules], whereas lexicography studies [words] one at a time. Both sciences contribute to the conventions [on which language is based]. (*fa-kamā lā yağūzu ʾiḥdāṯ lafẓ mufrad, kaḏālika lā yağūzu fī al-tarākīb;* [...] *wa-l-farq bayna ʿilm al-naḥw wa-ʿilm al-luġa ʾanna ʿilm al-naḥw mawḍūʿuhu ʾumūr kulliyya, wa-mawḍūʿ ʿilm al-luġa ʾašyāʾ ğuzʾiyya, wa-qad ištarakā maʿan fī al-waḍʿ*, ʾAbū Ḥayyān [d. 745/1344], quoted by Suyūṭī [d. 911/1505] *Muzhīr* I, 37 l. 15, 17 f.)[11]

In short, the language needs to have impositions of grammatical rules as well as impositions of single words. This is not in fact what Fārābī says, but ideas like this take their time to emerge.

Instead Fārābī believes that he can capture what is needed by using the notion of similarity (*tašbīh*, e.g. 139 l. 15). Briefly, the construction of the lan-

11 Hodges's notes indicate that he is in debt to Khaled El-Rouayheb and Kees Versteegh for discussions of this passage in 2006.

guage requires that if C1 and C2 are compound concepts constructed in similar ways, then corresponding to them there are expressions E1 and E2 constructed in similar ways. The similarity of E1 to E2 must itself be similar to the similarity of C1 to C2.[12]

A version of this four-term relationship appears in the logic section of *ʾIḥṣāʾ*, where it is often taken to be a characteristic view of Fārābī. But in fact Fārābī is quoting Paul the Persian, with one significant addition. Paul had said:

(7) the relationship of the art of grammar to the expressions is like the relationship of the art of logic to the meanings, and just as grammar guides the language to correctness of speech and gives the rules by which one knows inflection, so likewise logic guides the mind to correctness of meanings and gives the rules by which one knows the facts. (*ʾinna nisbat ṣināʿat al-naḥw ʾilā al-ʾalfāẓ ka-nisbat ṣināʿat al-manṭiq ʾilā al-maʿānī wa-kamā ʾanna al-naḥw yusaddidu al-lisān naḥwa ṣawāb al-qawl wa-yuʿṭī al-qawānīn allatī yuʿarrafu bihā al-ʾiʿrāb fa-ka-ḏālika al-manṭiq yusaddidu al-ḏihn naḥwa ṣawāb al-maʿānī wa-yuʿṭī al-qawānīn allatī tuʿarrafu bihā al-ḥaqāʾiq*, Miskawayhi *Tartīb* 22 l. 5–8)

Take the grammar of a language as consisting of the rules for forming and using grammatical compounds in the language, and logic as consisting of the rules for forming and using compound meanings. (This comes close to ʾAbū Ḥayyān's description of grammar in (6) above.) Then Paul is telling us that the grammatical compounds of expressions are analogous to the logical compounds of meanings. Fārābī's version is:

(8) (this art [logic] is similar to the art of grammar: in fact) the relation of the art of logic to the intellect and the concepts is like the relation of the art of grammar to language and expressions. So for all the things that the science of grammar tells us about the rules of expressions, the science of logic gives us similar things (*naẓaʾirahā*) about concepts. (*wa-hāḏihi al-ṣināʿa tunāsibu ṣināʿat al-naḥw: ḏālika ʾanna nisbat ṣināʿat al-manṭiq ʾilā al-ʿaql wa-l-maʿqūlāt ka-nisbat ṣināʿat al-naḥw ʾilā al-lisān wa-l-ʾalfāẓ. fa-kull mā yuʿṭīnāhu ʿilm al-naḥw min al-qawānīn fī al-ʾalfāẓ fa-ʾinna ʿilm al-manṭiq yuʿṭīnā naẓāʾirahā fī al-maʿqūlāt*, Fārābī *ʾIḥṣāʾ* 54 l. 2–5)

12 So we have a proportionality: C1 is to C2 as E1 is to E2.

What Fārābī has added is that the analogy between grammatical and logical constructions is itself a form of similarity.[13]

The purpose of this requirement of similarities is presumably to make the class of impositions more internally coherent and less ad hoc, so that the language is more easily understood and learned (cf. *ʾIḥṣāʾ* 147 l. 15–18). Fārābī speaks of the system of similarity relations between concepts as an 'organization' (*intiẓām*, 139.3), and he speaks of a language being a 'copy' (*ḥikāya*) (140 l. 12, cf. *Šarḥ ʿibāra* 50 l. 4, 13, 18, 23; 51 l. 2) of this organization. He believes that the requirement applies also to single-word impositions: two similar simple concepts should be represented by similar words (139 l. 2 f.).

All of this is highly abstract, and Fārābī expounds it without giving concrete examples of what he counts as a similarity. But we will find that Sībawayhi's *Kitāb* contains many examples that fit Fārābī's formula.

3.3 *Example of a Successful Language: Arabic*

In *Ḥurūf* Fārābī comments that:

(9) When meanings are similar in respect of an accident or a feature which they share, they are rendered using expressions that are similar in shape and similar in their ends and their beginnings, and each of these ends or beginnings is taken as a single letter which is taken to signify the accident. (*wa-ʾiḏā kānat al-maʿānī mutašābihatan bi-ʿaraḍin ʾaw ḥālin mā taštariku fīhā, ǧuʿilat al-ʿibāratu ʿanhā bi-ʾalfāẓin mutašābihati l-aškāli wa-mutašābihatin bi-l-ʾawāḫiri wa-l-ʾawāʾili, wa-ǧuʿilat ʾawāḫiruhā kulluhā ʾaw ʾawāʾiluhā ḥarfan wāḥidan fa-ǧuʿila dāllan ʿalā ḏālika al-ʿaraḍi*, *Ḥurūf* 140 l. 3–6)

Here is one example out of many discussions in Sībawayhi that fit Fārābī's description. In *Kitāb* (II, 263, § 460) Sībawayhi mentions a number of words for the place where an action occurs: *maḥbis* where people are imprisoned, *maḍrib* where a tent is pitched, *maǧlis* where people sit. These three expressions share a feature of their meanings, and the words are similar in their beginnings; so naturally we take their common beginning *ma-* to signify the common meaning 'place where'. This is a well-known example which precisely fits Fārābī's recipe in (9).

13 One should not be surprised that Fārābī can express his similarity requirement in the words of a sixth-century Neoplatonist. The seed for this collection of ideas about language mirroring concepts is already planted in Plato's (d. 348–347 BC) *Sophist* (261d–263b).

Sībawayhi goes on to remark that since "time when" is similar to "place where", it can also be represented by this same form, as in *mantiǧ* "time of giving birth". A few pages later (*Kitāb* II, 267, § 465) Sībawayhi points out that "what is done" and "where it is done" are analogous ideas, allowing them both to be represented by the form *mafʿūl* (which illustrates Fārābī's point about both beginnings and ends). We will come back to these remarks of Sībawayhi in Section 3.4 below, in the context of Fārābī's claims about different kinds of similarity, some more remote than others.

It seems that classical Greek has no straightforward equivalent to Arabic *ma-*. (For Syriac, Persian and Sogdian we are not in a position to say.) English has "*-wards*" for "place towards which", though it is not a single letter. Fārābī could have known that classical Greek adds *e-* at the beginnings of verbs to express past tense. So in (9) Fārābī has identified a phenomenon that does occur in various languages. But did Fārābī really know this, or was he just drawing on what he knew was true about Arabic? His reference in (9) to letters and the beginning and ends of words does fit Arabic better than many languages. Again one wishes he had given examples of what he had in mind.

When Fārābī describes the science of language in *ʾIḥṣāʾ*, he is no longer in search of a general theory that fits all languages. At head (45 l. 1) and tail (52 l. 1) of this section he does speak of a single "science of language". But everywhere between these phrases he talks of language "of some nation" (*ʿinda ʾummatin mā*, 45 l. 3, cf. 46 l. 9 f.; 46 l. 17; 47 l. 8) or simply "that language" (*ḏālika al-lisān*, 47 l. 6; 47 l. 13; 49 l. 3 f.; 51 l. 1), or sometimes specifically of Arabic (49 l. 6; 49 l. 10 f.). The section contains no comparisons between one language and another, or any suggestion that a linguist might make such comparisons. The nearest he comes to such a suggestion is at 47 l. 6, where he seems to imply that a linguistic scientist studying a particular language might note that some feature is peculiar to that language while another feature is universal across languages—he gives no examples. In fact when he does state features that are peculiar to some languages, they are always features of Arabic. Examples are the classification of nouns as masculine or feminine, with no mention of neuters as in Greek (46 l. 15; 47 l. 16; 48 l. 10); the classification of verbs by number of letters in the root, and whether the verb is geminate or defective (48 l. 7 ff.); *ʾalif lām* in Arabic (49 l. 6); the phenomenon of *ʾidġām* between words (51 l. 8). There is no mention of features that are peculiar to Greek or Syriac or Turkish.

These facts should reinforce the suggestion we mentioned in Section 1 above, that this section of *ʾIḥṣāʾ* is based on a description of the grammar of Arabic by some earlier writer. The fact that the section uses some concepts and classifications from Greek grammar is not an argument against this suggestion (cf. our note 5). If the suggestion is correct, then this section of *ʾIḥṣāʾ* is evidence that Fārābī himself saw no conflict between his own philosophical view of grammar and a standard introductory treatment of Arabic grammar.[14]

At *Ḥurūf* (146 l. 8–10) Fārābī conjectures that town-dwellers, being more sophisticated than desert nomads, will find ways to make their vocal apparatus more flexible, and hence are more liable to alter established pronunciations. For this reason linguists will need to appeal to "people who live in houses made of hair" (*Ḥurūf* 146 l. 5) to establish the true forms of words. This is clearly an attempt at justification after the event for the Arabic linguists' appeal to Bedouins for authoritative forms.

This example shows Fārābī attempting justifications in general terms for features of Arabic linguistics. There is no hint of any conflict between his grammatical theories and those of Sībawayhi and his successors. Rather Fārābī is looking for explanations that could in principle apply to any languages, though the phenomena that he seeks to explain here are Arabic phenomena that he learned from the Arabic linguists.[15]

3.4 *Example of an Unsuccessful Language: Arabic*

Fārābī is also concerned that things can go wrong with a language, either because it violates the requirements of similarity, or because it obeys them in the wrong way. For example at *Ḥurūf* (141 l. 4–15) he worries that expressions can be similar or dissimilar in various ways, and a language might follow a "remote similarity" rather than a close one, giving rise to metaphors or ambiguous words. He seems to suggest that these are bad outcomes, but he gives no examples of harm that might be done. However, we can easily pick up examples of the phenomenon from the Arabic grammatical literature. Already in Section 4.2 we saw Sībawayhi discussing different kinds of similarity of meaning, and how they create cross-cutting similarities of expressions.

Sīrāfī (*Šarḥ* I, 443 l. 10–14, §17) records that grammarians have taken Sībawayhi to task for a wrong exposition of a line of the poet Sāʿida (d. 600? CE). Sībawayhi supposes that the word *kalīl* must be an active participle (meaning something like 'being weak but frequent') because of its formal similarity to active participles such as *raḥīm*, *ʿalīm*, *qadīr* and *samīʿ* (*Šarḥ* I, 440 l. 19). But in fact the word is a noun for sheet lightning (which is weak but repetitious).

---

14 Fārābī's description of Arabic in *ʾIḥṣāʾ* is almost neutral between different grammatical factions. The remark at 48 l. 5 that verbs are derived from *maṣdar*-s places it with the grammarians that later writers described as 'Basran' as opposed to 'Kufan'; certainly it is not a disagreement with Sībawayhi.

15 At *Ḥurūf* (147 l. 2 f.) he refers explicitly to the development of linguistics in Basra and Kufa in the eighth century.

Fārābī does give a concrete example where Arabic fails to supply a word to fit a similarity. Arabic logicians use *mawǧūd* to mean 'is'; but this usage violates the requirements of similarity, because *mawǧūd* is a passive participle, hence derived, whereas the concept 'is' is not derived in this sense. In fact Arabic compels this violation by not having a verb that means 'is' (*Ḥurūf* 110 l. 20–112 l. 3). But why does Fārābī care? Has he any evidence of logicians being misled by this violation? The simplest answer may well be the right one, namely that he doesn't care at all; the example is given purely to illustrate an abstract possibility. This is confirmed by the fact that in spite of his interest in terminological innovation (*Ḥurūf* 157 l. 5–161 l. 9), he takes no steps to repair any damage done by this particular violation of similarity.[16]

Why does Fārābī single out Arabic as a language that falls foul of the similarity requirement? Again the simplest answer may well be right: he chooses an example in Arabic because there is no other language that he knows well enough to find examples (see again our note 9). Versteegh's phrase "all other languages" in (1) above is revealing here: Fārābī repeatedly uses phrases meaning exactly this.[17] In no case does Fārābī draw a significant grammatical distinction between two languages that are not Arabic. Under these circumstances we should be wary of ascribing to him any interest in comparative linguistics.

4 The Disappearing Evidence of Conflict

4.1 *Zimmermann*

We return to part (b) of Zimmermann's remark (4) above. He seeks an explanation of why Ibn al-Sarrāǧ and Fārābī "never seems to refer to the other, and why the biographical tradition is virtually mute on the subject of their connexion". It is by no means clear that there is anything here that needs explaining. Medieval Arabic writers in logic hardly ever mention linguists, and vice versa; maybe nobody expected them to. The logicians almost never mention the Christian scholars who created the Arabic translation of the *Organon*, one of the essential tools of Arabic logic at least up to Ibn Sīnā. Also it would be very unreal-

16 Hodges and Druart (2019 Section 2) consider some possible reasons for Fārābī's objection to this feature in languages.

17 For example at *Ḥurūf* 80 l. 6; 80 l. 9f.; 111 l. 2; 111 l. 4; 111 l. 11f.; 111 l. 18; 112 l. 3; 165 l. 18; 212 l. 18. We agree with Menn (2008) that the role played by Greek in *Ḥurūf* is that of a language where supposedly the requirements of similarity are met ("where grammatical form tracks logical form", as Menn puts it on his page 68). But Menn might not agree with us that since Fārābī makes no linguistic distinction between any of the "other languages", the same applies to all of them.

istic to suppose that every fruitful conversation between scholars came to the attention of historians. But Zimmermann is not deterred; he crafts a theory to explain the silence.

In his theory, an early collaboration between Fārābī and Ibn al-Sarrāǧ led to a public estrangement between the two men, fortified by a

(10) campaign against Greek logic and philosophy [...] carried by the powerful religious wing of the grammatical community.

ZIMMERMANN 1981: CXXII

For his part Fārābī had

(11) a militant reaction to the opposition of those rejecting Greek thought principally because it was un-Arabic and un-Islamic. His indignation at what was unreasonable and noxious in the opposition's campaign made him impervious to justified criticism.

ZIMMERMANN 1981: CXXXVIIf

This is the context in which Fārābī allegedly challenges Arabic grammar by importing the number five (2).

Well, one must form one's own impressions. It seems to us that, far from having any vendetta against the grammarians, Fārābī was in general a tolerant and pacific writer. He believed that the teachings of Aristotle, interpreted in the light of the Neoplatonism of the Roman Empire philosophical academies, provided a useful general framework for understanding life and the universe in general, and grammar in particular. His writings were intended to transmit this belief to the Arabic-speaking intellectual world. Zimmermann's story of a feud between Fārābī and Ibn al-Sarrāǧ and other grammarians is not supported by any evidence at all, but it makes for lively reading in a discipline that can sometimes be dull and bookish.

Zimmermann's remark (2) on fives is particularly ironic in view of a more recent paper of Beata Sheyhatovitch (2019) on the role of the number five in medieval Arabic grammar. To quote from her conclusion (2019: 107):

(12) [...] in many cases the grammarians took pains to make the linguistic material fit into a fivefold division, while ignoring (or pretending to ignore) existing discrepancies. [...] The fact that even al-ʾAstarābāḏī, known for his non-conformism and originality, adheres to fivefold categorization of *tanwīn*-s and *tawābiʿ*, despite his own criticism of them, proves that the grammarians' engagement with number 'five' goes beyond mere respect for their predecessors' authority.

4.2 *Schöck*

So Zimmermann's account of an attack by Fārābī on traditional Arabic grammar has shrivelled under close inspection. We will find the same with Schöck's claim of opposition between Fārābī and Arabic grammarians, but for a very different reason. In her case we will conclude that her grasp of logic and its relation to grammar is too weak to allow her to provide reliable information about Fārābī's relation to the grammarians.

The central thesis of her book (Schöck 2006) is that three communities in the medieval Islamic empire, namely (a) early Muʿtazilite and Murǧiʿite thinkers, (b) some grammarians from Sībawayhi onwards, and (c) Aristotelian logicians, above all Fārābī, shared a number of concepts derived ultimately from Aristotle's logic, and this shared heritage allowed them to debate a number of issues across disciplinary boundaries.[18] This thesis may have truth in it and deserves to be examined. Schöck has assembled an impressive number of texts that could be relevant to the thesis.

Problems begin as soon as we move from her collected texts to her discussion of them. These problems lie at two levels. First there are her starting assumptions, which seem to us in some cases mistaken about the facts or confused in basic concepts, and in other places to go beyond what the known facts entitle her to assume. Second there are her detailed claims about opposition between Fārābī and the grammarians; these claims are flawed by both lack of essential explanations and lack of evidence.

We begin with the starting assumptions. We confine ourselves to just three examples of what are pervasive problems.

(i) One notion that she frequently calls on is proslepsis, as in the prosleptic sentences of Theophrastus.[19] She comments (2006: 432) that 'in the Arabic logic this kind of sentence is an interface between term-logic and propositional logic'; she refers to her section 14.4.3.3 for details. But Schöck fails to establish their relevance to Fārābī; the parallels that she draws in her 14.4.3.3 between proslepsis and remarks of Fārābī are too crude and commonplace to show that Fārābī had proslepsis in mind. In any case we know of no evidence that the notion of proslepsis ever reached Fārābī. If it had done it would probably have been through Alexander's *Commentary on Prior Analytics*, specifically his commentary on sections i.23 and i.29. But in 1013 Ibn Sīnā had not seen a translation

---

18 This is our summary, not hers. On her page 43 she speaks of the common property of the learned classes in late antiquity, which had reached the Arabic world long before the translations of Aristotle.

19 Fortenbaugh (1992:230–236) explains prosleptic sentences.

of Alexander of Aphrodisias's (150–215?) *Commentary* that went as far as i.23,[20] making it likely that Fārābī had not seen one either.[21]

(ii) The case of proslepsis illustrates her tendency to see detailed parallels where there are only vague resemblances. A vivid example of this tendency is her account of a discussion in which ʿUmar b. ʾAbī ʿUṯmān al-Šimmazī (sic, al-Šammarī, dates unknown) extracted from ʾAbū Ḥanīfa the view that people who professed belief in Allāh, but held wildly improbable beliefs about such things as the identity of Muḥammad, should still be counted as believers (Schöck 2005: 21f.). Schöck reports this as a refutation of ʾAbū Ḥanīfa which uses the (Aristotelian) concepts of homonymity and synonymity and "proves that ʾAbū Ḥanīfa violated the logical rules […]".[22] The source text (of ʾAšʿarī [d. 324/936]) doesn't refer to homonymity, synonymity or logic, and Schöck's reference to logical rules here must raise doubts about what she thinks a logical rule is.

(iii) These doubts are reinforced when she tells us that Sībawayhi has his own new "type of propositional logic", different from the Stoic form and the modern propositional logic (Schöck 2005: 88). Her basis for this claim seems to be that she assumes Sībawayhi would regard Arabic sentences from the Qurʾān as expressing necessary truths. But to belong to a "type of logic" the necessity would have to follow some formal rules, and Schöck gives no evidence that Sībawayhi had any such rules. There is a fundamental misunderstanding about logic here. A similar misunderstanding about logic may lie behind her claim (Schöck 2005: 358) that Sībawayhi took modus ponendo ponens to be a grammatical rule of Arabic.[23]

We turn to her more detailed claims about Fārābī's *Gegenposition* in relation to the grammarians. This is the topic of her ninety-page chapter 14, and there are some relevant references to Fārābī elsewhere in her book. In this lengthy

20 In *Muḫtaṣar* (146 l. 5–7) and the closely associated *Masāʾil* (101.21–102.5) Ibn Sīnā says that no Peripatetic logicians before him studied logical rules that yield hypothetical conclusions. Since Alexander's *Commentary* mentions such rules (viz. totally hypothetical syllogisms) at 265 l. 13, commenting on *Prior Analytics* I, 23, any copies available to Ibn Sīnā must have stopped before I, 23.

21 Ibn al-Nadīm (*Fihrist* 405) in the 980s has just two copies of Alexander's *Commentary*, one of them "incomplete" and the other running only "to the end of the three categorical figures" (i.e. to I, 7 or I, 22). Neither the texts cited in Fortenbaugh (1992:230–236) nor the further discussion in Huby (2007:131–135) yield any evidence that Arabic logicians knew of the notion of proslepsis.

22 Schöck 2005:21: "er nachwies, dass Abū Ḥanīfa die logischen Regeln verletzte, welche Voraussetzung für die Wahrheit oder Falschheit einer Aussage sind".

23 "[…] welchen Sībawaih zur grammatikalischen Regel des Arabischen erklärte". She refers to chapter 4 in support of this remark, but we found nothing relevant there. Grammatical rules are about being well-formed, not about being true or necessarily true.

discourse it is not easy to make out exactly what she thinks are the points on which Fārābī differs from the grammarians; but we found her making the following four points.

(1) Schöck devotes her chapter 4 (2005: 79–88) to the views of Sībawayhi, comparing them with the views of some other writers. On page 81 she sets out Fārābī's theory that in sentences such as Q. 5/38 (*wa-l-sāriqu wa-l-sāriqa fa-qṭaʿū ʾaydiyahumā* "The male and female thief, cut off their hands [...]") a word beginning with the definite article, such as "the thief", may be used as a substitute for a more restrictive description which is the one that the speaker or writer—in this case Allāh—intended. Writing "thief*" for the intended description, the sentence as a whole can then be read as referring to "every thief*".[24] She comments (2005: 82) that Sībawayhi "chose a completely different approach" to Q. 5/38, and goes on to explain that Sībawayhi regards the sentence not as universally quantified but as a conditional: "If a person steals then [...]".

There are two main problems with this contrast that Schöck draws between Fārābī and Sībawayhi. The first is that although on her page 82 Schöck claims to be talking about Sībawayhi's interpretation of Q. 5/38, there are in fact only two places where Sībawayhi mentions this Qurʾānic sentence in his *Kitāb*, and in neither place does he say anything like what Schöck attributes to him.[25] This is important for understanding Schöck, since it shows that her claim about Sībawayhi's "completely different approach" is relying on what Sībawayhi says about a larger class of sentences, not just Q. 5/38. But she doesn't tell us what this larger class is. One class of sentences that she might have in mind is the *waʿd* and *waʿīd* (Promise and Threat) verses from the Qurʾān, which she discusses in her chapter 5. But we found no place where she attributes to Sībawayhi any grammatical theory for this group of sentences.

The second problem will probably have already occurred to many readers. In common speech the universally quantified sentence "Every sinner is an X" and the conditional sentence "If anyone sins then he or she is an X" would normally be taken as conveying exactly the same information. Of course it would be possible for Schöck to argue that in Qurʾānic exegesis the choice of one sentence rather than the other should be understood as informative in some way;

24 This is indeed what Fārābī says in his essay on the application of syllogistic logic to *fiqh*, which appears at the end of some manuscripts of his *Qiyās* and some manuscripts of his work *Qiyās ṣaġīr*. See *Qiyās* 55 l. 13–56 l. 12. The passage is translated at Chatti and Hodges (2020:155f.) with explanatory notes.

25 At *Kitāb* I, 60 l. 9 he discusses how the noun "thief" can be in the nominative. At *Kitāb* II, 209 l. 9 he discusses the fact that this suffix is put in the dual rather than the plural.

but again we found no place where she offers such a suggestion. The outcome is that we are left with no idea what contrast she is aiming to draw between the approaches of Fārābī and Sībawayhi to this Qur'ānic sentence.

(2) On her page 299 she claims that Sībawayhi blurs the distinction between a name and what it is a name of, whereas Fārābī corrects this misunderstanding. To appreciate what the issue is here, we need to know more about what view she is attributing to Sībawayhi. Is it perhaps just that he adopts some locutions that are not strictly correct but are convenient and not likely to cause misunderstandings that interfere with his message? We never discover, because the only references that Schöck gives for this confusion in Sībawayhi are to secondary sources.[26]

(3) On her page 295 she claims that Fārābī "liberated participles from being linked to a determinate time", and that this move was of fundamental importance for the development of syllogistic.[27] There seems to be an implication here that Fārābī noticed possible relationships between participles and times, relationships which had not been noticed by the grammarians such as Sībawayhi. Since her claim is lacking in specifics about just what the grammarians were or weren't aware of, we confine ourselves to observing that Sībawayhi himself took it as clear that active participles sometimes act as nouns without attachment to any determinate time.[28]

(4) On her page 370 she claims that 'the grammarians' believe, and Fārābī denies, that it is legitimate to begin an induction from a single instance. This is not an issue of grammar.

Summing up, it seems unlikely that Schöck would find evidence of a grammatical disagreement between Fārābī and Sībawayhi or other classical Arabic grammarians, given her difficulties in formulating her claims without introducing confusions about the nature of logic, grammar or both. As we said, her case for Fārābī's *Gegenposition* against the grammarians shrivels under inspection.

26 She refers to note 29 in her chapter 7; this in turn refers to writings of Michel Allard (1924–1976), Gerhard Endress and Ulrike Mosel.

27 "Fārābīs Befreiung dessen, was ein Partizip anzeigen kann, von der Verknäpfung mit einer zeitlichen Bestimmung ist grundlegend für die Syllogistik." It was Ibn Sīnā, a century later than Fārābī, who first extended Aristotle's syllogistic to allow inferences involving quantification over times. Possibly he was influenced by Fārābī's writings on participles, but in *Masā'il* (83 l. 6f.) the sources that he himself names as leading to this extension are Alexander of Aphrodisias and Themistius (317?–388?), both much earlier than Fārābī.

28 Sībawayhi is of course aware of constructions where an active participle takes first place in an *'iḍāfa*; normally in these constructions the participle behaves as a noun with no time determination. He also knows that time quantifiers can be associated with active participles (*Kitāb* I, 48 l. 19–49 l. 3, § 30).

5 Conclusion

Sībawayhi collected a vast amount of detailed information about the Arabic language, its grammar, pragmatics and phonology. With its help he came as near as he could to a precise and accurate description of the language as a coherent whole.

Fārābī also described the Arabic language, but from a very different point of view. As a philosopher he preferred the big picture to the tiresome details, and he liked answering broad questions about Why and How. At some points he offered explanations for features of Arabic that we can verify from Sībawayhi's data. But no points of conflict between Fārābī's theories and those of Sībawayhi have come to light.

Although Fārābī cast his explanations in terms that should apply to any language, it is not established that he knew enough of any other language besides Arabic to test his views on that other language.

Comparing Fārābī to Sībawayhi, we see the contrast between the speculative philosopher and the linguistic scientist.

Bibliography

Primary Sources

Fārābī, *ʾAlfāẓ* = al-Muʿallim al-Ṯānī ʾAbū Naṣr Muḥammad b. Muḥammad b. Ṭarḫān b. ʾAwzaliġ al-Fārābī, *Kitāb al-ʾAlfāẓ al-mustaʿmala fī al-manṭiq*. Ed. by Muḥsin Mahdi. Bayrūt: Dār al-mašriq, 1968.

Fārābī, *Ḥurūf* = al-Muʿallim al-Ṯānī ʾAbū Naṣr Muḥammad b. Muḥammad b. Ṭarḫān b. ʾAwzaliġ al-Fārābī, *Kitāb al-Ḥurūf*. Ed. Muḥsin Mahdi. Bayrūt: Dār al-mašriq, 1990. A new edition with full translation by Charles E. Butterworth is reported to be near publication.

Fārābī, *ʾIḥṣāʾ* = al-Muʿallim al-Ṯānī ʾAbū Naṣr Muḥammad b. Muḥammad b. Ṭarḫān b. ʾAwzaliġ al-Fārābī, *ʾIḥṣāʾ al-ʿulūm*. Ed. by ʿUṯmān ʾAmīn. Paris: Dār bibliyūn, 2005.

Fārābī, *Qiyās* = al-Muʿallim al-Ṯānī ʾAbū Naṣr Muḥammad b. Muḥammad b. Ṭarḫān b. ʾAwzaliġ al-Fārābī, *Kitāb al-Qiyās*, in *al-Manṭiq ʿinda al-Fārābī*. Ed. by Rafīq al-ʿAǧam, vol. II, 11–64. Bayrūt: Dār al-mašriq, 1986. Trans. in Chatti and Hodges (2020).

Fārābī, *Qiyās ṣaġīr* = al-Muʿallim al-Ṯānī ʾAbū Naṣr Muḥammad b. Muḥammad b. Ṭarḫān b. ʾAwzaliġ al-Fārābī, *Kitāb al-Qiyās al-ṣaġīr*, in *al-Manṭiq ʿind al-Fārābī*. Ed. by Rafīq al-ʿAǧam, vol. II, 65–93. Bayrūt: Dār al-mašriq, 1986.

Fārābī, *Šarḥ ʿIbāra* = al-Muʿallim al-Ṯānī ʾAbū Naṣr Muḥammad b. Muḥammad b. Ṭarḫān b. ʾAwzaliġ al-Fārābī, *Šarḥ ʿibāra*. Ed. by W. Kutsch and S. Marrow. Bayrūt: Dār al-mašriq, 1986. Trans. in Zimmermann (1981: 1–219). We cite the page and line numbers in the Kutsch and Marrow edition; Zimmermann's translation gives these too.

Ibn al-Nadīm, *Fihrist* = Muḥammad b. ʾIsḥāq al-Muʿtazilī, *al-Fihrist*. Ed. by Yūsuf ʿAlī Ṭawīl. Bayrūt: Dār al-kutub al-ʿilmiyya, 2002.

Ibn al-Sarrāǧ, *ʾUṣūl* = ʾAbū Bakr Muḥammad b. al-Sarī b. Sahl Ibn al-Sarrāǧ al-Baġdādī, *al-ʾUṣūl fī al-naḥw*. Ed. by ʿAbd al-Ḥusayn al-Fatlī. Bayrūt: Muʾassasat al-risāla, 3 vol., 1996.

Ibn Sīnā, *Masāʾil* = ʾAbū ʿAlī al-Ḥusayn b. ʿAbd Allāh b. al-Ḥasan b. ʿAlī b. Sīnā, *al-Masāʾil al-ġarība al-ʿišrīniyya*. Ed. by M. Mohaghegh and T. Izutsu, *Collected Texts and Papers on Logic and Language*. Ṭahrān: Society for the Appreciation of Cultural Works and Dignitaries, 81–103, 2007.

Ibn Sīnā, *Muḫtaṣar* = ʾAbū ʿAlī al-Ḥusayn b. ʿAbd Allāh b. al-Ḥasan b. ʿAlī b. Sīnā, *al-Muḫtaṣar al-ʾawsaṭ fī al-manṭiq*. Ed. by Seyyed Mahmoud Yousofsani. Ṭahrān: Muassasah-i Pizhūhishī-i ḥikmat va Falsafan-i Īrān, 2017.

Miskawayhi, *Tartīb* = ʾAbū ʿAlī ʾAḥmad b. Muḥammad b. Yaʿqūb b. Miskawayhi, *Tartīb al-saʿāda wa-manāzil al-ʿulūm*. Ed. by ʾAbū al-Qāsim Emāmī. Ṭahrān: Mīrās-I Maktūb, 2017.

Sībawayhi, *Kitāb* = ʾAbū Bišr ʿAmr b. ʿUṯmān b. Qanbar Sībawayhi, *Le livre de Sîbawaihi. Traité de grammaire arabe par Sîboûya, dit Sîbawaihi*. Ed. by Hartwig Derenbourg. Paris: Imprimerie nationale, 2 vol., 1881–1889, reprint Hildesheim & New York: Georg Olms Verlag, 2 vol., 1970.

Sīrāfī, *Šarḥ* = ʾAbū Saʿīd al-Ḥasan b. ʿAbd Allāh al-Sīrāfī, *Šarḥ Kitāb Sībawayhi*. Ed. by ʾAḥmad Ḥasan Mahdalī. Bayrūt: Dār al-kutub al-ʿilmiyya, 5 vol., 2012.

Suyūṭī, *Muzhīr* = Ǧalāl al-Dīn ʿAbd al-Raḥmān b. Kamāl al-Dīn ʾAbī Bakr b. Muḥammad b. Sābiq al-Dīn Ḫaḍr al-Ḫuḍayrī al-Šāfiʿī al-ʾAsyūṭī al-mašhūr bi-l-Suyūṭī, *al-Muzhīr fī ʿulūm al-luġa wa-ʾanwāʿihā*. Ed. by Fuʾād ʿAlī Manṣūr. Bayrūt: Dār al-kutub al-ʿilmiyya, 1998.

ʾUṣaybiʿa, *ʿUyūn* = Muwaffaq al-Dīn ʾAbū al-ʿAbbās ʾAḥmad b. al-Qāsim b. Ḫalīfa Ibn ʾAbī ʾUṣaybiʿa, *ʿUyūn al-ʾanbāʾ fī ṭabaqāt al-ʾaṭibbāʾ*. Ed. by Nizār Riḍā. Bayrūt: Dār maktabat al-ḥayāt, 1965.

Secondary Sources

Chatti, Saloua & Wilfrid Hodges. 2020. *Al-Fārābī, Syllogism: An Abridgement of Aristotle's Prior Analytics, introduction and translation. Ancient Commentators on Aristotle*. London: Bloomsbury Academic.

Druart, Thérèse-Anne. 2019. "Al-Fārābī". *The Stanford Encyclopedia of Philosophy*, Fall 2020 Edition [online], ed. by Edward N. Zalta. URL: https://plato.stanford.edu/archives/fall2020/entries/al-farabi

Druart, Thérèse-Anne. 2020. "What does music have to do with language, logic, and rulership? Al-Farabi's answer". *The origin and nature of language and logic: Perspectives in medieval Islamic, Jewish, and Christian thought*, ed. by Nadja Germann and Steven Harvey, 193–210. Turnhout: Brepols.

Elamrani-Jamal, Abdelali. 1983. *Logique aristotélicienne et grammaire arabe (étude et documents)*. Paris: Librairie philosophique Vrin, coll. "Études musulmanes" 26.

Fortenbaugh, William W., Pamela M. Huby, Robert W. Sharples and Dimitri Gutas (eds.). 1992. *Theophrastus of Eresus: Sources for His Life, Writings, Thought and Influence*. Leiden: E.J. Brill.

Giolfo, Manuela E.B. & Wilfrid Hodges. 2018. "Syntax, semantics, and pragmatics in al-Sīrāfī and Ibn Sīnā". *The Foundations of Arabic Linguistics III. The Development of a Tradition: Continuity and Change*, ed. by Georgine Ayoub & Kees Versteegh, 115–145. Leiden: E.J. Brill. coll. "Studies in Semitic Languages and Linguistics" 94.

Giolfo, Manuela E.B. & Wilfrid Hodges. 2019. "Conditionality: Syntax and meaning in al-Sīrāfī and Ibn Sīnā". *The Foundations of Arabic Linguistics IV*, ed. by Manuela E.B. Giolfo & Kees Versteegh, 157–181. Leiden: E.J. Brill. coll. "Studies in Semitic Languages and Linguistics" 97.

Gutas, Dimitri. 1983. "Paul the Persian on the classification of the parts of Aristotle's philosophy: a milestone between Alexandria and Baghdād". *Der Islam: Zeitschrift für Geschichte und Kultur des Islamischen Orients* 60/2. 31–267; repr. in Dimitri Gutas, *Greek Philosophers in the Arabic Tradition*, Ashgate: Aldershot 2000, c. ix.

Hasnawi, Ahmad. 1985. "Fārābī et la pratique de l'exégèse philosophique (remarques sur son Commentaire au *De Interpretatione* d'Aristote)". *Revue de Synthèse Paris* 117. 27–59.

Hodges, Wilfrid & Thérèse-Anne Druart. 2019. "al-Fārābī's Philosophy of Logic and Language". *Stanford Encyclopedia of Philosophy*, Fall 2020 Edition [online], ed. by Edward N. Zalta. URL: https://plato.stanford.edu/archives/fall2020/entries/al-farabi-logic/

Huby, Pamela. 2007. *Theophrastus of Eresus: Sources for His Life, Writings, Thought and Influence. Commentary volume 2, Logic*. Leiden: E.J. Brill.

Menn, Stephen. 2008. "Al-Fārābī's *Kitāb al-ḥurūf* and his analysis of the senses of being". *Arabic Sciences and Philosophy* 18/1. 59–97.

Perkams, Matthias. 2019. "The Syro-Persian reinvention of Aristotelianism: Paul the Persian's treatise on the scopes of Aristotle's works between Sergius of Rēšʿaynā, Alexandria, and Baghdad". *Studia Graeca-Arabica* 9, 129–145.

Pingree, David. 2002. "Sirāfi, Abu Saʿid Ḥasan". *Encyclopaedia Iranica* [online]. URL: https://www.iranicaonline.org/articles/sirafi

Schöck, Cornelia. 2005. "Aussagenquantifizierung und -Modalisierung in der frühen Islamischen Theologie". *Logik und Theologie. Das* Organon *im arabischen und im lateinischen Mittelalter*, ed. by Dominik Perler & Ulrich Rudolph, 19–43. Leiden: E.J. Brill. coll. "Studien und Texte zur Geistesgeschichte des Mittelalters" 84.

Schöck, Cornelia. 2006. *Koranexegese, Grammatik und Logik. Zum verhältnis von arabischer und aristotelischer Urteils-, Konsequenz- und Schlußlehre*. Leiden: E.J. Brill. coll. "Islamic Philosophy, Theology and Science. Texts and Studies" 60.

Sheyhatovitch, Beata. 2019. "'Five' as a typological number in the medieval Arabic grammatical tradition". *Journal of Arabic and Islamic Studies* 19. 81–111.

Versteegh, Kees. 1977. *Greek elements in Arabic linguistic thinking*. Leiden: E.J. Brill. coll. "Studies in Semitic Languages and Linguistics" 7.

Versteegh, Kees. 2000. "Grammar and logic in the Arabic grammatical tradition". *Handbuch für die Geschichte der Sprach- und Kommunikationswissenschaft 1*, ed. by Sylvain Auroux et al., 300–306. Berlin & New York: Mouton de Gruyter.

Vidro, Nadia. 2020. "A Book on Arabic Inflexion According to the System of the Greeks: a Lost Work by ḤUNAYN B. ISḤĀQ". *Zeitschrift für Arabische Linguistik* 72/2. 26–58.

Zimmermann, Fritz W. 1981. *Al-Fārābī's Commentary and Short Treatise on Aristotle's* De Interpretatione. Oxford: British Academy and Oxford University Press.

CHAPTER 8

Ibn al-Sarrāǧ's Classification of Pseudo-Objects and the Grammatical Concept of *faḍla*

Hideki Okazaki

Introduction

This paper examines the classification of *mušabbah bi-l-mafʿūl* (resembling the *mafʿūl*, or pseudo-object) by Ibn al-Sarrāǧ (d. 316/929), using a chronological analysis of the development of the grammatical concept of *faḍla* (redundant element). Ibn al-Sarrāǧ divided the accusative complements of verbs into two categories: *mafʿūl* (object) and *mušabbah bi-l-mafʿūl*. In his treatise *al-ʾUṣūl fī al-naḥw*, he itemized five elements for each complement with specific terminologies. The framework of five *mafʿūl*-s has remained stable since then and has been dealt with as a principal category pertaining to a variety of accusative complements; in contrast, however, the framework of *mušabbah bi-l-mafʿūl* failed to gain traction among Ibn al-Sarrāǧ's followers, and was only inconsistently applied in later grammatical works. In the course of the recategorization of accusative complements according to the concept of *faḍla* in the 7th/13th century, it was found that the old framework of *mušabbah bi-l-mafʿūl* did not encompass all the accusative complements excluded from the long-established five *mafʿūl*-s. In this paper, we will consider the reasons why the framework proposed by Ibn al-Sarrāǧ did not become standard and why grammarians sought another way to categorize complements of accusative verbs, leading to rearrangement through *faḍla*.

1 *Mafʿūl*

The term *mafʿūl* has several meanings at different levels of grammar.[1] At the lexicological or morphological level, it is used to denote the word pattern of the passive participle. At the level of syntax, it denotes "the accusative noun/pronoun on which the act of the verb 'falls'" (Taha 2008: 100) and is sometimes

1 For three syntactic functions of *mafʿūl* (direct object, grammatical subject of a verb in the passive voice, and objective genitive) in Sībawayhi's (d. 180/796?) *Kitāb*, cf. Kasher 2012:4–13.

 | DOI:10.1163/9789004515895_010

translated as "object" or "patient".[2] *Mafʿūl* was also used to refer to the subject of a verb in the passive voice until the 7th/13th century, when this use was replaced by the term *al-nāʾib ʿan al-fāʿil* (substitute agent). Some grammarians, such as Sībawayhi and Mubarrad, used the term *mafʿūl* to denote the accusative verbal noun, which they called *maṣdar*,[3] in the same manner, the term *mafʿūl* was used as an abbreviation for *mafʿūl bihi* (direct object).[4] Besides these usages, *mafʿūl* functioned as an umbrella term to place five types of nominal complements of the verb into the same category: *mafʿūl muṭlaq*[5] (absolute object), *mafʿūl bihi* (direct object), *mafʿūl fīhi* (locative object), *mafʿūl lahu* (reason object), and *mafʿūl maʿahu* (accompaniment object).

Although each of these appears as a chapter title in *al-ʾUṣūl fī al-naḥw*, they are not always used in the text, being replaced instead by some single word or term without a prepositional phrase. The term *mafʿūl muṭlaq*,[6] for example, appears in *ʾUṣūl* only twice, in chapter titles; in the body text Ibn al-Sarrāǧ consistently uses *maṣdar* (verbal noun), which appears 308 times in this work. *Mafʿūl fīhi*,[7] which appears five times, alternates with the terms *ẓarf al-makān* and *ẓarf al-zamān*, used ten times each; moreover, plain *ẓarf* is used 192 times, including in non-technical, everyday vocabulary. *Mafʿūl* itself occurs 417 times, while *mafʿūl bihi* is used only 24 times across the three volumes of the work.[8]

2 Categorization of *mafʿūl* and *mušabbah bi-l-mafʿūl* by Ibn al-Sarrāǧ

The five categories into which Ibn al-Sarrāǧ classified *mafʿūl* used well-defined terminology: *mafʿūl muṭlaq*, *mafʿūl bihi*, *mafʿūl fīhi*, *mafʿūl lahu*, and *mafʿūl*

---

2 This subject is too involved to be treated here in detail. For further discussion, cf. Peled 1999:53–54, 58, 76; Kasher 2012:3; Carter 2016:143.

3 Cf. Sībawayhi *Kitāb* II, 267 l. 10–11; Mubarrad *Muqtaḍab* I, 74 l. 16; II, 122, l. 2; Ibn al-Sarrāǧ *ʾUṣūl* I, 159 l. 16; Levin 1991:919.

4 Mosel 1975:256; Owens 1989:218; Levin 1991:924.

5 For the word formation and the interpretation of *mafʿūl muṭlaq*, the post-Sībawayhian term used by Ibn al-Sarrāǧ, cf. Levin 1991.

6 In some later grammatical works, the term *mafʿūl muṭlaq* was replaced by the term *maṣdar* in chapter titles. Širbīnī (d. 977/1570) criticized the trend, pointing out that *maṣdar* may be in nominative and genitive form. Cf. Carter 1981:344; Peled 1999:85; Kasher 2019:206.

7 Ibn al-Sarrāǧ *ʾUṣūl* I, 159 l. 8; 190 l. 6; 190 l. 7; 218 l. 9; III, 149 l. 2. Although the term *mafʿūl fīhi* is used instead of *ẓarf* by Mubarrad (d. 285/898 or 286/899; cf. Mubarrad *Muqtaḍab* II, 120 l. 2; IV, 328 l. 3), *ẓarf* also continued to be widely used by him and later grammarians.

8 Ibn al-Sarrāǧ *ʾUṣūl* I, 35 l. 8; 58 l. 6; 99 l. 3; 107 l. 16; 122 l. 3; 122 l. 7; 134 l. 10; 159 l. 8; 169 l. 9; 171 l. 13; 196 l. 1; 196 l. 3; 206 l. 16; 210 l. 6; 212 l. 15; 254 l. 6; II, 18 l. 16; 18 l. 23; 315 l. 10; 315 l. 16; 315 l. 19; 317 l. 6; 344 l. 9; 345 l. 18. For the number of times each term appears in *ʾUṣūl*, cf. Okazaki 2003:21; 2008:35.

maʿahu (*ʾUṣūl* I, 158 ff.).[9] His treatise is characterized by the classification of grammatical categories based on the principle of comprehensive division, and the chapters are arranged according to this classification. However, his classification of what he calls "pseudo-objects", *mušabbah bi-l-mafʿūl*, is less well understood than his clear description of *mafʿūl*. A close look reveals that Ibn al-Sarrāǧ recognized five types of pseudo-objects: *ḥāl* (circumstantial qualifier), *tamyīz* (distinguishing element), *istiṯnāʾ* (exception), *ḫabar kāna wa-ʾaḫawātihā* (the predicate of *kāna* and its related verbs), and *ism ʾinna wa-ʾaḫawātihā* (subject-noun of *ʾinna* and its related particles).

In the grammatical treatises of the post-Sībawayhian era until the 9th/15th century, three technical terms, *manṣūb*, *mafʿūl*, and *faḍla*, complicate the overall picture of the basic theory of grammar. The *manṣūb* ("that which has been made accusative") is not a synonym for *mafʿūl* because the term *manṣūb* has a particular role in the organization of the chapters of *al-ʾUṣūl*. Beginning with the division of the parts of speech, the overall concepts of nouns, verbs, and particles are given (cf. *ʾUṣūl* I, 36 ff.). Following are chapters describing inflection, inflected parts of speech, invariability, and invariable parts of speech (cf. *ʾUṣūl* I, 45 ff.), a chapter on *niʿma* and *biʾsa* (cf. *ʾUṣūl* I, 111 ff.), and a chapter on nouns that were given the operative effect of the verb (cf. *ʾUṣūl* I, 122 ff.), among others. In parallel with this succession of chapters (*bāb* pl. *ʾabwāb*), another set of chapters follow under the group title of *ḏikr* (mention). In volume I, three *ḏikr*-s related to inflections are incorporated: mention of nouns in the nominative case, *ḏikr al-ʾasmāʾ al-murtafiʿa* (cf. *ʾUṣūl* I, 58 ff.); mention of nouns in the accusative case, *ḏikr al-ʾasmāʾ al-manṣūbāt* (cf. *ʾUṣūl* I, 158 ff.); and mention of the operator of genitive and nouns in the genitive case, *ḏikr al-ǧarr wa-l-ʾasmāʾ al-maǧrūra* (cf. *ʾUṣūl* I, 408 ff.). Most of the discussion of *mafʿūl*-s and *mušabbah bi-l-mafʿūl* occurs in *ḏikr al-ʾasmāʾ al-manṣūbāt*.

In *al-ʾUṣūl*, *mafʿūl* and *mušabbah bi-l-mafʿūl* are characterized as *al-ʾasmāʾ al-manṣūbāt*, that is, substantives or nouns in the accusative case. Compared to the categorization of *mafʿūl*, that of *mušabbah bi-l-mafʿūl* is not as clearly defined, as subtypes are not enumerated in a single paragraph, making it difficult to grasp the overall structure that Ibn al-Sarrāǧ had in mind. Regardless,

---

9 It was not always true that the classification of five *mafʿūl*-s before the age of Ibn al-Sarrāǧ was handed down and fully agreed to by later grammarians. Ibn Hišām al-ʾAnṣārī (d. 761/1360) mentioned that "Zaǧǧāǧ deleted *mafʿūl maʿahu* and then incorporated it into *mafʿūl bihi*", while the "Kufan school deleted *mafʿūl lahu* and then incorporated it into *mafʿūl muṭlaq*" and "Ǧawharī [d. 400/1009?] named *mafʿūl dūnahu* instead of *mustaṯnā*" (Ibn Hišām al-ʾAnṣārī *Qaṭr* 219 l. 6–12). The Kufan school maintains that the verb has only one *mafʿūl*, that is *mafʿūl bihi*, and the rest is *mušabbah bi-l-mafʿūl* (Suyūṭī *Hamʿ* II, 6 l. 1–2).

it is obvious that Ibn al-Sarrāǧ fundamentally recognized five *mušabbah bi-l-mafʿūl* in two classes, the first one being "a formal accusative [which] may be the same as the nominative in meaning" (*qad yakūnu fīhi al-manṣūb fī al-lafẓ huwa al-marfūʿ fī al-maʿnā*), and the second one "the formal accusative [which] is not the same as the nominative, while an accusative (noun) belongs to the same generic category as a nominative (noun)" (*mā yakūnu al-manṣūb fī al-lafẓ ġayr al-marfūʿ, wa-l-manṣūb baʿḍ al-marfūʿ*, *ʾUṣūl* I, 212).

The first class is further divided into three types, according to the operator (*ʿāmil*) that is used in the sentence. First, when the operator is a real verb, two types of *mušabbah bi-l-mafʿūl* are described: *ḥāl* and *tamyīz* (cf. *ʾUṣūl* I, 213). Second, for *ḫabar kāna wa-ʾaḫawātihā* (the predicate of *kāna* and related verbs), the operator is not a real verb but is conjugated as a verb (cf. *ʾUṣūl* I, 228). Third, for *ism ʾinna wa-ʾaḫawātihā* (a subject-noun for *ʾinna* and related particles), the operator is a non-inflective particle (cf. *ʾUṣūl* I, 229).

The second class of *mušabbah bi-l-mafʿūl* is not divided into subcategories consisting only of *mustaṯnā* (excepted element) and indicating that *mustaṯnā* is similar to *mafʿūl*, as it comes after the verb is satisfied with its agent or after the completion of an utterance (*al-mustaṯnā yušbihu al-mafʿūl ʾiḏā ʾutiya bihi baʿda istiġnāʾ al-fiʿl bi-l-fāʿil wa-baʿda tamām al-kalām*, *ʾUṣūl* I, 281).

Before Ibn al-Sarrāǧ, his teacher Mubarrad had already postulated that "nothing takes an accusative case unless it is a *mafʿūl* or a *mušabbah bi-l-mafʿūl*, structurally and semantically" (*iʿlam ʾannahu lā yantaṣibu šayʾ ʾillā ʿalā ʾannahu mafʿūl ʾaw mušabbah bi-l-mafʿūl fī lafẓ ʾaw maʿnā*, *Muqtaḍab* IV, 299). However, Mubarrad does not give explicit definitions of *mafʿūl* or *mušabbah bi-l-mafʿūl*, nor does he list the items each comprises. Although both categories are mentioned in treatises before Ibn al-Sarrāǧ, 2nd/8th- and 3rd/9th-century grammatical works lack certain grammatical terminology, classification (*taqsīm*) of subcategories of terms, and clear-cut chapter arrangements. For instance, the technical term *mafʿūl muṭlaq*[10] is not found in either *Kitāb Sībawayhi* or *al-Muqtaḍab*.

3 Rearrangement of *mafʿūl* and *mušabbah bi-l-mafʿūl*

Although Ibn al-Sarrāǧ's classification of the five *mafʿūl*-s was accepted by his successors in the 4th/10th century and afterwards, the framework of the five *mušabbah bi-l-mafʿūl* received some modifications.

10 For a full account of the term *al-mafʿūl al-muṭlaq*, cf. Levin 1991; Larcher 1991a; 1991b; Kasher 2019.

In his *al-ʾĪḍāḥ*, ʾAbū ʿAlī al-Fārisī (d. 377/987) included the same five accusative complements, *mafʿūl muṭlaq*, *mafʿūl bihi*, *mafʿūl fīhi*, *mafʿūl maʿahu*, and *mafʿūl lahu* (*ʾĪḍāḥ* 150 l. 3–4), as in the *mafʿūl* framework in al-Sarrāǧ's *al-ʾUṣūl*. Nevertheless, a slight change can be pointed out, namely the reversal of the order of the fourth and the fifth items, *mafʿūl maʿahu*, and *mafʿūl lahu*. As for the *mušabbah bi-l-mafʿūl* framework, Fārisī made a small change by adding *ḫabar mā*, the predicate of negative particle *mā* (*ʾĪḍāḥ* 171 l. 3).

In *Kitāb al-Lumaʿ fī al-naḥw*, Ibn Ǧinnī (d. 392/1002) followed Ibn al-Sarrāǧ's classification exactly. At the beginning of his description of nouns in the accusative (*al-ʾasmāʾ al-manṣūba*), Ibn Ǧinnī distinguishes *mafʿūl* and *mušabbah bi-l-mafʿūl* and enumerates the five subcategories of *mafʿūl* (*Lumaʿ* 20 l. 10–11). Each of these *mafʿūl* subcategories has a chapter further devoted to it.[11] Furthermore, Ibn Ǧinnī enumerated the five categories of *mušabbah bi-l-mafʿūl* more clearly than Ibn al-Sarrāǧ did, giving them as *ḥāl*, *tamyīz*, *istiṯnāʾ*, *ism ʾinna wa-ʾaḫawātihā*, and *ḫabar kāna wa-ʾaḫawātihā*[12] (*Lumaʿ* 26 l. 5–6). On the other hand, it should be noted that in *al-Ḫaṣāʾiṣ*, Ibn Ǧinnī does not refer to the framework of *mušabbah bi-l-mafʿūl*.

Like Ibn Ǧinnī's *Kitāb al-Lumaʿ fī al-naḥw*, Ǧurǧānī's (d. 471/1078) *Muqtaṣid*, a commentary on Fārisī's *al-ʾĪḍāḥ*, also maintains Ibn al-Sarrāǧ's framework, while by contrast, in *al-ʿAwāmil al-miʾa al-naḥwiyya*, Ǧurǧānī refers to five *mafʿūl*-s, with a section dedicated to each (*ʿAwāmil* 285–287), but does not use the term *mušabbah bi-l-mafʿūl*. He describes *ism ʾinna wa-ʾaḫawātihā*, *istiṯnāʾ*, *tamyīz*, and *ḫabar kāna wa-ʾaḫawātihā*, each dealt with in a separate section (*ʿAwāmil* 147, 189, 231, 251), but no section is dedicated to *ḥāl*.

In contrast, the subcategories of *mafʿūl* and *mušabbah bi-l-mafʿūl* in Zaǧǧāǧī's (d. 337/949) *Ǧumal*, a compendium of Arabic grammar written in the first half of the 4th/10th century, are not lineal descendants of Ibn al-Sarrāǧ's *ʾUṣūl*, as Zaǧǧāǧī's approach to the classification is different from that of Ibn al-Sarrāǧ. For instance, when Zaǧǧāǧī refers to five *mafʿūl*-s in the chapter on their division (*bāb ʾaqsām al-mafʿūlīn*, *Ǧumal* 305–310), he uses the term *mafʿūl min ʾaǧlihi* instead of *mafʿūl lahu*.[13] Likewise, Zaǧǧāǧī never uses the term *mušabbah bi-l-mafʿūl*, instead dealing with *ḥāl*, *tamyīz*, *istiṯnāʾ*, *ḫabar kāna wa-ʾaḫawātihā*,

11 Ibn Ǧinnī dedicated chapters 18 to 23 to describing *mafʿūl* subcategories. *Mafʿūl fīhi* was treated in two chapters: *ẓarf al-zamān* and *ẓarf al-makān* (cf. *Lumaʿ* 24 l. 1–25 l. 3).

12 Although chapters 24, 25, and 26 are devoted to *ḥāl*, *tamyīz*, and *istiṯnāʾ*, respectively, *kāna wa-ʾaḫawātuhā* and *ʾinna wa-ʾaḫawātuhā* are treated in chapters 15 and 16 (cf. Ibn Ǧinnī *Lumaʿ* 15–19).

13 For the terminologies of *mafʿūl min ʾaǧlihi* and *mafʿūl lahu*, cf. Carter 1981:327, 433, 439.

and *ism ʾinna wa-ʾaḫawātihā* in different places.[14] A disparity in the use of the term *ḥāl* between Zaǧǧāǧī and Ibn al-Sarrāǧ is apparent when *ḥāl* is presented as a synonym for *ẓarf* and *mafʿūl fīhi* in *Ǧumal*.[15]

> And *mafʿūl fīhi* is *ẓarf* and *ḥāl*, like your words: "Zayd came riding". It means that he came in such a way. Also, "he came rapidly", "he came riding", "I went out on Friday", "I sat in front of you", "I stayed at your home". These types of *ẓarf*-s are *mafʿūl fīhā* [lit. that in which the action is done]. (*wa-l-mafʿūl fīhi al-ẓarf wa-l-ḥāl naḥwa qawlika "ǧāʾa zaydun rākiban" maʿnāhu ǧāʾa fī miṯl hāḏihi al-ḥāl wa-kaḏālika "ǧāʾa musriʿan" wa-"ʾaqbala rākiban" wa-kaḏālika "ḫaraǧtu yawma l-ǧumʿati" wa-"ǧalastu ʾamāmaka" wa-"qaʿadtu ʿindaka" wa-mā ʾašbaha ḏālika min al-ẓurūf hiya mafʿūl fīhā*, *Ǧumal* 305 l. 10–13)

In the 5th/11th century, grammarians took a new approach to the categorization of accusative complements, considering any accusative complement of the verb, whether *mafʿūl* or *mušabbah bi-l-mafʿūl*, to be a non-essential item. Concerning "objectness" (*mafʿūliyya*), Zamaḫšarī (d. 538/1144; cf. *Mufaṣṣal* 18 l. 9–12) regards the five *mafʿūl*-s as one group, however, for remaining elements, he lists seven: *ḥāl, tamyīz, mustaṯnā, ḫabar kāna, ism ʾinna, lā li-nafy li-l-ǧins*, and *ḫabar mā wa-lā*, the last two being new to the framework.

Although Ibn al-Sarrāǧ's framework of *mušabbah bi-l-mafʿūl* was by and large accepted by Ibn Ǧinnī, Fārisī, and Ǧurǧānī, the framework itself was fundamentally changed, at least after the 7th/13th century, by the grammarians ʾAstarābāḏī (d. 688/1289?), Ibn Mālik (d. 672/1274), and their successors.

4 Instability of Ibn al-Sarrāǧ's Framework of *mafʿūl* and *mušabbah bi-l-mafʿūl*

4.1 *Distinction between* mafʿūl *and* mušabbah bi-l-mafʿūl

Owens (1990: 161; 1991: 230–231) admitted the limitations of a syntactic basis for distinguishing between *mafʿūl* and *mušabbah bi-l-mafʿūl*. He presented an alternative view, proposing that the term for object, *mafʿūl*, was taken directly from the *Kitāb*; all categories that Sībawayhi termed *mafʿūl* were converted into

14 Zaǧǧāǧī *Ǧumal* 44, 47, 53, 64, 108, 110, 146, 152, 235–240, 245–246.

15 For further examples of identification between *ḥāl* and *mafʿūl fīhi*, cf. Sībawayhi *Kitāb* I, 165 l. 4–5; 222 l. 2; 235 l. 11.

the class of "true" objects, while the accusatives that Sībawayhi did not designate as objects were consigned to the class of pseudo-objects.[16]

However, it remains unclear why the *mafʿūl maʿahu* was subsumed under the category of *mafʿūl*, while the *mafʿūl minhu*[17] ("that which is warned about") was not. Sībawayhi called it *mafʿūl minhu* with reference to the accusative form in *ʾiyyāka wa-l-ʾasada* ("beware of the lion!", *Kitāb* I, 116 l. 12–14). Although *mafʿūl minhu* appears in the *Kitāb*, it was never included among the standard object types by later grammarians; this accusative construction appears mostly in sections discussing warnings (*taḥḏīr*) without directly referring to *mafʿūl minhu*.[18]

Additionally, *mafʿūl minhu* is referred to by later grammarians, such as Ibn Hišām al-ʾAnṣārī and Suyūṭī (d. 911/1505) to denote the accusative in a passage from the Q. 7/155: *wa-ḫtāra mūsā qawmahu sabʿīna rağulan* ("and Moses chose from his people seventy men").[19] This construction is designated as *mafʿūl minhu* because the accusative noun *qawm-a*, people, can be interpreted in this sentence as synonymous with *min qawm-i*, from the people, in the genitive. Although this Qurʾānic quotation is also found in grammatical works by Sībawayhi, Mubarrad, Ibn al-Sarrāğ, and Zağğāğī, none of them mention *mafʿūl minhu* in relation to it.[20]

Another question remains unsolved: why does Ibn al-Sarrāğ exclude some of the *manṣūbāt* from *mušabbah bi-l-mafʿūl* ? The vocative noun (*munādā*, lit. "a person called") and the noun negated by *lā* (*ism lā*, lit. "a noun of *lā*") are generally listed among the *manṣūbāt* in grammatical works, but they are not regarded as *mušabbah bi-l-mafʿūl* by Ibn al-Sarrāğ.

The vocative noun which takes an accusative in a construction such as *yā ʿabda llāhi* (O ʿAbd Allāh!) is not regarded as *mušabbah bi-l-mafʿūl* even though its chapter in Ibn al-Sarrāğ's work is listed among the *manṣūbāt*. Ibn al-Sarrāğ explains that the vocative noun takes the accusative ending because the vocative particle *yā* acts as a representative of the verb *ʾunādī*[21](I call, *ʾUṣūl* I, 333 l. 2). However, the vocative noun ends in the vowel /u/ when it is a single noun,

16 Cf. Owens 1990:161.

17 For the *mafʿūl minhu*, cf. Mosel 1975:253; Carter 1981:447; Owens 1991:231.

18 Mubarrad *Muqtaḍab* III, 212–213; Ibn al-Sarrāğ *ʾUṣūl* II, 250; Zamaḫšarī *Mufaṣṣal* 48–49; Ibn al-ʾAnbārī *ʾAsrār* 168–170; ʾAstarābāḏī *ŠK* I, 180–183; Suyūṭī *Hamʿ* II, 17–19.

19 Tradition attributes the naming of the *mafʿūl minhu* to ʾAbū Saʿīd al-Sīrāfī (d. 368/979) (cf. Ibn Hišām al-ʾAnṣārī *Qaṭr* 219 l. 10–11; Suyūṭī *ʾAšbāh* III, 75 l. 16–18).

20 Sībawayhi *Kitāb* I, 12; Mubarrad *Muqtaḍab* II, 321, 342; IV, 330; Ibn al-Sarrāğ *ʾUṣūl* I, 178; Zağğāğī *Ğumal* 40.

21 Cf. Carter 1981:423; Owens 1988:189; Sheyhatovitch 2019:100. Ibn al-Sarrāğ additionally quotes Mubarrad's words indicating that the verbs that substitute for the particle are *ʾadʿū* and *ʾurīdu* (*ʾUṣūl* I, 340 l. 6). See also *Muqtaḍab* IV, 202 l. 2.

e.g. *yā zaydu* (O Zayd!). Ibn al-Sarrāǧ assumes that it is indeclinable (*mabnī*) not declinable (*muʿrab*), and is in the accusative grammatical position (*ʾUṣūl* I, 332 l. 2–4).

The noun negated by *lā* is also excluded from *mušabbah bi-l-mafʿūl*. The noun, *raǧula* takes an accusative marker without nunation in a construction such as *lā raǧula fi-l-dāri* (There is no man in the house). It is obvious that Ibn al-Sarrāǧ does not regard such an accusative as a real one as is clear in his expression: "the vowel /a/ that resembles the accusative" (*al-fatḥ allaḏī yušbihu al-naṣb*, *ʾUṣūl* I, 379 l. 1).

4.2 *Categorization of* ḥāl *and* mafʿūl fīhi

In the framework given by Ibn al-Sarrāǧ, *ḥāl* (circumstantial qualifier) is placed in the category of *mušabbah bi-l-mafʿūl*, while *mafʿūl fīhi* (locative object) is situated in the *mafʿūl* group. In an early stage of the development of Arab grammatical thought, a terminological confusion appeared concerning *ḥāl* and *mafʿūl fīhi*. In some contexts where *ḥāl* is discussed in the *Kitāb*,[22] some ambiguity can be observed in the use of the term *mafʿūl fīhi*, where expressions like *hāḏā ʿabdu llāhi munṭaliqan* "here is ʿAbd Allāh leaving" are discussed (*Kitāb* I, 221 l. 19–222 l. 2).[23]

Zaǧǧāǧī clearly distinguishes between *ḥāl* and *mafʿūl fīhi*, which he calls *al-ẓarf min al-zamān* and *al-ẓarf min al-makān* (*Ǧumal* 44 l. 9, 45 l. 13, 46 l. 10), while also identifying *mafʿūl fīhi* with *ḥāl*,[24] as in *wa-l-mafʿūl fīhi al-ẓarf wa-l-ḥāl naḥwa qawlika "ǧāʾa zaydun rākiban" maʿnāhu ǧāʾa fī miṯl hāḏihi al-ḥāl* (*Ǧumal* 305 l. 9–10).[25] This non-standard view, which places *ḥāl* in *mafʿūlāt*, is noted by Ibn ʿUṣfūr (d. 669/1271; *ŠǦ* II, 450 l. 11–15).

4.3 Ḫabar kāna

Ibn al-Sarrāǧ focuses on the concept of the operator, *ʿāmil*, when he classifies members within the *mušabbah bi-l-mafʿūl* framework. He maintains that *ḫabar kāna*, predicate of the verb *kāna*, shares a common feature with *ḥāl* and *tamyīz* in light of the fact that they take "the accusative case in form which may be the same as the nominative case in meaning" (*ʾUṣūl* I, 212 l. 17–18). He thereafter divides them into two categories on the basis of their operator, *ʿāmil*. *Ḥāl* and

22 The grammatical construction of *ḥāl* is commented on in Sībawayhi *Kitāb* I, 15–16, 158–159, 161–163, 168–170, 211–212, 218–224.

23 Cf. also Levin 1979b:194; Versteegh 2008:108. Peled (1999:77) pointed out that Mubarrad presents *ḥāl* as a grammatical category with the status of a *mafʿūl fīhi* (*Muqtaḍab* IV, 166).

24 The term *ḥāl* is also used by Zaǧǧāǧī to denote the present tense (*Ǧumal* 21–22).

25 Cf. also Owens 1988:150–151.

tamyīz have a real verb, *fiʿl ḥaqīqī* as an operator, whereas *ḫabar kāna* does not, because, while that the operator has some kind of verbal pattern and behaves the same as the verb, it is not a real verb, *al-ʿāmil fīhi šayʾun ʿalā wazn al-fiʿli, wa-yataṣarrafu taṣarrufahu wa-laysa bi-fiʿlin fī al-ḥaqīqa* (*ʾUṣūl* I, 213 l. 2–3).[26] In a construction such as *kāna zaydun munṭaliqan*, "Zayd was leaving", Ibn al-Sarrāǧ regards the verb *kāna* as a non-real verb, *fiʿl ġayr ḥaqīqī*,[27] which only denotes time, *zamān* (*ʾUṣūl* I, 74 l. 5–6; 82 l. 5–6).[28]

The above-discussed approach is appropriate for a design to consolidate the *mušabbah bi-l-mafʿūl* complements. Nevertheless, the members within the category do not share any stable syntactic or semantic grounds to create a framework. For instance, the essential distinction between *ḫabar kāna* and the rest of the categories in *mušabbah bi-l-mafʿūl*, including the adverbial accusatives, can be explained not only by the operator *ḫabar kāna* has but also by the sentence/clause structure itself, and Ibn al-Sarrāǧ does this in the chapter dealing with the five complements in the accusative case. He posits an underlying *mubtadaʾ–ḫabar*, or topic–comment, structure in a sentence. An example is, *kāna ʿabdu l-lāhi ʾaḫāka*, "Abdallah was your brother" in contrast to the *fāʿil–mafʿūl* structure in *ḍaraba ʿabdu l-lāhi ʾaḫāka*, "Abdallah hit your brother". Based on this premise, Ibn al-Sarrāǧ explains that *ʾaḫāka* in the former sentence (= *ḫabar kāna*) is in the accusative case by referring to its resemblance to *mafʿūl* in the latter sentence.[29] Such a description also shows that *ḫabar kāna* is distinguished from *ḥāl* and *tamyīz* by the status of the accusative complement. The predicate *ʾaḫāka* (= *ḫabar kāna*) in the sentence *kāna ʿabdu l-lāhi ʾaḫāka*, is indispensable, whereas *rākiban* (= *ḥāl*) is not in a construction such as *ǧāʾa ʿabdu l-lāhi rākiban*, "Abdallah came riding". Ibn al-Sarrāǧ explains that *rākiban* (= *ḥāl*) is put in the accusative by resemblance with *mafʿūl*, inasmuch as it was added after the completion of the predication. In addition, the *fāʿil* is complete with its verb (*istiġnāʾ al-fāʿil bi-fiʿlihi, ʾUṣūl* I, 213 l. 6–9).

It should also be noted that no more than six lines are devoted to the discussion of *ḫabar kāna* within the section on *mušabbah bi-l-mafʿūl* (*ʾUṣūl* I, 228–229). Most of the structures with the verb *kāna wa-ʾaḫawātuhā* are discussed in the section on *mušabbah bi-l-fāʿil fī al-lafẓ* (resembling the *fāʿil* on the surface

26 Cf. *Muqtaḍab* III, 33 l. 4–5.

27 Ibn al-Sarrāǧ also uses the term *ʾafʿāl fī al-lafẓ* (*ʾUṣūl* I, 74 l. 5), which can be interpreted as "verbs which conform to the category of verbs only in terms of their morphological patterns (Taha 1995:128–131)".

28 Cf. Levin 1979b:186; Taha 1995:106, 127, 302 ff.; 2008:105.

29 Cf. Ibn al-Sarrāǧ, *ʾUṣūl* I, 82 l. 9–12. Sībawayhi called a subject of *kāna* "*ism al-fāʿil*" or "*al-fāʿil*" and an object of *kāna* "*ism al-mafʿūl*" or "*al-mafʿūl*" (*Kitāb* I, 16, 17, 63). He also used the term *ḫabar kāna* (*Kitāb* I, 63). Cf. also Levin 1979b:187.

level), which is listed in the fifth of the five nominative complements (*ʾUṣūl* I, 58; 81ff.).

4.4 *Classification into Five Types*[30] *by Ibn al-Sarrāǧ*

As mentioned above, Ibn al-Sarrāǧ separates *mafʿūl* from *mušabbah bi-l-mafʿūl*, classifying the accusative elements into five types (*ʾUṣūl* I, 159 l. 8).

As for the nominative forms of nouns (*al-ʾasmāʾ al-murtafiʿa*), they are similarly divided into five types, expressly using the numeral *ḫamsa*, five (*ʾUṣūl* I, 58 l. 2): *mubtadaʾ* (lit. "that which is begun with"), *ḫabar* (lit. "the information"), *fāʿil* (lit. "the doer"), *mafʿūl allaḏī lam yusamma man faʿala bihi* (lit. "the object of which no agent has been named"), and *mušabbah bi-l-fāʿil* (lit. "resembling the *fāʿil*", *ʾUṣūl* I, 58, 62, 72, 76, 81). He follows a similar pattern when he illustrates the accusative nominals.

Furthermore, many other grammatical categories are classified into five types in *al-ʾUṣūl*.[31] For instance, Ibn al-Sarrāǧ enumerates five particles of swearing (*qasam*), *wa-*, *bi-*, *ta-*, *li-*, and *min*, which include some rare ones[32] (*ʾUṣūl* I, 430). He also itemizes five particles for calling, *yā*, *ʾayā*, *hayā*, *ʾay*, and *ʾa-* (*nidāʾ*, *ʾUṣūl* I, 329), whereas many later grammarians describe six.[33] Moreover, *ʾinna* and its related particles are regarded as making up a group of five, *ʾinna*, *lākinna*, *layta*, *laʿalla*, and *ka-ʾanna* (*ʾUṣūl* I, 229–230), excluding *ʾanna*, which is also included by many other grammarians.[34]

The examples mentioned above show that Ibn al-Sarrāǧ had a strong inclination to find a group of five for every grammatical category. It is probable that he classified *mafʿūl*-s and *mušabbah bi-l-mafʿūl* each into five types not only to create a purely linguistic framework according to the theoretical background but also to pursue beauty of form in his framework or to comply with pedagogical demands.

---

30 For a detailed study on fivefold divisions in medieval Arabic grammatical literature, cf. Sheyhatovitch 2019.

31 In *ʾUṣūl*, Ibn al-Sarrāǧ does not mention the "five/six nouns": *ʾabū*, *ʾaḫū*, *ḥamū*, *fū*, *ḏū*, and *hanū*. For the grammarians' positions on this issue, cf. Sartori 2010:36.

32 Zaǧǧāǧī enumerates four: *wa-*, *bi-*, *ta-*, and *li-* (*Ǧumal* 82 l. 4). Ibn Ǧinnī and Ǧurǧānī enumerate only three: *bi-*, *wa-*, and *ta-* (*Lumaʿ* 73 l. 3; *ʿAwāmil* 139–141). Zamaḫšarī enumerates four: *wa-*, *ta-*, *li-*, and *min* (*Mufaṣṣal* 345 l. 5).

33 Many grammarians, including Zaǧǧāǧī, Ibn Ǧinnī, Ǧurǧānī, and Ibn Mālik, itemize five (*Ǧumal* 168 l. 1; *Lumaʿ* 43 l. 17; *ʿAwāmil* 196; *ʾAlfiyya* v. 573). Others, like Zamaḫšarī and Ibn Hišām al-ʾAnṣārī, also added *wā*, for six (*Mufaṣṣal* 309 l. 10; *Qaṭr* 242–244).

34 Cf., for instance: Zaǧǧāǧī *Ǧumal* 64 l. 3; Ibn Ǧinnī *Lumaʿ* 17 l. 15; Ǧurǧānī *Muqtaṣid* I, 443 l. 3; Ǧurǧānī *ʿAwāmil* 147 l. 10; Zamaḫšarī *Mufaṣṣal* 292 l. 4; Ibn Mālik *ʾAlfiyya* v. 174; Ibn Hišām al-ʾAnṣārī *Qaṭr* 161 l. 10–11 For the process of subsuming *ʾanna* under the category of *ʾinna*, cf. Kasher 2010–2011:251–253.

5 Grammatical Concept of *faḍla*

Ibn al-Sarrāǧ's arrangement of *mafʿūl*-s and *mušabbah bi-l-mafʿūl* into groups of five was a turning point. Before his time, the accusative complements were not yet all theoretically established, and some had their own distinct conceptual terminology. However, Ibn al-Sarrāǧ's framework was not straightforwardly inherited by later grammarians, who instead sought a way to modify the framework and arrange it using the concept of *faḍla*, which is often translated as a redundant element.[35]

Before the 4th/10th century, the use of the term *faḍla* was limited. In early grammatical sources, various terms were used for redundant elements in an utterance, including *zāʾid*, *faḍl*, *tawkīd*, *ḥašw*, *ṣila*, and *laġw*.[36] While Sībawayhi did not use *faḍla* himself, he recognized the concept;[37] its use is also attested in the 3rd/9th-century grammatical work *al-Muqtaḍab*. Both Ibn al-Sarrāǧ and Ibn Ǧinnī use the term in their works, but Zaǧǧāǧī[38] does not.

In general, *faḍla* refers to accusative complements or non-predicative elements. Mubarrad describes it as *ʾiḏā ḏakartahu zidta fī al-fāʾida, wa-ʾiḏā ḥaḏaftahu lam tuḫlil bi-l-kalām*, (*Muqtaḍab* III, 116 l. 4), which Taha (2008: 100) interprets as "an element which adds to the meaning expressed by the verb and its agent and whose omission from speech does not affect the integrity of the text".[39] This includes structural items that are not requisite in a sentence or a clause because the meaning of the sentence or the clause is already complete (*baʿda tamām al-kalām*)[40] without them. This can be contrasted with the term *ʿumda* of later grammarians, which constitutes an essential part of the predication.

To all appearances, the term *faḍla* is related to other grammatical terms, such as *manṣūb* or *mafʿūl*, when it is viewed diachronically through the history of Arab traditional grammar.

35 A number of translations and explanations for the term *faḍla* have been suggested, including: "extraneous element" (Carter 1972:491; 2016:125), "structurally redundant" (Carter 1981:368–369), "redundant element" (Carter 1981:383); "non-predicative element" (Bohas et al. 1990:65), "optional item" (Owens 1988:60–61), "peripheral item" (Owens 1988:292).

36 Talmon 2003:222–223.

37 Cf. Carter 1981:369; 2016:183, 215.

38 Versteegh 1995:129.

39 Cf. Taha 1995:114. For a detailed discussion on the notion of *fāʾida*, cf. Sheyhatovitch 2015.

40 For example, cf. Ibn al-Sarrāǧ *ʾUṣūl* I, 281 l. 15–16. For another discussion of the notion, cf. Zaǧǧāǧī *Ǧumal* 47 l. 8–9.

5.1 Faḍla *in Ibn al-Sarrāǧ's* ʾUṣūl

Faḍla is seemingly not used in Ibn al-Sarrāǧ's *ʾUṣūl* to cover all complements in the category of *mafʿūl* and *mušabbah bi-l-mafʿūl*. Instead, he uses the term sporadically, without precisely defining it and without mentioning which complements of verbs belong to this category. It should be noted that his teacher Mubarrad provides a more detailed, though still incomplete, picture of the term; Mubarrad presents the three elements *ḥāl*, *ẓarf*, and *maṣdar*[41] as examples of *faḍla* (*Muqtaḍab* III, 116 l. 3–4; Taha 1995: 114. Cf. *Muqtaḍab* III, 121 l. 18).

Although Ibn al-Sarrāǧ only once relates *istiṯnāʾ* to *faḍla*, in a phrase, *ḥattā yakūna al-istiṯnāʾ faḍla*, "until (the accusative noun after) the exceptive particle becomes redundant" (*ʾUṣūl* I, 300 l. 16), he does not intend to indicate that *istiṯnāʾ* is included in the category of *faḍla*. It should be noted that Ibn al-Sarrāǧ does not assign a role to the term *faḍla* in the categorization of accusative complements. In several instances, he uses the term *faḍla* in the sense of "a redundant element". He implicitly correlates *faḍla* and *mafʿūl* in the context of a sentence with a verb and a subject, which is followed by silence, *sukūt* and the *fāʾida*[42] is completed with it to the addressee. He explains that the utterance, *kalām*, is completed without a *mafʿūl*, inasmuch as it is a *faḍla*, a redundant element (*ʾUṣūl* I, 74 l. 16–75 l. 2). In this context, the term *faḍla* is used to refer to the dispensable complement added to the complete sentence consisting of the verb and its agent. In other contexts that Ibn al-Sarrāǧ calls *mafʿūl* a *faḍla*, in expressions *al-mafʿūl faḍla* (the *mafʿūl* is a *faḍla*), or *al-mafʿūl allaḏī huwa faḍla* (lit. the *mafʿūl* which is a *faḍla*),[43] the term *faḍla* is not used to refer to the specific member within the *mafʿūl* framework.

Therefore, we cannot determine whether *faḍla* refers to the direct object (*mafʿūl bihi*) or to the object in a general sense, as an accusative element.[44] According to Taha, Ibn al-Sarrāǧ considered *mafʿūl bihi* to have a distinct status of other redundant items. Although the term *faḍla* implies that a verbal sentence can be represented by the verb and the agent only on the level of the surface structure, the semantic status of the object must not be considered to

41 Mubarrad does not use the term *mafʿūl muṭlaq*. Also, he uses the alternative term *ism al-fiʿl* (noun of the verb) to refer to *maṣdar* (*Muqtaḍab* IV, 299 l. 3).

42 Sheyhatovitch (2015:195) elucidates the term *fāʾida* in this context as 'a full message', while it is used frequently in the sense of 'communicative value'.

43 Ibn al-Sarrāǧ *ʾUṣūl* I, 89 l. 12; II, 121 l. 16, 241 l. 13, 242 l. 3, 242 l. 14, 243 l. 17.

44 Levin (1985:344) points out that Sībawayhi never refers to the *mafʿūl* in the *Kitāb* as *laġw*, his own term corresponding to *faḍla*.

be that of a redundant item because the meaning of a transitive verb is only complete with the inclusion of its direct object (Taha 1995: 149; 2008: 102). This interpretation is rooted in Ibn al-Sarrāǧ's description: "For the direct object of the verb [there exists] a share in the verb as [it is the case] for the agent [...]"[45] (*li-l-maf'ūl ḥiṣṣa min al-fi'l kamā li-l-fā'il*, *'Uṣūl* I, 412 l. 3). Ibn al-Sarrāǧ believes that the existence of the *maf'ūl* is indispensable for expression with transitive verbs (*'af'āl muta'addiya*) in sentences like: *ḍarabtu zaydan* "I hit Zayd" and *'akaltu al-ṭa'āma* "I ate the food". He says that *ḍarabtu* "I hit", and *'akaltu* "I ate", cannot be uttered without *maf'ūl*-s (cf. *'Uṣūl* I, 171 l. 11).[46] Therefore, Taha states, Mubarrad's description "may be taken to mean that the term *faḍla* does not apply to the direct object" (1995: 116).

5.2 *Ibn Ǧinnī's Eight* faḍalāt

In Ibn Ǧinnī's *al-Ḫaṣā'iṣ*, the term *faḍla* is more explicitly connected to the accusative case.[47] *Al-Ḫaṣā'iṣ* is one of the earliest treatises to enumerate the specific constituents of *faḍalāt*: *maf'ūl bihi*, *ẓarf*, *maf'ūl lahu*, *maf'ūl ma'ahu*, *maṣdar*, *ḥāl*, *tamyīz*, and *istiṯnā'* (*Ḫaṣā'iṣ* I, 197 l. 4–6).[48] However, it is not certain whether Ibn Ǧinnī regards all eight as constituting *faḍalāt*, as he mentions nothing about whether *ism 'inna wa-'aḫawātihā* and *ḫabar kāna wa-'aḫawātihā* constitute *faḍla*, both of which are included in *mušabbah bi-l-maf'ūl* in his *Luma'* (26 l. 5–6).

Although Ibn Ǧinnī states unequivocally that *maf'ūl bihi* is a *faḍla* (*Ḫaṣā'iṣ* I, 196 l. 16), he distinguishes it from other *faḍalāt* and assigns it a special status. Further, Ibn Ǧinnī makes no indication that *maf'ūl bihi* is a candidate *faḍla* that can be added after the completion of a sentence such as *inṭalaqa zaydun* ("Zayd has left", *Ḫaṣā'iṣ* II, 379 l. 7–8), excluding it while describing *maṣdar*, *ẓarf*, *ḥāl*, *maf'ūl lahu*, and *maf'ūl ma'ahu* as possible elements to be added to the sentence. This implies that he recognizes the difference between *maf'ūl bihi* and other *faḍalāt* with regard to syntactic and semantic structure.

Interestingly, in Ibn Ǧinnī's *Luma'*, in contrast to *Ḫaṣā'iṣ*, the word *faḍla* is used only twice (*Luma'* 20 l. 15, 67 l. 3), and only three elements: *maṣdar*, *ẓarf*, and *ḥāl*, appear in the context.

---

45 The translation is Taha's (cf. Taha 1995:150; 2008:102). The *maf'ūl* here is interpreted as *maf'ūl bihi*. On the problematic issue of the syntactic status of *maf'ūl bihi* within the framework of *faḍla*, cf. also Taha 2008:100.

46 Cf. also Taha 2008:103.

47 Ibn Ǧinnī *Ḫaṣā'iṣ* I, 173 l. 17–174 l. 2; 196 l. 16–19. Cf. also Owens 1988:60, 279.

48 Elsewhere, he mentioned four items as exemplifying *faḍalāt*: *ẓarf*, *ḥāl*, *tamyīz*, and *istiṯnā'* (Ibn Ǧinnī *Ḫaṣā'iṣ* II, 274 l. 12).

Faḍla continued to have limited use in grammatical works from the 4th/10th to the 6th/12th centuries: Zaǧǧāǧī, *al-Ǧumal* and *al-ʾĪḍāḥ fī ʿilal al-naḥw*; Ibn Ǧinnī, *Kitāb al-Lumaʿ fī al-naḥw*; Ǧurǧānī, *Kitāb al-Muqtaṣid fī šarḥ al-ʾĪḍāḥ*; Ibn al-ʾAnbārī (d. 577/1181), *ʾAsrār al-ʿarabiyya*; and Zamaḫšarī, *al-Mufaṣṣal fī ʿilm al-ʿarabiyya* (cf. *Mufaṣṣal* 61 l. 1, 69 l. 5).

5.3 Faḍla *in* Šarḥ Kāfiyat Ibn al-Ḥāǧib (d. 646/1249)

While Ibn al-Sarrāǧ's treatment of *mafʿūl* is characterized by a semantic approach, later grammarians adopted a structural approach, using *faḍla* to refer to any accusative complement (cf. Taha 2008: 103). From the 7th/13th century on, the term began to be used in the classification of *mafʿūlāt* or *manṣūbāt*, notably in ʾAstarābāḏī's *Šarḥ Kāfiyat Ibn al-Ḥāǧib*.[49] ʾAstarābāḏī paraphrases Ibn al-Ḥāǧib's saying "The accusatives are what comprises a marker of objectness" (*al-manṣūbāt huwa māištamala ʿalā ʿalam al-mafʿūliyya, šk* I, 112 l. 24) as "The accusative is a marker of *faḍla*", and based on this he enumerates twelve kinds of *manṣūbāt*. Thus, he writes, the *faḍalāt* are *ḥāl*, *tamyīz*, and *mustaṯnā* in addition to the five *mafʿūl*-s (*al-mafāʿīl al-ḫamsa*). The four *mušabbah bi-l-faḍalāt* are *ism ʾinna wa-ʾaḫawātihā*, *ism lā al-tabriʾa*, *ḫabar mā al-ḥiǧāziyya*, and *ḫabar kāna wa-ʾaḫawātihā* (*šk* I, 113 l. 3–5). Thus, the five *mafʿūl*-s and five *mušabbah bi-l-mafʿūl* in Ibn al-Sarrāǧ's *al-ʾUṣūl* are recategorized into eight *faḍalāt* and four *mušabbah bi-l-faḍalāt*. These eight elements correspond to what Ibn Ǧinnī describes as *faḍalāt* in *al-Ḫaṣāʾiṣ* (I, 197 l. 4–6).

Suyūṭī's set formula for the types of inflection is also based on the correlation between the framework of *faḍla* and the accusative case endings: *rafʿ li-l-ʿumad, wa-naṣb li-l-faḍalāt, wa-ǧarr li-mā baynahumā*, that is, a nominative to the *ʿumad* (pl. of *ʿumda*), an accusative to the *faḍalāt* (pl. of *faḍla*), and a genitive to the things between (*Hamʿ* I, 75 l. 2). It is safe to say that the *faḍla*, as far as ʾAstarābāḏī and Suyūṭī are concerned, is a hypernym for *mafʿūl* because five *mafʿūl*-s and three other items are included in the framework of *faḍla* (cf. *šk* I, 113 l. 3–5; *Hamʿ* I, 75 l. 1–8).

5.4 *Continual Rearrangement of* mafʿūl *and* mušabbah bi-l-mafʿūl

Although Ibn al-Sarrāǧ did not explicitly mention the arrangement of these elements, he was likely conscious of the order of the five *mafʿūl*-s, beginning with *mafʿūl muṭlaq* and ending with *mafʿūl maʿahu*, implying a hierarchy. Indeed, Ibn al-Sarrāǧ seems to prioritize *mafʿūl muṭlaq*, designating it *al-mafʿūl al-*

49 For a more detailed discussion of *faḍla* in the *Šarḥ Kāfiyat Ibn al-Ḥāǧib*, especially on numerals, cf. Druel 2018:103–109.

ṣaḥīḥ,[50] the true object (*ʾUṣūl* I, 159 l. 16). As this order did not change in the grammatical works written between the 4th/10th and 6th/12th centuries, it might imply the importance of the items.

The framework of the five *mafʿūl*-s as a subcategory of *faḍalāt* was maintained after the 7th/13th century, but the order changed to beginning with *mafʿūl bihi*. As far as we can determine, *al-ʾAlfiyya* by Ibn Mālik was, if not the oldest, certainly one of the oldest works to adopt this new order. The 8th/14th-century grammarian Ibn Hišām al-ʾAnṣārī also noted that the order begins with *mafʿūl bihi*: "I began among them with *mafʿūl bihi* just as Fārisī or others did such as the author of *al-Tashīl* or the author of *al-Muqarrib* (cf. *ŠT* II, 79, 107; *Muqarrib* 174, 194). I did not begin with *al-mafʿūl al-muṭlaq*, as Zamaḫšarī and Ibn al-Ḥāǧib did" (*Šuḏūr* 177 l. 5–7). The 9th/15th-century scholar Suyūṭī also began with *mafʿūl bihi* among the *faḍalāt*, indicating that beginning with *mafʿūl muṭlaq* was closely tied to the Basran school (*Hamʿ* II, 5 l. 14–15).

The 15-*manṣūbāt* framework began to be used in treatises in the 8th/14th century. In his *Šuḏūr al-ḏahab*, Ibn Hišām al-ʾAnṣārī mentioned that "*manṣūbāt* are restricted to 15 types"; the use of the number 15 was a new trend for classifying *mafʿūl* and *mušabbah bi-l-mafʿūl*. In *Šuḏūr al-ḏahab*, the traditional five-*mafʿūl* framework was maintained and the priority of *mafʿūl*-s among *manṣūbāt* was kept. In fact, Ibn Hišām al-ʾAnṣārī began his arrangement with the five *mafʿūl*-s because "*mafʿūl*-s are fundamental" (*Šuḏūr* 177 l. 4–5).

Furthermore, there was also a trend of significant change in the five-*mafʿūl* framework itself. While Ibn ʾĀǧurrūm (d. 723/1323) also adopted the 15-*manṣūbāt* framework, he made a drastic change in their order, placing *mafʿūl min ʾaǧlihi* tenth and *mafʿūl maʿahu* eleventh (Carter 1981: 326, 432, 440). These two *mafʿūl*-s were thus separated from the other three, which continued to enjoy priority in the arrangement.

6 Conclusion

We have analyzed how Ibn al-Sarrāǧ's subcategories of *mafʿūl* and *mušabbah bi-l-mafʿūl* were modified from the 4th/10th to the 7th/13th century. He managed to establish the framework for accusative complements using the term *mafʿūl* and *mušabbah bi-l-mafʿūl*, which were taken over by subsequent grammatical treatises. His system of categorizing and itemizing the elements seems well organized, and the framework of five *mafʿūl*-s and five *mušabbah bi-l-mafʿūl*

50 Cf. also Mubarrad *Muqtaḍab* IV, 299 l. 3; Zaǧǧāǧī *Ǧumal* 305 l. 4; Ǧurǧānī *Muqtaṣid* I, 580 l. 13; Suyūṭī *Hamʿ* II, 72 l. 4. For the term *mafʿūl ḥaqīqī*, cf. ʾAstarābāḏī *ŠK* I, 113 l. 6.

might have a considerable advantage, especially, for the purpose of pedagogy. However, his classification was not justified enough to convince later grammarians, partly because of his prioritizing the five-fold division in the classification of grammatical items. It seems quite probable that the limited availability of syntactic explanations regarding accusative complements led later grammarians to seek an alternative framework, in which the concept of *faḍla* played a significant role.

The term *faḍla* is seemingly not used in Ibn al-Sarrāǧ's *ʾUṣūl* to comprise all complements in the category of *mafʿūl* and *mušabbah bi-l-mafʿūl*. Indeed, the expression *al-mafʿūl faḍla* (the *mafʿūl* is a *faḍla*) is employed by Ibn al-Sarrāǧ, but the term *faḍla* is used in the sense of "a redundant element", and not used to refer to the specific member within the *mafʿūl* framework.

We can also confirm that, in the 4th/10th century, soon after Ibn al-Sarrāǧ, Ibn Ǧinnī attempted to describe accusative complements in terms of both *mafʿūl* and *faḍla*. Ibn Ǧinnī's description of the eight *faḍalāt* laid the foundations for the later modification of the framework by ʾAstarābāḏī. Further research on changes in the concept of *faḍla* between the 4th/10th and the 7th/13th century would help to clarify the modification of the framework of *mafʿūl* and *mušabbah bi-l-mafʿūl*.

Bibliography

Primary Sources

ʾAstarābāḏī, *ŠK* = Muḥammad b. al-Ḥasan Raḍī al-Dīn al-ʾAstarābāḏī, *Šarḥ Kāfiyat Ibn al-Ḥāǧib*. Bayrūt: Dār al-kutub al-ʿilmiyya, 2 vol., 1969.

Fārisī, *ʾĪḍāḥ* = ʾAbū ʿAlī al-Ḥasan b. ʾAḥmad al-Fārisī, *Kitāb al-ʾĪḍāḥ*. Ed. by Kāẓim Baḥr al-Marǧān. Bayrūt: ʿĀlam al-kutub, 1996.

Ǧurǧānī, *ʿAwāmil* = ʿAbd al-Qāhir b. ʿAbd al-Raḥmān b. Muḥammad ʾAbū Bakr al-Ǧurǧānī, *al-ʿAwāmil al-miʾa al-naḥwiyya*. Ed. by al-Badarāwī Zahrān. Al-Qāhira: Dār al-maʿārif, n.d.

Ǧurǧānī, *Muqtaṣid* = ʿAbd al-Qāhir b. ʿAbd al-Raḥmān b. Muḥammad ʾAbū Bakr al-Ǧurǧānī, *Kitāb al-Muqtaṣid fī šarḥ al-ʾĪḍāḥ*. Ed. by Kāẓim Baḥr al-Marǧān. Baġdād: Manšūrāt wizārat al-ṯaqāfa wa-l-ʾiʿlām, 2 vol., 1982.

Ibn al-ʾAnbārī, *ʾAsrār* = ʾAbū al-Barakāt ʿAbd al-Raḥmān b. Muḥammad al-ʾAnbārī, *ʾAsrār al-ʿarabiyya*. Ed. by Muḥammad al-Bayṭār. Dimašq: al-Maǧmaʿ al-ʿilmī al-ʿarabī, 1957.

Ibn al-Sarrāǧ, *ʾUṣūl* = Muḥammad b. al-Sarī b. Sahl ʾAbū Bakr Ibn al-Sarrāǧ al-Baġdādī, *al-ʾUṣūl fī al-naḥw*. Ed. by ʿAbd al-Ḥusayn al-Fatlī. Bayrūt: Muʾassasat al-risāla, 3 vol., 1985.

Ibn Ǧinnī, *Ḫaṣāʾiṣ* = ʿUṯmān b. Ǧinnī ʾAbū al-Fatḥ al-Mawṣilī, *al-Ḫaṣāʾiṣ*. Ed. by Muḥammad ʿAlī al-Naǧǧār. Al-Qāhira: Dār al-kutub al-miṣriyya, 3 vol., 1952–1956.

Ibn Ǧinnī, *Lumaʿ* = ʿUṯmān b. Ǧinnī ʾAbū al-Fatḥ al-Mawṣilī, *Kitāb al-Lumaʿ fī al-naḥw*. Ed. by Hadi M. Kechrida. Stockholm: Almqvist & Wiksell, 1976.

Ibn Hišām al-ʾAnṣārī, *Qaṭr* = Ǧamāl al-Dīn ʾAbū Muḥammad ʿAbd Allāh b. Yūsuf Ibn Hišām al-ʾAnṣārī, *Qaṭr al-nadā wa-ball al-ṣadā*. Ed. by Muḥammad Muḥyī al-Dīn ʿAbd al-Ḥamīd. Bayrūt: al-Maktaba al-ʿaṣriyya, 1988.

Ibn Hišām al-ʾAnṣārī, *Šuḏūr* = Ǧamāl al-Dīn ʾAbū Muḥammad ʿAbd Allāh b. Yūsuf Ibn Hišām al-ʾAnṣārī, *Šuḏūr al-ḏahab*. Ed. by Muḥammad al-Saʿdī Farhūd. Bayrūt: Dār al-kitāb al-lubnānī, 1999.

Ibn Mālik, *ʾAlfiyya* = Muḥammad b. ʿAbd Allāh b. ʿAbd Allāh ʾAbū ʿAbd Allāh Ǧamāl al-Dīn al-Ṭāʾī al-Ǧayyānī al-ʾAndalusī Ibn Mālik, *al-ʾAlfiyya*. Ed. by Antonin Goguyer [*La ʾAlfiyyah d'Ibnu-Malik*]. Bayrūt: Maktabat Lubnān, 1955.

Ibn Mālik, *ŠT* = Muḥammad b. ʿAbd Allāh b. ʿAbd Allāh ʾAbū ʿAbd Allāh Ǧamāl al-Dīn al-Ṭāʾī al-Ǧayyānī al-ʾAndalusī Ibn Mālik, *Šarḥ al-Tashīl : Tashīl al-fawāʾid wa-takmīl al-maqāṣid*. Ed. by Muḥammad ʿAbd al-Qādir ʿAṭā & Ṭāriq Fatḥī al-Sayyid. Bayrūt: Dār al-kutub al-ʿilmiyya, 3 vol., 2001.

Ibn ʿUṣfūr, *Muqarrib* = ʿAlī b. al-Muʾmin b. Muḥammad ʾAbū al-Ḥasan al-Ḥaḍramī al-ʾIšbīlī Ibn ʿUṣfūr, *al-Muqarrib wa-maʿa-hu Muṯul al-Muqarrib*. Ed. by ʿĀdil ʾAḥmad ʿAbd al-Mawǧūd & ʿAlī Muḥammad Muʿawwaḍ. Bayrūt: Dār al-kutub al-ʿilmiyya, 1998.

Ibn ʿUṣfūr, *ŠǦ* = ʿAlī b. al-Muʾmin b. Muḥammad ʾAbū al-Ḥasan al-Ḥaḍramī al-ʾIšbīlī Ibn ʿUṣfūr, *Šarḥ Ǧumal al-Zaǧǧāǧī*. Ed. by Ṣāḥib ʾAbū Ǧanāḥ. Baġdād: Dār al-kutub li-l-ṭibāʿa wa-l-našr, 2 vol., 1980.

Mubarrad, *Muqtaḍab* = Muḥammad b. Yazīd b. ʿAbd al-ʾAkbar ʾAbū al-ʿAbbās al-Ṯumālī al-ʾAzdī al-Mubarrad, *al-Muqtaḍab*. Ed. by Muḥammad ʿAbd al-Ḫāliq ʿUḍayma. Bayrūt: ʿĀlam al-kutub, 4 vol., n.d.

Sībawayhi, *Kitāb* = ʿAmr b. ʿUṯmān b. Qanbar ʾAbū Bišr Sībawayhi, *Kitāb Sībawayhi*. (*Le livre de Sîbawaihi. Traité de grammaire arabe par Sîboûya, dit Sîbawaihi*) Ed. by Hartwig Derenbourg. Paris: Imprimerie nationale, 2 vol., 1881–1889, reprint Hildesheim & New York: Georg Olms Verlag, 2 vol., 1970.

Suyūṭī, *ʾAšbāh* = ʿAbd al-Raḥmān b. ʾAbī Bakr b. Muḥammad b. Sābiq al-Dīn Ǧalāl al-Dīn al-Ḫuḍayrī al-Šāfiʿī al-Suyūṭī, *al-ʾAšbāh wa-l-naẓāʾir fī al-naḥw*. Bayrūt: Dār al-kutub al-ʿilmiyya, 4 vol., 1984.

Suyūṭī, *Hamʿ* = ʿAbd al-Raḥmān b. ʾAbī Bakr b. Muḥammad b. Sābiq al-Dīn Ǧalāl al-Dīn al-Ḫuḍayrī al-Šāfiʿī al-Suyūṭī, *Hamʿ al-hawāmiʿ fī šarḥ Ǧamʿ al-ǧawāmiʿ*. Ed. by ʾAḥmad Šams al-Dīn. Bayrūt: Dār al-kutub al-ʿilmiyya, 4 vol., 1988.

Zaǧǧāǧī, *Ǧumal* = ʾAbū al-Qāsim ʿAbd al-Raḥmān b. ʾIsḥāq al-Zaǧǧāǧī, *al-Ǧumal*. Ed. by Mohammed Ben Cheneb. Paris: Klincksieck, 2nd ed., 1957.

Zamaḫšarī, *Mufaṣṣal* = Ǧār Allāh ʾAbū al-Qāsim Maḥmūd b. ʿUmar b. Muḥammad b. ʾAḥmad al-Ḫawārizmī al-Zamaḫšarī, *al-Mufaṣṣal fī ʿilm al-ʿarabiyya*. Bayrūt: Dār al-ǧīl, n.d.

Secondary Sources

Bohas, George, Jean-Patrick Guillaume, and Djamel Eddine Kouloughli. 1990. *The Arabic Linguistic Tradition*. London & New York: Routledge, coll. "Arabic Thought and Culture".

Carter, Michael G. 1972. "'Twenty Dirhams' in the *Kitāb* of Sībawaihi". *Bulletin of the School of Oriental and African Studies* 35/3. 485–496.

Carter, Michael G. 1981. *Arab Linguistics. An Introductory Classical Text with Translation and Notes*. Amsterdam & Philadelphia: John Benjamins, coll. "Studies in the History of the Language Sciences" 24.

Druel, Jean N. 2018 "Blind Spots in Raḍī l-Dīn al-ʾAstarābāḏī's Grammar of Numerals". *The Foundations of Arabic Linguistics III. The Development of a Tradition: Continuity and Change*, ed. by Georgine Ayoub & Kees Versteegh, 96–114. Leiden & Boston: Brill, coll. "Studies in Semitic Languages and Linguistics" 94.

Kasher, Almog. 2010–2011. "Early Transformations of Theories about *anna* and *an* and the Standardization of Arabic Grammatical Tradition". *Zeitschrift für Geschichte der Arabisch-Islamischen Wissenschaften* 19. 243–256.

Kasher, Almog. 2012. "The Term *Mafʿūl* in Sībawayhi's *Kitāb*". *The Foundations of Arabic Linguistics. Sībawayhi and Early Arabic Grammatical Theory*, ed. by Amal E. Marogy, 3–26. Leiden & Boston: Brill, coll. "Studies in Semitic Languages and Linguistics" 65.

Kasher, Almog. 2019. "How to Parse Effective Objects according to Arab Grammarians? A Dissenting Opinion on *al-mafʿūl al-muṭlaq*". *The Foundations of Arabic Linguistics IV. The Evolution of Theory*, ed. by Manuela E.B. Giolfo & Kees Versteegh, 198–211. Leiden & Boston: Brill, coll. "Studies in Semitic Languages and Linguistics" 97.

Larcher, Pierre. 1991a. "Les *mafʿûl mutʿlaq* 'à incidence énonciative' de l'arabe classique". *L'adverbe dans tous ses états: Travaux linguistiques du CERLICO* 4, ed. by Claude Guimier and Pierre Larcher, 151–178. Rennes: PUR 2.

Larcher, Pierre. 1991b. "D'une grammaire l'autre: Catégorie d'adverbe et catégorie de *mafʿūl muṭlaq*". *De la grammaire de l'arabe aux grammaires des arabes*, ed. by Pierre Larcher, *Bulletin d'Études Orientales* 43. 139–159.

Levin, Aryeh. 1979a. "The Meaning of *taʿaddā al-fiʿl ilā* in Sībawayhi's *al-Kitāb*". *Studia Orientalia Memoriae D.H. Baneth Dedicata*, 193–210. Jerusalem: The Hebrew University.

Levin, Aryeh. 1979b. "Sībawayhi's view of the syntactic structure of *kāna wa ʾaxawātuhā*". *Jerusalem Studies in Arabic and Islam* 1. 185–213.

Levin, Aryeh. 1985. "The Syntactic Technical Term *al-mabniyy ʿalayhi*". *Jerusalem Studies in Arabic and Islam* 6. 299–352.

Levin, Aryeh. 1991. "What is Meant by *al-mafʿūl al-muṭlaq*?". *Semitic Studies: In Honor of Wolf Leslau on the Occasion of his eighty-fifth Birthday, November 14th, 1991*. Volume II, ed. by Alan S. Kaye, 919–926. Wiesbaden: Otto Harrassowitz.

Mosel, Ulrike. 1975. "Die syntaktische Terminologie bei Sībawayh". PhD dissertation, München Universität.

Okazaki, Hideki. 2003 "Arabu Dentou Bunpou niokeru *maf'ūl* no Kaihanchu: Ibn as-Sarrāǧ no Bunrui to soreikouno Hensen. [The Subcategory of *maf'ūl* in Arabic Grammatical Tradition: Ibn al-Sarrāǧ's Classification and the later Transition]". *Kansai Journal of Arabic and Islamic Studies* 3. 15–32. (in Japanese).

Okazaki, Hideki. 2008. "Arabu Bunpougaku niokeru "Gakuha" to Maṣdar no Ichizuke. [The Grammatical Schools and the Description of *Maṣdar*]". *Journal of Arabic and Islamic Studies* 6. 29–44. (in Japanese)

Owens, Jonathan. 1988. *The Foundations of Grammar. An Introduction to Medieval Arabic Grammatical Theory*. Amsterdam & Philadelphia: John Benjamins.

Owens, Jonathan. 1989. "The Syntactic Basis of Arabic Word Classification". *Arabica* 36/2. 211–234.

Owens, Jonathan. 1990. *Early Arabic Grammatical Theory. Heterogeneity and Standardization*. Amsterdam & Philadelphia: John Benjamins.

Owens, Jonathan. 1991. "Models for Interpreting the Development of Medieval Arabic Grammatical Theory". *Journal of the American Oriental Society* 111/2. 225–238.

Peled, Yishai. 1999. "Aspects of the Use of Grammatical Terminology in Medieval Arabic Grammatical Tradition". *Arabic Grammar and Linguistics*, ed. by Yasir Suleiman, 50–85. London & New York: Routledge Curzon.

Sartori, Manuel. 2010. "Les « six noms » : grammaire arabe et pudibonderie". *Synergies Monde Arabe* 7. 35–45.

Sheyhatovitch, Beata. 2015. "The Notion of *fā'ida* in the Medieval Arabic Grammatical Tradition: *Fā'ida* as a Criterion for Utterance Acceptability". *The Foundations of Arabic Linguistics II. Kitāb Sībawayhi: Interpretation and Transmission*, ed. by Amal E. Marogy & Kees Versteegh, 184–201. Leiden & Boston: Brill, coll. "Studies in Semitic Languages and Linguistics" 83.

Sheyhatovitch, Beata. 2019. "Five as a Typological Number in the Medieval Arabic Grammatical Tradition". *Journal of Arabic and Islamic Studies* 19. 81–111.

Taha, Zeinab A. 1995. "Issues of Syntax and Semantics: A Comparative Study of Sibawayhi, al-Mubarrad and Ibn as-Sarraj". PhD dissertation, Georgetown University.

Taha, Zeinab A. 2008. "*Maf'ūl*". *Encyclopedia of Arabic Language and Linguistics*, III, ed. by Kees Versteegh et al., 100–106. Leiden & Boston: Brill.

Talmon, Rafael. 2003. *Eighth-Century Iraqi Grammar: A Critical Exploration of Pre-Ḫalīlian Arabic Linguistics*. Winona Lake, In.: Eisenbrauns, coll. "Harvard Semitic Studies".

Versteegh, Kees. 1995. *The Explanation of Linguistic Causes. Az-Zaǧǧāǧī's Theory of Grammar*. Amsterdam & Philadelphia: John Benjamins.

Versteegh, Kees. 2008. "*Maf'ūl fīhi*". *Encyclopedia of Arabic Language and Linguistics*, III, ed. by Kees Versteegh et al., 106–110. Leiden & Boston: Brill.

CHAPTER 9

Suprasegmental Criteria in Medieval Arabic Grammar

Manuel Sartori

Introduction*

"What's the difference between *badal* and *ʿaṭf bayān*?".[1] Here is a student's question, quite legitimate, but which, interestingly enough, does not have an immediate answer, which seems to signal its "problematic" nature. The crux of the problem lies, in short, in how to tell them apart and account for the differences between *ʿaṭf bayān* on the one hand and *badal* on the other hand.

So let's pose the problem as it stands to the attentive reader: what is the difference between *muḥammad* of *al-ṣalātu wa-l-salāmu ʿalā nabiyyihi muḥammadin* and *ʿumar* of *ʾaqsama bi-l-llāhi ʾabū ḥafṣin ʿumar* (< *ʿumaru*[2]), the first being categorized by Arabic grammar as *badal* and the second as *ʿaṭf bayān*? What are the criteria for distinguishing what seems to be exactly the same, as will be shown in the following two examples borrowed from Ibn Ǧinnī (d. 392/1002) in his *Lumaʿ fī al-ʿarabiyya*:

(1) Ibn Ǧinnī *Lumaʿ* 144

qāma	*ʾaḫūka*	*zaydun*
to-stand-up.PAST	brother.NOM.-you	zayd.NOM.

categorized as *badal*

* Revised and expanded version of "La différence entre *badal* et *ʿaṭf bayān*. Mutisme et surdité des grammaires de l'arabe ?" published in French in *Al-Qanṭara* (2018).

1 In the rest of this article I will keep the terms *badal* (permutative), *mubdal minhu* (that for which the *badal* is substituted), *ʿaṭf al-bayān* (explanatory apposition), but sometimes also those of *ṣifa* (qualification, adjectival qualifier), *naʿt* (adjective) and *tawkīd* (corroboration) in transcription to simplify the translation. I will also keep the translation of the examples.

2 The pausal form is here necessitated by rhyme since it is a *rağaz* by ʾAbū al-Ǧaḥḥāf Ruʾba b. ʿAbd al-ʿAǧǧāǧ b. Ruʾba al-Tamīmī al-Saʿdī (d. 145/762).

 | DOI:10.1163/9789004515895_011

(2) Ibn Ǧinnī *Lumaʿ* 148

qāma	*ʾaḫūka*	*muḥammadun*
to-stand-up.PAST	brother.NOM.-you	muḥammad.NOM.

categorized as *ʿaṭf bayān*

These two structures are, from a written point of view, strictly identical and yet categorized differently to the point that even a grammarian and logician like Raḍī al-Dīn al-ʾAstarābāḏī (d. 688/1289?) comes to write this:

> I say: so far, no obvious difference has appeared to me between the *badal* of the whole for the whole and the *ʿaṭf al-bayān*, and I believe that *ʿaṭf al-bayān* is nothing but *badal*, as this is obvious in Sībawayhi's remark, since he does not mention the *ʿaṭf al-bayān*, but says: "as to substituting the definite expression for the indefinite expression, like *marartu bi-raǧulin ʿabdi llāhi* 'I passed by a man ʿAbd Allāh', it is as if someone has asked: *bi-man mararta* 'by whom did you pass?' or that [the speaker] has imagined that it was said to him and that consequently, he puts in its place what is more defined than it [the indefinite expression]". (*ʾaqūlu wa-ʾanā ʾilā al-ʾāna lam yaẓhar lī farq ǧalī bayn badal al-kull min al-kull wa-bayn ʿaṭf al-bayān bal lā ʾarā ʿaṭf al-bayān ʾillā al-badal ka-mā huwa ẓāhir kalām sībawayhi fa-ʾinnahu lam yaḏkur ʿaṭf al-bayān bal qāla "ʾammā badal al-maʿrifa min al-nakira fa-naḥwa "marartu bi-raǧulin ʿabdi llāhi" ka-ʾannahu qīla "bi-man mararta" ʾaw ẓanna ʾannahu yuqālu lahu ḏālika fa-ʾabdala makānahu mā huwa ʾaʿraf minhu"*, ʾAstarābāḏī ŠK II, 397; Sībawayhi *Kitāb* II, 12 and Sībawayhi *Kitāb*(*3*) II, 14, *hāḏā bāb badal al-maʿrifa min al-nakira wa-l-maʿrifa min al-maʿrifa*)

The fact that even such a distinguished grammarian and logician as ʾAstarābāḏī was confused by the problem suggests that it was unusually difficult, and indeed we find similar confusion in the works of other Arab grammarians. As we shall show, some of them reduce this difference to merely inflectional or, at best, pragmatic criteria, while others invoke an entirely different criterion, one which is more hinted at than explicitly stated. The latter approach has been largely overlooked in Western treatments of the phenomenon, which rely heavily on the traditional formal analysis, thereby increasing the need to rescue it from neglect.

1 The Traditional Approach

1.1 *The Reasons for This Embarrassment*

Let us recall briefly that the two types under study, *badal* and *ʿaṭf bayān*, belong to the generic category known as *tawābiʿ* that is to say to the class of appositives. In the terms of traditional Arabic grammar, these appositives are five in number: *ṣifa* (or *naʿt*), adjectival qualification; *taʾkīd* (or *tawkīd*), corroboration; *badal*, permutation; *ʿaṭf bayān*, explanatory apposition; and *ʿaṭf nasaq*, coordination (cf. Ġalāyīnī *Ǧāmiʿ* III, 169–190). Even if the last of these, unlike the first four, is not a juxtaposition, we can distinguish in each of them at least a categorized term as *tābiʿ*, that is to say an appositive, and preceding it, its *matbūʿ*, that is to say the term which is followed by the appositive, the *tābiʿ* following (generally) in declension its *matbūʿ*.

If the *ʿaṭf al-bayān* does not have subdivisions, the same is not true for the *badal* as stated by ʾAstarābāḏī in the quote above. The *badal* is subdivided into four types,[3] respectively *badal al-kull min al-kull* (substitution of the whole for the whole); *badal al-baʿḍ min al-kull* (substitution of the part for the whole); *badal al-ištimāl* (inclusive substitution); *al-badal al-mubāyin* (the contradictory substitution), itself subdivided into three sub-types which are *badal al-ġalaṭ* (substitution of error), *badal al-nisyān* (substitution of oversight) and *badal al-ʾiḍrāb* (substitution of retractation, cf. Ġalāyīnī *Ǧāmiʿ* III, 179–180 and Yaʿqūb 2006: IV, 88).[4]

According to Rafael Talmon (1948–2004), the *ʿaṭf al-bayān* would be a syntactic innovation (maybe we should rather say conceptual) which was introduced by Sībawayhi (d. 180/796?), who granted it a degree of autonomy approaching that of a *ṣifa* (cf. Talmon 1981: 279). According to an Arab grammarian, Ibn Barhān al-ʿUkbarī (d. 456/1064), the *ʿaṭf al-bayān* actually seems to be problematic since he writes in his *Šarḥ al-Lumaʿ*:

---

3 One of the first to mention them is Mubarrad (d. 285/898 or 286/899; *Muqtaḍab* I, 66–68 and IV, 528–530).

4 The translations given here to these terms are that of Carter (cf. Širbīnī *Nūr* 474). I will only note that for ʾAstarābāḏī *al-badal al-mubāyin* is, in fact, *al-badal al-ġalaṭ* and that under this latter, he distinguishes, in the order stated here, the types of *ġalaṭ ṣarīḥ muḥaqqaq* (substitution of a real error) then of *ġalaṭ nisyān* (substitution of oversight) and then finally of *ġalaṭ badāʾ* (substitution of second thought) (cf. ʾAstarābāḏī *ŠK* II, 403–404). On his side, Wright (1830–1889) reduces to two the sub-types of the *badal al-ġalaṭ*, subsuming *badal al-ʾiḍrāb* (the permutative of retractation) with *badal al-badāʾ* (the substitution of a new opinion, something one would like to substitute for the original statement), and subsuming under only one category *badal al-ġalaṭ wa-l-nisyān* (the permutative of error and forgetfulness, cf. Wright 1996:II, 286).

> Know, concerning the *ʿaṭf al-bayān*, that few grammarians know it, that Sībawayhi mentioned it only incidentally in some sections [...], and that he has not reserved for it any chapter. (*wa-ʿlam ʾanna ʿaṭf al-bayān lā yaʿrifuhu*[5] *kaṯīr min al-naḥwiyyīn wa-ʾinnamā ḏakarahu sībawayhi ʿāriḍan fī mawāḍiʿ* [...] *wa-lam yufrid lahu bāban*, Ibn Barhān al-ʿUkbarī *ŠL* I, 236)

A later grammarian, Baṭalyawsī (d. 521/1127), even points out the three features of *ʿaṭf al-bayān* which account for its "strangeness among grammarians" (*ġarābatihā ʿinda al-naḥwiyyīna*, Baṭalyawsī *Rasāʾil* 206): the vocative (*nidāʾ*), the vague terms (*mubhamāt*), that is to say the demonstratives (*ʾasmāʾ al-ʾišāra*), and the active participle (*ism al-fāʿil*).[6]

By cross-reading the presentations made by traditional Arab grammars, the *ʿaṭf al-bayān* represents, in fact, an intersection between *ṣifa* and *badal*, with which it shares some characteristics, but from which it is distinguished by others. This is why a grammarian like Baṭalyawsī devotes a study, in his *Rasāʾil*, to the difference between *naʿt*, *ʿaṭf bayān* and *badal* (cf. Baṭalyawsī *Rasāʾil* 195–226). As such, one of the best presentations, although not free from controversy, of the *ʿaṭf al-bayān* between *ṣifa* and *badal* is that of Ibn Yaʿīš (d. 643/1245) in his commentary on Zamaḫšarī's (d. 538/1144) *Mufaṣṣal* (cf. Ibn Yaʿīš *ŠM* II, 272–274).

However, none of the grammarians (ancient or modern) clearly explains the distinction that can be made between *badal* and *ʿaṭf bayān*, which may help us to understand the circumspection of ʾAstarābāḏī in the matter. What is important to bear in mind at this stage is that among the four types of *badal*, the *ʿaṭf al-bayān* would be confused with the *badal* of the whole for the whole. It is at least what grammarians say when they indicate that this equivalence is true under two conditions (*yaqūlu al-nuḥāt ʾinna kull mā ṣaluḥa ʾan yakūna ʿaṭf bayān ǧāza ʾan yakūna badalan bi-šarṭayn*, Yaʿqūb 2006: VI, 422, cf. also Howell 1880: I, 481).[7]

What should also be kept in mind is that the *ʿaṭf al-bayān*, representing an intersection between *badal* and *ṣifa*, obviously poses problems for gram-

5 The text gives *yāʾ-hāʾ-rāʾ-fāʾ* that could be read *yahrifu* "to praise excessively" (cf. Wehr 1994:1026a), but which does not make sense here. It is presumably a typo, *hāʾ* and *ʿayn* being side by side on a keyboard.

6 These considerations being once again only inflectional, and therefore more than suspicious in a language where the inflection by means of short vowels is not marked (cf. below, fn. 9), I will not deal with it here.

7 The two conditions in question here are that 1. the *tābiʿ* can take the place of the *matbūʿ* and thus that the operator on the *matbūʿ* can apply to the *tābiʿ* and 2. that no semantic impossibility results from the commutation of the two. The first of the two belongs precisely to the pragmatic criteria discussed by the grammarians (cf. below).

marians to define it precisely. As Esseesy says about the appositives, "the syntactic and semantic boundaries among these subclasses were not always drawn sharply […], leading to instances where syntactic ambiguity becomes inevitable, as in *ḍarabtu ʾabā ʿabdi llāhi zaydan* 'I hit ʾAbū ʿAbd Allāh, Zayd', which is bound to be construed either as *ʿaṭf bayān* 'explicative coordinating' or as *badal*" (Esseesy 2006: 124–125). Owens specifies indeed that "apparently grammarians found it difficult to define it clearly" (Owens 1990: 59).

However, there remains a question which should not be left unanswered, especially since some grammarians, as we will see, provide an implicit solution that must be made explicit: how to distinguish between (1) and (2) above? While Western Arabists do occasionally provide a explanation, albeit rarely,[8] our goal must be to focus on the view of the Arab grammarians, since we are here dealing with the *Foundations of Arab Linguistics*.

1.2 *Traditional Criteria of Distinction between* **ʿaṭf bayān** *and* **badal**

Let us first sum up very briefly the traditional criteria applied by the Arab grammarians to distinguish between *ʿaṭf bayān* and *badal*.

As for the differences between the two, the fact is that, when consulting ancient grammarians, there are at least two criteria of distinction between *badal* and *ʿaṭf bayān*, those criteria being widespread among ancient grammarians. The first one pertains to the linguistic belief in a consistent *ʾiʿrāb*, the difference made between the two from Mubarrad onwards being linked to inflection within the framework of the vocative, since he says that the *badal* is inflected in the nominative while the *ʿaṭf al-bayān* is to the accusative (cf. Mubarrad *Muqtaḍab* IV, 468 and 475). That is also what Ibn al-Sarrāǧ (d. 316/929) clearly states:

> The difference between the *ʿaṭf al-bayān* and the *badal* is that the implicit value (*taqdīr*) of the *ʿaṭf al-bayān* is that of the appositive adjective of the first noun while the implicit value of the *badal* is to replace the first [term], and you say in the framework of the vocative when you want to use the *ʿaṭf al-bayān*: *yā ʾaḫānā zaydan* by putting on the accusative with *tanwīn* since it is not the vocative element, and if you wish to use the *badal* you say: *yā ʾaḫānā zaydu*. (*wa-l-farq bayn ʿaṭf al-bayān wa-l-badal ʾanna ʿaṭf al-bayān taqdīruhu al-naʿt al-tābiʿ li-l-ism al-ʾawwal wa-l-badal taqdīruhu*

8 This is particularly the case of Larcher who indicates, following the Arab grammarians, that the *badal* represents the essential term compared to the *mubdal minhu* which is the accessory one (cf. Larcher 2017:35). For the details of the treatment of the *badal* and the *ʿaṭf al-bayān* by the Arabists, cf. Sartori 2018a:552–558.

ʾan yūḍaʿa mawḍiʿ al-ʾawwal wa-taqūlu fī al-nidāʾ ʾiḏā ʾaradta ʿaṭf al-bayān "yā ʾaḫānā zaydan" fa-tanṣubu wa-tunawwinu li-ʾannahu ġayr munādā fa-ʾin ʾaradta al-badal qulta "yā ʾaḫānā zaydu", Ibn al-Sarrāǧ *ʾUṣūl* I, 432)[9]

Ibn al-Dahhān al-Baġdādī (d. 569/1174) sums this up very briefly in his comment on *ʿaṭf al-bayān*: "it is recognized within the vocative explicitly and elsewhere implicitly" (*yuʿrafu fī al-nidāʾ lafẓan wa-fī ġayrihi taqdīran*, Ibn al-Dahhān al-Baġdādī *Šarḥ* 544).

However, these inflections do not appear in written Arabic with its scriptio defectiva, nor is inflection prominent in conventional pronunciation, where pausal forms predominate.[10] The appeal to inflection which is commonly made by the grammarians therefore has little explanatory value.

The second criterion raised by the grammarians is, in fact, twofold, invoking two pragmatic features which are discussed by Arab grammarians of all periods. The first concerns the *badal* and is linked to the speaker's intention: on him depends the fact that the *badal*, because being in a relation of *stricto sensu* referential uniqueness with its *mubdal minhu*, is conceived as the essential term while the term to which it is apposed is only as an accessory one; the second concerns the *ʿaṭf al-bayān* and again points to the speaker's intention: on him depends the restriction of the extension of the term to which the *ʿaṭf al-bayān* is apposed and, correlatively, the precision of its intension.[11] The *ʿaṭf al-bayān* is then not an essential term, but rather, as with adjectival qualification gener-

---

9 He also speaks about it in the context of the vocative (*nidāʾ*, cf. Ibn al-Sarrāǧ *ʾUṣūl* I, 300–302 and I, 327–328; cf. also II, 78–79; II, 116; II, 134–135). Ibn al-Sarrāǧ indicates that the categories of *badal* and *ʿaṭf bayān* are the terminologies of the so-called grammarians of Basra (cf. Ibn al-Sarrāǧ *ʾUṣūl* I, 328).

10 The pausal form is the default ending both in medieval and contemporary Classical Arabic, to which we may add that the full inflectional system of three cases is not found with every class of word—many have only two inflections, and others are invariable (e.g. *mūsā*, *ʿīsā*), or the inflections may be masked by suffixes (e.g. *kitābī*) or obscured by orthographical ambiguities. Even Qurʾānic Arabic can be seen to be "without desinential inflection, and that this syntactically irrelevant inflection was introduced for prosodic reasons, linked to the changing recitation of the Qurʾān (*taǧwīd*)" (Larcher 2021:37). In effect, overt inflection is the exception (only in the case of the "six nouns", cf. Sartori 2010 and Sartori 2018b:69) rather than the rule, and for a language known for inflection, this reduces to very few cases where it is actually performed!

11 "Intension" and "extension" are borrowed from Logic: "l'extension d'un terme est l'ensemble des référents qu'un terme est susceptibe de dénoter en langue [...]. L'intension (ou, plus traditionnellement, la compréhension) d'un terme correspond aux aspects pertinents de son contenu notionnel qui conditionnent ses emplois référentiels et qui rendent compte de ses relations avec les autres termes de la langue" (Riegel et al. 2004:179–180).

ally, only an accessory term and, like it, is not in a relation of strictly referential uniqueness with the term to which it is apposed,[12] unlike the *badal*.

However, there are grammarians whose inquiries go beyond these two criteria, challenging and extending both the distributional/inflectional and the semantic/pragmatic approach. As I shall show below, they introduce another criterion, this time of suprasegmental nature, arising from the fusion of the pragmatic and the syntactic approach…

2 A New Criterion of Suprasegmental Nature

The authors who follow do not abandon the presentation of *badal* as being the essential term and its *mubdal minhu* as the accessory one. Similarly, they still present the *ʿaṭf al-bayān* as a generally better-known element, clarifying the term to which it is associated, by restricting its extension. They even point to the inflectional criterion to distinguish between the two. However, those grammarians add something interesting that transcends the various branches of indegenous Arabic grammar and is therefore not specific to any one branch. In this section we introduce a syntactic criterion, that of repetition, resumption, or independence (i.e. beginning a new sentence), this last having the morphological consequence that by starting a new sentence a pausal ending appears on the preceding element.

2.1 *Repetition* (takrīr, takrār *or* tašdīd)

2.1.1 *Tašdīd*

I will begin with the most prevalent criterion among ancient grammarians, namely that of *repetition* which one finds in their works in the forms of *takrīr*, and more marginally *takrār* or *tašdīd*. It is with the latter that I will start this section since Ibn Ǧinnī begins by defining the *badal* as “following the course of the *tawkīd* in [factual] assertion and doubling” (*al-badal yaǧrī maǧrā al-tawkīd fī al-taḥqīq wa-l-tašdīd*, Ibn Ǧinnī *Lumaʿ* 144), which he is visibly the first to do so by using the term *tašdīd*. What needs to be understood here is actually twofold: *badal* and *mubdal minhu* being in a referential uniqueness relationship, it thus amounts to saying the same thing twice, both in intention and intension.

That is confirmed by Ibn al-Ḫabbāz (d. 637/1239), commentator of Ibn Ǧinnī’s *Lumaʿ*. Like Ibn Ǧinnī before him, he indicates about the *badal* that it

12 Suyūṭī (d. 911/1505) even states very clearly that “the explanatory apposition only exists after a multireferential [noun]” (*ʿaṭf al-bayān lā yakūnu ʾillā baʿd muštarak*, Suyūṭī *ʾAšbāh* III, 218).

follows the course of the *tawkīd* in [factual] assertion and doubling (*al-taḥqīq wa-l-tašdīd*) and specifies the meaning of *tašdīd*:

> It is because when you say *qāma ʾaḫūka zaydun* then the *badal* and the *mubdal minhu* are two expressions referring to a single meaning, so it is like you said *qāma ʾaḫūka ʾaḫūka*. (*fa-li-ʾannaka ʾiḏā qulta qāma ʾaḫūka zaydun fa-l-badal wa-l-mubdal minhu ʿābiratāni ʿan maʿnā wāḥid fa-ka-ʾannaka qulta qāma ʾaḫūka ʾaḫūka*, Ibn al-Ḫabbāz *Tawǧīh* 275)

But this is also equivalent to *repeating*, *qāma ʾaḫūka zaydun* amounting to saying *qāma ʾaḫūka qāma zaydun*, which Bāqūlī (d. 543/1148) and Ibn al-Faḫḫār (d. 754/1353) will express very clearly (cf. below).

2.1.2 *Takrīr*

As for ʿAbd al-Qāhir al-Ǧurǧānī (d. 471/1078), even though he does not expressly address the difference between *ʿaṭf bayān* and *badal*, he still has an interesting observation to make about the latter:

> Know that the *badal* virtually repeats the operator as it was before, so when you say *marartu bi-qawmika ṯulṯayhim* then *ṯulṯayhim* is in the genitive because of the preposition as if you had said *bi-ṯulṯayhim* [...]. The *badal* virtually repeats the operator only because the *mubdal minhu* is neglected in favor of the *badal* [...] and this is not the case with the *ṣifa* since when you say *ǧāʾanī zaydun al-ẓarīfu* then *zayd* is not virtually neglected, but rather both [terms] follow the course of the single noun. (*iʿlam ʾanna al-badal fī ḥukm takrīr al-ʿāmil ka-mā taqaddama fa-ʾiḏā qulta "marartu bi-qawmika ṯulṯayhim" kāna "ṯulṯayhim" maǧrūran bi-ḥarf ǧarr ḥattā ka-ʾannaka qulta "bi-ṯulṯayhim" [...] wa-ʾinnamā kāna al-badal fī ḥukm takrīr al-ʿāmil li-ʾaǧl ʾanna al-badal yutraku ʾilayhi al-mubdal minhu [...] wa-laysa ka-ḏālika al-ṣifa li-ʾannaka ʾiḏā qulta "ǧāʾanī zaydun al-ẓarīfu" lam yakun zaydun fī ḥukm al-matrūk bal kānā ǧāriyayni maǧrā ism wāḥid*, Ǧurǧānī *MŠĪ* II, 929)

What Ǧurǧānī adds in contrast to his predecessors is the *takrīr* element contained in the *badal* that, if we are to believe ʾUšmūnī (d. 900/1495?) used by Donat Vernier (1838–1917; cf. Vernier 1891: II, 176), the grammarians of the so-called school of Kufa partly called *takrīr*. Compared with the *takrīr*, which visibly presupposes a pause, he presents the case of the adjective (which we know the *ʿaṭf al-bayān* is close to) which, on the contrary, implies a lack of pause, that is to say a link, which is implied by its comparison with the single noun (*ism wāḥid*).

Baṭalyawsī, in the section which he devotes to the difference between *naʿt*, *badal* and *ʿaṭf bayān*, specifies four of them, the third of which being:

> that one supposes with the *badal* a reiteration of the operator, as if it belonged to another sentence, whereas one does not suppose that with the *ʿaṭf al-bayān* which is on the contrary in this respect like the adjective. (*ʾanna al-badal* […] *yuqaddaru maʿahu ʾiʿādat al-ʿāmil wa-ka-ʾannahu min ǧumla ʾuḫrā wa-ʿaṭf al-bayān lā yuqaddaru fīhi ḏālika bal huwa fī hāḏā al-waǧh ka-l-naʿt*, Baṭalyawsī *Rasāʾil* 204)

Thus Baṭalyawsī indicates both the element of repetition contained in the *badal* and, as a result, that the latter is then "as if it belonged to another sentence". By this reference to "another sentence", this author then indicates very clearly that the *badal* is preceded by a pause, which will be later on confirmed by Ibn Barhān al-ʿUkbarī (cf. below) who replaces *ǧumla* with his own term *kalām* "utterance".[13]

Despite what has been said, especially by Talmon, noting that Zamaḫšarī, like others, was only going by a pragmatic feature (the speaker's premeditation, cf. Talmon 1981: 291), ʾAbū al-Qāsim still devotes a section to the *independence* of the *badal*, an independence which he links to the concept of repetition when he says:

> And what indicates its independent character is that it may be judged as having its operator repeated. (*wa-llaḏī yadullu ʿalā kawnihi mustaqillan ʾannahu fī ḥukm takrīr al-ʿāmil*, Zamaḫšarī *Mufaṣṣal* 155)

This independent character (*mustaqill*) of the *badal* is thus seen to be closely related to repetition, and therefore implying the existence of a pause that precedes it.

Bāqūlī, known as Ǧāmiʿ al-ʿUlūm, specifies the same thing speaking also of "repetition". He does it a first time for the *badal*, for which he says that the operator is repeated and that, implicitly, the *badal* belongs to another sentence (*li-ʾanna al-ʿāmil mukarrar fī al-badal wa-l-badal fī al-taqdīr min ǧumla ʾuḫrā*, Ǧāmiʿ al-ʿUlūm *Kitāb Šarḥ al-Lumaʿ fī al-naḥw* 256). He gives for it as an example *zaydun ḏahaba ʿamrun ʾaḫūhu* that he paraphrases *zaydun ḏahaba ʿamrun ḏahaba ʾaḫūhu* (cf. Ǧāmiʿ al-ʿUlūm *Kitāb Šarḥ al-Lumaʿ fī al-naḥw* 257).

---

13 The sentences can indeed be segmented but also linked (or bound) (cf. below fn. 17) as is the case in subordinated constructions such as *yurīdu ʾan yatakallama* "he wants to speak" whereas the linguistic *kalām* (which one can render by 'utterance' or 'speech') "is bounded by silence" (Carter 2017:151 and cf. 148–149 for possible translations of *kalām*).

He once again addresses this aspect of repetition at the level of the *ʿaṭf al-bayān*, clearly indicating that, unlike the *badal*, no such repetition is found with *ʿaṭf al-bayān*:

> The *ʿaṭf al-bayān* resembles the *ṣifa* in that it is an appositive of the first [term] and that it clarifies it, except that it is not derived from the verb, unlike the *ṣifa*. It resembles the *badal* in its form, except that it differs from it because the *badal* is implicitly in the repetition of the operator, and that is unlike it [*ʿaṭf al-bayān*]. This is manifest in the chapter of the vocative: when you say *yā ʾaḫānā zaydan* "o our brother Zayd!", if you treat *zayd* as a *ʿaṭf bayān*, you put the accusative since you make it replace *ʾaḫānā*, and if you treat it as a *badal*, you suppose a repetition of *yā* and you say *yā ʾaḫānā zaydu* "o our brother, Zayd!", as if you said [*yā ʾaḫānā*] *yā zaydu*. (*ʿaṭf al-bayān yušbihu al-ṣifa fī kawnihi tabʿan li-l-ʾawwal wa-mubayyinan lahu ʾillā ʾannahu laysa bi-muštaqq min al-fiʿl bi-ḫilāf al-ṣifa wa-yušbihu fī al-lafẓ al-badal ʾillā ʾannahu yufāriquhu min ḥayṯu ʾanna al-badal fī taqdīr takrīr al-ʿāmil wa-hāḏā bi-ḫilāfihi wa-yatabayyanu ḏālika fī bāb al-nidāʾ ʾiḏā qulta "yā ʾaḫānā zaydan" ʾin ǧaʿalta "zaydan" ʿaṭf bayān naṣabta li-ʾannaka ʾaqamtahu maqām "ʾaḫānā" wa-ʾin ǧaʿalta badalan qaddarta takrīr "yā" fa-qulta "yā ʾaḫānā zaydu" ka-ʾannaka qulta "yā zaydu"*, Ǧāmiʿ al-ʿUlūm *Kitāb Šarḥ al-Lumaʿ fī al-naḥw* 261)

In his great commentary on the *Mufaṣṣal* Ibn Yaʿīš repeats the elements of *badal* by Zamaḫšarī, who, like other grammarians, emphasizes its syntactic independence and connects it with repetition, for which Ibn Yaʿīš then provides crystal clear examples:

> When you say *marartu bi-ʾaḫīka zaydin*, it is implicitly [saying] *marartu bi-ʾaḫīka bi-zaydin*, and when you say *raʾaytu ʾaḫāka zaydan*, its implicit meaning is *raʾaytu ʾaḫāka raʾaytu zaydan*. (*ʾiḏā qulta "marartu bi-ʾaḫīka zaydin" taqdīruhu "marartu bi-ʾaḫīka bi-zaydin" wa-ʾiḏā qulta "raʾaytu ʾaḫāka zaydan" fa-taqdīruhu "raʾaytu ʾaḫāka raʾaytu zaydan"*, Ibn Yaʿīš *ŠM* II, 264)

Ibn al-Ḥāǧib (d. 646/1249) also discusses the difference between the two and likewise connects it to the *takrīr*: "the *badal* is considered as the repetition in all of its cases" (*al-badal fī ḥukm al-takrīr fī ǧamīʿ ʾamṯālihi*, Ibn al-Ḥāǧib *ʾĪḍāḥ* I, 431).

As for the *badal*, Ibn ʿUṣfūr (d. 669/1271) also notes the feature of repetition since he says:

> When you say *qāma zaydun ʾaḫūka* […] it is as you said *qāma ʾaḫūka* having retracted what you first said, *zayd* […] and […] what indicates this is the repetition of the operator with the *badal* as in *marartu bi-zaydin bi-ʾaḫīka*. Allāh the Almighty said […] (Q. 7/75, cf. below). (*ʾiḏā qulta "qāma zaydun ʾaḫūka"* […] *fa-ka-ʾannaka qulta "qāma ʾaḫūka" fa-ʾaḍrabta ʿan qawlika ʾawwalan "zayd"* […] *wa-*[…] *allaḏī yadullu ʿalā ḏālika takrīr al-ʿāmil maʿa al-badal fī naḥw "marartu bi-zaydin bi-ʾaḫīka" qāla allāh taʿālā* […], Ibn ʿUṣfūr *ŠĞ* I, 251)

Ibn Hišām al-ʾAnṣārī (d. 761/1360), in his *Sabīl al-hudā*, deals with the two (cf. Goguyer 1887: 342 ff. for the *ʿaṭf al-bayān* and 358–361 for the *badal*). He even addresses the difference between the two (cf. Goguyer 1887: 344–346). He expressly takes into account only pragmatic and semantic aspects, but still specifies:

> De tout nom dont on peut dire qu'il est adjoint expositif, servant à élucider ou particulariser, on peut dire aussi qu'il est permutatif de tout en tout, servant à fixer et corroborer le sens, parce qu'il se trouve en effet comme si le régissant était répété pour lui. À cette règle les uns font une exception, les autres deux, d'autres même davantage, mais toutes se trouvent comprises dans l'expression que j'ai employée : « *s'il n'est pas impossible de lui faire remplacer son antécédent.* »
>
> GOGUYER 1887: 345

Further on *takrīr*, cf. also ʾUšmūnī and Ḫuḍarī (d. 1287/1870) (ʾUšmūnī *Manhaǧ* II, 435 and Ḫuḍarī *Ḥāšiya* II, 159).

2.1.3 *Takrār*

Ibn ʿUṣfūr, but this time in his *Muqarrib*, deals again with the two types of appositives (cf. Ibn ʿUṣfūr *Muqarrib* 321–326 for the *badal* and 327–328 for the *ʿaṭf al-bayān*), and, in the section devoted to the latter, he explains the difference between *ʿaṭf bayān* and *badal*, by expressly connecting it with the criterion of *takrār al-ʿāmil* (repetition of the operator):

> The difference between it [*ʿaṭf al-bayān*] and the *badal* is that you do not intend to reject the first [term] with the *ʿaṭf al-bayān* as you do with the *badal* […] because the purpose of the *badal* is to repeat the operator […] and that is not allowed in the case of the *ʿaṭf al-bayān* because no repetition is intended here. (*wa-l-farq baynahu* [*ʿaṭf al-bayān*] *wa-bayn al-badal ʾannaka lā tanwī bi-l-ʾawwal al-ṭarḥ fī ʿaṭf al-bayān ka-mā tafʿalu fī al-badal*

> […] *li-ʾanna al-badal fī niyyat takrār al-ʿāmil* […] *wa-ḏālika lā yaǧūzu* [*fī*] *ʿaṭf al-bayān li-ʾannahu laysa fī niyyat takrār al-ʿāmil*, Ibn ʿUṣfūr *Muqarrib* 327)

We find this use of *takrār* instead of *takrīr* among others in Ibn al-Faḫḫār, commentator of Zaǧǧāǧī's (d. 337/949) *Ǧumal*, who, although he sets out the five kinds of appositives, does not deal with the *ʿaṭf al-bayān* (cf. Ibn al-Faḫḫār *šǦ* and Ibn al-Faḫḫār *šǦ*(2)). As for the *badal*, he immediately indicates in the definition the aspect of repetition:

> The *badal* is the appositive whose implicit value is the repetition of the operator, so, when you say *qāma zaydun ʾaḫūka* it has the implicit value of *qāma zaydun qāma ʾaḫūka*. (*al-badal huwa al-tābiʿ ʿalā taqdīr takrār al-ʿāmil fa-ʾiḏā qulta "qāma zaydun ʾaḫūka" fa-ʾinnahu fī taqdīr "qāma zaydun qāma ʾaḫūka"*, Ibn al-Faḫḫār *šǦ* I, 190)

Ibn ʿAqīl finally (d. 769/1367) states that substitution (*badal*) occurs in the intention of repeating the operator (*al-badal ʿalā niyyat takrār al-ʿāmil*, Ibn ʿAqīl *šA* II, 59).

One last element to note is that this dimension is not totally ignored among Arabists. Wright (1830–1889), for example, for whom *ʿaṭf bayān* can be regarded as functionnong in a similar way to the adjectival qualifier, *ṣifa*, "This apposition is equivalent to the use of *wa-huwa, wa-hiya*, etc. (e.g. *ǧāʾanī ʾaḫūka wa-huwa zaydun*)" (Wright 1996: II, 287), which is basically approaching the solution by making of it a link of concomitant nature to be distinguished from the *badal* where there is a new start and therefore a break.

2.2 *Resumption* (istiʾnāf) *and Independence* (istiqlāl)

Regarding the distinction between *badal* and *ʿaṭf bayān*, the other distinguishing criterion that one can identify from reading the ancient grammarians, though it is less prominent than *takrīr*, is that of *istiʾnāf*, that is to say *resumption*[14] as well as that of *istiqlāl*, that is to say *independence*.

14 For this term in Farrāʾ (d. 207/822), cf. Kasher 2014 and also Larcher 2013:195, but also Kinberg 1996: 28–32 and notably his definition of *istʾanafa*: "to begin (a new unit which is: 1. Separated in pronunciation from the preceding unit…)" (1996:29) as well as the statement of Farrāʾ: *wa-qawluhu "wa-mā ʾarsalnā min rasūlin ʾillā bi-lisāni qawmihi li-yubayyina lahum"* […] *ṯumma qāla ʿazza wa-ǧalla "fa-yuḍillu -llāhu man yašāʾu" fa-rufiʿa li-ʾanna al-niyya fīhi al-istiʾnāf lā al-ʿaṭf ʿalā ma qablahu* (1996:30) where, here at least, Farrāʾ clearly contrasts *ʿaṭf* with *istiʾnāf*. In this paper, therefore, *resumption* will denote a new start, implying a pause before it.

I will start with Ibn Ǧinnī, who, when he writes about the *ʿaṭf al-bayān* "You say *qāma ʾaḫūka muḥammadun* as you say *qāma ʾaḫūka al-ẓarīfu*" (*taqūlu "qāma ʾaḫūka muḥammadun" ka-qawlika "qāma ʾaḫūka al-ẓarīfu"*, Ibn Ǧinnī *Lumaʿ* 148), significantly chooses the formulation *ka-qawlika* "as if you were saying". Could this be the trace of the fact that the apposed element and its *ʿaṭf bayān* must be pronounced as one does in the case of a *mawṣūf* and its *ṣifa*, that is to say in one breath, as a single noun (*ism wāḥid*, cf. ʿAbd al-Qāhir al-Ǧurǧānī above)? Such an idea cannot be ruled out, in view of the importance of the word *as* here,[15] especially in the light of what follows.

The first among the grammarians to be perfectly explicit on this subject is, it seems, Ibn Barhān al-ʿUkbarī who precisely links *takrīr* and *istiʾnāf*. About the *badal* he says indeed immediately this: "the *badal* is one of the appositives except that it has originally the implicit value of two sentences: when you say *ḍarabtu zaydan raʾsahu* the base is *ḍarabtu zaydan ḍarabtu raʾsahu*" (*al-badal ʾaḥad al-tawābiʿ ʾillā ʾannahu fī taqdīr ǧumlatayn fī al-ʾaṣl ʾiḏā qulta "ḍarabtu zaydan raʾsahu" fa-l-ʾaṣl "ḍarabtu zaydan ḍarabtu raʾsahu"*, Ibn Barhān al-ʿUkbarī *ŠL* I, 229). But further on, this time about the *ʿaṭf al-bayān*, he says:

> If you ask: why did you not treat this section of the appositives as a *badal*, we will say that the adjectival qualifier is directly joined in the utterance to the qualified element, that it is not considered as a new utterance and that the same is true of the situation of the *ʿaṭf al-bayān*. Also, when you say *qāma hāḏā zaydun* "this one Zayd got up" by constructing the utterance on the mention of *zayd*[16] and not disassociating it from *hāḏā*, it is a *ʿaṭf al-bayān*. If you make of it [utterance] a new one, as if you said *qāma hāḏā qāma zaydun* "this one got up, Zayd got up", it is then a *badal*. (*fa-ʾin qulta hallā ǧaʿalta hāḏā al-faṣl min al-tawābiʿ badalan qulnā ʾinna al-ṣifa yubnā lahā al-kalām ʿalā ḏikr bayān muttaṣil fī al-mawṣūf wa-laysat fī taqdīr kalām mustaʾnaf wa-ka-ḏālika manzilat ʿaṭf al-bayān fa-ʾiḏā qulta "qāma hāḏā zaydun" wa-banayta al-kalām ʿalā ḏikr zayd wa-lam taǧʿalhu munqaṭiʿan min "hāḏā" fa-huwa ʿaṭf al-bayān wa-ʾin ǧaʿaltahu mustaʾnafan wa-ka-ʾannaka qulta "qāma hāḏā qāma zaydun" fa-huwa badal*, Ibn Barhān al-ʿUkbarī *ŠL* I, 235)

15 It has the same importance elsewhere, notably for Émile Durkheim (1858–1917) when he says that we must treat social facts as things (cf. Durkheim 1988:77 and 120; Pouillon 1987:112 for French and Durkheim 1982:35 and 69 for English).

16 That is, with the intention of saying *zayd*.

Ibn Barhān al-ʿUkbarī could not be clearer, his recourse to *muttaṣil* on the one hand, to *mustaʾnaf* and *munqaṭiʿ* on the other hand, the first referring to *ʿaṭf al-bayān* and the second to *badal*, leaving no doubt about his concept of the difference between these two types of appositions: in addition to the traditional criteria already mentioned,[17] he adds one, suprasegmental in nature, which takes into account pronunciation in juncture or segmentation![18] This confirms, in my opinion, the reading of Ibn Ǧinnī's *as*, that is to say that an *ism* and its *ṣifa* are said in one breath.

This criterion of resumption, in the express form of *istiʾnāf*, is then found in particular in Ibn ʿUṣfūr who, in the section devoted to the *badal*, writes: "the *badal* is in the intention of a resumption of an operator, and when you say *qāma zaydun ʾaḫūka* the implicit value is that of *qāma ʾaḫūka*" (*al-badal fī niyyat istiʾnāf ʿāmil fa-ʾiḏā qulta "qāma zaydun ʾaḫūka" fa-l-taqdīr "qāma ʾaḫūka"*, Ibn ʿUṣfūr *Muqarrib* 321). What must be understood here, as elsewhere, is thus that *qāma zaydun ʾaḫūka* is equivalent to *qāma zaydun qāma ʾaḫūka* (cf. above, Bāqūlī and Ibn al-Faḫḫār).

This element of resumption (*istiʾnāf*), linked to that of repetition (*takrīr*), implies the recognition of a pause, exemplified by the existence of "two sentences", which Ibn al-Dahhān al-Baġdādī expresses very well when, as before him Bāqūlī, he clearly indicates that *badal* and *ʿaṭf bayān* contrast with each other in the feature of repetition, where again the "two sentences" are mentioned:

> Know that the *badal* and the element to which it is apposed are implicitly in two sentences, which is not the case of the qualifier and the qualified element (*ṣifa* and *mawṣūf*), nor of the corroborative and the corroborated element, nor of the *ʿaṭf al-bayān* and what precedes it. What confirms this to you is that the operator on the second element appears overtly in the words of the Almighty *qāla l-malaʾu llaḏīna -stakbarū min*

17 Note that he does not reject the traditional views, and nothing prevents him from contrasting the two structures purely in terms of their inflection: "*yā hāḏā zaydun* do you not see that the *tanwīn* of *zaydun* indicates that it is not a *badal* and against that you say *yā ʾayyuhā al-raǧulu zaydu* where *zaydu* is a *badal* of *ʾayy* and for that is indeclinable in *u* without bearing any *tanwīn*?" (*yā hāḏā zaydun ʾa-lā tarā ʾanna tanwīn zaydun qad dalla ʿalā ʾannahu laysa bi-badal wa-ʿalā hāḏā taqūlu yā ʾayyuhā al-raǧulu zaydu fa-zaydu* […] *yakūnu badalan min ʾayyu fa-li-ḏālika kāna mabniyyan ʿalā al-ḍamm ġayr munawwan*, Ibn Barhān al-ʿUkbarī *ŠL* I, 236).

18 This distinction is taken from the Swiss linguist Charles Bally (1865–1947) (cf. Bally 1965) and, for grammar and linguistics of Arabic, from Larcher (cf. especially Larcher 2008 and Larcher 2017).

> *qawmihi li-llaḏīna-stuḍʿifū li-man ʾāmana minhum* (Q. 7/75) "Said the Council of those of his people who waxed proud to those that were abased, to those of them who believed" (Arberry 1955: 180).[19] The overt expression of the *lām* indicates the correctness of our position. (*iʿlam ʾanna al-badal wa-l-mubdal minhu fī taqdīr ǧumlatayn wa-laysa al-ṣifa wa-l-mawṣūf wa-l-taʾkīd wa-l-muʾakkad wa-ʿaṭf al-bayān wa-mā qablahu ka-ḏālika wa-yuʾakkidu ḏālika ʿindaka ʾanna ʾiẓhār al-ʿāmil fī al-ṯānī qad ǧāʾa fī qawlihi taʿālā "qāla l-malaʾu llaḏīna -stakbarū min qawmihi li-llaḏīna -stuḍʿifū li-man ʾāmana minhum" fa-ʾiẓhār al-lām yadullu ʿalā ṣiḥḥat mā ḏahabnā ʾilayhi*, Ibn al-Dahhān al-Baġdādī *Ġurra* II, 817)

He then has a contrastive definition that is very interesting:

> Know that the purpose of the appositive is either to [syntactically] complete the antecedent or not. The one that does not complete the first is the element coordinated by a coordinating particle. The one that completes the first is either in the implicit value of two sentences or in that of a single sentence. The one that is in the implicit value of two sentences is the *badal* [...] and the one that is in the implicit value of a single sentence is of two types [...] the first is the *tawkīd* and the second is the *ʿaṭf al-bayān*. (*iʿlam ʾanna al-tābiʿ ʾimmā ʾan yakūna mukammilan li-l-ʾawwal wa-ʾimmā ʾallā yakūna mukammilan lahu fa-llaḏī lā yakūnu mukammilan li-l-ʾawwal huwa al-maʿṭūf bi-ḥarf al-ʿaṭf wa-llaḏī yakūnu mukammilan li-l-ʾawwal huwa ʾimmā ʾan yakūna fī taqdīr ǧumlatayn ʾaw fī taqdīr ǧumla wāḥida fa-llaḏī yakūnu fī taqdīr ǧumlatayn huwa al-badal* [...] *wa-llaḏī yakūnu fī taqdīr ǧumla wāḥida ʿalā ḍarbayn* [...] *fa-l-ʾawwal al-tawkīd wa-l-ṯānī ʿaṭf al-bayān*, Ibn al-Dahhān al-Baġdādī *Ġurra* II, 854)

We find here, once again through the mention of "two sentences" (*badal*), as opposed to "single sentence" (*ʿaṭf bayān*), the element of repetition, therefore of pause… This reference to "two sentences" is found later, explicitly in ʾUšmūnī who contrasts *badal* and *ʿaṭf bayān* according to eight criteria, the last could not be clearer: "[the *ʿaṭf al-bayān*] has not the implicit value of another sentence, unlike the *badal*" (*ʾannahu laysa fī al-taqdīr min ǧumla ʾuḫrā bi-ḫilāf al-badal*, ʾUšmūnī *Manhaǧ* II, 414).

19 "The chiefs among his people who were puffed up with pride, said unto those who were esteemed weak, *namely* unto those who believed among them" (Sale 1877:124).

This resumption is then linked to the independence of the *badal* from the *mubdal minhu*, unlike the relationship of dependence that exists between the *ʿaṭf al-bayān* and its *maʿṭūf*. On these, I already indicated that they were obviously to be considered as a single noun (*ism wāḥid*, cf. above ʿAbd al-Qāhir al-Ǧurǧānī) and as *muttaṣil* (cf. above Ibn Barhān al-ʿUkbarī). As for the independent relationship, it is apparently Ibn Mālik (d. 672/1274) who speaks of it first. Indeed, he writes concerning the *badal* that it is "like an independent element" (*ka-mustaqill*, Ibn Mālik *ŠKŠ* I, 579). Elsewhere, he further specifies that the *badal* is "the independent appositive because of the virtual requirement of the operator" (*al-tābiʿ al-mustaqill bi-muqtaḍā al-ʿāmil taqdīran*, Ibn Mālik *Tashīl* 172), which he says also in his own commentary on this book (cf. Ibn Mālik *ŠT* III, 186–188 for the *ʿaṭf al-bayān* and III, 189–201 for the *badal*).

It is, however, Ibn ʿAqīl who seems to be the first to link the *maṣdar istiqlāl* to the *badal*, writing about *ʿaṭf al-bayān* that it is: "the non-derived appositive similar to the qualifier in clarifying its antecedent and in its lack of [syntactic] independence" (*al-tābiʿ al-ǧāmid al-mušbih li-l-ṣifa fī ʾīḍāḥ matbūʿihi wa-ʿadam istiqlālihi*, Ibn ʿAqīl *ŠA* II, 57) where he addresses both the aspect of restriction of the extension (through *ʾīḍāḥ*) and where the non-independence that the *ʿaṭf al-bayān* shares with the qualifier contrasts indeed with the *badal* which, in turn, is conceived as independent.[20]

Finally, ʾAstarābāḏī, surprisingly, says he does not understand the difference between the total *badal* and the *ʿaṭf al-bayān*. This said, he, however, recognizes in the *badal* its *resumptive* quality, though without using the term, since he gives two examples going in this direction. The first is taken from the Qurʾān and shows the *badal* intervening after a *fāṣila*, that is to say in the verse following the one in which the *mubdal minhu* is located: *wa-ʾinnaka la-tahdī ʾilā ṣirāṭin mustaqīmin / ṣirāṭi l-llāhi*, Q. 42/52–53, "And thou, surely thou shalt guide unto a straight path—the path of God" (Arberry 1955: 198).[21]

The second is equally clear: "*marartu bi-qawmin ʿabdi llāhi wa-zaydin wa-ḫālidin* and the nominative is good, that is to say 'these are ʿAbd Allāh, Zayd and Ḫālid'" (*marartu bi-qawmin ʿabdi llāhi wa-zaydin wa-ḫālidin wa-l-rafʿ ǧayyid ʾay hum ʿabdu llāhi wa-zaydun wa-ḫālidun*, ʾAstarābāḏī *ŠK* II, 397). Thus ʾAstarābāḏī indicates here that the *badal* can follow the inflection of the *mubdal minhu*, but that it can also be in nominative by implying making a new start, which is neither more nor less than a resumption, which nowadays would be shown by the punctuation, as follows: "I went through a group of men: ʿAbd

20 A later author holds the same view (cf. Ḫuḍarī *Ḥāšiya* II, 159).

21 "and thou shalt surely direct *them* in to the right way, the way of God" (Sale 1877:397).

Allāh, Zayd and Ḫālid" where the colon serves to indicate a (strong) segmentation and therefore a pause.

3 Segmentation vs Juncture

So we see that many medieval Arab grammarians, when it comes to dealing with the *badal*, address the issue of *takrīr* (marginally *takrār* or *tašdīd*), in connection with *isti'nāf* and *istiqlāl*. The *takrīr* we are talking about is syntactic, non-morphological, and not unknown to Sībawayhi himself, since we find it twice in the *Kitāb* (Derenbourg's edition in I, 433 l. 11 and II, 152 l. 2, cf. Troupeau 1976: 182). More interestingly, one of the two occurrences of *takrīr* in the *Kitāb* is specifically related to the *badal*:

> You say *marartu bi-zaydin ibni ʿamrin* when you do not make of *al-ibn* a qualification but you make of it a *badal* or a *takrīr* like *ʾaǧmaʿīna*. (*wa-taqūlu "marartu bi-zaydin ibni ʿamrin" ʾiḏā lam taǧʿal "al-ibn" waṣfan wa-lākinnaka taǧʿaluhu badalan ʾaw takrīran ka-ʾaǧmaʿīna*, Sībawayhi *Kitāb*(2) II, 152 l. 2 = Sībawayhi *Kitāb* III, 566)

In the same way, it is interesting to note that of the three mentions in the *Kitāb* of the verb *istaʾnafa* in a syntactical meaning (cf. Troupeau 1976: 35), one is once more directly related to our topic. Indeed, at the very place of the single occurrence of the term *ʿaṭf al-bayān* in his *Kitāb*, Sībawayhi presents something that will, with rare exceptions as we have seen, be forgotten over time, and this element is in fact of suprasegmental nature: it is neither more nor less than the taking into account of a pause, marked by the *isti'nāf*. Making the difference between the *ʿaṭf al-bayān* and something that is not categorized at this point in the text as *badal*, Sībawayhi writes:

> As for what Ru'ba says, it is the fact that he made of *naṣran* a *ʿaṭf al-bayān* and he put it in the accusative as if he had said *yā zaydu zaydan*. As to what ʾAbū ʿAmr says, it is as if he had started the vocative again [i.e. *yā zaydu yā zaydu l-ṭawīlu*]. (*wa-ʾammā qawl ruʾba fa-ʿalā ʾannahu ǧaʿala "naṣran" ʿaṭf al-bayān wa-naṣabahu ka-ʾannahu ʿalā qawlihi "yā zaydun zaydan" wa-ʾammā qawl ʾabī ʿamr fa-ka-ʾannahu istaʾnafa al-nidāʾ*, Sībawayhi *Kitāb* II, 187)

Nevertheless, the author of the *Kitāb* indicates for one case that it can be a *badal* or a *ʿaṭf bayān*, which shows that he does not really have the idea of the segmentation by *istiʾnāf*… (cf. Sībawayhi *Kitāb* II, 191).[22] This correlation is, however, quite relevant, as Larcher recalls it:

> Especially remarkable is the case of "disjunction" called "resumption" (*istiʾnāf*), because the second clause is to be understood as a response (*jawāb*) to an implicit question (*suʾāl*) suggested by the first, as in the following verse: *qāla lī kayfa ʾanta qultu ʿalīlū/saharun dāʾimun wa-ḥuznun ṭawīlū* ("'How are you?' he asked me. 'Unwell! Permanent insomnia and prolonged melancholy!' I replied"); *saharun dāʾimun wa-ḥuznu ṭawīlū* responds in fact to a question like *mā bāluka ʿalīlan* ("What maladies do you have?") or else *mā sababu ʿillatika* ("What is the cause of your malady?"). We see, from these few examples, that if "conjunction" is defined as a *syntactic* coordination, then "disjunction" could be interpreted as a *semantic* coordination, in the sense of Bally (1965): the two disjoint clauses are in the semantic relation of topic to comment and the comment implicitly makes reference to the topic: "He is dead (and, because he is dead,) may Allah take pity on him!"; "(They say that they do nothing but mock, but) it is Allah who mocks them; [I am] sick; (you are going to ask me from what): from permanent insomnia and prolonged melancholy."
>
> LARCHER 2013: 195

The term "response" indeed implies that of "discourse's resumption" and therefore of segmentation. On the contrary, in the case of the *ʿaṭf al-bayān*, the juncture seems so strong that Talmon notes among the distinctions to be made between *ṣifa* and *ʿaṭf* (and thus *ʿaṭf al-bayān*) that the *ṣifa* can follow an implicit *ʾaʿnī* ("I mean"), which is impossible in the case of the *ʿaṭf* (cf. Talmon 1981: 287, fn. 14).[23]

4 Conclusion

In his *Syntaxe de l'arabe classique*, Pierre Larcher indicates that "the one thing missing element from traditional Arabic grammar is intonation" (Larcher 2017: 97).[24] We have just seen that this is true concerning the difference between

22 *Fa-hāḏihi al-ʾasmāʾ al-mubhama ʾiḏā fassartahā taṣīru bi-manzilat "ʾay" ka-ʾannaka ʾiḏā ʾaradta ʾan tufassirahā lā yağuzu laka ʾan taqifa ʿalayhā wa-ʾinnamā qulta "yā hāḏā ḏā l-ğumma" li-ʾanna "ḏā l-ğumma" lā tūṣafu bihi al-ʾasmāʾ al-mubhama ʾinnamā yakūnu badal ʾaw ʿaṭfan ʿalā al-ism.*

23 He refers to Sībawayhi *Kitāb*(2) I, 265 l. 5 where nevertheless the verb *ʾaʿnī* is not present.

24 "L'intonation est la grande absente de la grammaire arabe traditionnelle".

ʿaṭf bayān and *badal al-kull min al-kull*, where the main element taken into account is of pragmatic nature. However, as I have just shown, the suprasegmental aspect can still be identified, and join a dichotomy which, once we have it in mind, we can no longer leave out of account: the distinction between segmentation and juncture.

If a grammarian and logician like ʾAstarābāḏī is doubtful about the distinction between *badal al-kull* and *ʿaṭf bayān*, it is because at the written level, a fortiori at a time when punctuation did not exist, both can only be distinguished orally, and this is the strength of Ibn Barhān al-ʿUkbarī who was the first to go beyond a literary analysis and frankly integrates the rhythm of speech in his reflexion.

But make no mistake, in the perspective of the Arabic grammatical tradition, as elsewhere, this suprasegmental criterion is in fact conditioned by the semantic and pragmatic criterion and is therefore secondary to it: as for the *badal*, it is because there is a referential uniqueness which makes the *tābiʿ* the primary element (semantic and pragmatic criterion) that there is *takrīr*, therefore *istiʾnāf*, that is to say pause and therefore segmentation (suprasegmental criterion); as for the *ʿaṭf al-bayān*, it is because there is a referential multiplicity (semantic and pragmatic criterion) that *matbūʿ* and *tābiʿ* are considered as a single noun (*ism wāḥid*) and as linked (*muttaṣil*) and that therefore no pause is made possible between the two, indicating then a juncture (suprasegmental criterion). This second criterion would, therefore, come (the addressee ignoring for example whether what is referred to is unique or multiple) to highlight objectively the semantic and pragmatic criterion which remains only subjective.

Without giving into precursorism, we still have to note that the description made by these medieval Arab grammarians can indeed match what contemporary linguists of French[25] say when they distinguish between close apposition (*apposition liée*) and loose apposition (*apposition détachée*). Indeed, in French grammar, among expansions of the noun (also called its modifiers) including the attributive adjective, the construct state, etc., Riegel et al. indicate that they "have with the noun two types of relationships" (Riegel et al. 2004: 179,[26] also cf. 150) depending on whether these modifiers do restrict or not the extension of the noun. The first category includes the attributive adjective and among the second ones, which they generically call appositives "because non-restrictive modifiers are often separated from the rest of the utterance by

25 Being French, the author of these lines naturaly refers to French grammar and linguistics.

26 "entretiennent avec le nom deux types de relations".

intonation or by a pause, and in standard writing by a comma" (Riegel et al. 2004: 150).[27] These modifiers are then said to be "in detached position" (*en position détachée*, cf. Neveu 1998 and Caddéo 2000), a position that is "manifested in writing by the frame between two commas and orally by pauses (and sometimes by a 'bracketed' melody)" (Riegel et al. 2004: 190).[28] In the second category, the authors note that the appositive and its antecedent are in a relationship of referential uniqueness, which they illustrate with the example *Paris, la capitale de la France*, where "it is undeniable that the two defined expressions refer to the same reality" (Riegel et al. 2004: 190[29]).[30]

Even if, in French (or other languages like English or Swedish for example), things are not so clear-cut (cf. Rioul 1983, Lindqvist 2013 and Lindqvist 2015), we will recognize in the non-restrictive modifiers the description of the Arabic *badal al-kull min al-kull*, not only because of its explicit description by the medieval grammarians who make it an element in a relationship of referential uniqueness with the term to which it is apposed, but also because of their use of *takrīr* and *istiʾnāf* which effectively imply their separation from the term to which they are apposed through starting again and the associated pause.

We will then recognize in the first category, that of restrictive modifiers, those features which *ʿaṭf al-bayān* shares with the *ṣifa*, that is to say the adjective, namely its function of restricting the extension of the noun, the *ʿaṭf al-bayān* being the most often described as *ʾaḫaṣṣ min al-ʾawwal*, as *ʾašhar al-*

27 "parce que les modificateurs non restrictifs sont souvent séparés du reste de l'énoncé par l'intonation ou par une pause, et dans l'écrit standard par une virgule".

28 "matérialisée à l'écrit par l'encadrement entre deux virgules et à l'oral par des pauses (et parfois par une mélodie "parenthétique")". We can add here an example from Yusuf Idris in his short story *Riḥla* where he writes *kay ʾuḥissa ʾannī* [...] *wa-ʾannī ʾašʿuru bi-l-ʾamān, ʾaḥlā wa-ʾaʿḏab wa-ʾamtaʿ ʾamān* "so that I feel [...] that I know the peace, the most beautiful, pleasant and delightful peace". Here, the presence of a comma is the manifestation in the written expression of the pause between the *mubdal minhu* and the *badal*.

29 "il est indéniable que les deux expressions définies désignent la même réalité".

30 Paradigmatically, it is a matter of distinguishing 1) *at the G20 summit, President Biden and President Macron met...* where "President", in an international context, is a multiple referent from 2) *during his trip to the Lot (French area), the President, Macron, declared...* where "President", in a national context, is a unique referent. It could also explain what Mejdell points out when dealing with the pronunciation of demonstratives without juncture. According to her, pronunciations like *hāḏihi ʾal-madīna*, that is to say without the elision of "the *hamzat al-waṣl* of the article on the head noun following" (Mejdell 2006:212–213), would reflect "the search for the right expression, *le bon mot* to be the head noun" (Mejdell 2006:221). This said, this nonjuncture could also make of the head noun a *badal*, then to be read as *this, the town* for example. I wish here to warmly thank Michael G. Carter for this reference as well as for his reading of this article, drastically approving its English, and also to our colleague, Emilie Coulon.

ismayn (cf. Ǧurǧānī *ŠǦ* 277, Zamaḫšarī *ʾUnmūḏaǧ* 20), and *ʾaʿraf minhu* (cf. Ǧurǧānī *ŠǦ* 277), but which also shares with the *ṣifa* the feature of not being orally separated from the term to which it is apposed.

In grammatical traditions like the French one for instance, this recognition of the double status of the apposition as either close or loose only manifests itself during 16th century (cf. Neveu 1998: 20). So here, again without giving in to precursorism, we have, in Arabic grammar, the early trace of a distinction between these two types of apposition, according to the same semantic and pragmatic criteria and with therefore the same suprasegmental consequences.

Bibliography

Primary Sources

ʾAstarābāḏī, *ŠK* = Raḍī al-Dīn Muḥammad b. al-Ḥasan al-ʾAstarābāḏī, *Šarḥ Kāfiyat Ibn al-Ḥāǧib*. Ed. by ʾImīl Badīʿ Yaʿqūb. Bayrūt: Dār al-kutub al-ʿilmiyya, 5 vol., 1419/1998.

Baṭalyawsī, *Rasāʾil* = ʾAbū Muḥammad ʿAbd Allāh b. Muḥammad Ibn al-Sīd al-Baṭalyawsī, *Rasāʾil fī al-luġa*. Ed. by Walīd Muḥammad al-Sarāqabī. Al-Riyāḍ: Markaz al-Malik Fayṣal li-l-buḥūṯ wa-l-dirāsāt al-ʾislāmiyya, 1428/2007.

Ġalāyīnī, *Ǧāmiʿ* = Muṣṭafā b. Muḥammad Salīm al-Ġalāyīnī, *Ǧāmiʿ al-durūs al-ʿarabiyya*. Ed. by ʿAbd al-Munʿim Ḫalīl ʾIbrāhīm. Bayrūt: Dār al-kutub al-ʿilmiyya, 1421/2000.

Ǧāmiʿ al-ʿUlūm, *Kitāb Šarḥ al-Lumaʿ fī al-naḥw* = ʾAbū al-Ḥasan ʿAlī b. al-Ḥusayn b. ʿAlī al-ʾAṣfahānī al-Bāqūlī al-maʿrūf bi-Ǧāmiʿ al-ʿUlūm, *Kitāb Šarḥ al-Lumaʿ fī al-naḥw*. Ed. by Muḥammad Ḫalīl Murād al-Ḥarbī. Bayrūt: Dār al-kutub al-ʿilmiyya, 1428/2007.

Ǧurǧānī, *MŠĪ* = ʾAbū Bakr ʿAbd al-Qāhir b. ʿAbd al-Raḥmān b. Muḥammad al-Ǧurǧānī, *Kitāb al-Muqtaṣid fī šarḥ al-ʾĪḍāḥ*. Ed. by Kāẓim Baḥr al-Marǧān. Baġdād: Manšūrāt wizārat al-ṯaqāfa wa-l-ʾiʿlām, 2 vol., 1402/1982.

Ǧurǧānī, *ŠǦ* = ʾAbū Bakr ʿAbd al-Qāhir b. ʿAbd al-Raḥmān b. Muḥammad al-Ǧurǧānī, *Šarḥ al-Ǧumal fī al-naḥw*. Ed. by Ḫalīl ʿAbd al-Qādir ʿĪsā. Bayrūt & ʿAmmān: Dār Ibn Ḥazm & al-Dār al-ʿuṯmāniyya, 10th ed., 1432/2011.

Ḫuḍarī, *Ḥāšiya* = Muḥammad b. Muṣṭafā al-Ḫuḍarī, *Ḥāšiyat al-Ḫuḍarī ʿalā šarḥ Ibn ʿAqīl ʿalā ʾAlfiyyat Ibn Mālik*. Ed. by Turkī Farḥān al-Muṣṭafā. Bayrūt: Dār al-kutub al-ʿilmiyya, 5th ed., 2 vol., 1434/2013.

Ibn al-Dahhān al-Baġdādī, *Ġurra* = ʾAbū Muḥammad Saʿīd b. al-Mubārak b. ʿAlī al-ʾAnṣārī al-maʿrūf bi-Ibn al-Dahhān al-Baġdādī, *al-Ġurra fī šarḥ al-Lumaʿ min ʾawwal bāb ʾinna wa-ʾaḫawātihā ʾilā ʾāḫir bāb al-ʿatf*. Ed. by Farīd ʿAbd al-ʿAzīz al-Zāmil al-Sulaym. Al-Riyāḍ: Dār al-tadmuriyya, 2 vol., 2011.

Ibn al-Dahhān al-Baġdādī, *Šarḥ* = ʾAbū Muḥammad Saʿīd b. al-Mubārak b. ʿAlī al-ʾAnṣārī al-maʿrūf bi-Ibn al-Dahhān al-Baġdādī, *Šarḥ al-durūs fī al-naḥw*. Ed. by ʾIbrāhīm Muḥammad ʾAḥmad al-ʾIdkāwī. Al-Qāhira: Maṭbaʿat al-ʾamāna, 1411/1991.

Ibn al-Faḫḫār, *ŠĞ* = ʾAbū ʿAbd Allāh Muḥammad b. ʿAlī b. ʾAḥmad Ibn al-Faḫḫār, *Šarḥ al-Ǧumal*. Ed. by Rawʿa Muḥammad Nāǧī. Bayrūt: Dār al-kutub al-ʿilmiyya, 2 vol., 1434/2013.

Ibn al-Faḫḫār, *ŠĞ(2)* = ʾAbū ʿAbd Allāh Muḥammad b. ʿAlī b. ʾAḥmad Ibn al-Faḫḫār, *Šarḥ al-Ǧumal*. Ed. by Ḥammād b. Muḥammad Ḥāmid al-Ṯamālī. n.p.: n.p., 3 vol., 1410/1989.

Ibn al-Ḫabbāz, *Tawǧīh* = Šams al-Dīn ʾAbū al-ʿAbbās ʾAḥmad b. al-Ḥusayn b. ʾAḥmad al-maʿrūf bi-Ibn al-Ḫabbāz al-ʾIrbilī al-Mawṣilī al-Naḥwī al-Ḍarīr, *Tawǧīh al-Lumaʿ*. Ed. by Fāyiz Zakī Muḥammad Diyāb. Al-Qāhira: Dār al-salām, 2nd ed., 1428/2007.

Ibn al-Ḥāǧib, *ʾĪḍāḥ* = Ǧamāl al-Dīn ʾAbū ʿAmr ʿUṯmān b. ʿUmar b. ʾAbī Bakr b. Yūnus Ibn al-Ḥāǧib al-Miṣrī al-Dimašqī al-Mālikī, *al-ʾĪḍāḥ fī šarḥ al-Mufaṣṣal*. Ed. by ʾIbrāhīm Muḥammad ʿAbd Allāh. Dimašq: Dār Saʿd al-Dīn, 3rd ed., 1431/2010.

Ibn al-Sarrāǧ, *ʾUṣūl* = ʾAbū Bakr Muḥammad b. al-Sarī b. Sahl Ibn al-Sarrāǧ al-Baġdādī, *al-ʾUṣūl fī al-naḥw*. Ed. by Muḥammad ʿUṯmān. Al-Qāhira: Maktabat al-ṯaqāfa al-dīniyya, 2 vol., 1430/2009.

Ibn ʿAqīl, *ŠA* = Bahāʾ al-Dīn ʾAbū Muḥammad ʿAbd Allāh b. ʿAbd al-Raḥmān b. ʿAbd Allāh b. Muḥammad al-Qurašī al-Hāšimī al-ʿAqīlī al-Hamdānī al-Miṣrī Ibn ʿAqīl, *Šarḥ Ibn ʿAqīl ʿalā ʾAlfiyyat Ibn Mālik*. Ed. by ʾImīl Badīʿ Yaʿqūb. Bayrūt: Dār al-kutub al-ʿilmiyya, 7th ed., 2 vol., 1431/2010.

Ibn Barhān al-ʿUkbarī, *ŠL* = ʾAbū al-Qāsim ʿAbd al-Wāḥid b. ʿAlī al-ʾAsadī Ibn Barhān al-ʿUkbarī, *Šarḥ al-Lumaʿ*. Ed. by Fāʾiz Fāris. Al-Kuwayt: al-Silsila al-turāṯiyya, 2 vol., 1404/1984.

Ibn Ǧinnī, *Lumaʿ* = ʾAbū al-Fatḥ ʿUṯmān b. Ǧinnī al-Mawṣilī, *al-Lumaʿ fī al-ʿarabiyya*. Ed. by Ḥāmid al-Muʾmin. Bayrūt: ʿĀlam al-kutub & Maktabat al-nahḍa al-ʿarabiyya, 2nd ed., 1405/1985.

Ibn Mālik, *ŠKŠ* = Ǧamāl al-Dīn ʾAbū ʿAbd Allāh Muḥammad b. ʿAbd Allāh b. ʿAbd Allāh al-Ṭāʾī al-Ǧayyānī al-ʾAndalusī Ibn Mālik, *Šarḥ al-Kāfiya al-šāfiya suivi de al-Kāfiya al-šāfiya*. Ed. by ʿAlī Muḥammad Muʿawwaḍ & ʿĀdil ʾAḥmad ʿAbd al-Mawǧūd. Bayrūt: Dār al-kutub al-ʿilmiyya, 2nd ed., 2 vol., 1431/2010.

Ibn Mālik, *ŠT* = Ǧamāl al-Dīn ʾAbū ʿAbd Allāh Muḥammad b. ʿAbd Allāh b. ʿAbd Allāh al-Ṭāʾī al-Ǧayyānī al-ʾAndalusī Ibn Mālik, *Šarḥ al-Tashīl: Tashīl al-fawāʾid wa-takmīl al-maqāṣid*. Ed. by Muḥammad ʿAbd al-Qādir ʿAṭā & Ṭāriq Fatḥī al-Sayyid. Bayrūt: Dār al-kutub al-ʿilmiyya, 2nd ed., 3 vol., 1430/2009.

Ibn Mālik, *Tashīl* = Ǧamāl al-Dīn ʾAbū ʿAbd Allāh Muḥammad b. ʿAbd Allāh b. ʿAbd Allāh al-Ṭāʾī al-Ǧayyānī al-ʾAndalusī Ibn Mālik, *Tashīl al-fawāʾid wa-takmīl al-maqāṣid*. Ed. by Muḥammad Kāmil Barakāt. n.p.: Dār al-kitāb al-ʿarabī, 1386/1967.

Ibn ʿUṣfūr, *Muqarrib* = ʿAlī b. al-Muʾmin b. Muḥammad ʾAbū al-Ḥasan al-Ḥaḍramī al-ʾIšbīlī Ibn ʿUṣfūr, *al-Muqarrib wa-maʿahu Muṯul al-Muqarrib*. Ed. by ʿĀdil ʾAḥmad ʿAbd al-Mawǧūd & ʿAlī Muḥammad Muʿawwaḍ. Bayrūt: Dār al-kutub al-ʿilmiyya, 1418/1998.

Ibn ʿUṣfūr, *ŠĞ* = ʾAbū al-Ḥasan ʿAlī b. al-Muʾmin b. Muḥammad al-Ḥaḍramī al-ʾIšbīlī Ibn ʿUṣfūr, *Šarḥ Ǧumal al-Zaǧǧāǧī*. Ed. by Fawwāz al-Šaʿʿār & ʾImīl Badīʿ Yaʿqūb. Bayrūt: Dār al-kutub al-ʿilmiyya, 3 vol., 1419/1998.

Ibn Yaʿīš, *ŠM* = Muwaffaq al-Dīn ʾAbū al-Baqāʾ Yaʿīš b. ʿAlī b. Yaʿīš b. ʾAbī al-Sarāyā Muḥammad b. ʿAlī al-ʾAsadī al-Ḥalabī Ibn Yaʿīš, *Šarḥ al-Mufaṣṣal li-l-Zamaḫšarī*. Ed. by ʾImīl Badīʿ Yaʿqūb. Bayrūt: Dār al-kutub al-ʿilmiyya, 2nd ed. 6 vol., 1432/2011.

Mubarrad, *Muqtaḍab* = ʾAbū al-ʿAbbās Muḥammad b. Yazīd b. ʿAbd al-ʾAkbar al-Ṯumālī al-ʾAzdī al-Mubarrad, *al-Muqtaḍab*. Ed. by Ḥasan Ḥamad & ʾImīl Badīʿ Yaʿqūb. Bayrūt: Dār al-kutub al-ʿilmiyya, 5 parts in 3 vol., 1420/1999.

Sībawayhi, *Kitāb* = ʾAbū Bišr ʿAmr b. ʿUṯmān b. Qanbar Sībawayhi, *al-Kitāb*. Ed. by ʾImīl Badīʿ Yaʿqūb. Bayrūt: Dār al-kutub al-ʿilmiyya, 5 vol., 1420/1999.

Sībawayhi, *Kitāb*(2) = ʾAbū Bišr ʿAmr b. ʿUṯmān b. Qanbar Sībawayhi, *Le livre de Sîbawaihi. Traité de grammaire arabe par Sîboûya, dit Sîbawaihi*. Ed. by Hartwig Derenbourg. Paris: Imprimerie nationale, 2 vol., 1881–1889, reprint Hildesheim & New York: Georg Olms Verlag, 2 vol., 1970.

Sībawayhi, *Kitāb*(3) = ʾAbū Bišr ʿAmr b. ʿUṯmān b. Qanbar Sībawayhi, *al-Kitāb*. Ed. by ʿAbd al-Salām Muḥammad Hārūn. Al-Qāhira: Maktabat al-ḫānǧī, 3rd ed., 5 vol., 1408/1988.

Širbīnī, *Nūr* = Šams al-Dīn al-Ḫaṭīb Muḥammad b. ʾAḥmad al-Širbīnī, *Nūr al-saǧiyya fī ḥall ʾalfāẓ al-ʾĀǧurrūmiyya*. Ed. by Sayyid Šaltūt al-Šāfiʿī. Ǧadda: Dār al-minhāǧ, 1429/2008.

Suyūṭī, *ʾAšbāh* = Ǧalāl al-Dīn ʿAbd al-Raḥmān b. Kamāl al-Dīn ʾAbī Bakr b. Muḥammad b. Sābiq al-Dīn Ḫaḍr al-Ḫuḍayrī al-Šāfiʿī al-ʾAsyūṭī al-mašhūr bi-l-Suyūṭī, *al-ʾAšbāh wa-l-naẓāʾir fī al-naḥw*. Ed. by ʿAbd al-ʿĀl Sālim Mukarram. Bayrūt: Muʾassasat al-risāla, 9 vol., 1407/1987.

ʾUšmūnī, *Manhaǧ* = Nūr al-Dīn ʾAbū al-Ḥasan ʿAlī b. Muḥammad b. ʿĪsā al-ʾUšmūnī, *Šarḥ al-ʾUšmūnī ʿalā ʾAlfiyyat Ibn Mālik al-musammā Manhaǧ al-sālik ʾilā ʾAlfiyyat Ibn Mālik*. Ed. by Muḥammad Muḥyī al-Dīn ʿAbd al-Ḥamīd. Bayrūt: Dār al-kitāb al-ʿarabī, 3 vol., 1375/1955.

Zamaḫšarī, *Mufaṣṣal* = Ǧār Allāh ʾAbū al-Qāsim Maḥmūd b. ʿUmar b. Muḥammad b. ʾAḥmad al-Ḫawārizmī al-Zamaḫšarī, *al-Mufaṣṣal fī ṣanʿat al-ʾiʿrāb*. Ed. by ʾImīl Badīʿ Yaʿqūb. Bayrūt: Dār al-kutub al-ʿilmiyya, 1420/1999.

Zamaḫšarī, *ʾUnmūḏaǧ* = Ǧār Allāh ʾAbū al-Qāsim Maḥmūd b. ʿUmar b. Muḥammad b. ʾAḥmad al-Ḫawārizmī al-Zamaḫšarī, *al-ʾUnmūḏaǧ fī al-naḥw*. Ed. by Sāmī b. Muḥammad al-Manṣūr. n.p.: n.p., 1420/1999.

Secondary Sources

Arberry, Arthur John. 1955. *The Koran Interpreted*. London & New York: George Allen & Unwin LTD & The Macmillan Company.

Bally, Charles. 1965 [1944]. *Linguistique générale et linguistique française*. Berne: A. Francke. 4th ed [1st edition 1932, 2nd edition Berne: Francke].

Caddéo, Sandrine. 2000. “L’apposition : analyse syntaxique de l’apposition nominale détachée dans divers registres de la langue parlée et de l’écrit en français contemporain”. PhD dissertation. Université de Provence (Aix-Marseille I).

Carter, Michael G. 2016. *Sībawayhi’s Principles. Arabic Grammar and Law in Early Islamic Thought*. Atlanta, G.: Lockwood Press.

Durkheim, Émile. 1982. *The Rules of Sociological Method*, edited with an Introduction by Steven Lukes, translated by W.D. Halls. New York: The Free Press.

Durkheim, Émile. 1988 [1894^1/1895^2]. *Les règles de la méthode sociologique*. Paris: Flammarion, coll. “Champs”.

Esseesy, Mohssen. 2006. “Apposition”. *Encyclopedia of Arabic Language and Linguistics*, I, ed. by Kees Versteegh et al., 123–126. Leiden & Boston: Brill.

Goguyer, Antonin. 1887. *La pluie de rosée. Étanchement de la soif. Traité de flexion et de syntaxe par Ibnu Hiǧām*. Leiden: Brill.

Howell, Mortimer Sloper. 1880–1911. *A Grammar of the Classical Arabic Language. Translated and compiled from the works of the most approved native or naturalized authorities*. Allahabad: n.p., 2 vol.

Kasher, Almog. 2014. “The Term and Concept of *Isti’nāf* in al-Farrā”’s Qur’ānic Commentary and the Early Development of Arabic Grammatical Tradition”. *Ancient Near Eastern Studies* 51. 341–352.

Kinberg, Naphtali. 1996. *A Lexicon of al-Farrā”’s Terminology in his Qur’ān Commentary*. Leiden: E.J. Brill, coll. “Handbook of Oriental Studies. Section 1 The Near and Middle East” 23.

Larcher, Pierre. 2008. “Les « complexes de phrases » de l’arabe classique”. *Kervan. Rivista internazionale di studii afroasiatici* 6. 29–45.

Larcher, Pierre. 2013. “Arabic Linguistic Tradition II. Pragmatics”. *The Oxford Handbook* of *Arabic Linguistics*, ed. by Jonathan Owens, 185–212. Oxford: Oxford University Press.

Larcher, Pierre. 2017. *Syntaxe de l’arabe classique*. Aix-en-Provence: Presses Universitaires de Provence.

Larcher, Pierre. 2021. “Une rime « cachée » dans Cor. 23, 12–14 ? Histoire du texte et histoire de la langue”. *Arabica* 67/1. 36–50.

Lindqvist, Karin. 2013. “Apposition détachée ou liée ? Étude contrastive français-suédois sur des combinaisons de Npr et de Nc”. *Revue Romane. Langue et littérature* 48/2. 254–283.

Lindqvist, Karin. 2015. “Sur le rôle du nom commun dans le choix entre les appositions des trois types « le président Obama », « Obama, le président » et « le président, Obama » en français et en suédois”. *Festival Romanistica*, ed. by Gunnel Engwall & Lars Fant, 273–290. Stockholm: Stockholm University Press.

Mejdell, Gunvor. 2006. *Mixed Styles in Spoken Arabic in Egypt. Somewhere between order and chaos*. Leiden & Boston: Brill, coll. “Studies in Semitic Languages and Linguistics” 48.

Neveu, Franck. 1998. *Études sur l'apposition: Aspects du détachement nominale et adjectival en français contemporain, dans un corpus de textes de J.-P. Sartre*. Paris: Honoré Champion, coll. "Grammaire et Linguistique".

Owens, Jonathan. 1990. *Early Arabic Grammatical Theory: Heterogeneity and standardization*. Amsterdam & Philadelphia: John Benjamins.

Pouillon, Jean. 1987. "L'œuvre de Claude Lévi-Strauss". *Race et histoire*, Claude Lévi-Strauss, 87–127. Paris: Gallimard, coll. "Folio/Essais", réédition Unesco 1952.

Riegel, Martin et al. 2004 [1994]. *Grammaire méthodique du français*. Paris: P.U.F., coll. "Quadrige", 3rd ed.

Rioul, René. 1983. "Les appositions dans la grammaire française". *L'information grammaticale* 18. 21–29.

Sale, George. 1877. *The Koran: or, Alcoran of Mohammed with explanatory notes. Various readings from Savary's version of the Koran; and a preliminary discourse on the religion and political condition of the Arabs before the days of Mohammed*. Londres: William Tegg and Co.

Sartori, Manuel. 2010. "Les « six noms » : grammaire arabe et pudibonderie". *Linguistique arabe*, ed. by Henda Dhaoudi and Antonella Ghersetti. *Synergies Monde arabe* 7. 35–45.

Sartori, Manuel. 2018a. "La différence entre *badal* et *ʿaṭf al-bayān*. Mutisme et surdité des grammaires de l'arabe ?". *La lengua árabe a través de la historia. Perspectivas diacrónicas*, ed. by Ignacio Ferrando. *Al-Qanṭara* 39/2. 581–620.

Sartori, Manuel. 2018b. "La flexion désinentielle et l'arabe. État de la question et discussion d'arguments récents". *Case and Mood Endings in Semitic Languages—Myth or Reality? Désinences casuelles et modales dans les langues sémitiques—mythe ou réalité ?*, ed. by Lutz Edzard et al., 68–94. Wiesbaden: Harrassowitz, coll. "Abhandlungen für die Kunde des Morgenlandes" 113.

Talmon, Rafael. 1981. "*ʿAṭf*: An inquiry into the History of a Syntactic Category". *Arabica* 28/2–3. 278–292.

Troupeau, Gérard. 1976. *Lexique-index du* Kitāb *de Sībawayhi*. Paris: Klincksieck, coll. "Études arabes et islamiques".

Vernier, Donat S.J. 1891. *Grammaire arabe composée d'après les sources primitives*. Beyrouth: Imprimerie catholique, 2 vol.

Wehr, Hans. 1994 [1979]. *Arabic-English Dictionary*. Urbana, Illinois: Spoken Language Services. J. Milton Cowan. 4e éd., revue et augmentée.

Wright, William. 1996 [1896–1898 [1859–1862]]. *A Grammar of the Arabic Language*. Translated from the German of Caspari and edited with numerous additions and corrections. Third edition revised by W. Robertson Smith and M.J. de Goeje with a preface and addenda et corrigenda by Pierre Cachia. Cambridge: Cambridge University Press, 2 vol., reprint Librairie du Liban.

Yaʿqūb, ʾImīl Badīʿ. 2006. *Mawsūʿat ʿulūm al-luġa al-ʿarabiyya*. Bayrūt: Dār al-kutub al-ʿilmiyya, 10 vol.

CHAPTER 10

On Interpretation of the Pronoun *huwa* in 112/1 of the Qur'ān: *Tafsīr* and Grammar

Haruko Sakaedani

Introduction

The pronoun *huwa* in *qul huwa llāhu 'aḥad allāhu l-ṣamad* (Q. 112/1) is often interpreted as a topic, *allāh* its comment, and *'aḥad*[1] its apposition or the second comment, as shown below[2] :

Sahih International	"Say, 'He is Allah, [who is] One,'"
Muhsin Khan	"Say (O Muhammad (Peace be upon him)): 'He is Allah, (the) One."
Pickthall	"Say: He is Allah, the One!"
Yusuf Ali	"Say: He is Allah, the One and Only"
Shakir	"Say: He, Allah, is One"
Dr. Ghali	"Say, 'He is Allah, The Only One,'.

As for John A. Arberry (1905–1969; Arberry 1955: 361), he translates this verse as "Say: 'He is God, One,'. This paper examines the proposition that *huwa* is a pronoun of the matter (*ḍamīr al-ša'n*), as evidenced by descriptions in *tafsīr*-s and grammar books.

1 Previous Studies

1.1 *The Pronoun of the Matter* (ḍamīr al-ša'n)

The pronoun of the matter (*ḍamīr al-ša'n*) is a kind of cataphoric pronoun that refers to the sentence that follows the pronoun.

1 On the meaning of *'aḥad* as "anyone", while *wāḥid* is "one, unique", and as a possible foreign word of Hebrew origin, *e(ḥ)ḥād*, cf. Dye 2017:343–344.

2 https://legacy.quran.com/112 (accessed on September 13, 2018). Shakir's translation regards Allāh (*allāhu*) as an apposition of He (*huwa*). Refer to the interpretation of Bāqūlī/Zağğāğ *'I'rāb* (II, 564) described in the beginning of § 4.

 | DOI:10.1163/9789004515895_012

According to Badawi & Abdel Haleem (2008: 994), at the entry of *huwa*, *huwa* of Q. 112/1 is referred as pronoun of the fact (*ḍamīr al-šaʾn*) or pronoun of the story (pronoun that anticipates a whole subsequent clause) (*ḍamīr al-qiṣṣa*) and is translated as 'the fact is…', and 'the situation is…'. 'The fact of the matter is: God is One' is shown as an interpretation of the verse *huwa llāhu ʾaḥad*.

Ziyādī (2006: 237) stated that *ḍamīr al-šaʾn* is characterized by its ambiguity (that is, its referent does not precede it), its clarity in the sentence that follows it (*al-ʾamr*), and its emphasis of the matter (*al-šaʾn*). He also states that *ḍamīr al-šaʾn* in the Qurʾān is divided into three categories: independent pronouns, suffix pronouns, and omitted (*maḥḏūf*) pronouns, and that examples of *ḍamīr al-šaʾn* in independent forms without 'sudden *ʾiḏā*' (*ʾiḏā al-fuǧāʾiyya*)[3] can be found in Q. 18/38, Q. 34/27,[4] and Q. 112/1 (Ziyādī 2006: 243).

As for Modern Arabic, Bloch (1990) and Badawi et al. (2004; 2016) describe *ḍamīr al-šaʾn* limiting it to suffixed pronouns attached to *ʾinna* etc., as independent pronouns are scarcely used as *ḍamīr al-šaʾn* in Modern Arabic.[5]

Bloch (1990) claims that *ḍamīr al-šaʾn* is not a referential pronoun, but a 'dummy' pronoun that has no content or referentiality, that is, that such pronouns are used after *ʾinna* and its sisters (*ʾinna wa-ʾaḫawātuhā*) to keep the verb-subject word order, as in: *ʾannahu laysat tuġannī ḥamāmatun* ("that no dove cooed"), which cannot be a correct or sound clause without the pronoun *-hu*: **ʾanna laysat tuġannī ḥamāmatun*. In his opinion, *huwa* in the verse (Q. 112/1) must not be confused with *ḍamīr al-šaʾn*; it is another kind of pro-

3 There are a total of 12 examples of *ḍamīr al-šaʾn* with 'sudden *ʾiḏā*' given by Ziyādī (2006), that is, Q. 7/107, 108, 117, 16/4, 20/20 (Ziyādī writes 20/19), 21/18, 97, 26/32, 33, 45 (Ziyādī writes 40), 36/77 (Ziyādī writes 36/57), and 67/16, but in eight of them (Q. 7/107, 108, 16/4, 20/20, 21/18, 26/32, 33, and 36/77), the pronouns (*huwa* and *hiya*) are followed only by indefinite noun phrases, as can be seen in the following examples: *fa-ʾalqā ʿaṣāhu fa-ʾiḏā hiya ṯuʿbānun mubīnun* (Q. 7/107, "So he threw his staff, and suddenly it was a serpent, manifest"); *fa-nazaʿa yadahu fa-ʾiḏā hiya bayḍāʾu li-l-nāẓirīna* (Q. 7/108, "And he drew out his hand; thereupon it was white for the observers"). I question the inclusion of such pronouns in *ḍamīr al-šaʾn*, which introduces a sentence. Regarding Q. 7/117, 26/45, and 67/16, the pronoun *hiya* is followed by a verb or a verb and its object. Since the expression *fa-ʾiḏā* must be followed by a nominal sentence, it is inevitable that the anaphoric pronoun *hiya* is used just after *fa-ʾiḏā* in these verses. With regard to Q. 21/97: […] *fa-ʾiḏā hiya šāḫiṣatun ʾabṣāru allaḏīna kafarū* "[…] then suddenly the eyes of those who disbelieved will be staring", the pronoun *hiya* is followed by a complete nominal sentence in which a comment precedes its topic. Ibn Hišām al-ʾAnṣārī (d. 761/1360) uses such a pronoun, *hiya*, in this verse as an example of *ḍamīr al-šaʾn* in his *Muġnī al-labīb* (II, 103). We have avoided an in-depth discussion of this issue here. (The translations of the verses are from Sahih International.)

4 For these two verses, cf. *infra* § 5.

5 According to Ziyādī (2006), pronouns of the fact (*ḍamīr al-šaʾn*) in suffix pronoun form following *ʾinna* and *ʾanna* occur thirty times in the Qurʾān.

noun with an obscure function. Bloch (1990: 34) also regards the pronoun *-nī*[6] as *ḍamīr al-šaʾn*, because its usage is parallel to *-hu*, which is *ḍamīr al-šaʾn*:[7]

a. yā Mūsā innahu anā llāhu l-ʿazīzu l-ḥakīmu
"Moses, I am God, the All-mighty, All-wise" Q 27: 9
b. yā Mūsā innī anā rabbuka fa-ḫlaʿ naʿlayka
"Moses, I am your Lord; put off your shoes" Q 20: 12
c. innanī anā llāhu lā ilāha illā anā
"I am God, there is no God but I" Q 20: 14
d. yā Mūsā ʾinnī anā llāhu rabbu l-ʿālamīn
"Moses, I am God, the Lord of all being" Q 28: 30

On the other hand, Badawi et al. (2004: 337; 2016: 382) call *ḍamīr al-šaʾn* an anticipatory pronoun, and state that after the sentence modifiers *ʾinna*, *ʾanna*, etc. (that is, *ʾinna* and its sisters), a default *-hu*[8] (masculine singular, but rarely feminine *-hā*) must be used when the modifier is followed by a verbal sentence, and that this *-hu* is an anticipatory pronoun representing the sentence to come.

William Wright (1830–1889; Wright 1955) also describes *ḍamīr al-šaʾn*, limiting it to suffixed pronouns attached to *ʾinna*, among others. In his discussion of *ʾinna* and *ʾanna*, Wright (1955: respectively I, 285 and I, 293) also states that the pronoun *-hu* often represents and anticipates a subsequent clause. He calls it *ḍamīr al-šaʾn* or *ḍamīr al-qiṣṣa* and states that it is masculine or feminine according to the gender of the subject in the following sentence. He gives the following verse as an example of the feminine (II, 299): *fa-ʾinnahā lā taʿmā al-ʾabṣāru* (Q. 22/46,[9] "For it is not the eyes that become blind").

Based on Ǧurǧānī (d. 471/1078; *Muqtaṣid* I, 421) and Zamaḫšarī (d. 538/1144; Ibn Yaʿīš *ŠM* III, 114), Peled (2009: 212–213) summarised the basic constructions of *ḍamīr al-šaʾn* as follows:

---

6 In a precise sense, *-n-* is *nūn al-wiqāya* (*nūn* of protection), so the pronoun is only *-ī*.

7 He refuses to state that the pronoun *-nī* is a subject and *ʾanā* is its emphasis in Q. 20/11–12 (*yā mūsā ʾinnī ʾanā rabbuka* "Oh, Musa, I am your lord"), Q. 20/14, and Q. 28/30, claiming that these contexts do not suggest contrastiveness like 'I alone am God'.

8 Badawi et al. (2004:338; 2016: 383) also refer to the unusual occurrence of a feminine pronoun *-hā*. It can be considered that *-hā* occurs by attraction to the subject of the verbal sentence when it is a grammatically feminine singular, or sometimes it may be simply cataphoric.

9 Wright writes Q. 22/45, according to Flügel's version.

		Ǧurǧānī	Zamaḫšarī
(A)	*mubtadaʾ+ḫabar*	*huwa zaydun munṭaliqun.*	
(B)	*kāna* (and its sisters)	*kāna ḫaraǧa ʾaḫawāka.*	*laysa ḫalaqa llāhu miṯlahu.* (verbal sentence)
			kāna ʾanta ḫayrun minhu. (nominal sentence)
(C)	*ʾinna* (and its sisters)	*ʾinnahu man yaʾti rabbahu muǧriman…* (Q. 20/74) (conditional sentence)	
			ʾinnahu ʾamatu llāhi ḏāhibatun. (nominal sentence)
(D)	*ẓanna* (and its sisters)	*ẓanantuhu zaydun ḫāriǧun.*	*ẓanantuhu zaydun qāʾimun.* (nominal sentence)
			ḥasibtuhu qāma ʾaḫūka. (verbal sentence)

Ḍamīr al-šaʾn may occur as a separate pronoun as in (A), an implicit pronoun as in (B), or as an omitted (or implicit) pronoun as in (C) and (D) (Peled 2009: 213).

As for *huwa* in *huwa llāhu ʾaḥadun* (Q. 112/1), Peled (2009:214) insists that the analysis of *huwa* in this case, as *ḍamīr al-šaʾn*, was not universally accepted.

Peled (1990: 5) regards *huwa* in Q. 112/1 as non-referential. He shows three major types of syntactic interpretations of Q. 112/1, as follows:

ḍamīr al-šaʾn—mubtadaʾ | *ḫabar*

mubtadaʾ | *ḫabar*

(A) *huwa* | *allāhu* | *ʾaḥadun*

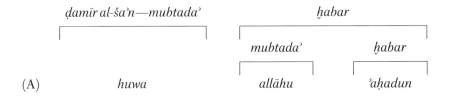

(B) 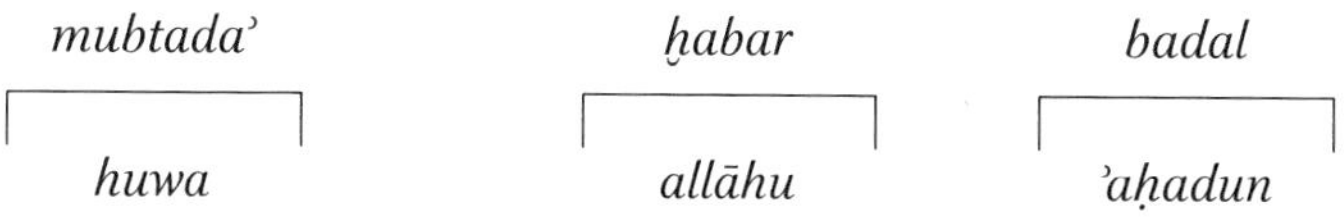

(C) 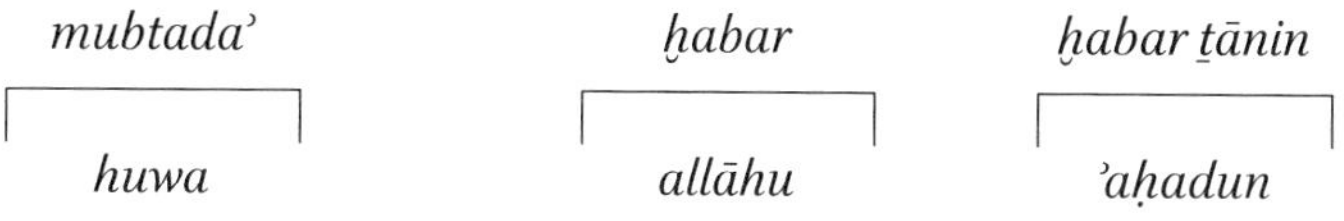

Peled (1990: 6) rejects these three because (A) does not explain the function of *huwa*,[10] as the indefinite noun (*'aḥadun*) in (B) is regarded as an apposition of the definite noun (*allāhu*), and because the term *ḫabar ṯānin* in (C) does not specify the topic; furthermore, the relationship between the two comments is unclear.

He also rejects the following analysis as it is unsuitable in this context (Peled 1990: 6, fn. 7):

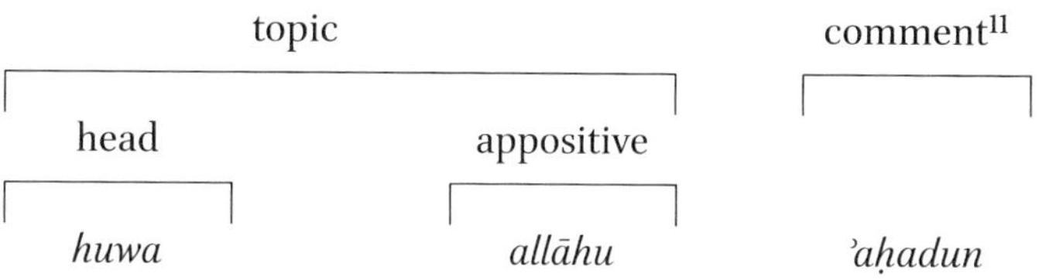

Peled (1990: 14) presents the analysis (D) that accounts for the function *ḫabar ṯānin* assigned to *'aḥadun*:

(D) 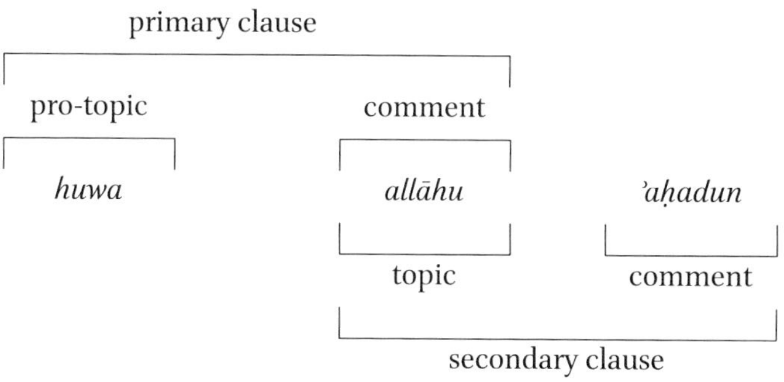

He claims that *huwa* is a pro-topic, a non-referential pronoun that cannot be replaced by a referential nominal, and its function is to fill the topic slot in the

10 Peled (1990) also insists that the exponent for non-referential pronoun consists of one word rather than a full clause.

11 Peled (1990) writes respectively "subject" and "predicate".

primary clause so as to create a comment position readily available for *allāhu*; because of this, *huwa* and *allāhu* can function as full topics in the secondary clause, and that *allāhu* shows new information in the primary clause and *ʾaḥadun* shows new information in the secondary clause (Peled 1990: 14–15).

1.2 Naming the Pronoun of the Matter (*ḍamīr al-šaʾn*)

Ziyādī (2006) mentions, as names of the pronoun of the matter, names other than *ḍamīr al-šaʾn* such as *ḍamīr al-maǧhūl*, *ḍamīr al-ʾamr*, *ḍamīr al-ḥadīṯ*, *ḍamīr al-qiṣṣa*, *ḍamīr al-ʿimād*, and *ḍamīr al-ḥāla*. According to him, three of these names—*al-šaʾn* (matter), *al-ḥadīṯ* (speech), and *al-qiṣṣa* (story)—are terms of the Basra school of grammarians. On the other hand, *al-maǧhūl* (unknown) is a Kufan term. This description almost concurs with that of Ibn Hišām al-ʾAnṣārī, who states that *ḍamīr al-šaʾn* and *ḍamīr al-qiṣṣa* are called *ḍamīr al-maǧhūl* by the Kufan grammarians (cf. *Muġnī* II, 103).

Wright, however, regards *ḍamīr al-maǧhūl* as a name of a pronoun *-hu* following *rubba* ("many a…") because the noun to which it relates has not previously been mentioned: *wa-rubbahu ʿaṭiban ʾanqaḏta min ʿaṭabih*[12] ("and many a perishing (man) hast thou saved from destruction" (Wright 1955: II, 214).

Peled (2006: 558) points out that grammarians present the pronoun *-hu* in *rubbahu raǧulan* 'many a man'. Zamaḫšarī describes this pronoun as indefinite, vague, and non-referential (*yurmā bihi min ġayri qaṣdin ʾilā muḍmarin lahu* 'it is thrown without aim at anything kept for it') (Ibn Yaʿīš *ŠM* III, 118), and that, though this is similar to *ḍamīr al-šaʾn*, as both of them require *tafsīr* (exponent), Ibn Yaʿīš explains the difference between them as that *ḍamīr al-šaʾn* is expounded by a sentence while the pronoun attached to *rubba* is expounded by a single word (*ŠM* III, 118).

Wright uses the term *ḍamīr al-ʿimād*, which serves as a prop or support to the sentence, with a similar meaning to *ḍamīr al-faṣl* (the pronoun of separation, that is, the pronoun that separates the topic *mubtadaʾ* and the comment *ḫabar*, cf. Wright 1955: II, 259). According to Peled (2006: 557), some grammarians regarded *ʾiyyā* as *ʿimād*, a prop word for the pronoun attached to it.

ʿAbābnih (2006: 30–31) summarizes transitions of the terms. As for *ʿimād*, Basran grammarians like Ibn al-Sarrāǧ (d. 316/929), Zaǧǧāǧ (d. 311/923), and Zamaḫšarī used the Kufan term *ʿimād* to express *ḍamīr al-faṣl*. Though they were tracing this usage to Kufan grammarians, ʾAbū Ǧaʿfar al-Naḥḥās (d. 338/950) used it as if it were his term.[13]

12 *ʿaṭabihi* becomes *ʿaṭabih* to rhyme in the end (cf. Wright 1955:II, 214).

13 See footnote 17 for a discussion of the usages of the term *ʿimād* with a focus on Ṭabarī.

ʿAbābnih does not mention that *ḍamīr al-ʿimād* means *ḍamīr al-šaʾn*. According to him, *ḍamīr al-šaʾn*, *al-qiṣṣa*, and *al-ḥadīṯ* are Basran terms that correspond to the Kufan term *al-maǧhūl*. The terms *ḍamīr al-šaʾn*, *al-qiṣṣa*, and *al-ḥadīṯ* had already been mentioned in the books of Ibn al-Sarrāǧ, who used the term *al-maǧhūl*, which he traced to Kufan grammarians. Zamaḫšarī made the same connections. This pronoun was named *ḥadīṯ* and *qiṣṣa* because it may stand for the speech or the story that is mentioned after the pronoun. Moreover, this pronoun is always in the 3rd person, because ambiguity is intended. Thus, the Kufan grammarians called it *maǧhūl*.

2 Descriptions in *Tafsīr*-s

2.1 *Preceding Contexts of the Verse*

Many *Tafsīr*-s state that the verse Q. 112/1 is an answer to a question or a request such as 'Describe your Lord' as found in Ṭabarī (d. 310/923):

1. The polytheists asked the Messenger of God about the origin of Lord of the might. God revealed this chapter as an answer to them.
2. [The chapter] was revealed as Jews asked him. They said to him: 'This is God, He created the creatures. Then who created God?'. Thus, it was revealed as an answer to them.
3. [The chapter] was revealed as an answer to the polytheists who asked him to trace for them the Lord the Blessed and Sublime [to his origin].
4. […] The polytheists said to the Prophet 'trace for us your Lord [to his origin]' so God revealed *qul huwa llāhu ʾaḥad allāhu l-ṣamad*.
5. […] The polytheists said 'Muḥammad, let us know about your Lord. Describe for us your Lord. What is he? What is he made of?'. Thus, God revealed *qul huwa llāhu ʾaḥad* to the end of the chapter.
6. […] The leaders of the factions said that [= the following words]: 'Trace for us your Lord [to his origin]'. Thus, Ǧibrīl brought this.
7. […] The polytheists said to the Prophet, 'Trace for us your Lord [to his origin]'. Thus, God the Blessed and Sublime revealed *qul huwa llāhu ʾaḥad*.
8. […] According to the [man] who said 'He revealed that for the Jews' question', a group of the Jews came to the Prophet and said 'Muḥammad, this is God. He created creatures. So, who created Him?'. Thus, the Prophet got angry and the colour of his face changed. He attacked them because of anger for the sake of his Lord.

Then Ǧibrīl came to him and made him calm, and said 'Make lower your wing on you, Muḥammad'. The answer for what they asked him about came to him from God. He said, God says, *qul huwa llāhu ʾaḥad*. When the Prophet recited it for them, they said, 'Describe for us your Lord. How is his creation? How is his upper arm? How was his forearm?'. Thus, the Prophet became angrier and attacked them. Then, Ǧibrīl came to him and said to him something like his words and brought to him the answer of what they asked him about [Q. 39/67].

9. [...] Some people of the Jews came to the Prophet and said 'Trace for us your Lord [to his origin]'. Then *qul huwa llāhu ʾaḥad* was revealed until the end of the chapter.

ṬABARĪ *Ǧāmiʿ* XXIV, 727–729[14]

In Zamaḫšarī, almost the same as mentioned above, that is, "Qurayš said, 'Muḥammad, describe for us your Lord that you are calling him to'. Then it [Q. 112/1] was revealed" (*qālat qurayš: yā muḥammad ṣif lanā rabbaka allaḏī tadʿūnā ʾilayhi fa-nazalat, Tafsīr* 1228). Afterwards, he explains the meaning of *ʾaḥad* of *qul huwa llāhu ʾaḥad* and some differences in the recitation of this verse (cf. *Tafsīr* 1228).

Bayḍāwī (d. 685/1288 or 691/1292) says the same: "Qurayš said, 'Muḥammad, describe for us your Lord that you are calling him to'. Then it [Q. 112/1] was revealed" (*ʾiḏ ruwiya ʾanna qurayš qālū: yā muḥammad ṣif lanā rabbaka allaḏī tadʿūnā ʾilayhi fa-nazalat, ʾAnwār* V, 347).

For Maḥallī (d. 864/1459–1460) and Suyūṭī (d. 911/1505), the Prophet was asked about his Lord, then *qul huwa llāhu ʾaḥad* was revealed. For them, *allāhu* is *huwa*'s comment and *ʾaḥad* is its apposition or the second comment (they do not refer to *huwa* as *ḍamīr al-šaʾn*, cf. Maḥallī & Suyūṭī *Ǧalālayn* 604).

2.2 Ḍamīr al-šaʾn *in* Tafsīr-s

Ṭabarī introduces some opinions of people of the Arabic language about Q. 112/1:

> [1] What makes it [*ʾaḥad*] nominative is *allāh*, and *huwa* is a prop or support (*ʿimād*) at the rank of *-hu* in *ʾinnahu ʾanā llāhu l-ʿazīzu l-ḥakīmu*.[15]

---

14 Cf. the text in the appendix *infra*.

15 Q. 27/9: "Oh Mūsā, surely it is I, Allah (or I am Allah), the Mighty, the Wise". Ṭabarī explains *-hu* in this verse as follows: "*hāʾ* [he means *-hu*] in *ʾinnahu* is a prop *hāʾ*. It is a noun (*ism*) which does not appear in the speech of some people of the Arabic language. Some

> [2] No, it [*ʾaḥad*] is—even though it was indefinite—nominative by recommencement like *hāḏā baʿlī šayḫun*.[16] He said *huwa llāhu* ("He is God"). An answer to words of people who said to him, 'What is your object of worship?' then he said 'He is God'. Then it is said to him: 'What is he?' He said 'He is one'. (*bal huwa marfūʿ—wa-ʾin kāna nakira—bi-li-stiʾnāf, ka-qawlihi: "hāḏā baʿlī šayḫun" wa-qāla "huwa llāhu". ǧawāb li-kalām qawm qālū lahu: mā allaḏī taʿbudu? fa-qāla: huwa llāhu. ṯumma qīla lahu: fa-mā huwa? qāla: huwa ʾaḥad*, Ṭabarī *Ǧāmiʿ* XXIV, 729–730)

Though he does not use the term *ḍamīr al-šaʾn* in (1), he explains the verse quite a bit closer to it, using the term *ʿimād*.[17] On the other hand, he interprets *huwa* as an anaphoric pronoun based on the preceding context of the verse.

Zaǧǧāǧ, after dealing with the issue of whether the end of *ʾaḥadun* is read with *tanwīn* or not,[18] states the following:

> *huwa* may be for the fact (*ʾamr*) as you say *huwa zaydun qāʾimun* "(It is that) Zayd is standing", that is, *al-ʾamr zayd qāʾim* "the fact is that Zayd is standing". Its meaning is *al-ʾamr allāh ʾaḥad* "the fact is that God is one". (*wa-yaǧūzu ʾan yakūna "huwa" li-l-ʾamr kamā taqūlu "huwa zay-*

---

grammarians of Kufa said that it is 'unknown (*maǧhūl*) *hāʾ*'. It means that the fact (*al-ʾamr*) and the matter (*al-šaʾn*) are that 'I am God'" (*wa-l-hāʾ allatī fī qawlihi "ʾinnahu" hāʾ ʿimād, wa-huwa ism lā yaẓharu fī qawl baʿḍ ʾahl al-ʿarabiyya. wa-kāna baʿḍ naḥwiyyī al-kūfa yaqūlu: hiya al-hāʾ al-maǧhūla, wa-maʿnāhā: ʾinna al-ʾamr wa-l-šaʾn, ʾanā allāh, Ǧāmiʿ* XVIII, 13–14).

As mentioned above, Kufan grammarians call the pronoun of the matter *ḍamīr al-maǧhūl*, so 'unknown (*maǧhūl*) *hāʾ*' can be considered as an expression that came from that.

16 Q. 11/72: "This, my husband, is an old man".

17 Note that this is not a 'prop, support' as Wright said (1955:II, 259). ʾAbū Ḫuḍayr (2014:139–141) notes that the term *ʿimād* is referred to as *ḍamīr al-faṣl*, that is, what divides (*faṣala*) between topic (*mubtadaʾ*) and comment (*ḫabar*), which the Kufan grammarians called *ʿimād*; with regard to Ṭabarī, the term *ʿimād* includes more than a meaning, and its function in the sentence is to divide (*faṣl*) between the affairs as follows: (1) topic and comment, (2) topic of *kāna* and its sisters (and their comment), (3) two objects of *ẓanna* and its sisters, and (4) topic, comment, and circumstantial expression (*ḥāl*). The term *ʿimād* in his *Tafsīr*-s has two main meanings: (1) *ḍamīr al-šaʾn* and (2) *ḍamīr al-faṣl*. With regard to the former, the Kufan grammarians sometimes call it *al-maǧhūl*, 'unknown'. It includes pronouns used in a sentence that begins with *mā* for negation, as in Q. 2/96. In this case, Ṭabarī allows for *ḍamīr al-šaʾn* and the comment to precede the topic, following the ideas of the Kufan grammarians.

18 While this paper does not treat this theme, it is an important argument that other interpreters have dealt with.

dun qāʾimun", ʾay al-ʾamr zayd qāʾim, al-maʿnā al-ʾamr allāh ʾaḥad, Zaǧǧāǧ *Maʿānī* V, 377)

He does not use the term *ḍamīr al-šaʾn*, either, but regards the pronoun *huwa* as something for the fact (*ʾamr*), so his explanation is very close to *ḍamīr al-šaʾn*.

Zamaḫšarī, who is a grammarian, describes this verse as an answer to a question from Qurayš as mentioned in the previous section, but in addition, he explains *huwa* as a *ḍamīr al-šaʾn*, as shown below:

> *huwa* is a pronoun of the matter (*ḍamīr al-šaʾn*) and *allāhu ʾaḥadun* is the matter (*al-šaʾn*), as your utterance: *huwa zaydun munṭaliqun* "(It is that) Zayd is going on / Zayd is away", as if it is said that *al-šaʾn hāḏā wa-huwa ʾanna allāha wāḥidun lā ṯāniya lahu* "the matter is this and it is that God is one, without an alternative for him".
>
> If you say 'What is the role of *huwa*?', I say 'Nominative because of its being a topic [of the nominal sentence] and the comment is the sentence'.
>
> If you say 'then the sentence that exists as a comment must have in itself what returns to the topic.[19] Where is *rāǧiʿ* ?', I maintain that the status for this sentence [as a comment] is the same as that for a single word in the utterance *zaydun ġulāmuka* 'Zayd is your lad' because it [*ġulāmuka*] has a meaning that is equal to the topic [*zaydun*]. This means that His saying *allāhu ʾaḥad* regards the matter (*al-šaʾn*), about which *huwa* is an expression.
>
> *Zaydun ʾabūhu munṭaliqun* "As for Zayd, his father is going on / his father is away" is not the same. *Zaydun* and the sentence [*ʾabūhu munṭaliqun*] refer to two different referents; thus, they need to be connected [by something (that is, a pronoun)].
>
> (*"huwa" ḍamīr al-šaʾn wa-"allāhu ʾaḥadun" huwa al-šaʾn. ka-qawlika: "huwa zaydun munṭaliqun": ka-ʾannahu qīla: al-šaʾn hāḏā wa-huwa ʾanna llāha wāḥidun lā ṯāniya lahu.*
>
> *fa-ʾin qulta: mā maḥall huwa? qultu: al-rafʿ ʿalā al-ibtidāʾ, wa-l-ḫabar al-ǧumla.*
>
> *fa-ʾin qulta: fa-l-ǧumla al-wāqiʿa ḫabaran lā budda*[20] *fīhā min rāǧiʿ ʾilā al-mubtadaʾ fa-ʾayna al-rāǧiʿ! qultu: ḥukm hāḏihi al-ǧumla ḥukm al-mufrad fī qawlika zaydun ġulāmuka fī ʾannahu huwa al-mubtadaʾ fī al-maʿnā. wa-ḏālika ʾanna qawlahu: allāhu ʾaḥadun huwa al-šaʾn allaḏī huwa ʿibāra ʿanhu*

19 *Rāǧiʿ*, what returns to the topic, is a pronoun that refers to the topic, though this term is usually used for a "resumptive pronoun" of a relative clause.

20 This part is revised as "*ḫabar al-ʾabad*" but it is not correct.

wa-laysa ka-ḏālika zaydun ʾabūhu munṭaliqun, fa-ʾinna zaydan wa-l-ǧumla yadullāni ʿalā maʿnayayni muḫtalifayni fa-lā budda mimmā yaṣilu baynahumā, Zamaḫšarī *Tafsīr* 1228)

3 *Ḍamīr al-šaʾn* in Grammatical Studies

Sībawayhi (d. 180/796?) quotes in his *Kitāb* Q. 112/1 only in the section about the ways to read *tanwīn* at the end of *ʾaḥadun* (*Kitāb* IV, 152, cf. ʿIbāda 2002: 244–246). He mentions pronouns equivalent to *ḍamīr al-šaʾn*, but the term *ḍamīr al-šaʾn* itself is not used. He explains it using the expression *mā fī ʾinnahu* (what is in *ʾinnahu*). Moreover, *ḍamīr al-šaʾn* in independent forms is ignored.

Sībawayhi describes *ḍamīr al-šaʾn* (though he never uses this term, as mentioned above) as suffix pronouns and omitted (*maḥḏūf*) pronouns in order to explain verb conjugations and noun inflections.

Examples of suffix pronouns (cf. *Kitāb* I, 69):

> *ʾinnahu man yaʾtinā naʾtihi* "(It is that) as for the man who comes to us, we come to him"
>
> *ʾinnahu ʾamatu llāhi ḏāhibatun* "(It is that) God's slave girl is going"

Examples of omitted pronouns (*Kitāb* I, 70–71):

> *laysa ḫalaqa llāhu miṯlahu* "It is not that God created his equivalent [= God did not create his equivalent]"
>
> *wa-laysa kulla l-nawā tulqī l-masākīnu* "It is not that the miserable people threw all the date pits [= The miserable people did not throw all the date pits]"
>
> *kāda tazīġu qulūbu farīqin minhum*[21] "(It is that) the hearts of a party of them had almost inclined"

In his *Muqtaḍab*, Mubarrad (d. 285/898 or 286/899) does not use the term *ḍamīr al-šaʾn*, either, and he also ignores *ḍamīr al-šaʾn* in independent forms. For instance, he gives some examples of *ḍamīr al-šaʾn* as an omitted pronoun, such as: *kāna ġulāmahu zaydun ḍāribun* "It was that Zayd is hitting his lad [= Zayd was hitting his lad]" (cf. *Muqtaḍab* IV, 99). In this sentence, the pronoun is hidden in *kāna*.

---

21 Q. 9/117. According to Hārūn's footnote (cf. Sībawayhi *Kitāb* I, 71, fn. 3), this way of reading (*tazīġu*) is mainstream, and Ḥamza (d. 156/772) and Ḥafṣ (d. 180/796) read it as *yazīġu*.

The example Sībawayhi quoted, too, is quoted: *wa-laysa kulla l-nawā yulqī l-masākīnu* (however, *yulqī* is masculine, cf. *Muqtaḍab* IV, 100, the pronoun hidden in *laysa*).

Ibn Ǧinnī (d. 392/1002) also mentions the verse Q. 112/1 *huwa llāhu ʾaḥadun* in the section where he explains *ḍamīr al-šaʾn*. He says that (*a*)*llāhu ʾaḥadun* is a *tafsīr* (exponent) of *huwa*. For a similar example, he gives the verse Q. 22/46 *ʾinnahā lā taʿmā al-ʾabṣāru* (lit. 'She is that the eyesight is not blind') and explains that *lā taʿmā al-ʾabṣāru* 'the eyesight is not blind' is the exponent of *-hā* so it is also regarded as *ḍamīr al-šaʾn*. (I, 105). He also points out that the verse *huwa llāhu ʾaḥadun*, (*a*)*llāhu ʾaḥadun* does not contain any personal pronouns that return to *huwa* (I, 106).

Zamaḫšarī also refers to the example of *ḍamīr al-šaʾn* of Q. 112/1. He states in *al-Mufaṣṣal*:

> They let a pronoun called *ḍamīr al-šaʾn* (the matter) or *al-qiṣṣa* (the story), which is [*ḍamīr*] *al-maǧhūl* (the unknown) in the Kufan school, precede before the sentence. That is like your utterance *huwa zaydun munṭaliqun*, that is, the matter and the speech (*al-ḥadīṯ*) is that Zayd is going on. One of the examples of such a pronoun is the word of the Sublime *qul huwa llāhu ʾaḥad*. Such a pronoun saliently appears in your utterance.
>
> *ẓanantuhu zaydun qāʾimun* "I thought that (it is that) Zayd was standing", *ḥasibtuhu qāma ʾaḫūka* "I thought that (it is that) your brother had stood", *ʾinnahu ʾamatu llāhi ḏāhibatun* "(It is that) God's slave girl is going", *ʾinnahu man yaʾtinā naʾtihi* "(It is that) as for the man who comes to us, we come to him", and in the revelation *ʾannahu lammā qāma ʿabdu llāhi*[22] "(It is that) when God's slave stood…". (*wa-yuqaddimūna qabla al-ǧumla ḍamīran yusammā ḍamīr al-šaʾn wa-l-qiṣṣa wa-huwa al-maǧhūl ʿinda al-kūfiyyīna wa-ḏālika naḥwa qawlika huwa zaydun munṭaliqun ʾay al-šaʾn wa-l-ḥadīṯ zaydun munṭaliqun wa-minhu qawluhu taʿālā "qul huwa llāhu ʾaḥad" wa-yattaṣilu bārizan fī qawlika "ẓanantuhu zaydun qāʾimun" wa-"ḥasibtuhu qāma ʾaḫūka" wa-"ʾinnahu ʾamatu llāhi ḏāhibatun" wa-"ʾinnahu man yaʾtinā naʾtihi" wa-fī al-tanzīl "wa-ʾannahu lammā qāma ʿabdu llāhi"*, Ibn Yaʿīš *ŠM* III, 114)

Thus, he mentions the verse Q. 112/1, that is, the example of *ḍamīr al-šaʾn* is also as an independent pronoun (cf. Ibn Yaʿīš *ŠM* III, 114). Ibn Yaʿīš (d. 643/1245) also explains it as a cataphoric pronoun in his *Šarḥ al-Mufaṣṣal* (III, 114–118).

---

22 Q. 72/19.

Ibn Mālik (d. 672/1274), who studied *al-Mufaṣṣal* under Ibn Yaʿīš, does not mention *ḍamīr al-šaʾn* in the section of personal pronouns in his *ʾAlfiyya*, but in the sections of *kāna* and its sisters (*ʾAlfiyya*, v. 153, 144) as *muḍmar al-šaʾn*,[23] and *ẓanna* and its sisters (*ʾAlfiyya*, v. 211, 219).

Ibn ʿAqīl (d. 769/1367), who wrote a commentary (*Šarḥ*), refers to *ḍamīr al-šaʾn* in the section of *ʾinna* and its sisters, that is, in his interpretation for v. 193 (*ʾAlfiyya*, v. 193, 193). However, none of them use *ḍamīr al-šaʾn* as an independent pronoun.

Ibn Hišām al-ʾAnṣārī gives seven kinds of the cataphoric pronouns in his *Šarḥ Šuḏūr al-ḏahab*, and shows *ḍamīr al-šaʾn* at the top, using the example of Q. 112/1:

> One of them [that is, cataphoric]: *ḍamīr al-šaʾn* category. Like *huwa*—or *hiya*—*zaydun qāʾimun* "(It is that) Zayd is standing" that is, the matter, the speech (*al-ḥadīṯ*) or the story (*al-qiṣṣa*). It is explained by the sentence that comes after it; It [the sentence] is the same speech and story. Some examples are: *qul huwa llāhu ʾaḥad, fa-ʾinnahā lā taʿmā al-ʾabṣāru.*[24] (*ʾaḥaduhā: bāb ḍamīr al-šaʾn, naḥwa: "huwa—ʾaw hiya—zaydun qāʾimun" ʾay: al-šaʾn wa-l-ḥadīṯ ʾaw al-qiṣṣa, fa-ʾinnahu mufassar bi-l-ǧumla baʿdahu; fa-ʾinnahā nafs al-ḥadīṯ wa-l-qiṣṣa, wa-minhu: "qul huwa llāhu ʾaḥad" "fa-ʾinnahā lā taʿmā al-ʾabṣāru"*, Ibn Hišām al-ʾAnṣārī *ŠŠ* 136)

4 Q. 112/1 in *ʾiʿrāb al-Qurʾān* Books

By and large, *huwa* in Q. 112/1 is mainly explained as *ḍamīr al-šaʾn*, or what is close to *ḍamīr al-šaʾn*, in the early *ʾiʿrāb al-Qurʾān* books, as follows:

---

23 ʿAbābnih (2006:27) summarizes the change of the terms which indicate personal pronouns as follows: first, Sībawayhi used *ʾiḍmār*, as well as the term *muḍmar*, many times in his *Kitāb*. On the other hand, the term *ḍamīr* seems to appear after Sībawayhi. ʿAbābnih supposes that it may be used for the first time in *Maʿānī al-Qurʾān* of al-ʾAḫfaš al-ʾAwsaṭ (d. 215/830). Afterwards, Basran scholars began to use *ḍamīr* as a well-known term while the usage of the term *muḍmar* was also common until the age of Zamaḫšarī, though it has become less used. However, Ayoub (2019:35) points out that the term *ḍamīr* occurs in Sībawayhi's *Kitāb* six times. Five of them clearly mean personal pronouns, though one of them refers to the mind of a speaker. According to one of the reviewer, *muḍmar al-šaʾn* is only found in the *ʾAlfiyya*, and the reason for choosing *muḍmar* instead of *ḍamīr* plausibly lies in the meter of the *ʾAlfiyya*.

24 Q. 22/46.

> [1] *huwa* in Q. 112/1 is the pronoun of the fact and the matter (*al-ḍamīr li-l-ʾamr wa-l-šaʾn*), so this verse means "say, the matter and the fact are 'Allāh is One'". [2] *huwa* refers to Allāh, and *allāhu* is an apposition of *huwa* and explains it. (*fa-ʾammā qawluhu "qul huwa llāhu ʾaḥad" fa-qīla: al-ḍamīr li-l-ʾamr wa-l-šaʾn, ʾay: qul al-ʾamr wa-l-šaʾn "allāhu ʾaḥad" wa-qīla: "huwa" ʾišāra ʾilā "allāh", wa-qawluhu "allāhu" badal minhu, mufassir lahu,* Bāqūlī/Zaǧǧāǧ *ʾIʿrāb* II, 564)

Naḥḥās explains that *huwa* of Q. 112/1 is nominative because of its *ibtidāʾ* (being a topic of a nominal sentence), and it means speech (*ḥadīṯ*), that is, the speech which is the truth that Allāh is One (cf. Naḥḥās *ʾIʿrāb* V, 194).

Ibn Ḫālawayhi (d. 370/980) does not regard *huwa* in Q. 112/1 as *ḍamīr al-šaʾn*, but as a nominative because of its *ibtidāʾ* (being a topic of a nominal sentence). Here *allāhu* is its comment (cf. Ibn Ḫālawayhi *ʾIʿrāb* 242), and *ʾaḥadun* is the apposition of *allāhu* (cf. Ibn Ḫālawayhi *ʾIʿrāb* 243). He regards this verse as an answer to the question 'inform us about Allāh the sublime, is he made of gold, silver or musk?' (cf. Ibn Ḫālawayhi *ʾIʿrāb* 243).

For ʾAbū ʿAlī al-Fārisī (d. 377/987), the pronoun *huwa* in Q. 112/1 is explained, with *hiya* in Q. 21/97,[25] as what is explained by a sentence; that is, the verse Q. 112/1 means *al-ʾamr allāhu ʾaḥadun* ("the fact is that Allāh is One"). He does not use the term *ḍamīr al-šaʾn*, but he explains it as *ḍamīr al-šaʾn* (cf. *ʾIġfāl* 333).

Ḫaṭīb al-Tabrīzī (d. 502/1109) does not mention Q. 112/1 (cf. *Mulaḫḫaṣ*) but Zamaḫšarī says about *huwa* in Q. 112/1 that it is nominative because of its *ibtidāʾ* (being a topic of a nominal sentence), and its comment is the sentence (*Nukat* 375); that is, he does not use the term *ḍamīr al-šaʾn*, but he explains it as *ḍamīr al-šaʾn*.

ʿUkbarī (d. 616/1219) presents two explanations for *huwa* in Q. 112/1; that is, (1) it is *ḍamīr al-šaʾn*, and (2) the verse is an answer to the question 'is your Lord made of copper or gold?'. Thus, *huwa* is a topic, *allāhu* is its comment and *ʾaḥadun* is an apposition or a comment of an omitted topic. It may be accepted that *allāhu* is an apposition and *ʾaḥadun* is its comment, too (cf. *ʾImlāʾ* II, 297).

Finally, Zakariyyā al-ʾAnṣārī (d. 926/1520?) clearly states that *huwa* in Q. 112/1 is *ḍamīr al-šaʾn* (cf. ʾAnṣārī *ʾIʿrāb* 505).

---

25 Refer to footnote 3.

5 *Ḍamīr al-šaʾn* in Q. 18/38 and Q. 34/27

Here, let us take a brief look at *ḍamīr al-šaʾn* other than one in Q. 112/1. According to Ziyādī (2006), there are two more pronouns of the matter in the Qur'ān, namely Q. 18/38 and Q. 34/27:

> *lākinnā*[26] *huwa llāhu rabbī* (Q. 18/38)
> But as for me, He is Allāh, my Lord [= It (the matter) is that Allāh is my Lord];

> *bal huwa llāhu l-ʿazīzu l-ḥakīmu* (Q. 34/27)
> Rather, He is Allāh, the Exalted in Might, the Wise [= It (the matter) is that Allāh is the Exalted in Might, the Wise].

Let us look at the explanations of these two pronouns in 1. *Tafsīr*-s, 2. *ʾiʿrāb al-Qurʾān* books, and 3. grammar books.

5.1 *Q. 18/38 and Q. 34/27 in* Tafsīr*-s*

As for Q. 18/38, Ṭabarī explains that its meaning is *wa-lākin ʾanā ʾaqūlu: huwa llāhu rabbī* "although I say: he is Allāh, my Lord". However, he mostly leaves the pronoun *huwa* (cf. *Ǧāmiʿ* XV, 263–264), and *huwa* of Q. 34/27 (cf. *Ǧāmiʿ* XIX, 288), unexplained.

Zamaḫšarī clearly states that *huwa* in Q. 18/38 is *ḍamīr al-šaʾn*, and that the fact (*ʾamr*) is *allāhu rabbī* "Allāh is my Lord", but he regards this sentence (*allāhu rabbī*) as a comment of (*ʾa*)*nā*, not *huwa*,[27] and the pronoun which returns to (*ʾa*)*nā* is *-ī* of *rabbī* (cf. *Tafsīr* 620). For Q. 34/27, he states that *huwa* is a pronoun which returns only to *allāhu* or *ḍamīr al-šaʾn*, the same as *huwa* in Q. 112/1 (cf. *Tafsīr* 874).

For Bayḍāwī the pronoun *huwa* in Q. 18/38 is *ḍamīr al-šaʾn* and it is a comment of (*ʾa*)*nā* because of the sentence which is regarded as the comment of *huwa*. This *huwa* may also be a pronoun for *allāhu*, and *allāhu* is its apposition and *rabbī* is the comment. This sentence is the comment of (*ʾa*)*nā*. (cf. *ʾAnwār* III, 281). As for the pronoun *huwa* in Q. 34/27, it is for *allāhu* or for the fact (*ʾamr*) (cf. *ʾAnwār* IV, 247).

Maḥallī & Suyūṭī say that *huwa* of Q. 18/38 is *ḍamīr al-šaʾn* and that the sentence after it explains this *huwa*. (*Lākin*)-*nā huwa* means "I say *ʾanā ʾaqūlu*". (cf. *Ǧalālayn* 298). They do not explain *huwa* of Q. 34/27 (cf. *Ǧalālayn* 431).

---

26 *wa-lākinnā* < *wa-lākin-ʾanā*, *ʾa* is omitted according to many *Tafsīr*-s.
27 This matter needs more investigation but it may be interpreted close to *ḍamīr al-faṣl*.

As for the two *huwa*-s which appear in the middle of the chapters, being different from *huwa* of Q. 112/1, their preceding contexts are not discussed in *Tafsīr*-s.

Broadly speaking, Zamaḫšarī began to interpret these *huwa*-s as *ḍamīr al-šaʾn* in *Tafsīr*-s; however, Zamaḫšarī's explanation of *huwa* in Q. 18/38 contains a description which does not fully explain *ḍamīr al-šaʾn* (cf. above fn. 27), meaning it requires more investigation.

5.2 *Q. 18/28 and Q. 34/27 in* ʾiʿrāb al-Qurʾān *Books*

Zaǧǧāǧ does not mention either Q. 18/38 or Q. 34/27 (cf. *ʾIʿrāb*). As for Q. 18/38, Naḥḥās explains about *-nā* that it is (*ʾa*)*nā* of *wa-lākinnā* (cf. *ʾIʿrāb* II, 295) but he says nothing about Q. 34/27. Ibn Ḫālawayhi does not mention either Q. 18/38 or Q. 34/27. ʾAbū ʿAlī al-Fārisī mentions Q. 18/38 (cf. *ʾIġfāl* 375–376) but only explains the *-nā* in *wa-lākinnā* (that is, (*ʾa*)*nā*) and does not say anything about Q. 34/27.

Ḫaṭīb al-Tabrīzī only mentions Q. 18/38 (cf. *Mulaḫḫaṣ* 206–208); however, his explanation is mainly about the *-nā* in *wa-lākinnā* (that is, (*ʾa*)*nā*). He says nothing about *huwa*. As for Zamaḫšarī, his explanation about Q. 18/38 does not contain anything about *huwa* (cf. *Nukat* 257), and he does not refer to Q. 34/27.

In ʿUkbarī's explanation for Q. 18/38, (*ʾa*)*nā* is regarded as a topic (*mubtadaʾ*), *huwa* as a second topic, *allāhu* as a third topic, and *rabbī* as its comment; the *-ī* of *rabbī* is a pronoun which returns to the first topic, that is, (*ʾa*)*nā* (cf. *ʾImlāʾ* II, 103), but he says nothing about Q. 34/27.

Finally, Zakariyyā al-ʾAnṣārī says that, as for Q. 18/38, (*ʾa*)*nā* is a topic (*mubtadaʾ*), *huwa* is a second topic, *allāhu* is a third topic and *rabbī* is its comment. This sentence (*allāhu rabbī*) is a comment of *huwa*, and *huwa* and what follows it are a comment of (*ʾa*)*nā* (cf. *ʾIʿrāb* 262). This explanation, that *huwa* is the topic of the sentence *allāhu rabbī*, shows that this is a *ḍamīr al-šaʾn* sentence structure, though he does not use the term *ḍamīr al-šaʾn*. His explanation about Q. 34/27 (cf. *ʾIʿrāb* 354) is only on *kallā*, which occurs at the beginning of the verse, but he says nothing about the pronoun *huwa*.

By and large, Q. 18/38 and Q. 34/27 are not standing out in the *ʾiʿrāb al-Qurʾān* books, and we hardly find explanations about *huwa* in them. Even Zamaḫšarī does not deal with these two *huwa*-s. However, ʿUkbarī and Zakariyyā al-ʾAnṣārī after Zamaḫšarī make some explanations close to *ḍamīr al-šaʾn* for *huwa* in Q. 18/38.

5.3 *Q. 18/28 and Q. 34/27 in Grammar Books*

Sībawayhi never mentions these two verses in his *Kitāb* (cf. ʿIbāda 2002). Mubarrad, the head of the Basran school, does not refer to them in his *Muqtaḍab* either. As for *Šarḥ al-Mufaṣṣal*, the commentary on Zamaḫšarī's grammar book, Ibn Yaʿīš does not refer to Q. 34/27 in it. He mentions Q. 18/38, but the description is not about *huwa* but *wa-lākinnā*.

Ibn Mālik, who studied *al-Mufaṣṣal* under Ibn Yaʿīš, does not refer to the two verses in his *ʾAlfiyya*, and Ibn ʿAqīl does not in his commentary on it either.

Ibn Hišām al-ʾAnṣārī gives seven kinds of cataphoric pronouns in his *Šarḥ Šuḏūr al-ḏahab*. *Ḍamīr al-šaʾn* is the first one which includes the example of Q. 112/1 (cf. *šš* 136), but he mentions neither Q. 18/38 nor Q. 34/27, at least not in this passage.

In contrast to *Tafsīr*-s, principal grammar books do not refer to the two verses. Even after Zamaḫšarī, who began to explain *huwa* as an independent pronoun in Q. 122/1 as *ḍamīr al-šaʾn*, Q. 18/38 and Q. 34/27 still have no presence.

5.4 *Roundup*

The pronoun *huwa* in Q. 112/1, as seen in § 2.2, § 3 and § 4, began to be recognised as a cataphoric *ḍamīr al-šaʾn* in Zamaḫšarī's time in *Tafsīr*-s, slightly earlier than that, in Ibn Ǧinnī's time in grammar books, and in even earlier times in *ʾiʿrāb al-Qurʾān* books.

As for *huwa* in Q. 18/38 and Q. 34/27, the following two points have become plain:

1. we find some differences between the explanations of the two verses in *Tafsīr*-s and those in grammar books, and
2. in *ʾiʿrāb al-Qurʾān* books, the way of dealing with *huwa* in the two verses is clearly different from the way of dealing with *huwa* in Q. 112/1.

Generally, *huwa* in the verses Q. 18/38 and Q. 34/27 are not explained clearly as *ḍamīr al-šaʾn* many times. The reasons may be:

1. *ḍamīr al-šaʾn* in the Qurʾān mainly appear as suffix pronouns, and
2. these two verses have preceding contexts, so *huwa* can be interpreted as an anaphoric pronoun.

6 Conclusion

This paper has examined the interpretations of *huwa* in descriptions in Q. 112/1. It may be said that in *Tafsīr*-s, *huwa* in Q. 112/1 came to be recognised as a cataphoric *ḍamīr al-šaʾn* around the time of a Zamaḫšarī; however, in Arabic grammar books, Ibn Ǧinnī had already covered it as *ḍamīr al-šaʾn*, and in *ʾiʿrāb al-Qurʾān* books, it had long ago been explained as *ḍamīr al-šaʾn*. Nonetheless, this *huwa* has been interpreted as an anaphoric pronoun until now because:

1. many preceding contexts of the verse 112:1 are mentioned in many *Tafsīr*-s; and
2. in Modern Arabic, independent pronouns are not used as *ḍamīr al-šaʾn*, and even in the Qurʾān, *ḍamīr al-šaʾn* in suffix pronouns are found more than independent forms (only three examples of independent forms are found in the Qurʾān).

ʾIʿrāb books, as grammar books, emphasize grammatical explanations. In contrast, the *Tafsīr*-s, which aim to interpret and comment on Qurʾānic texts, contain more descriptions of the traditions surrounding the verse rather than syntactic explanations.

The difference in interpretation of the *huwa* in Q. 112/1 can be attributed to the difference in purpose between the *ʾIʿrāb* books and grammar books that aim to explain syntax and the *Tafsīr*-s, which aim to interpret the meaning of the verses. Symbolically, it was not until the time of Zamaḫšarī, who was also a grammarian, that *huwa* came to be recognised as *ḍamīr al-šaʾn* in *Tafsīr*-s. In other words, the grammatical research that had been done up to that point came to be utilized in the interpretations of the *Qurʾān*.

Appendix

1. *ḏukira ʾanna al-mušrikīna saʾalū rasūl allāh ṣallā allāh ʿalayhi wa-sallama ʿan nasab rabb al-ʿizza, fa-ʾanzala allāh hāḏihi al-sūra ǧawāban lahum.*
2. *wa-qāla baʿḍuhum: bal nazalat min ʾaǧl ʾanna al-yahūd saʾalūhu, fa-qālū lahu: hāḏā allāhu ḫalaqa al-ḫalq, fa-man ḫalaqa allāha? fa-ʾunzilat ǧawāban lahum.*
3. *ḏikru man qāla: ʾunzilat ǧawāban li-l-mušrikīna allaḏīna saʾalūhu ʾan yansuba lahum al-rabb tabāraka wa-taʿālā.*
4. [...] *qāla al-mušrikūna li-l-nabī ṣallā allāh ʿalayhi wa-sallama: unsub lanā rabbaka. fa-ʾanzala allāh: "qul huwa llāhu ʾaḥad allāhu al-ṣamad".*
5. [...] *ʾinna al-mušrikīna qālū: yā muḥammad, ʾaḫbirnā ʿan rabbika, ṣif lanā rabbaka mā huwa? wa-min ʾayy šayʾ huwa? fa-ʾanzala allāhu: "qul huwa llāhu ʾaḥad" ʾilā ʾāḫir al-sūra.*
6. [...] *qāla ḏālika qādat al-ʾaḥzāb, unsub lanā rabbaka. fa-ʾatāhu ǧibrīlu bi-hāḏihi.*
7. [...] *qāla al-mušrikūna li-l-nabī ṣallā allāh ʿalayhi wa-sallama: unsub lanā rabbaka. fa-ʾanzala allāh tabāraka wa-taʿālā: "qul huwa llāhu ʾaḥad".*
8. *ḏikru man qāla: nazala ḏālika min ʾaǧl masʾalat al-yahūd* [...] *ʾatā rahṭ min al-yahūd al-nabīya ṣallā allāh ʿalayhi wa-sallama, fa-qālū: yā muḥammad, hāḏā allāh ḫalaqa al-ḫalq, fa-man ḫalaqahu? fa-ġaḍiba al-nabī ṣallā allāh*

ʿalayhi wa-sallama ḥattā untuqiʿa lawnuhu, ṯumma sāwarahum ġaḍaban li-rabbihi, fa-ǧāʾahu ǧibrīlu ʿalayhi al-salāmu fa-sakkanahu, wa-qāla: iḫfiḍ ʿalayka ǧanāḥaka yā muḥammad. wa-ǧāʾahu min allāhi ǧawāb mā saʾalūhu ʿanhu. qāla: yaqūlu allāh: "qul huwa llāhu ʾaḥad". fa-lammā talā ʿalayhim al-nabī ṣallā allāh ʿalayhi wa-sallama, qālū: ṣif lanā rabbaka kayfa ḫalquhu, wa-kayfa ʿaḍuduhu, wa-kayfa ḏirāʿuhu? fa-ġaḍiba al-nabī ṣallā allāh ʿalayhi wa-sallama ʾašadda min ġaḍabihi al-ʾawwali, wa-sāwarahum ġaḍaban, fa-ʾatāhu ǧibrīlu fa-qāla lahu miṯla maqālatihi, wa-ʾatāhu bi-ǧawāb mā saʾalūhu ʿanhu: "wa-mā qadarū llāha ḥaqqa qadrihi wa-l-ʾarḍu ǧamīʿan qabḍatuhu yawma al-qiyāmati wa-l-samāwātu maṭwīyātu bi-yamīnihi subḥānahu wa-taʿālā ʿammā yušrikūna" [al-zumar: 67]

9. [...] *ǧāʾa nāsun min al-yahūdi ʾilā al-nabī ṣallā allāhu ʿalayhi wa-sallama, fa-qālū: unsub lanā rabbaka. fa-nazalat: "qul huwa llāhu ʾaḥad" ḥattā ḫatama al-sūrata.*

ṬABARĪ *Ǧāmiʿ* XXIV, 727–729

Bibliography

Primary Sources

ʾAnṣārī, *ʾIʿrāb* = Zakariyyā Muḥammad b. ʾAḥmad al-Miṣrī al-Šāfiʿī al-ʾAnṣārī, *ʾIʿrāb al-Qurʾān*. Ed. by Muḥammad ʿUṯmān. Al-Qāhira: Maktabat al-ṯaqāfa al-dīniyya, 2009.

Bāqūlī/Zaǧǧāǧ, *ʾIʿrāb* = ʿAlī b. al-Ḥusayn al-Bāqūlī (Ǧāmiʿ al-ʿUlūm) / Dubious author: ʾIbrāhīm b. al-Sarī b. Sahl ʾAbū ʾIsḥāq al-Zaǧǧāǧ, *ʾIʿrāb al-Qurʾān*. Ed. by ʾIbrāhīm al-ʾAbyārī. Al-Qāhira: al-Hayʾa al-ʿāmma li-šuʾūn al-maṭābiʿ al-ʾamīriyya, 3 vol., 1963–1965.

Bayḍāwī, *ʾAnwār* = Nāṣir al-Dīn ʾAbū al-Ḫayr ʿAbd Allāh b. ʿUmar b. Muḥammad al-Šīrāzī al-Šāfiʿī al-Bayḍāwī, *ʾAnwār al-tanzīl wa-ʾasrār al-taʾwīl*. Ed. by Muḥammad ʿAbd al-Raḥmān al-Marʿašlī. Bayrūt: Dār ʾiḥyāʾ al-turāṯ al-ʿarabī, 5 vol., n.d.

Fārisī, *ʾIġfāl* = al-Ḥasan b. ʾAḥmad b. ʿAbd al-Ġaffār b. Muḥammad b. Sulaymān b. ʾAbān ʾAbū ʿAlī al-Fasawī al-Fārisī al-Naḥwī, *al-ʾIġfāl: wa-huwa al-masāʾil al-muṣlaḥa min kitāb Maʿānī al-Qurʾān wa-ʾiʿrāb li-ʾAbī ʾIsḥāq al-Zaǧǧāǧ*. Ed. by ʿAbd Allāh b. ʿUmar al-Ḥāǧǧ ʾIbrāhīm. Madīnat ʾAbū Ẓaby: al-Maǧmaʿ al-ṯaqāfī, 2 vol., 1424/2003.

Ǧurǧānī, *Muqtaṣid* = ʿAbd al-Qāhir al-Ǧurǧānī, *Kitāb al-Muqtaṣid fī šarḥ al-ʾĪḍāḥ*. Ed. by al-Marǧān. 2 vol. Dār al-Rašīd li-l-našr, 1982.

Ḫaṭīb al-Tabrīzī, *Mulaḫḫaṣ* = ʾAbū Zakariyyā Yaḥyā b. ʿAlī b. Muḥammad al-Šaybānī al-Tabrīzī al-maʿrūf bi-l-Ḫaṭīb al-Tabrīzī, *al-Mulaḫḫaṣ fī ʾiʿrāb al-Qurʾān*. Ed. by Yaḥyā Murād. Al-Qāhira: Dār al-ḥadīṯ, [2004].

Ibn ʿAqīl, *Šarḥ* = ʿAbd Allāh b. ʿAbd al-Raḥmān b. ʿAbd Allāh b. Muḥammad Bahāʾ al-Dīn al-Qurašī al-Hāšimī al-ʿAqīlī al-Hamdānī al-Miṣrī Ibn ʿAqīl, *Šarḥ Ibn ʿAqīl ʿalā ʾAlfiyyat*

Ibn Mālik. Ed. by ʾAḥmad Salīm al-Ḥumṣī & Muḥammad ʾAḥmad Qāsim. Ṭarābulus (Lubnān): Dār ǧarrūs, 1990.

Ibn Ǧinnī, *Ḫaṣāʾiṣ* = ʾAbū al-Fataḥ ʿUṯmān b. Ǧinnī, *al-Ḫaṣāʾiṣ*. Ed. by Muḥammad ʿAlī al-Naǧǧār. n.p.: Dār al-kutub al-miṣriyya/al-Maktaba al-ʿilmiyya, 3 vol., 1959.

Ibn Ḫālawayhi, *ʾIʿrāb* = ʾAbū ʿAbd Allāh b. al-Ḥusayn b. ʾAḥmad b. Ḫālawayhi, *ʾIʿrāb ṯalāṯīna sūra min al-Qurʾān al-karīm*. Ed. by Muḥammad ʾIbrāhīm Salīm. Al-Ǧīza: Maktabat al-Qurʾān, 1989.

Ibn Hišām al-ʾAnṣārī, *Muġnī* = ʿAbd Allāh b. Yūsuf b. ʾAḥmad b. ʿAbd Allāh b. Yūsuf ʾAbū Muḥammad Ǧamāl al-Dīn al-ʾAnṣārī Ibn Hišām, *Muġnī al-labīb ʿan kutub al-ʾaʿārīb*. Ed. by Muḥammad al-ʾAmīr. Al-Qāhira: Dār ʾiḥyāʾ al-kutub al-ʿarabiyya, 2 vol., n.d.

Ibn Hišām al-ʾAnṣārī, *Šarḥ* = ʿAbd Allāh b. Yūsuf b. ʾAḥmad b. ʿAbd Allāh b. Yūsuf ʾAbū Muḥammad Ǧamāl al-Dīn al-ʾAnṣārī Ibn Hišām, *Šarḥ Šuḏūr al-ḏahab fī maʿrifat kalām al-ʿArab*. Ed. by Muḥammad Muḥyī al-Dīn ʿAbd al-Ḥamīd. Ṣaydā & Bayrūt: al-Maktaba al-ʿaṣriyya, n.d.

Ibn Mālik, *ʾAlfiyya* = Muḥammad b. ʿAbd Allāh b. Mālik ʾAbū ʿAbd Allāh Ǧamāl al-Dīn al-Ṭāʾī al-Ǧayyānī al-ʾAndalusī, *ʾAlfiyyat Ibn Mālik fī al-naḥw wa-l-ṣarf*. See Ibn ʿAqīl.

Ibn Yaʿīš, *ŠM* = Yaʿīš b. ʿAlī b. Yaʿīš b. ʾAbī al-Sarāyā Muḥammad b. ʿAlī ʾAbū al-Baqāʾ Muwaffaq al-Dīn al-ʾAsadī al-Ḥalabī Ibn Yaʿīš, *Šarḥ al-Mufaṣṣal*. Bayrūt: ʿĀlam al-kutub, 10 vol., n.d.

Maḥallī & Suyūṭī, *Ǧalālayn* = Ǧalāl al-Dīn al-Maḥallī wa-Ǧalāl al-Dīn al-Suyūṭī, *Tafsīr al-Ǧalālayn al-muyassar*. Ed. by Faḫr al-Dīn Qabāwa. Bayrūt: Maktabat Lubnān. 2003.

Mubarrad, *Muqtaḍab* = Muḥammad b. Yazīd b. ʿAbd al-ʾAkbar ʾAbū al-ʿAbbās al-Ṯumālī al-ʾAzdī al-Mubarrad, *al-Muqtaḍab*. Ed. by Muḥammad ʿAbd al-Ḫāliq ʿUḍayma. Al-Qāhira: Wizārat al-ʾawqāf, 2nd ed., 4 vol., 1979.

Naḥḥās, *ʾIʿrāb* = ʾAḥmad b. Muḥammad ʾAbū Ǧaʿfar al-Naḥḥās, *ʾIʿrāb al-Qurʾān*. Ed. by ʿAbd al-Munʿim ʾIbrāhīm. Bayrūt: Dār al-kutub al-ʿilmiyya, 2nd ed., 5 vol., 2004.

Sībawayhi, *Kitāb* = ʿAmr b. ʿUṯmān b. Qanbar ʾAbū Bišr Sībawayhi, *al-Kitāb*. Ed. by ʿAbd al-Salām Muḥammad Hārūn. Al-Qāhira: Maktabat al-ḫānǧī, 3rd ed., 5 vol., 1988.

Ṭabarī, *Ǧāmiʿ* = Muḥammad b. Ǧarīr ʾAbū Ǧaʿfar al-Ṭabarī, *Ǧāmiʿ al-bayān ʿan taʾwīl ʾāy al-Qurʾān*. Ed. by ʿAbd Allāh b. ʿAbd al-Muḥsin al-Turkī. Al-Qāhira: Dār haǧar, 25 vol., 2001.

ʿUkbarī, *ʾImlāʾ* = ʾAbū al-Baqāʾ ʿAbd Allāh b. al-Ḥusayn b. ʿAbd Allāh al-ʿUkbarī, *ʾImlāʾ mā min bihi al-Raḥmān min wuǧūh al-ʾiʿrāb wa-l-qirāʾāt fī ǧamīʿ al-Qurʾān*. Ed. by ʾIbrāhīm ʿAṭuwwa ʿAwḍ. Al-Qāhira: Dār al-ḥadīṯ, 2 vol., 1992.

Zaǧǧāǧ, *Maʿānī* = ʾIbrāhīm b. al-Sarī b. Sahl ʾAbū ʾIsḥāq al-Zaǧǧāǧ, *Maʿānī al-Qurʾān wa-ʾiʿrābuhu*. Ed. by ʿAbd al-Ǧalīl ʿAbduh Šalabī. Bayrūt: ʿĀlam al-kutub, 5 vol., 1988.

Zamaḫšarī, *Nukat* = Ǧār Allāh ʾAbū al-Qāsim Maḥmūd b. ʿUmar b. Muḥammad b. ʾAḥmad al-Ḫawārizmī al-Zamaḫšarī, *Nukat al-ʾiʿrāb fī ġarīb al-ʾiʿrāb fī al-Qurʾān al-karīm*. Ed. by Muḥammad ʾAbū al-Futūḥ Šarīf. Al-Qāhira: Dār al-maʿārif, 1985.

Zamaḫšarī, *Tafsīr* = Ǧār Allāh ʾAbū al-Qāsim Maḥmūd b. ʿUmar b. Muḥammad b.

ʾAḥmad al-Ḫawārizmī al-Zamaḫšarī, *Tafsīr al-kaššāf ʿan ḥaqāʾiq al-tanzīl wa-ʿuyūn al-ʾaqāwīl fī wuǧūh taʾwīl*. Ed. by Ḫalīl Maʾmūn Šīḥā. Bayrūt: Dār al-maʿrifa, 3rd ed., 2009.

Secondary Sources

ʿAbābnih, Yahyā ʿAṭiyya. 2006. *Taṭawwur al-muṣṭalaḥ al-naḥwī al-baṣrī min Sībawayhi ḥattā al-Zamaḫšarī*. ʾIrbid: ʿĀlam al-kutub al-ḥadīṯ.

ʾAbū Ḫuḍayr, Nāṣir al-Dīn. 2014. *al-Ruʾya al-naḥwiyya ʿinda al-Ṭabarī: qirāʾa fī Ǧāmiʿ al-Bayān ʿan Taʾwīl al-Qurʾān*, Irbid: ʿĀlam al-kutub al-ḥadīṯ (Modern Book's World).

Arberry, Arthur John. 1955. *The Koran Interpreted*. London & New York: George Allen & Unwin LTD & The Macmillan Company.

Ayoub, Georgine. 2019. "Pronouns in Sībawayhi's *Kitāb* and related concepts: *ḍamīr, ʾiḍmār, muḍmar*". *The Foundations of Arabic Linguistics IV. The Evolution of Theory*, ed. by Manuela E.B. Giolfo & Kees Versteegh, 30–60. Leiden & Boston: Brill, coll. "Studies in Semitic Languages and Linguistics" 97.

Badawi, El-Said & Muhammad Abdel Haleem. 2008. *Arabic-English Dictionary of Qurʾanic Usage*. Leiden & Boston: Brill, coll. "Handbook of Oriental Studies. Section 1, The Near and Middle East" 85.

Badawi, El-Said., Michael G. Carter and, Adrian Gully. 2004. *Modern Written Arabic: A Comprehensive Grammar*. London & New York: Routledge.

Badawi, El-Said., Michael G. Carter and, Adrian Gully. 2016. *Modern Written Arabic: A Comprehensive Grammar*. Ed. revised by Maher Awad. London & New York: Routledge.

Bloch, Ariel A. 1990. "*Ḍamīr al-šaʾn*". *Zeitschrift für Arabische Linguistik* 21. 30–39.

Dye, Guillaume. 2017. "Traces of Bilinguism/Multilingualism in Qurʾānic Arabic". *Arabic in Context. 400 Years of Arabic at Leiden University*, ed. by Ahmad Al-Jallad, 337–371. Leiden & Boston: Brill, coll. "Studies in Semitic Languages and Linguistics" 89.

ʿIbāda, Muḥammad ʾIbrāhīm. 2002. *al-Šawāhid al-qurʾāniyya fī kitāb Sībawayhi: ʿarḍ wa-tawǧīh wa-tawṯīq*. Al-Qāhira: Maktabat al-ʾādāb.

Peled, Yishai. 1990. "Non-referential pronouns in topic position in medieval Arabic grammatical theory and in modern usage". *Zeitschrift der Deutschen Morgenländischen Gesellschaft* 140/1. 3–27.

Peled, Yishai. 2006. "Ḍamīr". *Encyclopedia of Arabic Language and Linguistics*, Vol. 1, ed. by Kees Versteegh et al., 555–559. Leiden & Boston: Brill.

Peled, Yishai. 2009. *Sentence types and word-order patterns in written Arabic: medieval and modern perspectives*. Leiden & Boston: Brill, coll. "Studies in Semitic Languages and Linguistics" 52.

Wright, William. 1955. *A grammar of the Arabic Language*. Cambridge: Cambridge University Press, 3rd ed., 2 vols.

Ziyādī (al-), ʿAmmār Niʿma. 2006. "Ḍamīr al-šaʾn fī al-Qurʾān al-karīm: dirāsa naḥwiyya balāǧiyya". *Maǧallat Ǧāmiʿat Karbalāʾ* (*Journal of Kerbala University*) 4/3. 237–275.

Index Operum

al-ʾAlfāẓ al-mustaʿmala fī al-manṭiq (by al-Fārābī) 159–160
al-ʾAlfiyya (by Ibn Mālik) 106, 193, 235, 239
ʾAsrār al-ʿarabiyya (by Ibn al-ʾAnbārī) 107, 192
al-ʿAwāmil al-miʾa al-naḥwiyya (by ʿAbd al-Qāhir al-Ǧurǧānī) 183
al-ʿAyn (by al-Ḫalīl) 14–15, 27, 119

Barnāmaǧ šuyūḫ al-Ruʿaynī (by al-Ruʿaynī) 45
al-Bayān wa-l-tabyīn (by al-Ǧāḥiẓ) 65

Commentary on Prior Analytics (by Alexander of Aphrodisias) 171

al-Ḍarūrī fī ṣināʿat al-naḥw (by Ibn Rušd) 138

al-Fihrist (by Ibn al-Nadīm) 69, 135, 160

Ǧāmiʿ al-bayān ʿan taʾwīl ʾāy al-Qurʾān (= *Tafsīr*, by al-Ṭabarī) 231
al-Ǧawāb al-lāʾiḥ al-muʿtamad ʿalayhi fī al-radd ʿalā man nasaba rafʿ al-ḫabar bi-lā ʾilā Sībawayhi (by Ibn al-Faḫḫār al-ʾArkušī al-Ǧuḏāmī) 139
al-Ǧumal fī al-naḥw (by al-Zaǧǧāǧī) 7, 135–136, 139, 142, 145–147, 149–151, 183–184, 192, 209, 249

al-Ḫaṣāʾiṣ (by Ibn Ǧinnī) 108, 110–111, 121, 183, 191–192
al-Ḥayawān (by al-Ǧāḥiẓ) 65
al-Ḥulal fī ʾiṣlāḥ al-ḫalal al-wāqiʿ fī al-Ǧumal (by Ibn al-Sīd al-Baṭalyawsī) 136, 139, 142, 146
al-Ḥulal fī šarḥ ʾabyāt al-Ǧumal (by Ibn al-Sīd al-Baṭalyawsī) 139
al-Ḥurūf (by al-Fārābī) 159–160, 163, 166, 168–169, 250

al-ʾĪḍāḥ fī ʿilal al-naḥw (by al-Zaǧǧāǧī) 107, 192
al-ʾĪḍāḥ fī al-naḥw (by al-Fārisī) 7, 135, 145–146, 149–151, 183, 249
ʾIḥṣāʾ al-ʿulūm (by al-Fārābī) 159–160, 165, 167–168, 250
Iḫtiṣār al-intiṣār li-kitāb al-ʾĪḍāḥ min risālat al-ʾIfṣāḥ (by Ibn al-Faḫḫār al-ʾArkušī al-Ǧuḏāmī) 139
al-ʾInṣāf (by Ibn al-ʾAnbārī) 54, 124–125, 129
al-Intiṣār (by Ibn Wallād) 37, 61, 135
→ *al-Radd ʿalā al-Mubarrad*
al-Iqtirāḥ fī ʿilm ʾuṣūl al-naḥw (by al-Suyūṭī) 107
ʾIṣlāḥ al-ḫalal al-wāqiʿ fī al-Ǧumal li-l-Zaǧǧāǧī
→ *al-Ḥulal fī ʾiṣlāḥ al-ḫalal* [...]
ʾIṣlāḥ al-manṭiq (by Ibn al-Sikkīt) 54

al-Kāfī fī al-naḥw (by ʾAbū Ǧaʿfar al-Naḥḥās) 137, 141, 145
al-Kitāb (by Sībawayhi) 4–9, 13, 15–16, 18, 21–22, 24–27, 31–32, 37–38, 41–42, 45–47, 49, 52, 54–55, 57–66, 68–74, 76, 81, 83, 85, 97–102, 104–105, 111, 114–128, 130–131, 135, 139, 145–146, 148–151, 157, 160, 166, 173, 179, 182, 184–186, 190, 214, 233, 235, 238, 244–251

Lexique-Index du Kitāb *de Sībawayhi* (by Gérard Troupeau) 13, 21, 116
Lumaʿ al-ʾadilla (by Ibn al-ʾAnbārī) 107
al-Lumaʿ fī al-naḥw / fī al-ʿarabiyya (by Ibn Ǧinnī) 183, 191–192, 198, 204

Maʿānī al-Qurʾān (by al-ʾAḫfaš al-ʾAwsaṭ) 6, 52, 55, 70, 72–74, 76, 81, 83, 85–86, 89, 235, 246
Maʿānī al-Qurʾān (by al-Farrāʾ) 21
al-Maʿārif (by Ibn Qutayba) 66, 70
Maǧālis al-ʿulamāʾ (by al-Zaǧǧāǧī) 56
Maǧāz al-Qurʾān (by ʾAbū ʿUbayda) 72
Marātib al-naḥwiyyīn (by ʾAbū al-Ṭayyib al-Luġawī) 60
al-Masāʾil al-ġarība al-ʿišrīniyya (by Ibn Sīnā) 172, 174
al-Masʾala al-rašīdiyya (by al-ʾAʿlam al-Šantamarī) 137–138, 141
al-Minhaǧ al-muʿarrib fī al-radd ʿalā al-Muqarrib (by al-Ǧazarī al-Ḫazraǧī al-Maġribī) 139

al-Mufaṣṣal (by al-Zamaḫšarī) 31, 138, 142, 192, 201, 207, 234–235, 239
Muġnī al-labīb (by Ibn Hišām al-ʾAnṣārī) 224
al-Muḫtaṣar al-ʾawsaṭ fī al-manṭiq (by Ibn Sīnā) 172
al-Muqaddima (by Ibn Ḫaldūn) 119
al-Muqaddima al-ǧazūliyya (by al-Ǧazūlī) 147
al-Muqaddimāt ʾilā ʿilm al-Kitāb (by Ibn al-Ṭarāwa) 138–139, 142, 145
al-Muqarrib (by Ibn ʿUṣfūr) 139, 142, 147–149, 193, 208
al-Muqtaḍab (by al-Mubarrad) 6, 38, 54, 102–104, 111, 127, 182, 189, 233, 238
al-Muqtaṣid fī šarḥ al-ʾĪḍāḥ (by al-Ǧurǧānī) 183, 192
al-Mušriq fī al-naḥw (by Ibn Maḍāʾ) 137

Nukat ʿalā Kitāb Sībawayhi (by ʾAbū Yaʿlā b. ʾAbī Zurʿa) 61

Organon (by Aristotle) 169

Prior Analytics (by Aristotle) 171–172

al-Qiyās (by al-Fārābī) 173
al-Qiyās al-ṣaġīr (by al-Fārābī) 173

al-Radd ʿalā ʾAbī Ǧaʿfar al-Naḥḥās fī kitāb al-Kāfī (by Ibn al-ʿArīf) 137
Radd ʿalā ʾAbī Muḥammad Ibn al-Sīd al-Baṭalyawsī (by Ibn Ḫalaṣa) 137
Radd ʿalā ʾAbī al-Walīd Ibn Rušd (by Ibn Ḫarūf al-ʾIšbīlī) 138
Radd ʿalā ʾAbī Zayd al-Suhaylī (by Ibn Ḫarūf al-ʾIšbīlī) 138
al-Radd ʿalā al-ʾaʾimma fī-mā yaqaʿu fī al-ṣalāt min al-ḫaṭaʾ wa-l-laḥn fī šahr ramaḍān wa-ġayrihi (by Makkī b. ʾAbī Ṭālib) 136
Radd ʿalā al-ʾAʿlam fī risālatihi al-Rašīdiyya wa-ġayrihā (by Ibn Ḫarūf al-ʾIšbīlī) 138
Radd ʿalā Ibn Ḫarūf muntaṣiran li-šayḫihi al-Suhaylī (by ʾAbū ʿAlī al-Rundī) 138
Radd ʿalā Ibn Ḥazm fī baʿḍ maqālātihi (by Ibn Ḫarūf al-ʾIšbīlī) 137
Radd ʿalā Ibn Malkūn (by Ibn Ḫarūf al-ʾIšbīlī) 138
Radd ʿalā Ibn Sirāǧ bi-risāla farīda (by al-ʾAʿlam al-Šantamarī) 137
Radd ʿalā Ibn al-Ṭarāwa fī Muqaddimātihi ʿalā ʾabwāb al-Kitāb (by Ibn Ḫarūf al-ʾIšbīlī) 138
al-Radd ʿalā al-Mubarrad (= *al-Intiṣār li-Sībawayhi*, by Ibn Wallād) 38, 61, 135–136
Radd ʿalā Muqarrib Ibn ʿUṣfūr (by Ibn al-Ḍāʾiʿ) 139
al-Radd ʿalā al-nuḥāt (by Ibn Maḍāʾ) 7, 107, 136–137, 140, 149, 249
al-Radd ʿalā Sībawayhi (by Mubarrad) 38, 60–61, 135
al-Radd ʿalā al-Zamaḫšarī fī Mufaṣṣalihi (= *al-Tanbīh ʿalā ʾaġlāṭ al-Zamaḫšarī fī al-Mufaṣṣal wa-mā ḫālafa fīhi Sībawayhi*, by Ibn Maʿzūz) 138
Radd iʿtirāḍāt Ibn al-Sīd al-Baṭalyawsī ʿalā al-Zaǧǧāǧī (by Ibn al-Ḍāʾiʿ) 139
Radd iʿtirāḍāt Ibn al-Ṭarāwa ʿalā al-Fārisī (by Ibn al-Ḍāʾiʿ) 139
Radd iʿtirāḍāt Ibn al-Ṭarāwa ʿalā Sībawayhi (by Ibn al-Ḍāʾiʿ) 139
Radd al-Mubarrad ʿalā Sībawayhi (by Ibn al-Ḥaǧǧ al-ʾAzdī) 142
Rasāʾil fī al-luġa (by Ibn al-Sīd al-Baṭalyawsī) 201
Risāla fī iḫtilāfihi ʾilā ʾAbī ʿAbd Allāh Ibn Ḫalaṣa (by Ibn al-Ǧazzār) 137
Risāla fī-mā ǧarā baynahu wa-bayna ʾAbī al-Ḥasan [*Ibn*] *al-Bāḏiš fī masʾala naḥwiyya* (by Ibn al-Ṭarāwa) 137
Risālat al-ʾIfṣāḥ bi-baʿḍ mā ǧāʾa min al-ḫaṭaʾ fī al-ʾĪḍāḥ (by Ibn al-Ṭarāwa) 136, 139, 142, 145
Risāla ʾilā ʾAbī ʿAbd Allāh Muḥammad Ibn Ḫalaṣa (by Ibn al-Sīd al-Baṭalyawsī) 137
Risālat al-Kitāb (by Sībawayhi) 117

Sabīl al-hudā (by Ibn Hišām al-ʾAnṣārī) 208
Šadd al-ziyār ʿalā ǧaḥfalat al-ḥimār (by Ḥāzim al-Qarṭāǧannī) 139
Šarḥ ʿalā ʾAlfiyyat Ibn Mālik (by Ibn ʿAqīl) 235
Šarḥ ʿalā ʾAlfiyyat Ibn Mālik (by Ibn al-Nāẓim) 129
Šarḥ Ǧumal al-Zaǧǧāǧī (by Ibn Ḫarūf) 146, 150

Šarḥ ʿIbāra (by al-Fārābī) 159–161
Šarḥ Kāfiyat Ibn al-Ḥāǧib (by Raḍī al-Dīn al-ʾAstarābāḏī) 192
Šarḥ Kitāb Sībawayhi (by al-Sīrāfī) 63, 160–161, 168
Šarḥ al-Lumaʿ (by Ibn Barhān al-ʿUkbarī) 200
Šarḥ al-Mufaṣṣal (by Ibn Yaʿīš) 234, 239
Šarḥ nukat Kitāb Sībawayhi (by ʾAbū ʾIsḥāq al-Ziyādī) 63
Šarḥ Šuḏūr al-ḏahab (by Ibn Hišām al-ʾAnṣārī) 235, 239
Sophist (by Plato) 166
Šuḏūr al-ḏahab (by Ibn Hišām al-ʾAnṣārī) 193
Syntaxe de l'arabe classique (by Pierre Larcher) 215

Ṭabaqāt fuḥūl al-šuʿarāʾ (by Ibn Sallām al-Ǧumaḥī) 65, 71
Ṭabaqāt al-naḥwiyyīn wa-l-luġawiyyīn (by al-Zubaydī) 125
al-Tabyīn ʿan maḏāhib al-naḥwiyyīn al-baṣriyyīn wa-l-kūfiyyīn (by al-ʿUkbarī) 124
Tafsīr al-Ṭabarī → *Ǧāmiʿ al-bayān* [...]
Talḫīṣ radd al-Mubarrad ʿalā Sībawayhi wa-ntiṣār Ibn Wallād lahu (by Ibn al-Ḥāǧǧ al-ʾAzdī) 139, 142–143
al-Tanbīh ʿalā ʾaġlāṭ al-Zamaḫšarī fī al-Mufaṣṣal wa-mā ḫālafa fīhi Sībawayhi (by Ibn Maʿzūz) → *al-Radd ʿalā al-Zamaḫšarī fī Mufaṣṣalihi*
Tanqīḥ al-ʾalbāb fī šarḥ ġawāmiḍ al-Kitāb (by Ibn Ḫarūf) 37, 45, 47–49
Tanzīh al-Qurʾān ʿammā lā yalīqu bi-l-bayān (by Ibn Maḍāʾ) 137–138, 142
Tartīb al-saʿāda wa-manāzil al-ʿulūm (by Ibn Miskawayhi) 159
Tashīl al-fawāʾid wa-takmīl al-maqāṣid (by Ibn Mālik) 193
Ṭurar ʿalā al-ʾĪḍāḥ (by Ibn al-ʾAḫḍar) 150

al-ʾUṣūl fī al-naḥw (by Ibn al-Sarrāǧ) 6, 8, 104–106, 108, 111, 115, 160, 162, 179–181, 183, 188, 190, 192, 194, 251

Index Nominum

ʿAbābnih, Yaḥyā ʿAṭiyya 228–229, 235
ʿAbd Allāh b. ʾAbī ʾIsḥāq (d. 117/735) 71
Abdel Haleem, Muhammad 224
ʾAbū ʿAmr b. al-ʿAlāʾ (d. 154/771?) 85, 214
ʾAbū al-Dardāʾ (d. 32/652) 57
ʾAbū Ḥanīfa (d. 150/767) 65, 172
ʾAbū Ḥayyān al-Ġarnāṭī (d. 745/1344) 24, 165, 244
ʾAbū Ḫuḍayr, Nāṣir al-Dīn 231
ʾAbū Šamir (fl. 2nd/8th–3rd/9th centuries) 84
ʾAbū Tammām (d. 231/845) 24
ʾAbū ʿUbayda (d. 207/825) 62, 72
ʾAbū Zayd al-ʾAnṣārī (d. 215/830?) 62, 64
ʾAḫfaš, al- ~ al-ʾAwsaṭ (d. 215/830) 5–6, 52, 55–57, 60–62, 65–66, 68–77, 79–86, 88, 90–91, 97, 124, 235, 246
ʾAḥmar, ʿAlī b. Ḥasan al- (d. 194/809) 67
ʾAḥmar, Ḫalaf al- (d. 180/796) 67
ʾAʿlam al-Šantamarī, al- *see* Šantamarī
Alexander of Aphrodisias (150–215?) 171–172, 174
ʿAlī b. ʾAbī Ṭālib (d. 40/661) 65, 82
Allard, Michel (1924–1976) 174
Amharar, Ilyass 5, 151
ʾAnṣārī, ʾAḥmad Makkī al- 124
Arberry, Arthur John (1905–1969) 223
Aristotle (384–322 BC) 158–159, 170–171, 174
ʾAšʿarī, al- (d. 324/936) 172
ʾAṣmaʿī, al- (d. 213/828) 62, 68
ʾAstarābāḏī, Raḍī al-Dīn al- (d. 688/1289?) 8, 38, 44, 170, 184, 192, 194, 199–201, 213, 216, 251
ʿAttāb b. ʾAsīd (d. 23/644?) 65
Ayoub, Georgine 1, 235

Baalbaki, Ramzi 23, 54, 100, 102, 148
Badawi, El-Said (1929–2014) 224–225
Badīrī, Ḫalīfa 45
Bally, Charles (1865–1947) 211, 215
Bannā, Muḥammad ʾIbrāhīm al- 137
Bāqūlī, Ǧāmiʿ al-ʿUlūm al- (d. 543/1148) 205–206, 211
Baššār b. Burd (d. 167/783) 59
Baṭalyawsī, Ibn al-Sīd al- (d. 521/1127) 136, 139–142, 144, 146–147, 149, 151, 201, 206, 249
Bayḍāwī, al- (d. 685/1288 or 691/1292) 230, 237
Bernards, Monique 37, 55, 60–63, 67, 83, 102
Bettini, Lidia 26
Binaghi, Francesco 7
Bloch, Ariel A. 224–225
Bohas, Georges 115
Bongianino, Umberto 42

Carter, Michael G. 1–4, 53, 57, 83–84, 99, 116–117, 119, 122, 124, 130, 200, 217
Chatti, Saloua 161–162, 173
Chomsky, Noam 164
Crone, Patricia (1945–2015) 85

Dayyeh, Hanadi 6
Derenbourg, Hartwig (1844–1908) 13, 38, 42–43, 49, 214
Dimašqī, ʾAbū ʿUṯmān al- (d. 302/914) 162
Druart, Thérèse-Anne 169
Druel, Jean N., 5, 151
Durkheim, Émile (1858–1917) 210

Elamrani-Jamal, Abdelali 160
El-Rouayheb, Khaled 164
Endress, Gerhard 174
Esseesy, Mohssen 202

Fārābī, al- (d. 350/961) 7, 124, 157–175, 250
Farazdaq, al- (d. 114/732?) 128
Fārisī, ʾAbū ʿAlī al- (d. 377/987) 7, 20, 38, 44, 135, 145–146, 149–151, 183–184, 193, 236, 238, 249
Farrāʾ, al- (d. 207/822) 21–23, 27, 53–55, 59–60, 64–65, 67–68, 72, 82–83, 124, 135, 209, 244
Fleisch, Henri (1904–1985) 53
Fortenbaugh, William Wall 171
Frolov, Dmitry 25

Ǧāḥiẓ, al- (d. 255/868–869) 33, 64–65, 67, 85
Ǧāmiʿ al-ʿUlūm al-Bāqūlī *see* Bāqūlī

Ġāmidī, Ṣāliḥ b. ʾAḥmad al- 45
Ǧarmī, al- (d. 225/839) 5, 37, 68–69, 245
Ǧawharī, ʾAbū Naṣr ʾIsmāʿīl al- (d. 400/1009?) 181
Ǧazarī, ʾAbū ʾIsḥāq ʾIbrāhīm b. ʾAḥmad al-Maġribī al- (d. 709/1309) 139
Ǧazūlī, ʾAbū Mūsā al- (d. 607/1211) 147
Ghersetti, Antonella 26, 31
Giolfo, Manuela E.B. 1–2, 7
Goguyer, Antonin (1846–1909) 15
Guillaume, Jean-Patrick 115
Ǧurǧānī, ʿAbd al-Qāhir al- (d. 471/1078) 8, 129, 183–184, 188, 192, 205, 210, 213, 225–226, 251
Gutas, Dimitri 159
Ǧuzūlī *see* Ǧazūlī

Ḥadīṯī, Ḫadīǧa al- 57
Ḥafṣ b. Sulaymān (d. 180/796) 233
Ḫalaf al-ʾAḥmar *see* ʾAḥmar, Ḫalaf al-
Ḫalīl, b. ʾAḥmad al-Farāhīdī al- (d. 170/786 or 175/791) 5, 13–15, 18–22, 24–28, 30–33, 39, 54, 56–58, 63–64, 68, 84, 119–121, 135, 244
Ḥāmiḍ, ʾAbū Mūsā al- (d. 305/918) 59
Ḥammād b. Salama (d. 167/784) 56–57, 84, 97
Ḥamza b. Ḥabīb (d. 156/772) 233
Hārūn, ʿAbd al-Salām Muḥammad (1909–1988) 13, 49, 233
Hārūn al-Rašīd (r. 170/786–193/809) 53, 58, 62, 68
Hāšimī, ʿĪsā b. Ǧaʿfar al- 62
Hasnawi, Ahmad 162
Ḫaṭīb al-Tabrīzī (d. 502/1109) 236, 238
Ḥātim al-Ṭāʾī (d. 578 CE) 24
Ḥāzim al-Qarṭāǧannī (d. 684/1285) 139, 142, 144
Hodges, Wilfrid 7, 161–162, 164, 169
Ḫuḍarī, al- (d. 1287/1870) 208
Humbert, Geneviève 37, 42–43, 45, 55, 60, 70–71, 83, 151
Ḥunayn b. ʾIsḥāq (d. 260/873) 159
Ḫwānsārī, Muḥammad Bāqir al- (d. 1313/1895) 138

Ibn al-ʾAbbār (d. 658/1260) 137–138
Ibn ʿAbd al-Malik (d. 703/1303) 138
Ibn ʾAbī ʾUṣaybiʿa, al- (d. 668/1270) 158, 160–161
Ibn ʾĀǧurrūm (d. 723/1323) 193
Ibn al-ʾAḫḍar (d. 514/1120) 150
Ibn al-ʾAnbārī (d. 577/1181) 54, 69, 107, 124
Ibn ʿAqīl (d. 769/1367) 209, 213, 235, 239
Ibn al-ʿArīf (d. 390/1000) 137, 141
Ibn al-Bāḏiš (d. 528/1133) 137, 141, 144, 146, 149
Ibn Barhān al-ʿUkbarī (d. 456/1064) 129, 200, 206, 210–211, 213, 216
Ibn Barrī (d. 582/1187) 147
Ibn al-Dahhān al-Baġdādī (d. 569/1174) 203, 211
Ibn al-Ḍāʾiʿ (d. 680/1281) 139, 142–146, 148–149
Ibn al-Faḫḫār al-ʾArkušī al-Ǧuḏāmī, ʾAbū Bakr Muḥammad b. ʿAbd al-Raḥmān (d. 723/1323) 139, 142–146, 149
Ibn al-Faḫḫār [al-Bayrī al-Ḫawlānī], ʾAbū ʿAbd Allāh Muḥammad b. ʿAlī (d. 754/1353) 205, 209, 211
Ibn al-Faqīh (d. 300/913?) 33
Ibn al-Furāt, ʾAbū al-Fatḥ al-Faḍl b. Ǧaʿfar (d. 327/939) 160
Ibn al-Ǧazzār (d. 540/1145) 137, 141, 144
Ibn Ǧinnī (d. 392/1002) 6, 8, 108–111, 121, 183–184, 188–189, 191–192, 194, 198, 204, 210–211, 234, 239, 247, 251
Ibn al-Ḫabbāz (d. 637/1239) 204
Ibn al-Ḥāǧǧ al-ʾAzdī (d. 647/1249 or 651/1253) 139, 142–143
Ibn al-Ḥāǧib (d. 646/1249) 192–193, 207
Ibn Ḫalaṣa (d. 519/1125 or 521/1127) 137, 140–141, 144
Ibn Ḫālawayhi (d. 370/980) 135, 236, 238
Ibn Ḫaldūn (d. 808/1406) 119
Ibn Ḫallikān (d. 681/1282) 64
Ibn Ḫarūf al-ʾIšbīlī (d. 609/1212) 37–38, 42, 45–49, 137–138, 140–146, 149–150, 245, 249
Ibn Ḫayr al-ʾIšbīlī (d. 575/1179) 137, 140
Ibn Ḥazm (d. 456/1064) 137, 141, 144, 151
Ibn Hišām al-ʾAnṣārī (d. 761/1360) 181, 185, 188, 193, 208, 224, 228, 235, 239
Ibn Kaysān (d. 299/911 or 320/932) 60, 125
Ibn Maḍāʾ al-Qurṭubī (d. 592/1196) 7, 107, 136–138, 140–142, 144–145, 148–151, 249
Ibn Mālik (d. 672/1274) 8, 106, 184, 188, 193, 213, 235, 239, 251
Ibn Malkūn (d. 581/1185 or 584/1188) 138, 142, 144

Ibn Maʿzūz (d. 625/1227) 138, 142, 144–145
Ibn al-Nadīm (d. 385/995) 59, 61, 63, 68–69, 135, 160, 172
Ibn al-Naṭṭāḥ (d. 252/866) 64
Ibn al-Nāẓim (d. 686/1287) 129
Ibn Qutayba (d. 270/889) 58, 64, 66–67, 70–71
Ibn Rušd (d. 595/1198) 138, 142, 144, 151
Ibn Sallām al-Ǧumaḥī (d. 231/845?) 64–65, 71, 85
Ibn al-Sarrāǧ (d. 316/929) 6–8, 31, 104–106, 108, 115, 129, 160–162, 169–170, 179–194, 202–203, 228–229, 247, 251
Ibn al-Sīd al-Baṭalyawsī *see* Baṭalyawsī
Ibn Sīda (d. 458/1066) 38, 128
Ibn al-Sikkīt (d. 244/858) 54
Ibn Sīnā (d. 427/1037) 157, 159, 169, 171–172, 174
Ibn Sirāǧ (d. 489/1096) 137, 141, 144
Ibn Ṭāhir al-Ḫidabb (d. 580/1184) 45–49
Ibn al-Ṭarāwa (d. 526/1132 or 528/1134) 136–138, 141–142, 144–150, 249
Ibn ʿUṣfūr (d. 669/1271) 139, 142, 144, 147–149, 186, 207–208, 211
Ibn Wallād (d. 332/944) 5, 37–38, 61, 135, 139, 143, 245
Ibn Yaʿīš (d. 643/1245) 38, 44, 201, 207, 228, 235, 239
Ibn al-Zubayr (d. 708/1308) 147
Idris, Yusuf (1927–1991) 217
Imruʾ al-Qays (d. 540? CE) 25, 46, 65
ʿĪsā b. ʿUmar al-Ṯaqafī (d. 149/766) 19, 56–57

Jahn, Gustav (1837–1917) 13–14, 16, 21, 125

Kalāʿī, al- (fl. 6th/12th century) 137
Kasher, Almog 127
Kinberg, Naphtali (1948–1997) 21, 27
Kisāʾī, al- (d. 189/805) 22, 53, 58–60, 65, 67–69
Kouloughli, Djamel Eddine (1947–2013) 115

Lancioni, Giuliano 5, 26, 52
Larcher, Pierre 2, 122, 202, 211, 215
Levin, Aryeh 190
Luġawī, ʾAbū al-Ṭayyib al- (d. 351/962) 58, 60, 63, 70–71

Mabramān (d. 326/938) 125
Maḥallī, Ǧalāl al-Dīn al- (d. 864/1459–1460) 230, 237
Mahdī, al- (r. 158/775–169/785) 58
Makkī b. ʾAbī Ṭālib (d. 437/1045) 136
Mālik b. ʾAnas (d. 179/795) 65
Maqqarī, al- (d. 1041/1632) 139
Marogy, Amal Elesha 1, 16, 127, 157
Marzubānī, al- (d. 384/994) 59, 64
Mattā b. Yūnus (d. 328/939) 160
Māzinī, al- (d. 249/863) 5, 61–62, 68–69, 124, 245
Mejdell, Gunvor 217
Menn, Stephen 169
Miskawayhi (d. 421/1030) 159–160
Mosel, Ulrike 174
Moses 185, 225
Mubarrad, al- (d. 285/898 or 286/899) 5–6, 18, 23–24, 29, 31, 37–38, 53–55, 60–62, 67, 69, 82–83, 102–105, 124–125, 127, 129, 135, 139, 142, 180, 182, 185–186, 189–191, 200, 202, 233, 238, 244–245, 247
Muḥammad (d. 11/632) 172, 223, 229–230

Nābiġa, al- ~ al-Ḏubyānī (d. 604 CE) 65
Naḥḥās, ʾAbū Ǧaʿfar al- (d. 338/950) 141, 145, 228, 236, 238
Naẓẓām, ʾIbrāhīm al- (d. 221/836) 84

Okazaki, Ideki 7
Olivieri, Simona 6
Owens, Jonathan 105, 184, 202

Paul the Persian (fl. 6th century CE) 159, 165
Peled, Yishai 186, 225–228
Perkams, Matthias 159

Qarrāʿa, Hudā Maḥmūd 52, 70, 78
Qarṭāǧannī, Ḥāzim al- (d. 684/1285) 139, 142, 144
Qifṭī, al- (d. 646/1248) 59, 61, 147
Qurayš 230, 232
Quṭrub (d. 206/821) 84

Raḍī al-Dīn al-ʾAstarābāḏī *see* ʾAstarābāḏī
Rašīd, Hārūn al- (r. 170/786–193/809) 53, 58, 62, 68
Reuschel, Wolfgang (1924–1991) 21

Riegel, Martin 216
Riyāšī, al- (d. 257/871) 70
Ruʿaynī, al- (d. 666/1268) 45, 138, 140
Ruʾba b. ʿAbd al-ʿAǧǧāǧ, ʾAbū al-Ǧaḥḥāf al-Tamīmī (d. 145/762) 198, 214
Rundī, ʾAbū ʿAlī al- (d. 616/1219) 138, 140, 142, 144–145

Sahl b. Muḥammad 62
Sāʿida (d. 600? CE) 168
Sakaedani, Haruko 9
Šammarī, ʿUmar b. ʾAbī ʿUṯmān al- 172
Šantamarī, al-ʾAʿlam al- (d. 476/1084) 38, 44, 137–138, 141, 144–145
Sartori, Manuel 8
Schöck, Cornelia 157–158, 171–174, 250
Sheyhatovitch, Beata 170, 190
Sībawayhi (d. 180/796?) 3–9, 13–19, 21–24, 26, 28–29, 32, 37–41, 44, 46–47, 49, 52–77, 79, 81–85, 89–91, 97–106, 111, 114–131, 135, 139, 145, 149–151, 157, 160, 166–168, 171–175, 179–181, 184–185, 187, 189–190, 199–201, 214, 233–235, 238, 244–251
Siǧistānī, ʾAbū Ḥātim al- (d. 255/869) 61–62, 64
Silvestre de Sacy, Antoine-Isaac (1758–1838) 31
Sīrāfī, ʾAbū Saʿīd al- (d. 368/979) 7, 27, 38, 44, 58, 61–64, 69–70, 125, 129, 157, 160–162, 168, 185, 245, 250
Širbīnī, al- (d. 977/1570) 180
Suhaylī, al- (d. 581/1185) 138, 142, 144–145 148–150
Sulamī, ʾAbū ʿAbd al-Raḥmān al- (d. 74/693) 82
Suleiman, Yasir 107
Suyūṭī, al- (d. 911/1505) 24, 107, 124, 129, 164, 185, 192–193, 204, 230, 237

Ṭabarī, al- (d. 310/923) 228–231, 237
Tabrīzī, Ḫaṭīb al- (d. 502/1109) 236, 238
Taha, Zaynab 189–191
Ṯaʿlab (d. 291/904) 53–55, 59–60, 67, 125, 127, 135
Talmon, Rafael (1948–2004) 54, 57, 67, 84, 116, 200, 206, 215
Themistius (317?–388?) 174
Theophrastus (371?–288? BC) 171
Troupeau, Gérard (1927–2010) 13, 16, 21, 53, 57, 116

ʿUkbarī, ʾAbū al-Baqāʾ al- (d. 616/1219) 124, 236, 238
ʿUkbarī, Ibn Barhān al- *see* Ibn Barhān al-ʿUkbarī
ʿUlaymī, ʾAḥmad b. Muʿāwiya b. Bakr al- 58
ʿUrwa b. al-Ward (d. 607 CE) 24
ʾUšmūnī, al- (d. 900/1495?) 205, 208, 212
ʿUṯmān b. ʿAffān (d. 35/656) 65
ʿUyūnī, Sulaymān b. ʿAbd al-ʿAzīz al- 37, 45

Vernier, Donat (1838–1917) 205
Versteegh, Kees 4, 54, 157–158, 164, 169
Vidro, Nadia 159–160
Villano, Raoul 5

Weil, Gotthold (1882–1960) 53–55
Wolfe, Ronald Gary 137
Wright, William (1830–1889) 200, 209, 225, 228, 231

Yaḥyā b. Ḫālid (d. 190/806) 67–69
Yaʿqūb al-Ḥaḍramī (d. 205/821) 57–58, 84–85
Yāqūt al-Ḥamawī (d. 626/1229) 59, 69
Yūḥannā b. Ḥaylān (d. 328/941) 158
Yūnus b. Ḥabīb (d. 182/798?) 56–57, 64, 68, 71

Zaǧǧāǧ, al- (d. 311/923) 59, 125, 129, 151, 181, 223, 228, 231, 238
Zaǧǧāǧī, al- (d. 337/949) 7, 56, 61, 64, 67, 107, 120, 128, 135, 139, 145–147, 149–151, 183–186, 188–189, 192, 209, 249
Zakariyyā al-ʾAnṣārī (d. 926/1520?) 236, 238
Zamaḫšarī, al- (d. 538/1144) 9, 31, 38, 129, 142, 144, 184, 188, 192–193, 201, 206–207, 225–226, 228–230, 232, 234–240
Zayyāt, Muḥammad b. ʿAbd al-Malik al- (d. 233/847) 64
Zimmermann, Fritz 157–158, 160–162, 169–171, 250
Ziyādī, ʾAbū ʾIsḥāq al- (d. 249/863) 63
Ziyādī, ʿAmmār Niʿma al- 224, 228, 237
Zubaydī, al- (d. 379/989) 58, 125
Zurʿa, ʾAbū Yaʿlā b. ʾAbī (d. 257/871) 61

Index Rerum

Abbasid 66
accusative 57, 67, 76–77, 79, 81, 179–194, 202, 207, 214
see also naṣb
acoustic 14, 25, 32, 244
act
~ of imposition 164
speech ~ 22, 26
active participle *see under* participle
Adab 85
adjective 22, 198, 202, 205–206, 216–217
attributive ~ 216
adjectival 16, 22, 30, 200, 203, 209–210
see also naʿt; ṣifa
adverbial 187
affix 16
affixation 30
ʾaʿǧam 59
agent 17–18, 74, 180, 182, 188–191
see also fāʿil
agreement (linguistic ~) 18–19, 22–23, 30
agreement (scholarly ~) 122–124, 148, 161, 248
disagreement (scholarly ~) 54, 63, 138, 150, 168, 174
ʿalāma *see under* proper name
Alexandria 159
allocation (case and mood ~) 136
see also ʿamal; government
allomorph 28–29
Almohades 136
alphabet 163
ʿām *see under* year
ʿamal 78, 136, 146, 148, 150
ʿāmil 8, 103, 182, 186–187, 205–209, 211–213, 251
see also governor (*under* government)*;* operator
ʾiʿādat al-ʿāmil 206
ʾiẓhār al-ʿāmil 212
see also allocation; government
ambiguity 52, 115, 186, 202–203, 224, 229
ambiguous 126–127, 129, 168, 248
Ambrosiana (Milan) 5, 37, 42, 51, 245
ʾamr 76–78, 81, 99
see also under ḍamīr
ʾams *see under* yesterday
analogy 102, 110, 127, 166
analogical 107, 148
see also qiyās
anaphoric 9, 224, 231, 239, 253
Andalus (al-) 7, 135–137, 139–140, 143, 149–150, 249
Andalusi(an) 7, 37, 136, 140–141, 143, 145–146, 149, 249
anecdote 66–67, 120–121
annexation 16, 18, 30
annexed 21, 102
antecedent 208, 212–213, 217
antepose 101, 103
anticipation 129
anticipatory pronoun *see under* pronoun
aorist (*élabon*) 162
apposition 9, 21, 198, 200, 204, 209, 211, 216, 218, 221–223, 227, 230, 236–237, 252–253
close ~ 216, 218, 252
explanatory ~ 198, 200, 204, 252
loose ~ 216, 218, 252
apposed 203–204, 210–211, 217–218, 252
appositive 200, 202, 207–210, 212–213, 216–217, 227
see also ʿatf; badal; tābiʿ
ʾaqsām
~ al-kalām 123
see also kalim; parts of speech
~ al-mafʿūlīn 183
see also mafʿūl
ʿarab 146
kalām al-~ 6, 105–106, 118, 124–126, 130, 248
luġat al-~ 108
maḏhab al-~ 146
Arab(s) 1–4, 8–9, 24, 57, 97, 99–101, 105, 108–111, 117–121, 123, 125, 148, 150, 157, 186, 189, 199, 200–203, 214, 216
Arabic 1–9, 25–26, 28, 33, 37, 39, 52–53, 55–58, 60–61, 63–67, 71–72, 81, 83–85, 97–99, 102, 105–111, 114–126, 130–131, 133, 135–136, 138, 141, 146, 148–150, 157–160, 162, 166–172, 174–175, 183, 188, 198,

200, 203–204, 211, 215–218, 224, 230, 239–240, 246–250, 252–253
Arabic grammatical tradition 3, 6–9, 52, 61, 65, 83–84, 102, 105–107, 136, 146, 148–150, 168, 188, 216, 249
Arabists 2–4, 8, 202, 209
ʿarabiyya 56, 64, 81, 111, 121–122, 138, 231
arbiter (speaker as ~) 6, 98–99, 101–102, 108, 112, 247
argument (linguistic ~) 6, 115, 117, 119–120, 122, 124, 126, 128–130, 161–162, 167, 231, 248
Aristotelian 158, 171–172
article 16, 30, 46–48, 173
ʾaṣl 77, 161, 210
ʾasrār al-naḥw *see under naḥw*
asseverative 20
ʿaṭf 8–9, 198–217, 252
 ~ bayān 8–9, 198–217, 252
 ~ nasaq 200
 maʿṭūf 212–213
 see also under apposition
attribute *see taḥliya*
audible 25, 32, 244
augment 110
authority (intellectual, grammatical ~) 5, 45, 52, 55–56, 58, 60, 62, 64, 67, 69–71, 82–83, 102, 118, 123, 126, 170, 246
 authoritative 117–120, 125–126, 145, 168
autograph (manuscript) 45
ʾAzraqism 85

badal 8, 17, 103, 198–217, 227, 236, 252
 ~ al-baʿḍ min al-kull 200
 ~ al-badāʾ 200
 ~ al-ġalaṭ 200
 ~ al-ʾiḍrāb 200
 ~ al-ištimāl 200
 ~ al-kull min al-kull 8, 199–200, 216–217
 ~ al-mubāyin 200
 ~ al-nisyān 200
 mubdal minhu 8, 198, 202–205, 212–213, 217
badāʾ 200
bāriḥa *see under* yesterday
Basra 6, 52–57, 59, 64–65, 84–85, 97, 129, 168, 203, 228, 246
 Basran 6, 53–54, 56, 60–61, 63–66, 69, 71, 76, 82–85, 102, 123, 125, 168, 193, 228–229, 235, 238
bayān *see under ʿaṭf bayān*
Bedouin 59, 66–68, 99, 109, 117–121, 125, 146, 168
Bibliothèque nationale de France (BnF, Paris) 5, 37, 42–43, 245
bio(biblio)graphical sources *see under* sources
biographers 70, 97, 105
biography 52, 56, 58, 97
 biographical x, 5–6, 55, 58, 61, 63–64, 66, 68, 72, 83–84, 161, 169, 246, 249
boundary 5, 13, 26, 28–29, 32, 72, 202, 244
 bound 17, 20, 40, 42, 202, 206
break 27, 209
brevity *see ʾīǧāz*

canon 65–66
 canonical 5, 37–38, 41, 49, 56–57, 84, 245
case 17, 19, 21–22, 31, 46, 57, 67, 76–77, 79–82, 136, 181–182, 186–187, 191–192
cataphoric pronoun *see under* pronoun
cause 99, 102, 105, 107, 215, 247
choice (speaker's ~) 100, 103
circumstantial *see ḥāl*
classification 7–8, 124, 167, 177, 179, 181–183, 188, 192, 194, 251
clause 17, 187, 189, 215, 224–225, 227–228, 232
 see also ǧumla; sentence
cluster 25, 32
codex 37–38, 42
collocation 30
comma 28, 217
commentary 5, 38, 44–47, 49, 61, 63, 72, 106, 135–137, 139, 146, 150, 159–161, 171–172, 183, 201, 207, 213, 235, 239, 245
 commentator 44, 69, 97, 125–126, 204, 209, 248
 šarḥ / šurūḥ 63, 106
comment 223–224, 227–228, 230–232, 236–238
 see also ḫabar; predicate
compendium 135, 145–146, 183
complement 46, 179–180, 183–184, 187–190, 192–194
 see also mafʿūl; mušabbah bi-l-mafʿūl
completeness *see under tamām*
completion 18–19, 22, 28–29, 182, 187, 191
compound 15, 17, 19, 24, 27–30, 163, 165
conditional *see under* sentence

conjugation 129, 233
conjugated 182
conjunction 215
consonant 14, 21, 25
constituent 17, 20, 25, 27–29, 32, 191, 244
construct 77, 104, 216
construction 5, 19, 76, 78, 81, 122, 129, 137, 150, 164, 166, 174, 185–187, 206, 225
coordination 16–17, 30, 200, 215
coordinated/-ing 15, 202, 212
correct (way of speaking) 33, 57–59, 77–78, 118–119, 224
correctness (linguistic ~) 29, 67, 121, 165
ḥusn 29, 78
qubḥ 29
corruption (language ~) 119
criticism 37–38, 49, 60–61, 63, 71, 83, 85, 135, 137, 139, 144, 146, 148–149, 170

ḍamīr 9, 161, 223–226, 228–240, 253
~ *al-ʾamr* 224, 228, 231–232, 236–237
~ *al-faṣl* 228, 231, 237
~ *al-ḥadīṯ* 228–229, 234–236
~ *al-ḥāla* 228
~ *al-ʿimād* 228–231
~ *al-maǧhūl* 228–229, 231, 234
~ *al-qiṣṣa* 224–225, 228–229, 234–235
~ *rāǧiʿ* 232
~ *al-šaʾn* 223–226, 228–240, 253
see also pronoun
day *see under yawm*
declension 128, 200
declinable 129, 186
see also inflection; *ʾiʿrāb*
definiteness 16, 18
definite 16, 19, 30, 46–48, 161–162, 173, 199, 227
muḥaṣṣal 161–162
deictic 16, 41, 47–49
deixis 41
deletion 100–101, 103, 106, 110
see also ellipsis; *ḥaḏf*
demonstrative 5, 31, 59, 201, 217
dependent 17–19, 21–22, 29, 99–100, 103, 127
desinential 203
detached position *see under* position
dialect 122
dialectal 19

didactic approach 53, 104, 106
taqrīb al-naḥw 106
diminutive 5, 38–41, 44–49, 245
diptote 59
diptotic 128
mamnūʿ min al-ṣarf 148
direct object *see under* object
discourse 25–26, 215
see also kalām
disjunction *see under istiʾnāf*
disjunctive exception *see istiṯnāʾ*
dispute (intellectual ~) 66–67, 139–140
see also public debate
doubling *see tašdīd*
doxographical sources *see under* sources
dual 48, 173
dummy pronoun *see under* pronoun
durative verbs 21–22

eîlēpha see perfect
élabon see aorist
ellipsis 57
elliptical 17, 24, 29–30
see also deletion; *ḥaḏf*
English 24, 26, 167, 217
epistemology 145, 151, 163
epistemological 1, 7, 150, 249
error 32, 60, 119, 121, 200
Escorial (Real Biblioteca del Monasterio de San Lorenzo) 42
etymology 57
etymological 137
exception 57, 181, 251
exceptive 19, 137, 190
see also istiṯnāʾ
exclamation 17
exegesis (Qurʾānic ~) 72, 84, 173, 246
see also tafsīr
extension (semantic ~) 203–204, 213, 216–217

faḍl see under faḍla
faḍla / *faḍalāt* 8, 29, 179, 181, 183, 185, 187, 189–194, 251
faḍl / *ḥašw* / *laġw* / *ṣila* / *tawkīd* / *zāʾid* 189
fāʿil 74, 105, 180, 182, 187–188, 191, 201
see also agent; participle (active ~); subject

fāṣila 213
fiʿl 18, 38, 74, 76–77, 79–81, 99, 103, 109, 123, 182, 187, 190–191, 207, 251
see also verb
fiqh 53, 173
flexibility 5, 40–41, 245
flexible 44, 168
see also tamakkun
foundations of grammar *see under naḥw* (*ʾuṣūl al-* ~)
French 2, 26, 28, 160, 198, 210, 216–218
frequency of usage *see under kaṯrat al-istiʿmāl*
fuǧāʾiyya *see ʾiḏā al-fuǧāʾiyya*
fuṣḥā 122–123

ġad *see under* tomorrow
ġalaṭ *see under badal*
ġarāʾib 63
ǧarr 181, 192, 205
genitive 179–181, 185, 192, 205
gloss 37–38, 45–49, 60, 70–72, 147
government 103
governed/-s 78–79, 103
governor 148
see also ʿāmil (*under ʿamal*)*;* operator
see also allocation*; ʿamal*
grammar 1–3, 5, 7–9, 28–29, 31, 33, 52–56, 58, 62–64, 66, 71, 83–85, 97–98, 102, 104–108, 115, 119–120, 123–125, 135–139, 141, 145–150, 157–160, 163–165, 167–168, 170–171, 174–175, 179, 181, 183, 189, 198, 200–201, 204, 211, 215–216, 218, 223, 237–240, 244, 246, 249–250, 252–253
see also naḥw
grammarian 2–4, 6–9, 13, 19, 21–22, 25, 29–31, 33, 37, 41, 45, 53–54, 57–58, 60–61, 63, 66–68, 71, 84, 98, 102, 104, 106–108, 115–124, 126–130, 135–137, 140–143, 145–150, 157, 159–163, 165, 167–174, 179–181, 184–185, 188–189, 192–194, 199–205, 207, 209–210, 214, 216–217, 228–229, 231–232, 240, 248–253
see also naḥwiyyūn
grammatical tradition *see* Arabic grammatical tradition
Greek 3, 157–160, 162, 167, 169–170
ǧumla 206, 212
~ *ʾuḫrā* 206, 212
~ *wāḥida* 212
ǧumlatayn 210, 212
see also clause*;* sentence

ḫabar 57, 74–75, 77–78, 127, 139, 142, 161, 187–188, 226–228, 231–232
~ *kāna wa-ʾaḫawātihā* 8, 129, 181–184, 186–187, 191–192, 251
~ *lā al-nāfiya li-l-ǧins* 184
see also comment*;* predicate
ḥadf 57, 99–101, 110, 189
maḥḏūf 224, 233
see also deletion*;* ellipsis
ḥadīṯ 56–57, 66, 79, 83–84, 118, 126, 228–229, 234–236
ḥaḏw 82
haǧar 127–128
ḥāl 8, 75, 181–184, 186–187, 190–192, 231, 251
ḫālifa / *ḫawālif* 124
ḥarf / *ḥurūf* 14, 27, 76–77, 123, 162, 166, 205, 212, 251
see also particle
Ḫāriǧism 85
ḥašw *see under faḍla*
Hebrew 149, 223
Hedjaz 55
hidden pronoun *see under* pronoun
hierarchy 18, 122, 192
ḫiffa 109
ḥikma 108, 111
ḫilāfāt tradition 124
historiographical sources *see under* sources
history of Arabic grammar 31, 52, 55, 83, 98, 115, 124, 136, 189
history (textual ~) 7, 37, 63, 139, 151, 249
homonymity 172
ḥuǧǧa 117
ḥukm 205–207
ḥusn *see under* correctness
hypercorism 32
hypernym 192
hysteron *see taqdīm wa-taʾḫīr*

ʾIbāḍism 85
ibtidāʾ 77, 80, 82, 232, 236
ʾiḏā al-fuǧāʾiyya 224

ʾidġām 167
ʾiḍmār 40, 79, 81, 106, 235
ʿalāmat al- ~ 40
muḍmar 78, 80, 228, 235
ʾīǧāz 100–101, 105, 146–147
iḫtilāfāt 54, 66
iḫtiṣār *see ʾīǧāz*
ʿilla / ʿilal 51, 99, 105, 107, 136, 148, 192, 209
ʿilm
~ *al-lisān* 159
~ *al-luġa* 164
~ *al-manṭiq* 165
~ *al-naḥw* 105, 164–165
ʿimād 228–231
implicit
~ meaning/value 77, 202, 207, 209–212, 215
~ pronoun *see under* pronoun
implicitly 203, 206–207, 211, 215
see also taqdīr
inaudibility 26
incorrect 17, 119
indeclinable 186, 211
indefiniteness 19, 28
indefinite 18, 59, 199, 224, 227–228, 231
independence (semantic ~) 21, 100, 127, 204, 206–207, 209, 213
independent case 46
independent mood 127
independent pronoun *see under* pronoun
indeterminate length 25, 29
indirect sources *see under* sources
Indo-Iranian language 158
inflection 24, 30–31, 165, 181, 192, 201–203, 211, 213, 233, 252
inflected 21, 162, 181, 202
inflectional 1, 8–9, 15, 26, 199, 201, 203–204, 252
see also declension; *ʾiʿrāb*
informants (linguistic ~) 118, 120–121
ʾinna wa-ʾaḫawāt-hā 8, 127, 181–184, 188, 191–192, 224–226, 235, 251
see also under ism
innovation (terminological ~) 162, 169
innovation (syntactic ~) 200
Institute of Oriental Manuscripts (Saint Petersburg) 43
intention (speaker's ~) 148, 203, 209–211
intension (semantic ~) 203–204
interrogative *see under* sentence
intonation 8, 26, 215, 217
invariable *see under mabnī*
inversion 17
ʾiʿrāb 8, 59, 132, 136–137, 148, 165, 202, 235, 237–240, 252–253
see also declension; inflection
Iraqi (Old ~ School) 54, 116
ʾišbāʿ 26
Islamic law *see* law
Islamic(ate) civilization 3, 33, 65–66, 71, 115–116, 118–120, 135, 143, 150, 170–171, 248
ism 18–19, 23, 28, 38, 43, 47, 57, 76–77, 79, 123, 202, 211, 215, 218, 230
~ *al-fāʿil* 187, 201
see also under participle (active ~)
~ *al-fiʿl* 38, 190
~ *ʾinna wa-ʾaḫawātihā* 8, 181–184, 188, 191–192, 251
~ *al-ʾišāra* 201
see also demonstrative
~ *kāna wa-ʾaḫawātihā* 57
~ *lā al-nāfiya li-l-ǧins* 185–186, 231
~ *lā al-tabriʾa* 192
~ *al-mafʿūl* 187
see also under participle (passive ~)
~ *wāḥid* 27–29, 32, 205, 210, 213, 216
see also noun
ʾišmām 26
isolated form 30, 43
istifhām *see under* sentence (interrogative ~)
ištiġāl 76, 81, 146
istiġnāʾ 100, 182, 187
mustaġnī 29
istiʾnāf 209–211, 214–217, 231
disjunction / disjoint clauses 215
mustaʾnaf 211
resumption 204, 209, 211, 213, 215
istiqlāl 209, 213–214
mustaqill 206, 213
istiṯnāʾ 8, 57, 161, 181, 183, 190–191, 251
mustaṯnā 181–182, 184, 192
iʿtirāḍāt 63, 139
see also radd; refutation
ittisāʿ al-kalām 101, 106
ʿiwaḍ 20, 23–24, 31

juncture 13, 25, 211, 214–217
  junctural 25, 30
  nonjuncture 217
justifications *see ʿilla*

kalām 5–6, 13, 15, 17–27, 29, 31–33, 76, 78, 84, 99, 101, 103, 105–106, 110, 118, 123–126, 130, 182, 189–190, 199, 206, 210, 231, 244, 248
  see also under ʾaqsām; ʿarab; ittisāʿ; tamām; ṭūl
kalim 26, 123
  see also ʾaqsām al-kalām; parts of speech
kalima 26–28, 31
  ~ wāḥida 27–28
kāna wa-ʾaḫawāt-hā 8, 129, 161–162, 181–184, 186–187, 191–192, 226, 231, 233, 235, 251
  see also under ḫabar; ism
kaṯrat al-istiʿmāl 99–100
  frequency of usage 100, 103, 106
Kazan *see* Milan-Kazan codex
Kufa 52–55, 65–66, 124, 129, 168, 205, 231, 246
  Kufan 6, 27, 53–54, 59–60, 63, 65–67, 82–83, 123, 168, 181, 228–229, 231, 234

lā al-nāfiya li-l-ǧins 29–30, 185–186, 231
  see also under ḫabar; ism
lafẓ 28, 99, 108, 164, 182, 187, 203, 207
laġw 8, 29, 189–190, 251
  see also under faḍla
lambánō *see under* present
language 1–3, 5, 7–8, 21, 24, 26, 30, 33, 38, 72, 81, 97, 99, 101, 105, 107–111, 114–122, 135–136, 138, 150, 157–160, 162–169, 175–177, 201, 203, 217, 230, 250
  see also lisān; luġa
law 25, 56, 66, 83–85, 97
laysa 43–44, 49, 57, 127, 129–130, 226, 234
learner 6, 97–98, 102, 104–111, 247
legitimacy 122, 126, 128, 130, 150, 248
length 5, 14, 16, 19–25, 27, 29, 31–32, 244
  see also ṭūl
lexicography 25, 84, 164
  lexicographer 128
  lexicographic(al) 120, 128, 158
lexicological 179
linguistics 2–3, 26, 28, 158, 160, 168–169, 211, 216
  linguistic 1–2, 4, 6, 13, 22, 32, 64, 83, 97–99, 101–109, 111, 114–126, 130–131, 136–138, 151, 157, 159–162, 167, 169–170, 175, 188, 202, 206, 247–248, 250
  linguist 2, 158, 160, 162, 167–169, 211, 216
lisān 119, 159, 165, 167, 209
  see also language*; luġa*
listener 19–20, 25–26, 28–29, 31–32, 110, 244
literary (genre, etc.) 26, 53, 55, 66, 125, 140, 216
literary sources *see under* sources
locative object *see under* object
loci probantes *see šawāhid*
logic 40, 84, 158–161, 165, 169–174, 203
  logical 119, 123, 157, 162, 165–166, 169, 172
  logician 8, 123, 160, 162, 169, 171–172, 199, 216, 250
long (sound, compound, etc.) 13–20, 22–24, 29, 244
luġa 105, 108–109, 122, 164, 218
  see also language*; lisān*

mā al-ḥiǧāziyya 192
madd 14–15
  madda 26
  mamdūda 15
mabnī 31, 78, 186, 211
  invariable 181, 203
maḏhab 53, 84, 146
mafʿūl 8, 74–75, 103, 107, 167, 179–194, 251
  ~ bihi 180–181, 183, 190–191, 193, 251
  ~ dūnahu 181
  ~ fīhi 180, 183–184, 186, 251
  ~ lahu / min ʾaǧlihi 180–181, 183, 191, 193, 251
  ~ maʿahu 180–181, 183, 185, 191–193, 251
  ~ minhu 185
  ~ muṭlaq 180–183, 190, 192–193, 251
  ~ ṣaḥīḥ 192–193
  mafʿūliyya 184, 192
  see also mušabbah bi-l-mafʿūl; object
Maghrib 139, 146
mahmūs 13
Maktaba ʾAḥmadiyya (Tunis) 139
mamnūʿ min al-ṣarf *see under* diptote
maʿnā 103, 110, 148, 150, 182, 205, 232–233
manṣūbāt 181, 183, 185, 192–193

manṭiq 54, 160, 165
manuscript 5, 37–38, 41–43, 49, 60, 63, 70, 72, 78, 139–140, 173, 245
manzila 27, 38, 43, 47–49, 75, 210, 215
marfūʿāt / *al-ʾasmāʾ al-murtafiʿa* 181, 188
marker (grammatical ~) 18–19, 25, 28, 30–31, 76, 186, 192
masʾala zunbūriyya 58, 66–67, 97
maṣdar 168, 180, 190–191, 213
maṯal 79–82
maṭl 13–15
maṭṭa 13–15
  see also prolongation
mawḍiʿ 82, 203
Medina 55
melody 217
metalanguage 21, 27, 30
metrics 61–62, 84
  metrical 25, 32, 244
Milan-Kazan codex (of *Kitāb Sībawayhi*) 37–38, 42
mistake (grammatical ~) 60, 97, 109
modifier 216–217, 225
Monday 5, 38, 245
month (names of the ~) 5, 41, 46–48, 245
mood 127, 136
morpheme 5, 26, 244
morphology 15, 25, 39, 72
  morphological 1, 13, 15–16, 21–22, 27–28, 30–32, 38–39, 110, 128, 137, 179, 187, 204, 214
morphosyntactic 27
muʾakkad *see under tawkīd*
mubdal minhu *see under badal*
mubtadaʾ 77–78, 127, 187–188, 226–228, 231–232, 238
  see also topic
mufrad 30–32, 232
muǧādala *see* dispute
Muḥarram 48
muḥaṣṣal *see under* definiteness
mukarrar *see takrār*
multireferential 204
  multiple referent 216–217, 252
munāẓara *see* dispute
munqaṭiʿ 210–211
munṣarif 28
muntahā al-ism 28
muʿrab 186
murakkab 31
Murǧiʾite (thinkers) 171
mušabbah bi-l-mafʿūl 7–8, 179–194, 251
  see also under object (pseudo- ~)
musammā 47–48
mustaʾnaf *see under istiʾnāf*
mustaqill *see under istiqlāl*
muštaqq 207
muštarak 204
mustaṯnā *see under istiṯnāʾ*
mutaʿallim *see* learner
mutakallim *see* speaker
Muʿtazila 85
  Muʿtazilite 83–84, 171, 176
muttaṣil 211, 213, 216

nafy 8, 161, 184, 251
  see also negation
Nahḍa 33
naḥw 6, 33, 56, 58, 60, 63–64, 67–68, 71, 105–107, 123–124, 148, 150, 159–160, 164–165, 192, 208, 251
  ʾasrār al- ~ 107
  ʾuṣūl al- ~ 105–107, 123
  see also grammar
naḥwiyyūn / *nuḥāt* 6–7, 55, 57–58, 66, 76, 83–85, 107, 116–117, 136–137, 140–141, 149, 201, 231, 246, 249
  see also grammarian
nahy 76–77, 81, 99
nāʾib ʿan al-fāʿil 180
nakira *see* indefiniteness
naṣb 67, 76, 81, 103, 186, 192
  manṣūb 8, 181–183, 189, 251
  see also accusative
naʿt 13, 22, 82, 198, 200–202, 206
  see also adjective; *ṣifa*
National Archives (Kazan) 37
National Library of Tunisia (Tunis) 139
native speaker 2, 26, 56, 66, 119
negation 8, 43–44, 48–49, 231, 251
  negative 29–30, 161, 183
  see also nafy
Neoplatonism 170
  Neoplatonist 159, 166
  Neoplatonic 158

nidāʾ 8, 99–100, 102–103, 188, 201, 203, 207, 214, 251
munādā 185, 203
see also vocative
nominative 57, 67, 77, 79–82, 105, 173, 180–182, 186, 188, 192, 202, 213, 230–232, 236
see also rafʿ
noun 15–19, 26–30, 38, 40–41, 46, 76–77, 79, 100, 102–103, 124, 128–129, 148, 157, 167–168, 173–174, 179–183, 185–186, 188, 190, 202–205, 210, 213, 216–217, 224–225, 227–228, 230, 233
see also ism
nuḥāt *see naḥwiyyūn*
nukat 63
nūn al-wiqāya 225
nunation *see under tanwīn*

object 8, 17, 74–76, 101, 103, 179–180, 184–188, 190–191, 193, 224, 231, 251
direct ~ 17, 179–180, 190–191, 251
see also under mafʿūl (~ *bihi*)
locative ~ 180, 186, 251
see also under mafʿūl (~ *fīhi*)
pseudo- ~ 7–8, 179, 181, 185, 251
see also mušabbah bi-l-mafʿūl
see also mafʿūl
operator 8, 127, 181–182, 186–187, 201, 205–209, 211, 213, 251
see also ʿāmil (*under ʿamal*)*;* governor (*under* government)
oral 25–26, 32–33, 70, 140, 148, 216–218, 234
order (word ~) 18, 101, 103, 106, 110, 183, 192–193, 224
originator (speaker as ~) 6, 98–111, 247
orthography 26
orthographic(al) 26–27, 32, 203, 244

parsing 25
participle 16, 162, 174
active ~ 168, 174, 201
see also under ism (~ *al-fāʿil*)
passive ~ 169, 179
see also under ism (~ *al-mafʿūl*)
particle 38, 40, 44, 162, 181–182, 188, 251
~ of swearing 188
coordinating ~ 212
exceptive ~ 57, 137, 190
see also istiṯnāʾ
negative ~ 183
see also nafy; negation
vocative ~ 185, 188
see also nidāʾ; vocative
see also ḥarf
parts of speech 27, 123, 160, 181
see also ʾaqsām al-kalām; kalim
passive
~ participle *see under* participle
~ voice 179–180
past 41, 47, 161–162, 167
patient 180
see also mafʿūl
pause 5, 25–26, 28, 32, 205–206, 209, 211–212, 214, 216–217
see also waqf
pedagogy 107, 194
pedagogical 125, 150, 188
perfect (*eîlēpha*) 162
performative 29
Peripatetic 160, 162, 172
permission (grammatical ~)
permissible 5, 38, 44, 80, 106, 245
permitted 17, 19, 21, 24–25, 30
permutation 200
permutative 198, 200, 208
Persian 56, 97, 158–159, 165, 167
philology 62, 84–85
philologist 66, 84
philosophy 7, 147, 170
philosopher 175
philosophical 2, 85, 150, 162, 168, 170
phoneme 5, 244
phonology 25, 72, 175
phonological 13, 21, 25–26, 28
phrase 14, 19, 21, 29–31, 117, 167, 169, 180, 190, 224
Physicians 158, 160
pioneering terminology 6, 248
plural 31, 39, 48, 109, 173
poetry 25, 31–32, 49, 61–62, 65–66, 99, 117, 120, 244, 248
poet 56, 59, 66, 168
poetic 16, 21–22, 24, 45, 47, 62–63, 79, 81, 85, 139
point
~ of articulation 14
pointing 163–164
see also under ism (~ *al-ʾišāra*)

polemics 136, 149
  polemical (attitude) 138, 143, 149
position
  detached ~ 216–217
  syntactical ~ 17–18, 21, 30, 77, 82, 186, 228
pragmatics 175
  pragmatic 8–9, 16, 98, 146, 149, 199, 201, 203–204, 206, 208, 216, 218, 252
predicate 9, 20, 74, 77–79, 81, 104, 129, 181–183, 186–187, 227, 251, 253
  predicating 75
  predication 187, 189
  predicative 189
  see also comment; *ḫabar*
prefixes 110
preposition 205
  prepositional 180
prescriptive (grammar) 53, 123
  prescriptivist 114
present (time / tense) 41, 46–48, 106, 162, 186
  lambánō 162
prestige 123–124, 147
  prestigious 149
profile of the speaker 6, 98, 101–106, 108, 111, 247
prohibition *see nahy*
prolongation (phonetic ~)
  prolong 13, 15, 26
  see also maṭṭa
pronoun 9, 16–17, 20, 40, 44, 146, 179, 223–229, 231–240, 253
  anticipatory ~ 224–225
  cataphoric ~ 9, 223, 225, 234–235, 239, 253
  dummy ~ 224, 253
  hidden ~ 233–234
  implicit ~ 226
  independent ~ 224, 233–235, 239–240, 253
  referential ~ 17, 20, 224, 226–228, 253
  resumptive ~ 232
    see also istiʾnāf
  see also ḍamīr
pronunciation 5, 15, 21, 168, 203, 209, 211, 217
  pronounced/-ing 13, 25–26, 30, 210
prop *see ʿimād*
proper name 5, 16, 38–41, 44–49, 148, 245
  ʿalāma 46–47
prose 20, 25, 31–32, 85
proslepsis 171–172
prosody 25, 32, 252
  prosodic 25, 203
  prosodist 25, 32, 244
prósōpa see wuǧūh
proteron *see taqdīm wa-taʾḫīr*
pseudo-object *see under* object
public debate 56, 58, 66, 69, 160, 170
  see also dispute
punctuation 28, 213, 216
pupil 5, 52–53, 56, 60, 65–66, 68, 70, 72, 84, 143–144, 149, 246

Qadarite 84
qasam 188
qirāʾāt / Qurʾānic readings 26, 54, 72
qiṣṣa see under ḍamīr; ṭūl
qiyās 102, 107, 110, 117, 148
  see also analogy
qualification 16, 30, 198, 200, 203, 214
  qualified 40, 210–211
  qualifier 16, 21–22, 30, 181, 186, 198, 209–211, 213, 251
qubḥ see under correctness
Qurʾān 6, 9, 17, 20–21, 25, 47, 49, 52, 55–56, 63, 66, 70, 72, 74, 85–86, 99, 117–120, 126, 137–138, 142, 148, 150, 172–173, 203, 213, 223–224, 235, 237–240, 246, 248, 253
  Qurʾānic 1, 6, 15, 20, 22–23, 25, 29, 52, 54–55, 57, 72–74, 76, 79, 81–82, 84–86, 88, 118, 137, 173–174, 185, 203, 240, 246, 253
qurʾān al-naḥw 6, 63, 148, 150
quwwa see strength

radd / *rudūd* 7, 63, 135–137, 139–143, 145, 149, 158, 249
  see also refutation
rafʿ 77, 80–82, 139, 142, 192, 213, 232
  marfūʿ 8, 43, 105, 127, 182, 231, 251
  see also nominative
reader (Qurʾānic ~) 57–58, 84, 116
rearrangement (grammatical ~) 179, 182, 192
reception (of a text) 4, 102, 114, 248
recitation 15, 25, 203, 230, 244
redundant element 29, 179, 189–191, 194

referentiality 224
referent 44, 48, 217, 224, 232
referential multiplicity 216, 252
referential pronoun *see under* pronoun
referential uniqueness 203–204, 216–217, 252
refutation 4–5, 7, 27, 37, 60, 63, 135–141, 143–144, 146, 148, 172, 245, 249
see also radd
reiteration 206
relative 16, 20, 30, 232
repetition 204–209, 211–212
see also takrār; tašdīd
reputation 5–6, 52, 55, 58, 63, 66, 83, 102, 246
restriction (of the extension) 203, 213
resumption *see under istiʾnāf*
resumptive pronoun *see under* pronoun
rhyme 24–25, 106, 198, 228
rhythm of speech 216
risāla 63, 137, 140
Roman Empire philosophical academies 170
rubba 24, 228
rule 5, 25, 29, 32, 106, 109–110, 115, 119, 123, 150, 164–165, 172, 203

sāʿa 41
saʿa 111
sabt 48
Ṣafar 48
šaǧāʿa 110–111
šahr 41, 46
ʾasmāʾ al-šuhūr 47–48
samāʿ 102, 148
sana *see under* year
šarḥ *see under* commentary
Saturday 48
šawāhid 63, 73–74, 76, 81, 88, 106
school (grammatical ~) 6, 52–55, 71–72, 82–83, 85, 116, 123–124, 129, 181, 193, 205, 228, 234, 238, 246
see also Basra*;* Iraqi*;* Kufa
scriptio defectiva 203
segmentation 28, 211, 214–216
segment 28, 30
segmented/-ing 27, 32, 206
semantics 159, 163
semantic 8–9, 27, 29–30, 40, 44, 62, 72, 81, 110, 182, 187, 190–192, 201–202, 204, 208, 215–216, 218, 251–252
sentence 17, 27, 29, 39–40, 62, 75–77, 79, 81, 99, 104, 117, 128, 161–162, 171–174, 182, 187, 189–191, 204, 206, 210–212, 223–226, 228, 231–238
conditional ~ 173, 226
interrogative ~ 76–77, 253
nominal ~ 17, 67, 146, 224, 226, 232, 236
verbal ~ 29, 146, 190, 225–226
see also clause*; ǧumla*
short (phonetic value) 16, 23, 26, 201
ṣifa 8, 82, 198, 200–201, 205, 207, 209–213, 215, 217–218
mawṣūf 210–212
see also adjective*; naʿt*
ṣila *see under faḍla*
silence 27, 190, 206
silent 26, 29
šīn 14, 21
ṣināʿa
~ al-naḥw 159–160, 165
~ al-manṭiq 165
sisters (of *kāna* or *ʾinna*) 129, 224–226, 231, 235
see also ʾinna wa-ʾaḫawāt-hā; kāna wa-ʾaḫawāt-hā
Sogdian 158, 167
sound 5, 13–15, 21, 26–27, 109, 164, 224
sources
bio(biblio)graphical ~ 7, 55, 61, 72, 83, 135–136, 138, 246
doxographical ~ 72
grammatical ~ 3, 6, 54, 118, 145, 189
historiographical ~ 55, 61, 63, 72, 83–84, 246
indirect ~ 7, 116, 136, 249
literary ~ 55, 61, 72, 83, 246
speaker 2, 6, 26, 28, 31, 41, 47–48, 56, 58, 66, 97–112, 119–120, 148, 173, 199, 203, 206, 235, 247
see also arbiter*;* choice*;* intention*;* native speaker*;* originator*;* profile of the speaker
speculative 7, 32, 53, 148–150, 175, 249

speech 14, 22, 24–27, 55, 57–59, 78, 84, 97, 99, 105, 110, 118–120, 122–123, 125, 160, 165, 173, 181, 189, 206, 216, 228–230, 234–236, 246
spelling 25, 56
standardization 7, 98, 105, 119
stem 13, 100
Stoic 172
strength 40, 81, 109, 123
  strong (segmentation) 214
stress 26
structure 17–18, 22, 25, 28, 32, 103–104, 110, 114, 116, 120, 122–123, 127, 129, 146, 150, 152, 158–159, 181, 187, 190–191, 196, 199, 211, 238
  structural 29, 182, 189, 192
style 100, 106, 108
subject 9, 17, 20, 77–78, 101, 105, 127–129, 179–180, 187, 190, 224–225, 227, 253
  see also fāʿil
substitution *see badal*
sufficiency *see istiġnāʾ*
suffix 9, 18, 26, 110, 173, 203, 224–225, 233, 239–240, 253
Sunday 48
support *see ʿimād*
suppression *see ʾiḍmār*
suprasegmental 8–9, 25–26, 32, 198, 204, 211, 214, 216, 218, 244, 252
swearing *see qasam*
syllable 25–26, 28, 32
syllogism 172
  syllogistic 173–174
synonymity 172
syntax 17, 72, 157, 179, 240
  syntactic(al) 9, 13, 16–17, 25, 27–30, 82, 110, 148, 179, 184, 187, 191, 194, 200, 202–204, 207, 213–215, 226, 240, 252
syntagm 29
syntagmeme 5, 244
Syriac 157–159, 167

taʿaddā 74, 103, 191
tābiʿ / *tawābiʿ* 170, 200–202, 209–210, 212–213, 216
  matbūʿ 200–201, 213, 216
  see also apposition; *ʿaṭf; badal*
tafsīr / *tafāsīr* 9, 63, 73, 223, 228–231, 233–234, 237, 240, 253
  see also exegesis
taǧwīd 203
taḥḏīr 185
taḫfīf 100
taḥliya 82
taḥqīq wa-tašdīd 204–205
taḥrīf 110
taʾkīd *see tawkīd*
takrār / *takrīr* 204–211, 214, 216–217
  mukarrar 206
  see also repetition
ṯalāṯāʾ 41, 45
taʿlīl 102, 107
tamakkun 5, 19, 28, 40, 245
  see also flexibility
tamām 29, 32
  ~ *al-ism* 19, 28
  ~ *al-kalām* 22, 182, 189
  completeness 28–30
Tamīmī (variety) 122
tamyīz 8, 181–184, 186–187, 191–192, 251
tanwīn 16, 18–19, 27–30, 32, 35, 128, 148, 170, 202, 211, 231, 233
  nunation 186
taqdīm wa-taʾḫīr 101, 103, 106, 110
taqdīr 82, 129, 148, 202–203, 206–207, 209–213
  see also implicit
taqrīb al-naḥw *see under* didactic approach
taqsīm 182
tarḫīm 32
tašbīh 83, 164
tašdīd 204–205, 214
  see also repetition
taṣġīr *see* diminutive
tawkīd 189, 198, 200, 204–205, 212
  muʾakkad 212
  see also under faḍla
taxonomy 3, 8, 149
  taxonomic 7, 145–146
teacher 57, 65, 68, 102, 116, 138–139, 145–146, 151, 160, 182, 190
teaching 5–6, 37–38, 47, 49, 54–55, 83, 106–107, 117, 121, 123, 143–146, 150, 159, 170, 245–246, 249
tense 47, 159, 162, 167, 186

terminology 3, 5–6, 8, 14, 54, 70, 85, 160–162, 179–180, 182–183, 189, 203, 244, 248, 251
terminological 54, 81, 83–84, 169, 186
textual (tradition, history, etc.) 5, 7, 45, 54, 63, 83, 139, 151, 249
theology 84–85, 137
theologian 66, 84, 158
theological 76, 83–85
thought 2, 4, 8, 71, 130, 137, 170, 186
ṯiqal 109
tomorrow 5, 41, 245
ġad 43, 46–48
topic 73, 127, 129, 187, 215, 223–224, 227–228, 231–232, 236, 238, 244
see also mubtadaʾ
tradition *see* Arabic grammatical tradition; *ḥadīṯ*
traditionist 56, 66
transitive *see taʿaddā*
transmission 56, 70, 83–84, 115, 119–120, 122, 124–126
transmitter 6, 65, 68–70, 123
triptote 59
triptotic 128
Tuesday 5, 38, 41, 245
ṭūl 21, 23–24
~ *al-ism* 23
~ *al-kalām* 5, 13, 15, 18, 20–24, 26–27, 29, 31–32, 244
~ *al-kalima* 26–27
~ *al-qiṣṣa* 23
~ *al-ṣila* 23
ṭāla 13, 21–22, 27
mamṭūl 14–15
ṭawwala 13, 15, 17
taṭwīl 16
muṭawwal 31
ʾaṭāla 13, 22
taṭāwala 22
see also length
ṯulayṯāʾ 5, 245
ṯunayyāni 5, 245
Turkic 158
Turkish 167

ʿumda 29, 189, 192
uniqueness (referential ~) 203–204, 216–217, 252
unique referent 216–217, 223
unstressed 26
unvowelled 13
usage 23, 100, 103, 106, 110, 119, 148, 162, 169, 180, 225, 228, 235
ʾuṣūl al-naḥw see under naḥw
utterance 5, 18–24, 27–32, 47, 67, 98–104, 106, 110, 118, 182, 189–190, 206, 210, 216, 232, 234, 244
ʿuyūn 63

value 4, 85, 118, 147, 190, 202–203, 209–212
variation 121–122
variant (linguistic ~) 118–122
variant reading 5, 37, 43–45, 65, 72, 81, 85, 245
verb 15, 17–18, 21–22, 24, 26, 29, 38, 47, 75–77, 79–81, 99–100, 103–104, 109, 124, 127, 146, 160–162, 167–169, 179–182, 184–187, 189–191, 207, 214–215, 224, 233, 251
verbal 16, 29, 38, 77, 146, 180, 187, 190, 225–226
see also fiʿl
verse 9, 19–20, 22, 24–25, 29, 45, 47, 59, 62, 73–74, 79, 81–82, 85, 106, 137, 173, 213, 215, 223–225, 229–232, 234, 236, 238–240
vocabulary 119–120, 159, 180
vocalisation 41
vocative 5, 8, 15, 18–19, 21, 27–30, 99, 185, 201–203, 207, 214, 251
see also nidāʾ
vowel 14–15, 26, 185–186, 201

waʿd and *waʿīd* 173
waqf 5, 27–28
see also pause
wasaṭ al-ism 19, 28
waṣf 30
see also qualification
waṣl 1, 217
weak (consonant) 14, 21, 109
Wednesday 41
week 5, 38, 41, 45, 47, 245
West 2–3, 33, 143, 149
Western 1–2, 26, 33, 52, 116, 135, 151, 199, 202
wuǧūh (*prósōpa*) 160

yawm 18, 23, 30, 39–41, 43, 46, 48, 71, 184, 241
~ *al-ʾaḥad* 48
~ *al-ʾarbiʿāʾ* 41
~ *al-iṯnayni* 47
ʾasmāʾ al-ʾayyām 48
day 5, 38–41, 44–48, 245
year 41, 46
ʿām 46–47
sana 41
yesterday 5, 37, 41, 47, 245
ʾams 41, 43–49
ʾawwal min ʾams 46–47
bāriḥa 41, 45–48

Ẓāhirī 136, 148
zāʾid *see under faḍla*
zamān 161, 180, 183, 186–187
ẓarf / *ẓurūf* 46, 180, 183–184, 186, 190–191
ziyāda *see* augment
zunbūriyya *see masʾala zunbūriyya*